READING THE BIBLE:

AN INTRODUCTION

by

RICHARD G. WALSH, PH.D.

READING THE BIBLE:

AN INTRODUCTION

by

RICHARD G. WALSH, PH.D.

Cross Cultural Publications, Inc.

CrossRoads Books

Published by **CROSS CULTURAL PUBLICATIONS, INC.**
Cross Roads Books
Post Office Box 506
Notre Dame, Indiana, 46556, U.S.A.
Phone: (219) 273-6526, 1-800-561-6526
FAX: (219) 273-5973

For Jennifer,
Susan, Megan Marie, Michael, and Megan Elizabeth

PREFACE

Reading the Bible encourages beginning students to read the Bible. Reading presents a literary-critical reading which emphasizes the Bible as an ancient religious text. Because the Bible is a Western classic, Reading also calls attention to its continuing influence and diverse interpretations. Thus, four dominant motifs unify Reading: literary criticism, the conflict between ancient and modern cultural codes, myth, and the plurality of biblical readings.

Reading's first four chapters offer a theoretical introduction to literary-criticism. They discuss key terms (e.g., scripture, ancient near eastern text, and myth), set literary-criticism in the context of other important criticisms, and outline a literary-critical approach attending to both story (plot, character, atmosphere) and discourse (medium, genre, narrator, narrative time, style, and implied reader).

Chapters five through twenty-three apply the literary-critical approach to the various sections of the Bible. In addition to literary matters, each chapter also discusses that biblical section's religious function (myth), its world-view (cultural code), and its later cultural or critical use (see the numerous figures in each chapter). Two appendices offer introductory reading guides to the Latter Prophets and to the NT letters.

The last chapter discusses the relevance and truth of the Bible. This chapter provides a counter-point to the text's discussion of the Bible as ancient and as myth.

As the Bible is an extremely long work, teachers may wish to use Reading in a piecemeal fashion. A teacher might well concentrate on the first four chapters and the numerous figures in chapters five through twenty-three in order to encourage students to offer their own readings of the Bible. Alternatively, a teacher might focus on chapters five through twenty-three and use the introduction and the glossary as an explanatory resource for key terms. Of course, any teacher can think of a number of better strategies.

It might help students to know that chapters one through four are the most difficult section of the text. For that reason, those four chapters have previews and summaries. Each chapter uses bold-facing and review questions to call attention to important issues. A glossary identifies the text's key terms which are bold-faced and italicized.

Most importantly, students should not be afraid to disagree with <u>Reading</u>. It is only an introduction which students should use and leave behind as they pursue their own informed readings of the Bible.

A number of people have assisted me in the production of this text and deserve thanks and acknowledgment. At the beginning, my mother, Colleen Walsh, taught me to love reading. Dr. Garland Knott insisted that I undertake this project. Various students and colleagues, notably Dr. Ken Collins, Dr. Jay Brabban, and Mrs. Catherine Shuford, suffered through earlier versions of this book. Various people read, proofed, and checked the work. In particular, I would like to thank Mrs. Virginia Rohrer, Mrs. Jennifer Rohrer-Walsh, Mrs. Margo Jarvis, Mrs. Mary Blewett, and Dr. Cyriac Pullapilly for their meticulous help. Mr. Michael Jerch provided valuable computer information and access. Ms. Megan Walsh used the delete key judiciously. Of course, all mistakes are my own.

My deepest thanks go to Jennifer who edited, provided constant support, offered necessary perspective and humor, encouraged me to finish the project, and loved me despite the book.

TABLE OF CONTENTS

LIST OF ABBREVIATIONS

ANE	Ancient Near East or Ancient Near Eastern
ANET	Ancient Near Eastern Text
BCE	Before the Common Era (cf. BC)
CBQ	Catholic Biblical Quarterly
CE	Common Era (cf. AD)
cf.	Compare
CTM	Currents in Theology and Mission
EH	Ecclesiastical History
EJ	Encyclopedia Judaica
ER	Encyclopedia of Religion
HB	Hebrew Bible
Interp	Interpretation
JAAR	Journal of the American Academy of Religion
JAOS	Journal of the Academy of Oriental Studies
JBL	Journal of Biblical Literature
JR	Journal of Religion
JSOT	Journal for the Study of the Old Testament
KJV	King James Version
LXX	Septuagint
NovT	Novum Testamentum
NRSV	New Revised Standard Version
NT	New Testament
NTS	New Testament Studies
OT	Old Testament
RSV	Revised Standard Version
SBLDS	Society of Biblical Literature Dissertation Series
SBLSP	Society of Biblical Literature Seminar Papers
SJT	Scottish Journal of Theology
ZAW	Zeitschrift fuer die alttestamentliche Wissenschaft

All biblical abbreviations and quotations follow the NRSV.

CHAPTER 1

WHAT IS THE BIBLE?

Chapter Preview

1) Bibles **differ from community to community**.
2) The Bible is the **product of the religious experience** of Israel and early Christian communities.
3) The Bible is an **ancient Near Eastern text**.
4) The Bible is **sacred literature**.

Bible: Definition

The word "Bible" comes from a Latin (and that from a Greek) word, **biblia**, which means "little scrolls." Today, of course, "Bible" means a special type of collection which for a particular religious community is a religious **authority** also known as *scripture*.

Diverse Communities and Diverse Bibles

The Bible, then, differs from community to community. The Bibles of Jews and Christians, for example, are both alike and different.

Judaism's scripture contains twenty-four books, divided into three parts: the Torah (or law), the prophets, and the writings. As the texts were originally written in Hebrew, a common name for the Jewish scripture is the *Hebrew Bible* (HB). Other names for the HB include *Torah* ("revelation") and *Tanak* (an acronym formed from the Hebrew names of the three parts of the HB).

The **Christian Bible** adds to the HB and arranges its material differently. The addition is another section of works called the *New Testament*. The addition of the NT "rewrites" the HB as the *Old Testament* (OT). Further, Christians arrange their OT differently than the HB. Following the *Septuagint* (an early Greek translation of the HB), the Christian OT has four sections: law, history, poetry and wisdom, and prophets. The final position of the prophets illustrates the early Christian tendency to read the entire HB as a prophecy of Jesus and the church.

Of course, within Christianity, Protestant and Catholic Bibles also differ. The Catholic Bible expands the HB more aggressively than does the Protestant. The Catholic OT includes books not in the HB (e.g.,

Figure 1: **Different Bibles**	
Jewish Bible	**Christian Bible**
	Old Testament
Torah	Pentateuch
Prophets	History
Writings	Poetry/Wisdom
	Prophets
	New Testament

Maccabees) and additions to books (Esther, Daniel) therein. These extra books come from the *Septuagint* which early Greek-speaking Christians used as scripture. Later, Jerome's influential Latin translation, the *Vulgate*, also incorporated these works. Realizing that the works were not in the HB, Jerome termed them the *apocrypha*, the church's "hidden" books. The apocrypha still appears in Catholic and in ecumenical Bibles. Protestant Bibles do not include it.

The Ancient Origins of the Hebrew Bible

None of these Bibles simply appeared. They are the fruit of the lengthy, rich religious experience of Israel and early Christianity.

Israel's ancestors were semi-nomads wandering from Mesopotamia through Palestine to Egypt in search of grass and water for their flocks. According to her own accounts, Israel's ancestors were enslaved by Egypt before their **miraculous release** (Exodus, 13th cent. BCE) led them to settle in Palestine.

There, they carved out a tenuous place among the natives and learned agriculture. Israel briefly dominated Palestine as she developed a **monarchy under David** and his sons (ca. 1000 BCE). Israel's dominance lasted, however, only as long as the power vacuum amongst the major Middle Eastern nation-states.

Internal strife soon divided Israel into two petty-states: Israel (Ephraim) and Judah (the Davidic Monarchy). These petty-states quickly fell prey to Middle Eastern empires. Assyria ruled the eighth and seventh centuries and ultimately destroyed Israel (722 BCE).

Judah survived until she met a similar fate (587 BCE) at the hands of Babylon, ruler of the sixth century. Babylon deported the leaders and upper classes (**the Exile**) and left Jerusalem and the temple in ruins. The exiles survived in Babylon adopting a new language (Aramaic) and new occupations (merchants).

The Persians usurped the Babylonians as rulers of the Middle East and allowed the exiles to return to their homeland (539 BCE) where they rebuilt a **temple-state** under Persian hegemony (fifth and fourth centuries).

The Greek conquest of the Persian empire in the late third century did not drastically change the status of this temple-state. However, later squabbles among the descendants of the Greek (Hellenistic) empire did effect her. After the Syrian-based Seleucid kingdom defeated the Egyptian-based Ptolemaic kingdom, a Seleucid king's (Antiochus IV Epiphanes) desire to rule the East led to more rigorous internal policies. In particular, Epiphanes outlawed native religions and imposed Greek worship in an attempt to foster cohesion.

Rural Jews revolted (Maccabean Revolt, 167 BCE). Their successes led to the establishment of a short-lived, independent Jewish kingdom under the Hasmoneans, the family name of the revolt's leaders. That kingdom ended with the arrival of the Romans (63 BCE) who reduced the Jews again to a petty temple-state.

Some Jews compromised with Rome. Others hoped for the arrival of God's kingdom. Others revolted. Ultimately, two ill-fated revolts led to the destruction of the second temple (70 CE) and to Jewish expulsion from Palestine (132-35 CE).

Throughout her history, Israel's **sense of belonging to** *Yahweh*, her God, dominated her religious experience. Her history divides that religious experience into three phases: tribal, monarchical, and exilic.

In both the tribal and monarchical periods, Israel's religion was a ***natural religion,*** a religion of "blood and soil." In such cases, religion and society are synonymous, so that to be in a certain place is to have a certain religion. Further, as society and religion are mutually supportive, being good (religiously correct) easily translates into having it good (political power, economic wealth). The result is an objective, ***ontological*** sense of the ***good*** (goodness = having goods).

The prophetic movement, of course, indicates that all was not idyllic during the monarchy. The leaders and people combined their worship of **Yahweh** with the worship of other gods. The prophets called the monarchy to pure **Yahwism** and explained the exile as God's judgment upon an apostate people.

The exile ended Israel's monarchy and natural religion. In a foreign land, without king or temple, the Jews turned increasingly to rituals symbolizing their sense of **separateness** such as circumcision, dietary regulations, and sabbath-worship.

```
┌─────────────────────────────────────────────────────┐
│ Figure 2: Israel's History                           │
│                                                       │
│ History                    Religion (Literature)      │
│                                                       │
│ Pre-history                                           │
│   semi-nomadic                                        │
│   exodus                   (Oral traditions)          │
│ Land (1200 BCE)            Natural Religion           │
│ Monarchy (1000)                                       │
│   Davidic                  (Early writings)           │
│   Israel & Judah           Prophets                   │
│   End of Israel (722)                                 │
│   End of Judah (587)                                  │
│ Exile (587-39)             Separatism (Collections)   │
│ Persian Rule (539-333)     Modified Natural Religion  │
│                                       (Torah/Prophets)│
│ Greek Rule (333-63)        (Writings)                 │
│   Brief independence       (Apocrypha)                │
│ Roman Rule (63-135 CE)     (Books of NT)              │
│                            Rabbinic Judaism           │
│                            (HB, 100 CE)               │
│                            (Mishnah, 200 CE)          │
└─────────────────────────────────────────────────────┘
```

The exile also spurred the collection and preservation of a national literature accounting for both Israel's election by God and her catastrophe. Despite Persian leniency, the rebuilt post-exilic temple, and brief Hasmonean independence, Judaism after exile was increasingly **a religion of the book**. The destruction of the second temple and the end of Palestine as the Jewish homeland solidified this trend.

The HB, then, is **a document of exile**. Not unfairly, one might refer to the pre-exilic period as the HB's prehistory. Given Israel's semi-nomadic ancestry, a situation hardly conducive to the amassing of stately libraries, that pre-history is predominantly oral.

For early Israel, tribal bards performed the family and tribal stories. Prayers, hymns, and oracles were all performed before they were written. During the monarchy, written records and texts became increasingly prominent. According to one theory, an early source of the Torah dates to the early monarchy. Nevertheless, texts approximating the canonical Torah and prophets did not appear until the exilic period. The writings are still later.

The move to revered scriptural status, a process known as **canonization**, occurred quite quickly. After the return from exile, a priest-scribe named Ezra reconstituted the people as a Torah-society, a move sponsored by the Persian government (400 BCE?, see Neh 8-9). With this event, Torah was nothing less than scripture.

The prophets quickly joined Torah. Ecclesiasticus, an early second century BCE work, refers to both the law and prophets as scripture. NT documents refer to Jewish scriptures in a similar way. The agreement between the HB and the LXX in the prophets' section also points to a fairly early canonization date.

The writings were the last books to be canonized. The disagreement here between the HB and the LXX, which includes the apocrypha, suggests a fairly late date. Though it is something of a critical tradition to say that the Jewish rabbis closed the Hebrew canon around 100 CE, present scholars deny such official action. The Jewish community did, however, harden its notion of scripture in response to the destruction of the second temple in 70 CE and against the growing Christian threat.

Even as scripture, the ancient Hebrew books were available only as separate, manuscript scrolls (not one book). Scribes provided copies as needed. Hebrew scribes followed exacting methods to insure accuracy. The dominant Hebrew textual tradition is the Masoretic, the work of the **Masoretes** (from the Hebrew word for tradition) who preserved a standardized consonantal text and its proper reading (both pronunciation and punctuation). Until recently, the oldest extant manuscript of the HB dated only to the tenth century

CE. Early manuscripts vanished because scribes would destroy the exemplar when a copy was complete to prevent the text from falling into profane hands. Recently, of course, the Dead Sea Scrolls have made available far older manuscripts of the HB (second and first century BCE). Interestingly, these scrolls have also demonstrated the accuracy of the Masoretes at many points.

The concretizing of sacred texts (canonization and standardization) renders them irrelevant to new ages. Not surprisingly, Jewish religious leaders supply "up-dating" interpretations. The oldest and most important are the oral traditions codified in the *Mishnah* (ca. 200 CE) and ultimately expanded to form the *Talmud* (fourth-fifth century). This text remains a major authority for modern Judaism.

The Hellenistic Origins of The Christian Bible

Frustration and alienation typify Hellenistic religious experience. The old religions could not cope with this larger world, and the empires despite some desperate attempts (like that of Antiochus Epiphanes) did not supply a new natural religion. Political and military power maintained order. The empires created more "have-nots" (or different "have-nots") than in previous times and a greater sense that religious belief and harsh reality did not mesh. Where religious belief continued, it did so by privatizing, conventicling, or appeasing the dominant empire (e.g., Second Temple Judaism). In short, religious experience tended to **disenchantment with the world**. *Sects* replaced natural religion groups.

The miracle-working, visionary **Jesus** attracted quite a following in this world. Whatever he meant by his message about the kingdom of God, Hellenistic religious frustration quickly gave it a *mystic* (spiritual) or *apocalyptic* (imminent end) meaning.

The message about Jesus' death and resurrection (or about

his apocalyptic return) quickly moved beyond Jewry and Palestine. **Missionaries**, like Paul, took the good news into the Mediterranean cities of the Roman empire. If the documents of the first two centuries are credible, this early Christianity was quite diverse.

Figure 3: **Early Christian History**

History	**Religion (Literature)**
Jesus (30 CE)	Jewish reform (Oral message)
Expansion	Jewish sect (Oral traditions)
Jew to Gentile	Mystery religion (Paul, 50s)
Into Mediterranean	(Gospels, 70+)
Consolidation	The Great Church (NT, 180)
Constantine	Council, Nicea (Creed, 325)

Rudimentary organization and uniformity began to overtake Christian growth in the second century. By the end of that century, the "**Great Church**," the ancestor of the Roman Catholic Church, was in place. A hundred years later, Constantine legalized Christianity. In that same century, Theodosius made Christianity the religion of the Roman Empire. In less than three hundred years, then, Christianity evolved from a frustrated Jewish sect into the empire's official religion. Shortly thereafter, it became the natural religion of Medieval Europe.

The earliest Christian Bible was the LXX interpreted in light of Jesus (his words/deeds, death/resurrection, or expected return). Paul was the first NT author. He penned letters to his urban, Mediterranean churches. The gospels, products of the second Christian generation, combined earlier diverse messages about Jesus into rudimentary cultic biographies. By the middle of the second century, the entire NT had been written.

At that point, these books were not truly the NT (a name first used in the third century). They remained independent manuscript scrolls or codexes. By the end of the second century, however, the Great Church had a rudimentary NT canon (including the four gospels, Acts, and Pauline letters). It employed this canon, seen as a corpus of apostolic writings, as part of its apostolic authority in its battle with other versions of Christianity.

Figure 4: **English Translations: Protestant**

Before the Reformation, the Bible in the English-speaking world was the Vulgate. Although not the first, the most important Reformation translation was that by **Tyndale** in 1525. The famous **King James Version** (1611) used his work. The Revised Version (1885) updated the KJV in light of new manuscript discoveries and changes in the English language. In 1901, Americans produced their version of this revision known as the American Standard Version. The Revised Standard Version (1952) continued and updated this translation tradition. Recently, the **New Revised Standard Version** (1990) moved this translation tradition toward inclusive language. British scholars have also continued revisions of the KJV tradition with the **New English Bible** (1970) and the Revised English Bible (1989).

Dispute continued over the NT's exact limits for some time. The oldest complete NT manuscript dates from the fourth century. At the beginning of that century, Eusebius divided NT scriptures into three categories: recognized, disputed, and spurious [Ecclesiastical History, 3.25]. By the end of that century, Athanasius' festal letter to his North African churches (367 CE) listed the twenty-seven books now considered the NT together for the first time. The eventual dominance of the Vulgate, containing the same 27 books, further ensured their recognition as scripture. Even the Reformation with its published translations in new national languages did not seriously challenge this NT canon.

Figure 5: **English Translations: Catholic and Jewish**

Important modern Catholic translations include the Rheims-Douai (1610) and the New Jerusalem Bible (1985). The New American Bible (1970) was the first American Catholic translation of the original languages.

The Jewish Publication Society Bible (1917) was for years the American Jewish Bible. The New Jewish Version (1962-81) differs more radically from the KJV tradition.

English readers obviously have several available options. Informed choices can be made by consulting the prefaces to the various translations and by comparing the translations on selected texts.

The Bible as an Ancient Near Eastern Text

The HB is a product of the Ancient Near East and the NT of the Hellenistic-Roman world. Although powerful institutions declare the Bible's relevance today, the Bible is an antique foreigner. The Bible's languages (Hebrew, Aramaic, Greek) require translation, and the Bible's settings are antique, exotic lands.

Far more importantly, the cultural codes by which the biblical books were written and read (for hundreds of years) are alien to modernity [see figure 6]. Quite simply, people explained events and life itself differently then than now. In particular, **modernity's explanatory code is rationalistic and individualistic while that of the biblical text relies instead upon *divine sovereignty* (rule).** If one grants the divine sovereignty, everything else in biblical literature follows. To navigate in the biblical world, then, the modern reader who relies upon scientific and/or philosophical reason for explanations must at least temporarily exercise "a willing suspension of disbelief."

Figure 6: Biblical and Modern World-View

Biblical	Modern
divine sovereignty	individualism
providence	chance, human effort
monarchy	democracy
sacred	secular
supernatural	natural
theistic	humanistic
pre-scientific	scientific
agricultural, pastoral	industrial
animals	machines
poetic, symbolic	prosaic, descriptive
patriarchal	egalitarian
parochial	universal
faith	reason
magic, ritual	technology

For example, modern "scientific" historians describe the destruction of Israel and Judah as the result of foreign imperialism. The modern reader comfortable with such an appraisal must "suspend disbelief" to grapple with the biblical assertion that the destruction was a divine judgment on the peoples' religious apostasy (cf. 2 Kings 17). Similarly, the poetic description of the Israelite infantry's victory over immobilized Canaanite chariots may evade modern historians:

> LORD, when you went out from Seir . . .
> the earth trembled, and the heavens poured,

> the clouds indeed poured water. . . .
> The stars fought from heaven,
>   from their courses they fought against Sisera. (Judg 5:4, 20)

Of course, the distinction between the world-views is not merely a matter of explaining individual events in different ways. For many, reason's successes have created a "sensate society" with an "empirical, this-worldly, secular, humanistic, pragmatic, utilitarian, contractual, epicurean . . ." orientation [Kahn and Wiener, in Berger, Rumor, 1]. One can hardly imagine a world-view which differs more radically from the frustrated Hellenistic religiosity of Jesus' kingdom of God or Paul's life in the spirit.

Reason applied technologically (the Industrial Revolution) and bureaucratically (secularization) created the radically new world of modern cities, nations, and governments drastically improving the average person's quality of life.   Certainly, its mechanistic, rationalized explanatory code differs from that of agrarian empires and natural religions.

Thus, for example, ancient authors often described evil using bestial images (Dan 7; Rev 12-13). Modern authors resort more often to mechanical imagery. One thinks at random of Hal the computer from 2001, of Darth Vader from Star Wars, of the Terminator, and of Robocop. Today, technology is the dangerous source of power. Even when film flirts with the ancient holy, as in Raiders of the Lost Ark, modern imagery transforms it into a mechanical, bomb-like device.

Further, religion today has become an institution separate from other institutions (e.g., government, the economy). The ancient biblical prophets made no such distinctions. Good economic (e.g., Am 2) and political advice were synonymous with religious advice. Thus, when Judah faced a military crisis, Isaiah recommended faith rather than reliance on military weaponry or alliances (Isa 7; 31). Although Americans once feared a Catholic President and although

Billy Graham has frequented the White House, contemporary military budgets indicate the foreignness of Isaiah's advice.

Finally, in America in particular, individualism and its corollaries render several aspects of the biblical world-view problematic: the exaltation of monarchy as the type of government properly modeling God's control of the world; the exaltation of society at the expense of the individual; the exaltation of Jews at the expense of other nationalities; and the exaltation of men at the expense of women. Although some Americans subscribe to these notions, most will not accept them. They cut too drastically across the modern American world-view of democracy, individualism, and equal rights.

Scripture, Word of God, and Myth

For Jewish and Christian religious communities, however, the Bible is not merely an ancient Near Eastern text. It is also *scripture*, the community's sacred literature. Western religious communities often refer to their scripture as the *word of God* [see figure 7].

Comparative religionists prefer the term *"myth"* as a synonym for scripture/word of God. A myth is **a community's master story** [see figures 8; 10] providing it with

    a. textual contact with the **sacred** (symbols, rituals);
    b. **social charters** (order, cohesion);
    c. **individual identity** (location, models, ethos); and
    d. **a world-view** (explanatory code, filter).

Myth is a community's narrative repository of the sacred, the awesome, attractive power providing both life and meaning. Enacted in ritual, myth provides safe, traditional **access to the sacred**. Together, myth and ritual recreate the founding *hierophany* for as long as the community survives.

Figure 7: **The Word of God**

The term, "the word of God," suggests that the Bible is divine speech or the record of such speech. Theologians have used three different theories to explain how God might speak through human authors. The **mechanical** view assumes that God used humans as tools overwhelming their finitude and preventing human error. The **dynamic** view asserts that the divine word is mysteriously and irretrievably mixed with mere human words. The **poetic** view declares the words to be merely those of human geniuses.

For outsiders, a community's assertion that a text is the word of God describes the community, rather than the Bible. To those outside, the declaration is the **community's confession of faith** and its designation of a text as its norm for its future polity, creed, ritual, and ethic.

A hierophany is a manifestation of the sacred in some ordinary (profane) artifact, event, or person. The event makes the ordinary a **vehicle for the transcendent**. Myth, then, is a vehicle for transcendence. Myth lifts humans above their captivity in the banal and allows them visions of better futures [Berger, cited in May, 25].

Combining the empirical with a transcendent world of value, myth is a *symbolic* narrative. One cannot gesture toward transcendence literally. One must forever "throw across" one's meaning. Because of its symbolic nature, myth is also an esoteric tale. It has meaning only within a particular community and its tradition. Only prophetic imagination (other hierophanies or symbols) or priestly mediation (ritual and interpretation) can clarify it.

In short, myth does not stand alone. It requires ritual to dramatize it, texts to enshrine it, institutions to protect and interpret it, and a community to incarnate it (that is, religion). Inextricably interwoven into the life of its community, a myth is a "community charter":

> It [myth] expresses, enhances, and codifies belief; it safeguards and enforces morality; it vouches for the efficiency of ritual and contains practical rules for the guidance of man.
>
> It is not an intellectual explanation or an artistic imagery, but a pragmatic charter of primitive faith and moral wisdom. [Malinowski, Myth, 81-83]

If myth is a fiction, then, it is **the culturally important fiction** [Doty, Mythography, 18]. With its bureaucracy (e.g., ritual), it assists cultural cohesion and survival by **transmitting a common identity**, by easing social transitions, and by providing a catharsis for social inequities [Malinowski, "Religion," 149-58].

In short, myth creates communal order. By creating order, it creates meaning or "world." Such orders, of course, provide individual as well as social identity. **Myth locates individuals** within a community and its tradition. Myth marks out boundaries. It indicates what to do and when (ethic). It provides paradigmatic models for all significant actions (e.g., eating, sexuality). Myth, then, specifies the self which individuals may legitimately become [Doty, Mythography, 28-29; May, 87].

Finally, myth **provides the community's basic world-view**, its explanatory code. It allows humans to see life whole and significantly:

> Myths are the instruments by which we continually struggle to make our experience intelligible to

ourselves. A myth is a large, controlling image that gives philosophical meaning to the facts of ordinary life; that is, which has organizing value for experience. [Murray, cited in Doty, Mythography, 10]

By providing a lens through which to view life, myth supplies the cultural answers to the "big questions," the basic *existential* questions of human life. In particular, myth offers identity and *theodicy* (a sense of meaning in the face of evil).

Figure 8: **Definitions of Myth**

Myth has multiple meanings [cf. Doty, 9]:

a. lie/fiction
b. stories about the gods
c. primitive science
d. etiologies

e. ritual texts
f. concrete universals
g. explanations of belief
h. social charters

Usages a-d are the most common. They pejoratively describe someone else's world-view as myth while insidiously implying that the speaker possesses truth. Usages e-h reflect the use of myth in an academic, comparative perspective. They reflect the academic attempt in a pluralist world to avoid *ethnocentrism* or to practice tolerance of the perspective of the other.

Summary

The Bible is the product of the religious experience of Israel and early Christian communities. As such, it is an ancient religious document. An informed reading, then, should recognize the Bible as both an Ancient Near Eastern text and as a myth.

Figure 9: **Myth and Reason**

Ancient Greeks sometimes distinguished **logos** ("reason") and **mythos** ("story"). Since the Enlightenment, **logos** (philosophy and science) has dominated the Western mind. This dominance, of course, closes off other avenues for accruing information (symbol, art). Not incidentally, many moderns misunderstand the Bible largely because they wish to read it as **logos** (rationally arranged argument), rather than as **mythos** (story). More importantly, a society confined to its own reason cuts itself off from possibilities of transcendence and courts death.

Review Questions

1. How does the HB differ from the Christian? How does the Catholic Bible differ from the Protestant?

2. Write a one-paragraph history of Israel. What are its three major periods?

3. When did the HB come into existence? What is the pre-history of the HB? Who preserved the text of the HB? What is the oldest text of the HB? In what form did the early Christian communities use the HB?

4. Write a one-paragraph history of early Christianity. Identify its three major periods. When did the NT come to be?

5. Identify the four most basic contrasts between the biblical and modern world-views.

6. What is scripture? What does it mean to say that the Bible is the word of God?

7. What is a myth? Explain the functions of myth.

Figure 10: **The Bible as Myth**

Modern biblical scholars first began to use myth to describe the Bible when they began to realize the distance between the Bible and themselves. D. F. Strauss used the term in the nineteenth century to describe the Bible as a repository of vivid, but primitive religious images. He wished to restate the biblical myth in terms of modern philosophy (in particular, Hegelianism). R. Bultmann advocated a similar approach in the twentieth century with a different modern philosophy (existentialism). Neither thought that modern readers could make "literal" sense of the Bible and live in the modern world. Further, both scholars privileged rational, cognitive **(logos)** language.

Beginning with biblical critics like Amos Wilder, however, recent scholars have tried to approach myth more aesthetically and to appreciate it as **mythos** without subjecting it to **logos** requirements. That is, one can term the Bible myth without prejudging its truth or relevance [see figures 8; 9]. In the pluralist twentieth century, this approach also has the benefit of encouraging rational, tolerant discussion of competing world-views.

Questions for Reflection

1. Why has the Western world associated the sacred with a text? What else might serve as a vehicle to the sacred?

2. Describe the text's understanding of the "word of God." How does this compare to popular opinions?

3. Are there other important Western scriptures? Are the Q'uran and the Book of Mormon Bibles? How do they function for their communities? Are they significant influences on Western history and culture? Are they as significant as the Judaeo-Christian Bible to the

West?

4. How does the text's understanding of myth differ from the popular definition? What is dangerous about the popular understanding? About the academic view?

5. Are there non-religious texts which function as myth in the West?

6. Is myth important in the modern world?

7. What is the American myth (world-view)? What incarnates this myth (text, other media)? Does it survive from one generation to the next?

For Further Reading

For a brief introduction to the history of Israel, see J. Miller, Historian. For a popular treatment, see M. Grant, History. For more technical treatments, see Bright; Noth; and Miller and Hayes.

On the history and diversity of early Christianity, see Duling and Perrin, 99-139; W. Bauer; Dunn, Unity, 235-366; and Koester, NT, vol. 2.

On the use of the OT in early Christianity, see Grant and Tracy, 28-51.

For discussions of canon, see Anderson, Understanding, 636-43; Duling and Perrin, 130-34; Kuemmel, Introduction, 475-510; Campenhausen; James Sanders, Canon; Blenkinsopp, Canon; and Gamble.

On texts and translation, see Bruce, Books; **idem**, English; Metzger, Text; and Kubo and Sprecht.

On the nature of scripture, see Stendahl, "Classic"; Detweiler, "Sacred"; and Kort, 6-23.

On the sacred, see Livingston, 53-73; Eliade, Profane; and

Otto. On transcendence in modernity, see Berger, <u>Rumor</u>.

For an introductory discussion of myth, see Livingston, 86-96. For more technical approaches, see Doty; <u>Mythography</u>; Malinowski, <u>Myth</u>; **idem**, "Religion"; Wheelwright, "Poetry"; Dundes; and Rogerson.

On the Bible and myth, see Strauss; and Bultmann, "Mythology." For a discussion of religious language as discursive **(logos)** and/or non-discursive **(mythos)**, see Capps, 209-65.

On symbol, see Tillich, 41-54; and Eliade, "Methodological."

On the evolution of society and religion, see Berger, <u>Canopy</u>; Bellah, "Evolution." On the changes in cultural code between antiquity and modernity, see Malina, <u>Anthropology</u>; Krentz, 1-32; Nineham, 1-39; and Harvey.

On the modern myth, see Berger, <u>Canopy</u>; Ellul; Richard E. Moore; and May. Berger, <u>Rumor</u>; May; and Huston Smith critique the modern myth for its over-emphasis on reason. Bellah, <u>Habits</u>; and M. Harrington critique it for its over-emphasis on individualism.

On the American mythos, see James Oliver Robertson; and Bellah, <u>Habits</u>. For critique, see Jewett, <u>Captain</u>; and Jewett and Lawrence.

CHAPTER 2

READING THE BIBLE: A THEORETICAL INTRODUCTION

Chapter Preview

The different reading strategies approach the Bible within different **contexts** (church or academy), for different **purposes** (spiritual, historical, aesthetic, anthropological, psychological, or political), and with different basic **images** of the Bible (word of God, antique myth, or literature). A conscious reading strategy should respect the Bible's status as **literature** and as **ancient myth**. Also, a critical approach should be open to **alternative readings**.

Conscious Reading and Factors Influencing Reading

As an **ancient myth**, the Bible is difficult to read in the modern world. In fact, one might hypothesize that one who does not have difficulty is misreading the text and appropriating it to his/her own world-view unconsciously. For the religious, their myth-ritual institution appropriates the Bible for them and makes it perennially relevant. In the pluralist academy, however, attention to a conscious, humble reading strategy is necessary.

After all, unless one remains within the safe confines of a myth-ritual community, readings differ dramatically because reading is an errant, willful process. Some contemporary scholars describe reading as a process of filling-in textual blanks [e.g., Iser]. Readers, of course, supply those blanks according to their world-views. That is, interpretations reflect psychological profiles [Holland] and socio-cultural locations [Robert Brown]. Masters and slaves, haves and have-nots, Republicans and Marxists, men and women, citizens of industrial societies and third-world peasants, Catholics and

Pentecostals all read differently. In fact, "every reader is, while he is reading, the reader of his own self" [M. Proust, cited by Genette, 261].

Apart from hidden psychological depths, several fairly obvious factors influence interpretation: **context, construing image, and purpose.**

Different **contexts** create different readings. Religious communities read the Bible in worship expecting an encounter with the sacred which will transform or empower life. The religious live and read "within the myth," within a context of faith and commitment to their text. By contrast, academic communities read the Bible in a context of reasoned debate. Academics read in a non-confessional, pluralistic context subjecting the text to alien questions and standards.

Different **images** of the text also effect reading. One reads novel, history, textbook, and poem differently. What one expects governs what one finds. Construing images filter some material in and others out. Reading communities share basic construing images. Thomas Kuhn has described such governing images as *paradigms* or the shared "constellation of beliefs, values, techniques, and so on" by which a community interprets data [Kuhn, viii, 17, 175; cf. Kelsey].

For the Bible, word of God and antique myth are radically different paradigms. One reads the word of God with "aggressive faith," subjecting all other material to it [Detweiler, 223-24]. By contrast, one reads antique myth dispassionately and critically in light of other more modern world-views.

Finally, **purposes** influence reading. Reading Paradise Lost or Great Expectations for entertainment and reading them to prepare for an exam yield vastly different results. Historians and literary critics read the same texts (e.g., the Iliad or the Bible) to different ends--history or aesthetics. Obviously, reading the Bible for entertainment (wiling time away with the hotel Gideon) is vastly different from reading for cultural advancement (academic pursuit). Further, reading the Bible for historical or literary answers differs from reading for spiritual guidance.

Review of Six Major Reading Strategies

Differing contexts, paradigms, and purposes create diverse reading strategies. Such strategies are the **conscious, rationalized reading systems** (rules) producing and governing disciplined readings. While any number of strategies is possible, only six historically important reading strategies are examined here: proof-text, traditional, historical-critical, fundamentalist, literary-critical, and reader-response.

Proof-Text

The proof-text strategy is the most popular approach. It **selectively appropriates bits and pieces** of the Bible for use in new contexts like worship, rhetoric, and personal crisis.

Thus, the church often proof-texts the Bible in **worship**. Preachers seldom have time to consider a biblical passage's historical and literary context. Rather, a passage is chosen according to a lectionary or at a pastor's whim for immediate application to worshipers' lives. The context, then, for interpretation is a liturgical calendar (or selected themes), a church or pastor's theology, and/or the dilemmas of the modern religious.

Educated, rhetorically adept persons also proof-text the Bible to win an **argument**. The biblical citation proves their point. Unfortunately, almost all sides (e.g., pro-life vs. pro-choice or women's rights vs. male chauvinists) can tailor the Bible to their argument. Such proof-texting does indicate, however, that the Bible remains an acknowledged authority in the West. The Bible is still worth citing in social and political debate.

The classic proof-texter, however, is the sincere believer in quest of **spiritual guidance**. Such readers open the Bible randomly (or to favorite passages) and find God's specific advice, often called "God's will," for their particular question. Their past successes with the method reinforce future use. Incidentally, the fact that Psalms deals with the entire gamut of human emotions, that it thus has relevance to most human problems, that Psalms is roughly in the middle of the Bible, and that a Bible opened randomly will often open near the middle (or to oft-used passages) may help explain some successes.

Except for liturgical uses, the context of proof-texting is intensely **personal and subjective**. Further, the method is normally employed in problematic or anxious situations. Its purpose is devotion, rhetoric, or "**self-help**." At the very least, the proof-texter construes the Bible as an authority which clinches arguments. Liturgical and private use, of course, understands the Bible as the **word of God**. The liturgical use requires the Bible to be a harmonious, canonical whole. The parts must agree if they are to be used piecemeal. The private use images the Bible as an **oracle**, a kind of biblical ouija board. Behind it all, of course, stands the assumption of God's superintending providence.

Traditional

Liturgical proof-texting resembles the traditional reading of the Bible. Historically the most important strategy, the traditional was the reading strategy from the end of the second century CE to the rise of the historical-critical method in the eighteenth century. As the name implies, a reader receives the Bible's proper interpretation as a **"tradition" handed down by the proper authorities.**

In the second century, a number of competing groups claimed to represent authentic Christianity. Each claimed to possess the genuine Christian truth either by virtue of their historical connection with some early Christian leader or by virtue of recent, esoteric revelations. The "Great Church," the ancestor of the Roman Catholic Church, emerged victorious by century's end because it convinced many that it was the legitimate bearer of the "**apostolic tradition**."

Figure 1: **Jewish Tradition**

Late Judaism produced its own traditional connections with earlier "golden ages." Of course, the Jewish tradition was not apostolic, but prophetic and rabbinic. The opening line of the Mishnaic tractate Pirke Aboth (1.1) neatly summarizes the Jewish tradition:

> Moses received Torah from Sinai and delivered it to Joshua, and Joshua to the Elders, and the Elders to the Prophets, and the Prophets delivered it to the men of the Great Synagogue. They said three things: Be deliberate in judgement; and raise up many disciples; and make a fence for the Torah.

This succession resembles the tripartite division of the HB: Torah, the Prophets, and the Writings. Beyond the succession implicit in the HB, Pirke Aboth lists a series of rabbinic pairs who transmitted the Mosaic tradition. The *Mishnah* and the *Talmud* ultimately codify that rabbinic tradition. This Rabbinic Judaism is the Jewish version of the Christian Great Church.

Modernity fractured Jewish tradition as it did Christian. Today, Judaism includes Orthodox (the most traditional), Conservative, and Reformed (comparable to liberal Protestants) Jews.

The Great Church claimed Jesus' twelve apostles as its heroic ancestors and portrayed them as harmoniously agreed on matters of church organization and eternal salvation (cf. Acts). This apostolic harmony was a "golden age" from which the later church ingloriously fell [cf. Eusebius, EH, 3.32.7-8].

The Great Church thus defined her opponents as late-arriving heretics. By contrast, the Great Church offered continuing contact with the apostles through a threefold "apostolic tradition" of men, faith, and writings.

In later years, if not immediately, the most important church was Rome. Rome traced her lineage to Peter, first of the apostles, to whom Jesus had entrusted the "keys of the kingdom" (Mt 16:19). Peter appointed his successor, who appointed his successor, and so forth down to the present pope. These leaders handed down the apostolic faith, the creed summarizing the harmonious apostolic teaching (cf. 2 Tim 2:2). Finally, the church possessed a written apostolic message (eventually the NT). This apostolic church declared itself the sole, proper reader of these texts (cf. 2 Pet 3:16; and below). The Bible meant only what the Great Church taught.

Apostolic tradition connected readers to the Bible. Cultural changes, however, soon severed the continuity. In response, the church allegorized. *Allegory* ignores an ancient tradition's literal meaning to discover **new, hidden meanings**. Through allegory, the church applied the Bible to new cultural situations and played down biblical material no longer thought worthy of God (e.g., anthropomorphisms, food laws, immorality). Through allegory, for example, the divine command to slaughter innocents became a command for Christians to purge their lives of sins. Further, allegory could find the church's whole teaching in any scripture. Thus, for example, in Augustine's reading of the "Good Samaritan" (cf. Lk 10:30-35), the man beset by thieves is Adam, the thieves are the devil and his angels, the priest and Levite represent the OT which is useless for salvation, the Good Samaritan is Jesus Christ, the inn is the church, and the innkeeper is Paul [cited in full in Dodd, Parables, 1-2].

Gradually, medieval interpreters found four levels of meaning in every scripture [cited in Grant and Tracy, 85]:

The letter shows us what God and our fathers did;
The allegory shows us where our faith is hid;
The moral meaning gives us rules of daily life;
The anagogy shows us where we end our strife.

Obviously, allegory leads to highly subjective meanings. Using such a method, one can find mysterious meanings in the phone book. The church's tradition, however, provided a controlling authority. Not surprisingly, then, the church demands readings in harmony with its "rule of faith" or the "catholic sense" [Grant and Tracy, 73-82].

The traditional reading's context is **ecclesiastical**. Outside the church, there is no reading. The strategy construes the Bible as the **word of God** entrusted to the apostolic church. That construal, of course, subordinates individual readings to the official interpretation. This official word functions as **myth**. The strategy's purpose, then, is to provide a **vehicle to the sacred** in which the religious can find life and meaning.

Historical-Critical

The traditional method persists where various religious groups read the Bible according to their respective theological traditions. Modernity, however, ended the traditional strategy's dominance.

The Reformation destroyed apostolic harmony. Suddenly, various christianities, with institutional and political support, were available. The competition made it difficult for any church to claim convincingly that it was the one true apostolic church.

Protestant readings became increasingly individualistic for both technical and theological reasons. The printing press and the

Reformers' vernacular translations made the Bible readily available. Further, the priesthood-of-the-believer theology made every believer his own interpreter of scripture. Readers no longer needed the church's controlling authority. Theoretically, the Reformers entrusted readers to reason and the Spirit.

Figure 2: **Tradition and Historical-Criticism**

Diverse interpretations of the divine command to kill the Canaanites (Ex 23:23-24; Deut 7:1-5; Josh 6:17-21) distinguish these approaches. Because the community's God would hardly demand such, tradition allegorizes these texts. Spiritualized, the command demands that the Christian purge her life (the promised land) of sins (the Canaanites).

By contrast, historical criticism explains the passages in light of holy war customs (including the ban, the practice of devoting all to the god who fights for the army) and natural religion ideology (in which ethical demands do not extend outside the community). This historicizing approach implies a progressive revelation assuming that Joshua's notion of God is more primitive than that of contemporary readers.

In short, where tradition reads difficult ancient texts in light of the community's faith, historical-criticism assigns difficult texts to the past.

The Enlightenment further eroded tradition. For the Enlightenment, reason, rather than allegiance to tradition, prevailed in area after area including the reading of the Bible [Krentz, 10-16].

These intellectual movements and the discovery of new worlds created a new perspective, the recognition of **relativity**. Connections with the past, long assumed, were broken. Modern readers looked at the Bible from afar.

Figure 3: **The History of the Texts**

The historical-critical method sees many texts as revised editions of earlier oral and written traditions, rather than the work of prophets or apostles.

Source critics detect in present texts earlier written sources. For example, most agree that Torah was the product of several (usually four) early sources stretching from the monarchy (the Yahwist) through the post-exilic period (the Priestly) [see chaps. 5, 7]. **Form critics** argue that a period of oral tradition preceded written sources and texts. They find in present texts stereotyped forms (e.g., oracles, laments, miracle stories) which they argue once circulated independently. These mnemonic forms were preserved in certain settings for specific purposes (e.g., legal, ritual, educational, missionary). The form critics often endeavor to write the history of the forms (in German **Formsgeschichte,** "form history") tracing them from event or poetic creation to text. Finally, **redaction critics** ask when, how, and why editors put together these earlier oral and written traditions. They investigate the theological concerns governing the final textual product.

Eighteenth and nineteenth-century scholars created the historical-critical method to deal with this new, distant Bible. In essence, historical-critics **read documents in light of their original circumstances**. To do so, these scholars have to reconstruct the documents' history. For these critics, this history is both whatever events the texts might refer to (e.g., the Exodus or Jesus), that is, "what actually happened," and the historical process which produced the texts (e.g., who wrote and when).

So described, of course, historical-criticism is an esoteric, professional activity. Few amateurs are likely to master the antiquarian (including languages) detail necessary to read so.

Even for trained scholars, the method is hardly simple. A scholar's historical recreation is a highly personal combination of data and interpretation. The method follows a *hermeneutical* circle. The primary evidence is the biblical text. After recovering history from the text, the scholar then interprets the same text in light of the recovered history. Further, crucial data is often simply unavailable. Scholarly imagination has to fill-in numerous gaps. Not surprisingly, scholars have arrived at numerous reconstructions of biblical history. The best scholarship arrives only at probabilities.

Nevertheless, historical-critics agree remarkably on many issues (or fall into recognizable camps). More importantly, historical-critical scholars have demonstrated the Bible's **ANE quality**. The Bible speaks, not in the gods' timeless language, but in historically conditioned, relative human language.

The Bible's distance creates relevance problems. After scholars uncover **what a text meant** in its ancient context, how are they to state **what the text means** now? Some scholars forego this issue and antiquate the Bible. Among those who search for relevance, the strictest solution demands the existence of similar situations then and now. By this standard, most of the Bible is irrelevant most of the time. A less rigorous, and more popular, solution attempts to uncover the eternal or lasting truth, the kernel in the biblical chaff. This process is, of course, highly subjective and generally reveals more about the individual scholar's world-view (myth, philosophy) than it does about the biblical text.

The context of historical-criticism is the modern academy and a **professional guild of antiquarian scholars**. Its purpose is the **recovery of history** hidden by a recalcitrant text. To recover historical truth, the strategy employs the rationalistic methodologies of modern historiography. Such an approach reads against the text's grain requiring it to answer questions framed by an alien perspective. Instead of a "suspension of belief," it practices a "hermeneutic of suspicion" [cf. Ricoeur, <u>Freud</u>, 32-36]. Historical-criticism construes the Bible as an **ancient myth**, the sacred literature of religious groups in the ANE and/or in the Hellenistic world.

Fundamentalist

In the late nineteenth and early twentieth century, a reaction against modernity began in American Protestantism. This movement called for a return to Christian fundamentals: the inerrancy of scripture, the virgin birth of Jesus, the substitutionary atonement, the bodily resurrection of Christ, and his bodily return. The common element is the miraculous. Fundamentalism, as in the machinations of creation science groups, **defends the supernatural against modern naturalism** (e.g., science). Not surprisingly, fundamentalism's first opponents were evolution (e.g., the Scopes Monkey Trial) and historical-criticism.

The early fundamentalist groups were *sects*, small counter-cultural groups withdrawing from an evil world in order to maintain their own purity. Fundamentalist groups often flesh out this *ethical dualism* in *apocalyptic* terms. That is, fundamentalists have often thought themselves to be living in the evil days just prior to the final struggle between good and evil.

This polemic mentality makes fundamentalism an aggressive purification movement. Fundamentalists reserve their most vicious attacks for the falsely religious, the mainline churches who have apostasized by accepting modernity. Thus, when fundamentalists have gained control of colleges and seminaries, widespread purges have followed.

Recently, fundamentalism's purification trends have overcome its withdrawal fantasies, and fundamentalism has become militantly involved in political and cultural life. Thus, fundamentalists have attacked communism (1950s), secular humanism (1980s), and godless school curricula (campaigning periodically for creation science). To date, their greatest popularity and cultural impact came in the eighties through an alliance with the Republican party.

Many fundamentalists equate Christianity and the American way. This trend supports the scholarly observation that fundamentalism's utopia is not NT Christianity, but rather nineteenth-century Protestant America before modernization and massive Catholic immigrations [Marsden, Religion, 168-205].

Figure 4: **Historical-Criticism and Fundamentalism**

Historical-criticism reads texts, like Gen 1, in light of their ancient contexts. Thus, historical-criticism would compare Gen 1 to ancient creation myths (like the Enuma Elish), rather than to modern science.

Fundamentalism, by contrast, endeavors to harmonize its inerrant word of God-Bible with modern science. At its most extreme, fundamentalism may demand that Gen 1 be taught in public schools as an alternative to modern science (in particular, evolution). Less extreme versions read Gen 1 in non-literal ways so that it harmonizes with science. For example, some read the six days of Gen 1 as six creative periods, rather than six twenty-four hour periods. Others find two creations in Gen 1:1-3 separated by a cosmic catastrophe (1:2) in which the dinosaurs perished. More sophisticated forms of fundamentalism harmonize more generally by restricting science and Gen 1 to separate compartments. Here, science is restricted to "how" questions and Genesis to "who" and "why" questions.

Despite their romanticism, the fundamentalist reading strategy is highly **rationalistic**. Their rhetoric often asserts that "the Bible teaches ____." For them, the Bible is a unified, rational whole easily summarized in creedal propositions (the fundamentals).

Similarly, *inerrancy* functions as the first principle of a philosophical system from which everything else is deduced. As such, it is above criticism. Nothing could sound more ridiculous to historical-critics. The Bible's transmission alone poses seemingly insuperable problems. The fundamentalist simply rejoins that it is the lost autographs, the authors' actual manuscripts, which are inerrant. The historical-critic despairs while the fundamentalist rests happily with his first principle.

Inerrancy means that nothing in the Bible can be read in such a way as to be in error, that is, in conflict with another biblical passage or what is otherwise known to be true. Although fundamentalists like to call their biblical readings *literal*, the need to **harmonize** internally, between various biblical passages, and externally, with other truths, frequently causes non-literal interpretations. For example, according to Gen 1, God created the world in six days. In the face of pressing geological evidence, most fundamentalists now reject this literal time-frame. Instead, they declare that long time-periods separated the six creative days or argue that the creative "days" were lengthy epochs rather than twenty-four hour periods.

Fundamentalist commitment to literal readings arises from their Protestant and American populist heritage. Nonetheless, the machinations required to harmonize the numerous apparent biblical errors are beyond an amateur reader. Like tradition and historical-criticism, fundamentalism requires professional experts, the fundamentalist clergy.

Given its relative lack of institutional organization and its anti-intellectualism, fundamentalism's authoritative readings tend toward the *charismatic*. Typically, an engaging television evangelist or the pastor of a mega-church leads the faithful through the thicket of apparent biblical error. As a result, of course, a particular biblical interpretation, rather than the Bible itself, is accorded inerrant status. This strategy makes the fundamentalist preacher incredibly authoritative.

This strategy's context is an **embattled religious sect**. Fundamentalism depicts the Bible as the **inerrant word of God** in defiance of modern naturalism. Like other "church-context" strategies, fundamentalism reads the Bible for religious (myth, ritual, etc.) reasons. Fundamentalism's militant context and rationalist program, however, makes its characteristic purpose the recovery of **creedal truth**. In short, for the fundamentalist, the Bible is a **textbook,** rather than a myth.

Literary-Criticism: Narrative, Structural, and Ideological

The reading strategies discussed to this point appeal to **external controls** to guarantee correct readings: providence, the institutional church, original historical circumstances, or charismatic individuals. By contrast, some twentieth-century forms of literary criticism--**New Criticism and narrative criticism**--have looked to the text's **internal** workings for clues to proper reading. Narrative criticism's basic construal of the text is aesthetic. Instead of asking how the text was produced, narrative criticism pursues a text's literary qualities: genre, plot, characters, setting, style, and so forth.

In short, where the previous strategies have attempted to use the text to recover the external reality to which it refers, narrative criticism focuses on the **text's own world**. That world's relationship to reality is no longer the premier question. The literary critic "suspends belief." He foregoes his understanding of "how the world wags" in order to understand the text's own reality.

Like historical-criticism, then, narrative criticism distances the Bible. Suspending the question of the relationship between the text's world and ordinary reality leaves the text's meaning indefinite. After all, what do the internal workings of an aesthetic world have to do with the critic's own reality?

For some, the aesthetic needs no external justification. It is an end in itself [cf. Sontag]. Others defend the aesthetic in terms of the cultural enhancement it provides. One can, of course, elaborate such justifications in terms of the Western tradition or in terms of the **perennial struggle with existential questions**.

Figure 5: **Historical-Criticism and Literary-Criticism**

Historical-criticism asks how the text came to be. In Gen 1-2, for example, historical-criticism argues that the present text is the product of two different sources because 1:1-2:4a and 2:4b-25) have different styles, vocabularies, and theologies.

By contrast, literary-criticism asks how the text works. It might observe the tensions between humans created "in the image of God" in 1:26-27 and man made "from the ground" in 2:7. The story of human mortality in Gen 3 resolves this literary tension.

Feminist literary criticism might also note a dichotomy between Gen 1:1-2:4a and 2:4b-25. In this case, however, the distinction would be between an egalitarian text (1:26-27) and a chauvinistic one (Gen 2:18-25). Of course, feminist readings would privilege the former.

Narrative criticism is not the only type of literary criticism in the modern, pluralistic academy. Structuralism, ideological criticism, and reader-response are also influential today.

Structuralism, like historical-criticism, is a suspicious reading. It searches for the text's **underlying structure**. Some structuralists look for the basic plot structure present with modifications in all stories and reduce all stories to relatively simple plot-diagrams [Propp; Greimas; cf. the myth criticism of J. Campbell, Hero; and N. Frye, Anatomy].

Other structuralists attempt to describe the world of **linguistic possibilities** from which a text is formed. Such critics treat any parable, for example, as one manifestation of the underlying structure "parable," the abstracted, generalized sum of all parables. Such structuralism produces complicated charts which elucidate particular parables by comparison to the abstraction parable [Via, Parables].

Finally, other structuralists try to find "behind" the text the **structure of the human mind**. Here, particular texts provide clues to the workings of the human mind. These workings are conceived in terms of **binary oppositions**. The reader tries to discover in the text the fundamental opposition and the way in which the text **mediates that opposition** [Levi-Strauss].

Structuralism finds behind the text the truly important world controlling interpretation. Unlike earlier strategies, its beyond is literary, linguistic, or mental. It seeks the super-text behind the text actually read. That beyond is human rather than divine (pace proof-text, traditional, fundamentalist). Further, it conceives the human generally, rather than as concretely individual (pace historical-criticism).

New Historicism is equally suspicious, but it finds a more "intermediate" beyond. Its concern is **the world which generates the text**. It conceives this world differently than either historical-criticism or structuralism, however. It is not concerned so much with the individual or the general as it is with larger cultural forces. Thus, it focuses on the **socio-economic cultural factors**, which unconsciously influence the creation of an artistic work. Quite simply, such ideological criticism is post-Marxist historical-criticism.

Of course, **ideological criticism** appears in other forms. The most popular is **feminist criticism** which seeks to uncover the sexual politics influencing works. In all its forms, ideological criticism is concerned with the **operations of power** which produce the text and which the text advances.

Literary-Criticism: Reader-Response

Reader-response criticism rejects the attempt to uncover a "world behind" the text. It turns away from questions of the text's production and inner aesthetic workings to **the text's reception, the experience of reading**. This shifts attention to a "world ahead" of the text, the reader's reality.

Figure 6: **Literary-Criticism and Reader-Response**

Where literary-criticism attempts to explain how texts work internally, reader-response concerns itself with texts' effects upon readers. Thus, literary-criticism explains Mark's abrupt end (at 16:8) in terms of Mark's generally abrupt style and in terms of Mark's earlier characterizations (of God, Jesus, and the disciples). By contrast, reader-response wants to know what the reader knows or does about the abrupt Markan ending. Reader-response may concern itself with the ideal Markan reader. If so, reader-response asks whether the reader is led to criticize, sympathize with, or replace the disciples. Other types of reader-response tell stories of particular readers' readings of Mark (e.g., the church, particular critics, Matthew).

This shift is a Copernican revolution in criticism. The text and the author vanish as centering points securing interpretation. The text ceases to be an unchanging artistic artifact. Now, **interpretation creates the text**. The (post-Kantian) reader molds, shapes, and creates the text.

While opponents decry the method's subjectivity, radical reader-response critics respond that objectivity does not exist and playfully multiply readings [cf. figure 7]. More traditional reader-response critics seek reading controls.

Rhetorical reader-response seeks textual controls. It examines literary works to uncover the reader expected by and elicited by the text's rhetorical clues. These interpretations seek to describe the text's **ideal reader** [Iser].

Figure 7: **Deconstruction**

Where structuralism reads texts as successful mediations of basic binary oppositions, deconstruction tries to demonstrate that texts are unstable entities threatening to fall apart. Deconstructionists, then, read texts to deliver the term suppressed by what structuralists see as mediation or they read at the margins of a text to seek what the text excludes. In every case, deconstruction reads playfully, creatively, and subversively.

By contrast, **psychological reader-response** foregoes correct readings. Instead, it describes the way **actual readers** read given texts. Ultimately, these critics concentrate on readers' psychological profiles, the fantasies and fears which readings reveal [Holland; Bleich]. The text becomes mere catalyst.

Institutional reader-response returns the controlling institution which owns the text. Such critics examine the rules governing reading and the rules determining the persons and readings to be admitted into the critical discourse. Interestingly, this secular strategy resembles the traditional approach. That is, proper readings depend upon external institutional control [Fish, Is].

The **modern academy**, however, is a less rigid authority than the traditional church. Modern academics are, at least, theoretically aware that their readings are relative and have moral and political consequences. This insight stems from the relatively recent arrival of women and non-Europeans as vocal, critical readers. Such plurality, as well as the plurality of methodologies, reduces the academy's ability to offer authoritative, correct readings.

Unlike the traditional strategy, then, which advances from an interpretative consensus, literary-criticism either revels in plurality or seeks to achieve consensus. When the purpose is consensus, the literary-criticisms focus on the aesthetic, rhetorical text; on its production by anthropological, socio-cultural, or ideological forces; or on its institutionally-governed reception. More simply, the literary-criticisms have **aesthetic** (narrative criticism) and **cognitive** purposes. The information sought comes either from the world "behind" or "ahead" of the text. The literary criticisms read the Bible as **literature**. Within the academy, the Bible has no privileged divine or mythic standing. Other words and myths provide competition.

Summary Comparison

The six major strategies have two strikingly different contexts: **the church or the academy**. These institutions adopt different attitudes toward the Bible. The ecclesiastical context is one of worship, devotion, and faith. The academic is one of debate, criticism, and reason.

A less obvious difference in the strategies' contexts arises from their relationship to **modernity**. The traditional strategy predates modernity. Historical-criticism and literary-criticism are at home in modernity's rationalism and secularism. Fundamentalism, on the other hand, reacts defensively against modernity. Finally, radical versions of reader-response, like deconstruction, suggest either the absurd extremities of modern individualism and pluralism or the arrival of postmodernism [McKnight, Post-modern; and S. Moore, Literary].

The strategies also have two quite different images of the Bible: **myth** or **literature**. The ecclesiastical strategies and historical-criticism perceive the Bible as myth. For the ecclesiastical strategies, of course, the Bible is the myth within which the worshipers live. It is not myth, then, but the word of God. By contrast, for historical-criticism, the Bible is an ancient myth.

Figure 8: **Comparing Strategies**

Strategy	Context, Image, Purpose, and Control
Proof-text	subjective, oracular Bible, self-help, and providence as control
Tradition	church, mythic Bible, access benefits of the sacred, and institution as control
Fundament	sect, inerrant textbook, uncover creedal truth, and pastor as control
Historical	antiquarian academy, antique myth, uncover production of texts, and original context as control
Narrative	academy of artists, literature, aesthetic, and textual controls
Structural	literature professors, Bible as reflection of deep structures, uncover deep structures, and such structure as control
Ideological	politicians, Bible as oppressive literature, identify powers that control, and ideology as control
Reader-Resp	readers, Bible as catalyst, understand reading experience, and the reader as control

For the literary-criticisms, the Bible is less unique. It is literature to be read as other literature. Of course, specific images differ. Various literary-criticisms conceive it as an artistic entity, as a product of deep structures or ideologies, or as a catalyst for reading experiences.

The strategies have three different purposes according to the realities which they seek to explore: the world "behind" the text, the textual world, or the world "ahead" of the text [see figure 9]. Most of the strategies seek to inhabit the sacred (ecclesiastical) or productive **world "behind" the text**. They read in order to find information (divine, historical, ideological) or in order to encounter the sacred (traditional). As the Bible is a religious text, those strategies seeking to find non-religious information read the text suspiciously or "against its grain."

Narrative criticism and rhetorical reader-response somewhat uniquely desire to inhabit **the text's own world**. To do so, these strategies suspend belief or consciously strive to become the text's ideal reader. The purpose of these strategies is more aesthetic than cognitive.

Other forms of reader-response focus on **the world "ahead" of the text**. They read in order to celebrate the experience of reading or to uncover the institutional, ideological controls on reading.

Not incidentally, the discussion of reading strategies uncovers **desires for the "correct" reading**. To achieve such, the strategies impose either **external or internal controls**. Traditional and institutional reader-response readings make obvious appeals to external, institutional control. Less obviously, fundamentalism and historical-criticism also depend respectively upon the external controls of charismatic pastors and an antiquarian guild.

In addition to institutional appeals, strategies also employ references to the forces producing texts as controls. Thus, historical-criticism contends that documents should be read in light of their original historical circumstances. Structuralism utilizes deep structures as a reading guide. Ideological criticism reads in light of the economic and political structures of power producing texts.

Only narrative criticism and reader-response differ here. Narrative criticism's emphasis upon the text itself is a unique attempt at an internal control (cf. rhetorical reader-response). Whether that is what actually happens in such criticism is a moot point. It is the rhetoric that matters. Radical reader-response, of course, is even more peculiar. It alone purports to forego controls and to celebrate the plurality of readings.

Figure 9: **Textual Worlds and Reading Strategies**

Production	**Text**	**Reception**
Proof-text	Narrative	Reader-Respon
Traditional	Rhetorical Reader	Deconstruction
Fundamentalist		Ideological
Historical-critical		
Structuralist		
Ideological		

Conclusion: A Modest Proposal

As the Bible is clearly literature, this text intends to adopt and adapt **narrative criticism** for an introductory reading of the Bible. The historical-critical insight that the Bible is an **ancient myth** will, however, modify this basic approach. In addition to genre, plot, and so forth, then, the text will frequently discuss the Bible's ancient and mythic features. Finally, the context of the modern, pluralistic academy also modifies the method. Given the plethora of readings and academic conventions, the text presents one introductory reading. As a corrective, then, the text will also call attention to **alternative readings** of important texts.

The reading's purpose is **cultural enhancement**. Liberal arts education hands on the Western tradition. To read the Bible, a significant part of that tradition, is to better understand the Western world. Further, the Bible deals pertinently with existential questions. Though moderns may not accept the biblical answers, the conscious struggle with those questions enhances life.

Review Questions

1. Why do readings differ?
2. Describe the various strategies' contexts, purposes, and images of the Bible.
3. What worlds do the various strategies seek to inhabit?
4. How do the various strategies seek to control readings?
5. Briefly describe the text's reading strategy.

Questions for Reflection

1. How do fundamentalist and traditional readings differ?
2. How do historical and literary-critical readings differ?
3. How do structuralist and deconstructionist readings differ?
4. What do the various church-reading strategies mean by saying that the Bible is the word of God?
5. Explain the different meanings of "myth" in the traditional reading strategy, historical-criticism, and narrative criticism.
6. Which reading strategy would a rugged individualist prefer? Which would a conservative prefer? Which would a liberal prefer?

For Further Reading

For an introductory overview of the history of biblical interpretation, see Grant and Tracy; Keegan; and Morgan. For definition of terms and criticisms, see also Coggins and Houlden.

For samples of readings from the different strategies, see Barton; Anderson and Moore; and Castelli, Postmodern.

On different theological images of the Bible, see Kelsey.

On the traditional reading strategy, see Grant and Tracy, 63-82; and Froelich.

For a brief introduction to historical-criticism, see Krentz. For more elaborate reviews, see Kuemmel, Problems; Neill and Wright; Clements, One; and Morgan. For criticism of it, see Smart; and Wink.

On fundamentalism, see Sandeen; Marsden, Fundamentalism; and Barr, Fundamentalism. The latter and Boone are particularly helpful with fundamentalist hermeneutic.

For general introductions to literary theory, see Berman; Adams; and Adams and Searle. For general discussions of biblical criticism and literary theory, see McKnight, Reader; McKnight, Postmodern; S. Moore, Literary; and Castelli, Postmodern.

On narrative criticism, see Genette; Chatman; and Rimmon-Kenan. For biblical criticism and narrative criticism, see Petersen, Literary Criticism; Beardslee; Powell, What; and Berlin.

On structuralism, see Culler, Structuralist. For biblical criticism and structuralism, see Patte, What; and Culley.

On ideological criticism, see Culler, Deconstruction; and Bal. For applications to biblical studies, see Robert Brown; Bal; and Letty Russell.

On reader-response criticism, see Culler, Deconstruction; Suleiman and Crosman; and Tompkins. For applications to biblical studies, see S. Moore, Literary; and Fowler, "Who."

CHAPTER 3

READING THE BIBLE: A LITERARY CRITICAL APPROACH
The Story in the Bible

Chapter Preview

1) Biblical story is about **Eden Lost and Restored** (or the hope thereof). The repetition of this story with different symbols creates a **story-telling tradition** (symbols, patterns), rather than one story.

2) Behind these stories is a **myth-ritual pattern rescuing order from chaos** by narratively connecting the ideal (Eden), the actual (Eden Lost), and the potential (Eden Restored).

3) God motivates biblical story. **Biblical plots depict God's action**: revealing Eden, taking Eden away, or restoring Eden.

4) Biblical story depicts humans in terms of a simple ethical dualism as **with God or apart from God**. Characters stand with God by **election** and/or **faith**.

5) Biblical story-worlds range from the **mythic** to the **ironic**.

6) Biblical story has a **mythic** character.

Story and Discourse

Texts are communications between authors and readers with significant contents and packages. Narrative criticism identifies content as *story* and packaging as *discourse* [Chatman, 19-26]. Important features of the biblical story include plot, characters, and atmosphere. While the entire Bible is not story in generic terms, its other genres (e.g, laws, proverbs, poetry) are normally set in a story-context or imply a story (at least, a world-view which can be narrated).

A Content Overview: "The Story in the Bible"

Seen as a whole, the biblical story is **the search for a lost Eden**. The Bible begins with creation and the loss of Eden (Gen 1-3). Subsequent stories rehearse that loss or respond to loss with various stories of Eden Found.

Figure 1: **Biblical Stories**		
Text	**Eden Lost**	**Eden Restored**
Torah	not yet Israel	Sinai covenant
Joshua	no land	Promised land
1-2 Sam	anarchy	human king
Prophets	God's judgments	God's salvation
Chronicles	exile	second temple
Psalms	apart from God	with God
Wisdom	folly	wisdom
1-2 Macc	foreign rule	Hasmonean kingdom
Apocalyptic	this evil age	the age to come
Jesus	this evil age	parables/miracles
Mark, Paul	the cross	the cross
NT	the cross	church
Paul	flesh	spirit

Despite this variety, the Bible is **a story-telling tradition using common symbols and patterns**. Thus, the various biblical stories agree on several points. First, humans live with a sense of loss. Eden, or some order, is gone. Second, as a result, human life is a quest for Eden. Third, whether one ever regains Eden or not, telling stories makes life meaningful and bearable. Fourth, one person's Eden is another's exile.

Figure 2: **Other Western Bibles**

The Western religious tradition continues the biblical story-telling tradition. Repeatedly, new reform movements have seen the immediate past as Eden Lost and have hoped for the restoration of Eden (e.g. monastic reforms, the Reformation). In this re-symboling of tradition, the Q'uran and the Book of Mormon deserve special mention.

Islam sees the Q'uran as the product of the angel Gabriel's revelation to Muhammed who recorded it. Compared to Judaism and Christianity, this revelation intensifies monotheism, divine determinism, and the emphasis upon scriptural revelation. Compared to the HB and the Christian Bible, the Q'uran emphasizes divine oracles and reduces narrative to a minimum.

The Book of Mormon continues biblical history in the ancient Americas. In that story, the lost tribes of Israel migrated to America where one group paganized and became the American Indians. The pagans, then, destroyed the faithful Israelites to whom the resurrected Jesus had just appeared. Before their destruction, their last prophet, Mormon, wrote down their story and hid it until the last days. In the nineteenth century, the angel Moroni communicated the revelation anew to Joseph Smith who wrote it down as the Book of Mormon.

Biblical Story's Myth-Ritual Patterns

The major biblical stories have a structure which resembles myth-ritual transformations. *Myth* narrates and *ritual* enacts the transition from one stage (e.g., childhood or the old year) through a dangerous liminal period to a new, better stage (e.g., adulthood or the new year). Thus, in the typical hero tale, the hero departs the world of common day into a region of supernatural wonder: fabulous forces are there encountered and a decisive victory is won: the hero comes back from this mysterious adventure with the power to bestow boons on his fellow man [Campbell, Hero, 30].

Schematized, the common pattern here is a **"mythic v,"** sketching the separation from Eden, the transition, and the finding of a new Eden [so Van Gennep, 2-3].

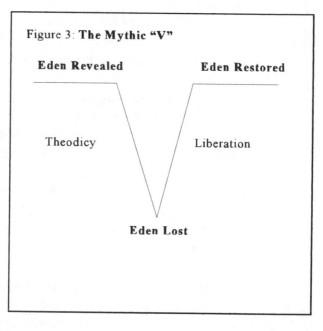

Figure 3: **The Mythic "V"**

Eden Revealed   Eden Restored

Theodicy   Liberation

Eden Lost

A l l biblical stories do not move clearly from one point to another on the mythic "v." Some **reveal an ideal mythic order** or the character of a mythic hero. The Sinai story, for example, expounds the covenant, the social order in which the people are to live (cf. Deut; Prov).

Ancient Near Eastern myths often depict creation as a battle between the gods (e.g., the Enuma Elish). Remnants of such creation stories are visible in some biblical passages (cf. Job 7:12; 26:12-13; 41; Isa 51:9):

> Thou didst divide the sea by thy might;
> thou didst break the heads of the dragons on the waters.
> Thou didst crush the heads of Leviathan . . . .

Thou hast fixed all the bounds of the earth;
thou has made summer and winter. (Ps 74:13-17)

By contrast, Gen 1, depicts creation as a divine revelation. God creates by fiat: "And God said . . . . And it was so." The resulting story dramatically reveals the divine sovereignty upon which the created order depends.

Stories revealing the character of mythic heroes provide mythic models. Abraham, for example, is a model of faith (Gen 12-25). Despite the divine promise of a son (Gen 12:1-3), Abraham grows old without issue. When he finally receives a son, God tests Abraham with the horrific demand to sacrifice the son (Gen 22). Throughout, Abraham is loyal to his sovereign.

Most biblical stories, however, are not revelations. Most are **conflict** stories which describe the transition from one point to another on the mythic "v" as the effect of some cause. The causal arrangement creates the story's *plot*:

"The king died and then the queen died," is a story.
"The king died, and then the queen died of grief" is a
plot. [Forster, 130]

A. J. Greimas describes plot abstractly as the resolution of a sender's goal to communicate an object to a receiver. To do so, the sender initiates a program of action and entrusts it to the subject. The subject attempts to give the object to the receiver. Events and characters assist (helpers) or retard (opponents) this goal [summarized in Patte, What, 41-43]. Thus, in biblical stories, God wishes to give his people an Eden in which to live [see figure 4]. The loss of Eden and the restoration of Eden are the major biblical conflict plots.

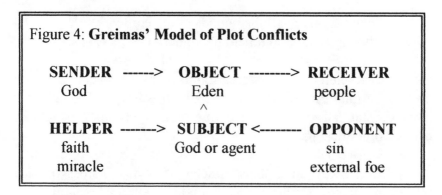

Figure 4: **Greimas' Model of Plot Conflicts**

SENDER ------>	**OBJECT** -------->	**RECEIVER**
God	Eden	people
	^	
HELPER ------->	**SUBJECT** <--------	**OPPONENT**
faith	God or agent	sin
miracle		external foe

The **basic Eden Lost story** is the story of human *sin* (Gen 3; the Former Prophets; etc.). In such stories, God's own people resist God's program. Adam and Eve eat the forbidden fruit and lose Eden. The people worship foreign gods and lose the land (the Former Prophets). The cause of such stories' tragic movements is sin, the human failure to live within the limits of the divinely established order.

Figure 5: **Alternative Edens**

While biblical story tends to explain Eden's loss in terms of human sin, other religious traditions explain the human predicament differently. For example, many Greek philosophers understood human loss in terms of **ignorance** and human redemption in terms of education. Western education owes much to this Greek notion. Romantics and reformers see the problem as **corrupt society** and the solution as either withdrawal from (e.g., Taoism, Thoreau) or revision of (e.g., Confucianism, Marx) society. Eastern religions identify the problem as **egoism** and the solution as the mystical loss of self in the ground of being (Hinduism) or in ego-extinction (Buddhism).

Sin stories are *theodicies*, explanations of the loss of order. While sin is the dominant biblical theodicy, others do occur [cf. Berger, Canopy, 73-80]. Some stories trace the loss of Eden to external evil forces (apocalyptic), to divine tests (Job 1-2), or to mysterious divine acts (Job, laments).

The **basic Eden Restored story** depicts God's defeat of his enemies. God delivers Eden by defeating a rival god (the exodus, apocalyptic) or a foreign nation (Joshua, apocalyptic). Such narratives are sovereignty contests or **holy wars**.

The biblical commitment to divine sovereignty makes holy wars hard to tell. God has to "prop up" the opposition. Hence, God continually hardens Pharaoh's heart (Ex 6-11). Similarly, in apocalyptic, God allows the rulers of this evil age a little while. Otherwise, there would be no story.

As a result, most Eden Restored stories are of a different type. They concern the identity of God's designated agent. Such narratives are **myth contests**. They debate conflicting claims to represent God: "Who is God's (the true) prophet?" "Who has God empowered to bring his people to Eden?" In the biblical tradition, such plots are quite common: Moses vs. Aaron and Miriam, David vs. Saul, Jeremiah vs. Haniniah, Jesus vs. the second temple powers, and so forth.

Such plots are mythic locators. They resolve when God favors one of the contestants. As mythic locators, these stories employ an *ethical dualism*. God and his agent are good while his opponents are bad.

Eden Restored stories highlight a divine liberation, a *deus ex machina*. That Latin phrase describes a dramatist's last-minute introduction of a deity to rescue his plot from hopeless entanglements (e.g., in Euripides' plays). An actor, lowered onto the stage from an elevated platform (the **ex machina**), plays the rescuing deity.

Figure 6: **The Modern Search for Eden**

The search for Eden continues today. Better futures live on in literary utopias and in art's alternative imagination. Further, various nineteenth and twentieth-century movements attempted to create **sectarian utopias** (e.g., Walden, hippie communes). The most notable is Marx's dream of a classless society at the end of the proletarian revolt.

More basically, Marx's economic and Darwin's biological theories are emblematic of the nineteenth-century **belief in progress**. Despite two world wars and alternative understandings of history (decadence or cyclical views), many still assume that human history is a progression toward some ideal (e.g., individual freedom) [cf. Nisbet, History]. Even when political and economic progress fails, most moderns still assume that human knowledge progresses. As modernity understands this knowledge narrowly as scientific or technological, counter-views occur (e.g., literary dystopias).

Biblical stories are replete with such last minute miraculous reversals. These deliverances are not incongruous, however, but arise naturally from the biblical God's character [Fretheim, Suffering, 24-29] whose "steadfast love endures forever" (Ps 136; cf. Ex 34:6-7).

Divine grace allows stories to continue beyond lost Edens. Although the first wilderness generation dies in the wilderness, the second continues to the land (Num 11-36). Eden Lost/sin plots do not stand alone. Salvation answers judgment. As a whole, then, biblical story includes both Eden Lost and Eden Restored. It includes both sin and liberation in a complete mythic "v" [see figure 3].

Characters: Divine: Tradition and Variation

The discussion of plot inevitably leads to *character*, the entities who act out or who are acted upon by the plot. The dominant biblical character is, of course, God. Revealed in story and its myth-ritual complexes, this story-God defies systematic (rational) expression. The story does, however, assert that he is **the holy, sovereign God of Israel.**

Historians of religion often define religion as a system of beliefs and activities oriented toward the *sacred* or the *holy*. These terms depict the mysterious power (or other) which is the source of life and meaning. Such power, of course, is both attractive and terrifying as it can take life (judge) as easily as grant it (save) [cf. Otto, 1-40]. The classic biblical expression of this "holy other" is Isaiah's temple-vision of singing, winged-snakes crying out:

> "Holy, holy, holy is the LORD of hosts; the whole
> earth is full of his glory." And the foundations of the
> thresholds shook at the voice of him who called, and
> the house was filled with smoke. And I said: "Woe is
> me! For I am lost; for I am a man of unclean lips, and
> I dwell in the midst of a people of unclean lips; for
> my eyes have seen the King, the LORD of hosts!" (Isa
> 6:3-5)

With respect to mere creatures the holy is **sovereign**. Thus, God controls, rules, or causes biblical story. The conception is not, however, philosophical. God's sovereignty is not that of an impersonal, inexorable First Cause (or of a closed continuum of materialistic cause and effect). God's effective rule, not determinism, is in mind. Biblical divine sovereignty is a **personal, relational conception** based upon human analogies. Hence, God is "LORD," "Father," or "King." Unlike philosophical determinism, then, divine sovereignty **never overturns human responsibility**. Humans remain accountable to their Lord.

Figure 7: **Cinematic Images of the Holy**

In Spielberg's <u>Raiders of the Lost Ark</u>, Indiana Jones and World War II Germans vie for the biblical ark of the covenant (see Ex 25). The Germans wish to use its awesome power (the holy) as a doomsday machine and are destroyed in the climax by the power they fail to respect (cf. Uzzah in 2 Sam 6:6-7). Indiana survives because he does not consider the holy ark a tool to be manipulated.

In <u>Grand Canyon</u>, "life" happens to the characters for good or for ill: one is rescued from a broken-down car in a ghetto by a savior; one finds a baby; one is shot; and so forth. The story, of course, turns on the meaning that these characters obtain from these *hierophanies*. The finale assembles the cast at the Grand Canyon for a transcendent experience summing up human life's insignificance and potential. Of course, this transcendence is American nature romanticism, rather than the biblical God.

The sovereign has a special relationship with Israel. He is the "**Holy One of Israel**," Israel's "LORD." Although such a national deity smacks of *ethnocentrism* today, it is completely at home in a *natural religion* environment. One needs, of course, a specific name to distinguish one's natural religion deity from others of the same class: Yahweh, Dagon, Baal, Marduk, and so forth. By contrast, of course, the pre-modern Western world needed no specific name for God. The generic designation, god, was also a specific name, God, as there was only one member of the class.

Israel's preferred, special name for God (there were others like the "fear of Isaac") is *Yahweh* (Ex 3:13-14). For this story-God, the name appropriately comes from the Hebrew verb "to be."

Unfortunately, its precise meaning is obscure. Exodus 3:14 (NRSV) renders it "I am who I am." Other renderings are possible: for example, "I will be what I will be" or "I cause to be what comes into existence."

In the Hebrew consonantal text, the name appears as "YHWH." The exact pronunciation is not known because Jewish tradition considered the name too sacred to pronounce (see Ex 20:7). When the Masoretes added vowels, they added the vowels from "**Adonai**," meaning "Lord," to indicate that "**Adonai**" should be read instead of "YHWH." "Jehovah" is a Latinized form of YHWH. The NRSV translates YHWH as "LORD."

According to Israel's story, this Yahweh **chose Israel**:

> Now therefore, if you obey my voice and keep my covenant, you shall be my treasured possession out of all the peoples. Indeed, the whole earth is mine, but you shall be for me a priestly kingdom and a holy nation. (Ex 19:5-6)

As a result, **Israel belonged to Yahweh**:

> You shall have no other gods before me. You shall not make for yourself an idol . . . . You shall not bow down to them or worship them; for I the LORD your God am a jealous God . . (Ex 20:3-5a)

The worship of one God as a choice among many is known as *henotheism* or *monolatry*. This attitude, rather than *monotheism* (the belief in the existence of only one god), animates most of the biblical text. Not incidentally, monolatry allows more room for stories about competing sovereignties and allegiances than does monotheism.

As it becomes advantageous for story, however, the biblical text moves toward monotheism. Monotheistic notions, for example, help prophets cope with Israel's exile. Where monolatry might suggest **Yahweh**'s defeat at the hands of Babylon's Marduk, monotheism stories **Yahweh**'s control over the nations whose fates now impinge upon Israel's. From **Yahweh**'s sovereignty over other nations (cf. the Exodus), it is not far to the denial of other gods' existence. Such monotheism can even foster **universalistic** notions. Thus, some stories portray God as the God of the whole earth and not just the God of Israel (the wisdom literature).

Figure 8: **The Satan**

While HB passages refer to "the adversary" ("the Satan") as a functionary in the divine court (Job 1-2; Zech 3:1; 1 Chr 21:1), Satan arrives as a personal, supernatural rival to God only in later apocalyptic and in the NT. At that point, the biblical divine cast threatens to disintegrate into polytheism.

Perhaps, the Satan notion developed as **ethical monotheism** made **theodicy** more difficult. If there was but one God, was that God the source of evil? **Zoroastrianism**, the Persian's dualistic religion, avoided that unhappy conclusion by explaining life as the battle between a god of light and a god of darkness. Some post-exilic Jews translated this as a conflict between God and Satan. Ultimately, monotheism will not allow this Satan-theodicy, for Satan can never be more than an underling. For monotheism, then, like the primitive holy, God remains the only terrifying, mysterious Other.

Monotheism does arise naturally from the biblical story's **divine sovereignty ideology**. Ultimately, not only will **Yahweh** brook no rival, he will also bear no comparisons. The biblical story does not chart a simple development, however, from particularistic monolatry to universalistic monotheism. Some stories even broaden the divine cast to meet the needs of story. When necessary, then, Israel's God has a court to whom to speak and to do his bidding (e.g., Gen 1:26; 3:22; 11:7; Job 1-2). When necessary, the story-God can also have supernatural opponents (e.g., Pharaoh or Satan). When necessary, God's agents can take on divine powers. Thus, kings are the sons of God (2 Sam 7:14; Ps 2:7), and prophets incarnate God's word (e.g., Jeremiah or Jesus).

In addition to differences in **number** and **universality**, story also depicts God variously because stories have different shapes. Stories of Eden Revealed or Lost tend to have **Gods of order** (e.g., creation, Sinai, or wisdom). Gods of Eden Restored tend to be **revolutionary Gods** (e.g., exodus or apocalyptic). That is, story-Gods can **support or subvert the story-status quo**. In the first case, the God of the establishment orders or maintains order. In the second case, the God of the underdog liberates his oppressed people from an unjust order.

Finally, stories depict God's control (his *providence*) either directly or indirectly. In the former case, **God is a story-character** (Gen 3). In the latter, God is **an unseen (off-stage) manipulator of events**. Dramatic miracles or auspicious divine agents are a half-way stage between direct and indirect conceptions of providence.

Divine appearances in the story are *theophanies* [Fretheim, Suffering, 79-106]. Anthropomorphic theophanies depict God as a human figure. His identity, however, is often suspect (cf. Gen 18; 32:24-32). Meterological theophanies depict God in terms of violent, powerful non-human forces: wind, fire, thunderstorm, earthquake, and so forth (e.g., Ex 19:16-18; 1 Kings 19:11-13; Judg 5:4-5; Ps 18:7-15).

The biblical tradition gradually moves away from the direct presentation of God [Patrick, God, 22-25]. The word (1 Kings 19:9-13), visions (cf. Am 1:1; Ezek 1), institutions (temple), texts (apocalyptic) and mediators (Moses, prophets, Jesus) gradually replace theophany. God the actor becomes God the speaker. Then, a spokesperson replaces God as the speaker. Finally, a message about the spokesperson replaces the spokesperson.

In summary, **continued story-telling varies God's depiction**. God is both one of a class and one of a kind. God is the God of Israel and the God of the whole earth. God is the establishment's orderer and the dispossessed's liberator. God is directly present as story-character and the absent, mysterious director of events. The **unity within this variety** is the portrayal of **Yahweh** as the holy, sovereign God of Israel who judges and saves [Patrick, God, 28-60]:

> The LORD passed before him, and proclaimed, "The LORD, the LORD, a God merciful and gracious, slow to anger, and abounding in steadfast love and faithfulness, keeping steadfast love for the thousandth generation, forgiving iniquity and transgression and sin, yet by no means clearing the guilty, but visiting the iniquity of the parents upon the children and the children's children, to the third and fourth generation." (Ex 34:6-7)

Characters: Humans Before God; Grace and Responsibility

For biblical story, humans are creatures before God. The Bible depicts them in terms of a simple *ethical dualism*. They are **with God** and, thus, enjoy the good things of life or they are **apart from God** and, thus, suffer and die [see figure 9].

Much of biblical characterization, then, is simply **locating everyone mythically**. Depending upon the particular story, those with God may be more specifically the people of the promise, of the covenant, of the king, and so forth. Outsiders also vary from story to story. They may be little more than plot functions, become tools in the hands of God, represent evil incarnate, or be simply and horribly the non-elect.

Figure 9: **The Basic Mythic Locations**

With God	Apart From God
sacred	profane
order	chaos
myth	mimesis
elect	not-elect
salvation	judgment
faith	apostasy
cleanness	uncleanness
life	death
light	darkness
health	sickness
righteousness	sin and guilt

The fundamental mythic identities, however, depend either upon **election** (typically, Eden Revealed or Restored) or upon **human responsibility** (typically Eden Lost).

In election-grace stories, identity depends solely upon God's sovereign choice: "Is not Esau Jacob's brother? says the LORD. Yet I have loved Jacob but I have hated Esau" (Mal 1:2b-3a). As such divine discriminations completely disregard human merit, they offend human dignity. Election does, however, have its own logic within the divine sovereignty ideology and a natural religion context.

First, election makes biblical sense because humans are mere creatures thrown into a situation in which they must live. The biblical stories treat this "thrownness," not as a harsh fatality, but as a fundamental benevolence. God graciously gives garden, promise, or covenant.

In fact, Eden Restored stories turn on senseless divine interventions. God liberates the unable, the unlovely, and the undeserving (cf. Rom 3:21-4:25). Such gifts (grace) come perilously close to moral chaos. In fact, **grace** makes sense only to those in mythic chaos. Grace offends those who accept life within its existing limits or those who believe they live within a stable order. Thus, in the famous parable of the prodigal, only the younger brother appreciates the father's graciousness. For the elder, it is moral chaos (Lk 15:11-32; cf. Mt 20:1-16).

Second, election makes sense within a natural religion community. **Yahweh** and Israel belong to each other. Other communities have their own life-giving holy. When such cultures encounter each other, they may define territory (your god is powerful in your land and mine in mine), merge gods (that which you call Baal I call **Yahweh**), strive to convert the other (accept my god), or begin holy war (my god will defeat yours).

If a mythic order is in place, human identity depends upon responsibility. That is, divine sovereignty (election-grace) does not eliminate **human responsibility**. It creates a world in which humans can live responsibly. In short, human responsibility depends upon divine sovereignty. The fundamental biblical demands of humans are faith and cleanness which correspond respectively to sovereignty and holiness.

Faith is commitment to the sovereign. God as Creator, King, and Father demands loyal subjects. They may not rebel by questioning or challenging the Eden Revealed (e.g., Gen 3). In essence, faith equals monolatry. The divine subjects may have no other gods before him (Ex 20:3). The divine jealousy will brook no other commitments.

Cleanness is variously understood as ritual *purity*, social justice, and individual morality [Gammie, 1-2]. Ultimately, the Holy

One demands complete cleanness:

> You shall be holy, for I the LORD your God am holy. You shall each revere your mother and father, and you shall keep my sabbaths: I am the LORD your God. Do not turn to idols or make cast images for yourselves: I am the LORD your God. (Lev 19:2b-4)

> You shall not hate in your heart anyone of your own kin; you shall reprove your neighbor, or you will incur guilt yourself. You shall not take vengeance or bear a grudge against any of your people, but shall love your neighbor as yourself: I am the LORD. (Lev 19:17-18)

Holiness, then, encompasses morality, one's relationship with one's fellows:

> . . . and one of them, a lawyer, asked him a question to test him. "Teacher, which commandment in the law is the greatest?" He said to him, "'You shall love the Lord your God with all your heart, and with all your soul, and with all your mind.' This is the greatest and first commandment. And a second is like it: 'You shall love your neighbor as yourself.'" (Mt 22:35-39)

The elect, faithful, and clean live with God. These characters have the good life which includes health and wealth (the *ontological good*). They live in or en route to Eden. By contrast, life away from God is perilous. Only the non-elect and the irresponsible live there.

Of course, all stories do not operate so neatly. After all, sometimes the good perish while the wicked prosper (see Ps 37; 39; 49; 73). Such stories complicate fundamental biblical patterns, but they also forge a way beyond both ethical dualism and the sin-theodicy.

The ethical dualism is foundational, however. Even heroes depend upon God for power, life, and status. Thus, many of them are **reluctant or unlikely heroes.** God uses whom he will. Further, even heroes fail if their association with God wavers. Thus, Moses dies outside the promised land; Solomon loses the kingdom; and Markan disciples betray, deny, and flee Jesus during his passion.

Figure 10: **Round Characters**

Literary critics describe characters as either **flat** or **round** [Forster, 103-18]. Flat characters are types embodying a "single idea or quality." Round characters are surprising, composite characters with "facets like a human being."

Biblical characters are not round. After all, they are only secondary biblical characters. The biblical character is God, who is the narrative standard and the plot causation. Further, biblical characters are mythic models typifying mythic locations and identities. Again, biblical characters are the aesthetic products of an ancient culture which understood humans primarily in terms of their solidarity with certain groups, rather than as independent individuals. Not surprisingly, then, ancient characters tend to be **types** [cf. the characters in Plutarch]. Only when biblical stories distance God, can they create round characters [cf. Alter, Narrative, 115; Sternberg, 325-41].

Atmosphere: Myth and Reality

Atmosphere is a story's setting or world. Atmosphere defines what is possible within the story. Biblical stories range **between mythic and *realistic*** atmospheres.

Eden stories have the most **mythic** atmosphere. Here, ordinary rules do not apply. God is a story-character (e.g., Gen 1-3).

He walks in the garden in the cool of the evening and eats with his friends. God talks with his divine court. Such story-worlds are the sacred, non-ordinary world dramatized by the community's myth and ritual. No reader, ancient or modern, lives in such a world.

Figure 11: **Fantasy**

Literary fantasies typically make only **one, crucial change** of the "normal world." For example, they assert that humans can fly, that humans can turn into flies, that humans are immortal, that life exists on other planets, or that God rules the world benevolently. Except for and in light of this single modification, fantasies create realistic worlds. In fact, many fantasies even offer "doors" between "reality" and the fantastic. One enters through a looking-glass, a wardrobe, a time-machine, a rocket, or a myth-ritual complex. Biblical story-worlds operate similarly. Grant the one impossibility--the divine sovereignty--and everything else follows quite naturally.

Stories en route to and away from Eden also have a mythic quality. These story-worlds do not have the direct divine presence, but they do have staggering miracles. God remains the obvious story-effector. Such story-worlds are the realistic, familiar world punctuated by strange, marvelous happenings, by hierophany and **deus ex machina**. Such stories have, then, **miraculous** atmospheres.

Other stories hide God's providence behind more **realistic** worlds. Here, characters struggle with mysterious events and with other human characters (e.g., the Joseph story). Often, only the reader is aware of the superintending divine providence at work. Narrators, prophets, or seers provide glimpses of the divine control. These realistic atmospheres are the real world seen through the lens of the divine sovereignty ideology.

Finally, some stories create worlds from which God's control seems absent. In these **ironic** worlds, being "with God" ceases to have obvious, material benefits. The righteous suffer and die. The wicked reign. These ironic stories escape the demonic only by declaring that the world is other than it seems, that God remains in charge (e.g., apocalyptic).

In summary, biblical stories create different worlds. Myth is an entirely strange, sacred realm. Miraculous story-world is a familiar world invaded temporarily by the sacred (hierophany). Realistic story-world is a familiar world read in light of the divine sovereignty. Ironic story-world subsumes even the horrific under hidden divine control.

Summary: The Mythic Character of Biblical Story

Biblical story is a **tradition of stories** about Eden Lost and Restored. With those dominant symbols, biblical story sketches a narrative connection between the ideal (Eden), the actual (Eden Lost), and the potential (Eden Restored). Such connections are the work of myth which thereby provides identity and meaning (theodicy, liberation). The shape of the stories is also clearly similar to basic myth-ritual patterns.

Biblical plots are also mythic. Thus, the causal agency is divine. God reveals Eden, removes it because of human offense, and graciously restores it. God dominates biblical story whether present as story-character or not. In short, biblical story gives narrative embodiment to the holy at the heart of biblical myth.

Human characters are equally mythic. They are characterized against the backdrop of an ethical dualism grounded in God. Those with God are positively valued. Those apart are negatively valued. The dualism imparts to characters a mythic identity through which they function as models of virtue or vice.

Finally, the atmosphere of the biblical stories ranges between the ideal world of myth, where God is intensely present, to realistic and ironic worlds, which continue to be read in light of the central ideology of the biblical myth--the divine sovereignty.

Review Questions

1. What is the "story in the Bible"? What are the recurring symbols in the biblical story-tradition?

2. Describe the myth-ritual pattern of biblical story.

3. Describe the basic biblical story plots. What causes biblical plots?

4. What is common to the divine depictions in the biblical story? What changes?

5. What does it mean to say that God is holy? Sovereign?

6. What is a theophany? What is providence?

7. How does the Bible characterize human characters? What part do election, faith, and holiness play?

8. Are biblical story-worlds mythic or realistic?

9. Describe the mythic character of the biblical story.

Questions for Reflection

1. Why do humans not live in Eden? How might one recover Eden?

2. Cite examples for the continuing quest for Eden in modernity.

3. Distinguish story and plot.

4. Compare sin to other conceptions of the human problem.

5. Why do biblical stories have different Gods?

6. If God is sovereign, are humans responsible? How does the Bible's conception of divine sovereignty differ from philosophical determinism?

7. Do modern religions operate in terms of natural religion and ethical dualism? Why might that be dangerous?

8. Does the modern world assume the ontological good? If so,

what religious or ethical activity is necessary to prosper?

9. Why are biblical characters not round? When are they round?

10. Are biblical worlds credible?

11. What literary features (both style and content) of biblical story are difficult for modern readers?

For Further Reading

Holman and Harmon provide concise definitions of literary terms. Perrine offers an introductory approach to the terms with narrative selections exhibiting their significance. Hoffman and Murphy have advanced theoretical discussions of the terms.

Chatman; Genette; and Rimmon-Kenan are important narrative critics. Alter, Narrative; Berlin; Josipovici; Sternberg; Alter and Kermode; Funk, Poetics; and Powell, What, apply narrative criticism to the Bible.

Anderson, Unfolding, is a simple introduction to the biblical story. Humphreys, Crisis, treats the Hebrew Bible as a story-telling tradition. Fishbane; and Childs, Scripture, treat it as an interpretative tradition.

Wheelwright, Metaphor; Tillich; and Eliade, "Methodological," are important works on symbols. Caird, Language; and Frye, Code, 139-68, are helpful introductions to biblical symbolism.

Livingston, 111-26; Van Gennep; Gaster, Thespis; Campbell, Hero; and Frye, Anatomy, 158-239, discuss myth-ritual patterns. Barbour, 20, describes this pattern as the narrative relationship of the ideal, actual, and potential. For myth, see the bibliography in chap. 1.

Aristotle, Poetics; Forster; Scholes and Kellogg, 207-39; Chatman, 43-48; and Greimas have helpful discussions of plot. For a concise introduction to Greimas, see Patte, Whaṯ, 41-43.

Forster, 103-18; Scholes and Kellogg, 160-206; and Chatman, 107-38, are interesting discussions of character.

On the name **Yahweh**, see "To the Reader," NRSV, xiii; Anderson, "Names"; **idem**, Understanding, 60-66.

Patrick, God; Sternberg, 322-25; and Fretheim, Suffering, discuss God's characterization in the HB. On the divine sovereignty, see Duling and Perrin, 531-34; and Perrin, Language, 15-32, 195-96. On God's holiness, see Jacob, 86; Otto, 1-40; and Gammie. On God's pathos, see Heschel; and Fretheim, Suffering. On God's presence or absence, see Terrien, Elusive; and Patrick, God, 22-25. On the biblical fondness for a revolutionary God, see Schneidau; and Gottwald, HB.

For brief introductions to theophanies, see Fretheim, Suffering, 79-106; Terrien, Elusive, 68-71; G. Henton Davies; Jeremias, "Theophany"; and Brueggemann, "Presence."

Berger, Sacred, 53-80, has a helpful introduction to theodicy.

W. C. Smith, Meaning, has an illuminating discussion of faith as commitment, rather than acceptance of creedal statements. Rad, Theology, 1:203-12, traces the demand for monolatry in the HB. Gammie presents different understandings of holiness and ethic in the HB. H. Wheeler Robinson, 1-20, is the classic treatment of "corporate personality."

CHAPTER 4

A LITERARY CRITICAL APPROACH (cont.)
Biblical Discourse

Chapter Preview

1) **Ritual** is the fundamental biblical discourse.

2) The Bible's formative medium is **orality**.

3) Functionally, the Bible's genre is **myth**.

4) The omniscience of the biblical narrator creates a **"word of God" effect**.

5) **Prophecy** and **typology** are key biblical manipulations of narrative time.

6) Biblical semantics are **symbolic** while biblical syntax tends to **parataxis**.

7) The biblical narratee is virtually inseparable from its myth-ritual community reader.

8) While the Bible has a **complementary** relationship with its myth-ritual community readers, it has a **confrontational** relationship with modern readers.

Discourse: The Drama of Ritual

Discourse, a narrative's packaging, includes medium, genre, narrator, time, style, and narratee. Stories may be packaged verbally, dramatically, cinematically, and so forth [Chatman, 26]. As a myth, the Bible's fundamental discourse is ritual. Ritual is symbolic, sacred act. Like myth, ritual is a sacred vehicle. Through ritual, worshipers participate in the sacred and rehearse the community's identity. In short, **ritual dramatizes myth. Without ritual, myths die**.

Clearly, much of the Bible was meant to be prayed, proclaimed, taught, or sung in worship (e.g., the psalms). Many stories also found important rituals (e.g., passover or the eucharist). More importantly, lectionaries and sermons have ritualized the entire Bible.

In ritual, the Bible's characters become mythic models and its story-shapes mirror ritual patterns [cf. chap. 3]. In this way, the ritual-Bible mythically locates the faithful as those who need to lament (repent, fast) or to praise (hope, feast).

Media: Orality, Repeated Performances of Stereotyped Content

The Bible's basic medium is **oral**. The Bible's roots are in the oral performance of family stories around campfires, of words chanted in worship, and of charismatic oracles. Even after manuscript Bibles became available, the oral Bible continued. After all, manuscripts were prohibitively expensive and many of the faithful were illiterate. Even today, worship provides an oral Bible. After all, religious communities nurture their young orally long before the young can read. Even today, then, the Bible as text is the medium primarily of the educated.

The oral Bible differs from text in **both experience and content**. In short, the oral Bible is the **repeated**, social performances of a stereotyped, patterned content.

Readers can possess texts, but oral performances are uncontrollable events. Readers read as they list. They begin, skip, reread, and stop at whim. By contrast, a **dominating other controls** oral performance for the listener. Texts are artifacts, but oral performances live through intonations, rhythm, gestures, and perhaps even music.

While texts find isolated readers, orality unites a teller and a listener in a social event. Instead of the reader and the object, an "I" speaks and a "thou" listens. Further, the "thou" is typically one of several listeners. The oral performance unites those listeners and **creates community**.

Finally, while the end of a book creates a sense of "once and done," oral stories keep on being told. Thus, small children beg for their favorite stories again and again at bedtime. Thus, the patterns of television dramas and situation comedies recur. Thus, the religious community gathers again to hear "the old, old story."

Figure 1: **Genre Films**

In one sense, there are only two major genres in popular fiction: the comedy and the melodrama. In the romantic comedy, a boy meets a girl, loses the girl, and gets the girl back (cf. Shakespearean comedy). In American film, the western is the classic melodrama (cf. gangster, disaster, and horror films). In the prototypical western, a mysterious hero arrives to save a threatened society (cf. Shane). The plot climaxes when the hero defeats the villain, rejects the girl, and leaves town.

These conventional forms do not aim to surprise. Instead, they comfort (secure a world) and educate (in a world-view) while they entertain. The appeal of an individual work depends upon slight twists, special effects, and/ or star appeal, rather than upon plot variations.

Oral performances tend to **stereotypical, repetitive content**. Myth, children's stories, popular literature, music, TV, and cinema depend upon such forms.

Children's stories, for example, have simple plots. Maurice Sendak's famous Where the Wild Things Are has a simple, circular plot. Sent to his room without supper because he acts like a wild thing, Max journeys to the land of the wild beasts, but he returns to find his supper warm and waiting. Biblical stories follow myth-ritual patterns with similar circular plots. Eden Lost is Restored. Moses returns to Sinai after battles with Pharaoh.

Figure 2: **Form Criticism**

Orality pressed the biblical content into pre-set forms like the prophets' judgment and salvation oracles or the psalmists' hymns and laments. Analysis of these forms can, of course, become far more complex. For example, critics find various kinds of stories (miracles, legends, and pronouncement stories) and sayings (proverbs, oracles, Torah-sayings, I-sayings, and parables) in the gospels alone.

While orality works with well-known forms, it also loves **reversals and contrasts** which subvert expectations. Jesus' parable of the seeds is typical (Mk 4:3-9). After three seeds fail, the fourth brings forth miraculous results. These results are expressed in a surprising series: thirty, sixty, a hundredfold (not ninety or one hundred twenty). In fact, in series of items, the most common reversal varies the third character/event significantly (cf. "Goldilocks and the Three Bears," "The Three Billy Goats Gruff," and the parable of the Good Samaritan in Lk 10:29-37) [cf. Orlik's "rule of three," discussed in Thompson, 35-37].

Characters also contrast. Thus, the wicked witch follows the good witches in "Briar Rose" (i.e., "Sleeping Beauty"). Similarly, biblical psalms and proverbs juxtapose the wise and the fool (e.g., Ps 1; Prov 10), or Pharaoh dreams of seven fat and seven thin, voracious cows (Gen 41:1-7).

Repetition is, of course, the fundamental pattern. Thus, Henny-Penny repeatedly asserts that the sky is falling. Alexander bemoans that it is "a terrible, horrible, no good, very bad day." Homer repeats the same epithets (descriptive tags) for his heroes: Achilles, the wrathful, and Odysseus, the cunning. The psalmist repeatedly intones "for his steadfast love endures forever" (Ps 118).

Figure 3: **Media and World-View**

The medium is not only the message, it is also the way the world is seen and explained. Orality and textuality, then, differ not only in technology, but also in world-view [chart from Fiske and Hartley, 124-25]:

Oral modes/worlds	**Literate modes/worlds**
dramatic	narrative
episodic	sequential
mosaic	linear
dynamic	static
concrete	abstract
ephemeral	permanent
social	individual
rhetorical	logical
dialectical	univocal

Even entire scenes repeat. Thus, the parable of the sheep and goats contrasts their respective works and destinies with almost exact wording (but note the significant variation; cf. Mt 25:34-40 with 41-45). In biblical narration, speeches often anticipate narrative reports verbatim (e.g., the speeches in Gen 24, divine speech in Exodus, and prophetic speech in 1-2 Kings).

Ultimately, repetition creates **type-scenes** or stereotyped forms [see figure 2]. For this reason, one expects country music to bewail the loss of pick-ups, trailers, dogs, sobriety, and girls. Viewers expect television comedies to pose some personal problem and to resolve it neatly within a thirty-minute time slot which includes four commercial breaks. Similarly, Homer's multitude of battle-scenes all rehearse formulaically the combatants' virtues, the reason for one's victory, the loser's terrible death, and the victor's great honor. Likewise, the gospels present Jesus' healing miracles according to a set form: the description of an insuperable difficulty, the miraculous cure itself, and Jesus' acclamation.

Figure 4: **Major Shifts in Media-Culture**

Culture and world-view change with technology [chart adapted from Scott, <u>Hollywood</u>, 45]:

Media	Social, Religion	Truth, Genre
Oral	Family, Israel	Presence, Myth
Text	Empire, Judaism Catholicism	Dualism, Allegory
Print	Nation, Protestant	Science, History
Electric	Corporation, Televangelism	Credibility, Photo

In sum, then, oral content differs from that of print. Orality is more **affective** than print. It creates an experience, rather than merely communicating information. Orality's content **emphasizes the whole** (structuring patterns), rather than details. Nevertheless, like the small child who corrects the parent's story-telling, an audience who had heard a story repeatedly would startle at variations.

In fact, orality's patterns focus attention on **significant variations**.

For modern readers, the oral Bible, encountered now in print, can be **annoyingly repetitive and simplistic**. Repetition, however, does **create a story-telling tradition**. The biblical story-tradition, then, is not merely the fruit of ritual discourse and institutional politics, but also of an oral medium.

Genre: Myth, Prose, and Poetry

Genre refers to **a literary work's type**. It describes a work's form, content, function, and reading conventions. Generic designations locate works comparatively. Such distinctions lead one to approach history differently from fiction or poetry differently from prose.

Functionally, the Bible is a myth. As a community's sacred, master-story [cf. chap. 1], the Bible is comparable to the Q'uran, the Book of Mormon, the Upanishads, and so forth. The Bible's reading conventions, then, are those of myth. Myths are symbolic, affective texts, not discursive (e.g., textbooks) or historical material. Myths resist literalization [Campbell, "Masks," 161-66] and allegorization. They do not attempt to achieve verisimilitude, but to convey the experience of the sacred.

Torah and the gospels are the premier examples of myth in the Bible. They found their respective communities' world-views. As such, they are not true or false. Instead, they provide the ground by which a community makes such distinctions.

Other biblical materials are less foundational, so they do fall into a fact-fiction spectrum. That is, they desire to present a past reality (e.g., history) or tell a story (fiction) [Scholes and Kellogg, 12-16; Frye, Anatomy, 51-52, 73-82].

Broadly speaking, the Former Prophets, 1-2 Chronicles,

Ezra-Nehemiah, and Acts are **ancient histories** [Aune, NT, 77-115]. In contrast to modern history's natural, human world of cause and effect, ancient histories presume worlds under a divine sovereignty which may, on occasion, become directly obvious in theophany and miracle.

Figure 5: **Myth as Literary Genre**

Chapter one defined myth functionally. By contrast, a traditional **literary definition** of myth is **a story of the gods**. Using such a definition, very little of the Bible is myth (e.g., Gen 1-3; 18). Using that standard, much of Torah and the gospels would be legend, rather than myth.

Further, in contrast to modern histories, ancient histories generally follow one prior source wherever possible. To this "pony," they add other materials as appropriate. Again, ancient histories are entertaining or moralistic. The biblical histories, of course, tend to moralism. Finally, ancient histories are not intended for academicians and, therefore, do not have scholarly paraphernalia (e.g., footnotes).

Fiction presents what might happen, not what did happen. In the guise of story, fiction can communicate aesthetic, moral, or religious truth. In fact, it may do that far more easily and effectively than history. Biblical examples of fiction include the gospel parables, Ruth, Jonah, Esther, and Dan 1-6.

In addition to story, the Bible contains **other kinds of prose**. In particular, various lists occur. The most famous, of course, are the extensive genealogies. At the other extreme from the lists, are discursive essays (homilies) which reflect logically upon the significance of founding myths (e.g., the NT letters).

```
┌─────────────────────────────────────────────────────────────┐
│                                                             │
│  Figure 6: Biblical Genres                                  │
│                                                             │
│  Prose        Story:  Myth (Torah; Gospels)                 │
│                       History (Former Prophets; Acts)       │
│                       Fiction (Esther; Ruth; Jonah)         │
│               Discursive (Ecclesiastes; NT Letters)         │
│               Lists (Genealogies)                           │
│                                                             │
│  Sayings      Traditional (Law; Proverbs)                   │
│               Oracular (Prophecy)                           │
│                                                             │
│  Poetry       Some Sayings; Psalms; Job                     │
│                                                             │
└─────────────────────────────────────────────────────────────┘
```

Beyond basic prose genres, the Bible also contains sayings and poetry [cf. e.g., chaps. 8, 12]. The Bible is replete with poetry [cf. Kugel, 85-95]. Most modern translations print Psalms, Proverbs, Job, the Song of Solomon, and large portions of the Latter Prophets as poetry.

Biblical poetry, however, does not follow modern Western rules. Although it is rhythmic, it does not use typical Western rhythms or end-rhyme. In translation, biblical poetry's most obvious feature is **parallelism**, a peculiar form of repetition sometimes described as "thought-rhyme" [see style below]. In parallelism, the second line of a couplet, the most typical biblical poetic form, extends the thought of the first line by restating it (synonymous parallelism), opposing it (antithetical parallelism), or building upon it (stair-step parallelism) [cf. Gottwald, "Poetry"; Kugel].

Biblical **sayings** stand between poetry and prose. The sayings are the isolated or collected words of important figures: particularly, **Yahweh**, the prophets, and the sages. They claim divine, traditional, or charismatic authority. Traditional sayings have long-standing social legitimacy (those of **Yahweh**, Moses, sages) and are, thus, distinct from oracular sayings which must gain acceptance (those of the Latter Prophets).

Narrator: The Omniscience Effect

In a narrative, an author creates an *implied author* and a narrator in order to communicate with a reader [Chatman, 151]. The implied author is the author's "second self," a persona adopted for the writing of a particular text [Booth, Fiction, 70-76]. Readers can infer the implied author from a text by analyzing the text's norms and standards or, more simply, its **perspective**. The *narrator* is **the voice** through which the tale is told.

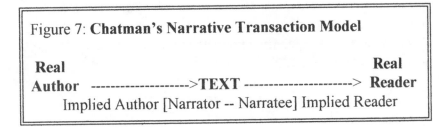

Figure 7: **Chatman's Narrative Transaction Model**

Real   **Real**
Author -------------------->TEXT ---------------------> **Reader**
Implied Author [Narrator -- Narratee] Implied Reader

Biblical narrators are generally anonymous voices telling a story from an external, **omniscient vantage point** [see figure 8]. This virtually unrestricted narrator knows the characters' inmost secrets, is aware of events where no one is present, and is aware of events greatly separated by space and time.

Most importantly, the narrator's knowledge includes the divine realm. The narrator moves freely in the divine world (Job 1-2) and time (Gen 1; Rev 20-22). The narrator even knows the divine mind. Thus, narrators know God's valuation of creation (Gen 1:4, 31), are aware of changing divine purposes (Gen 6:5-6; Ex 32:10), and recognize God's hidden actions (Mk 15:33-39; apocalyptic visions). The result of the narrator's knowledge of God's purposes is an **omniscience effect** [cf. Sternberg, 84-128, 153-63]. The

c

anonymous narrator speaks for God. More traditionally, the story is the **word of God**.

Figure 8: **Narrative Voice and Perspective**

Modern criticism distinguishes the implied author and the narrator in order to analyze modern stories with unreliable narrators (narrators whose viewpoint differs from the textual norms) [cf. Booth, Fiction, 304-09]. One of Booth's famous examples is Huckleberry Finn whose narrator claims wickedness while the story betrays his virtues. Although the Bible does not have unreliable narrators, the distinction between implied author and narrator can help the reader understand how an **anonymous human voice** can claim to offer the **divine perspective**. Brooks and Warren have identified possible combinations of voice and perspective [cited in Genette, 186]:

	Internal Analysis	**External Report**
Narrator as story-character	1. Main character tells story	2. Minor character reports story
Narrator not in the story	3. Omniscient author tells story	4. Author observes/ reports story

---

This **divine eye** view frees God from textual confines. God, although character, is never merely character. He is also the perspective by which events and humans are judged. This discourse style is, of course, appropriate to a sacred text and to the Bible's divine sovereignty ideology. God, for whom the anonymous narrator speaks, remains transcendent and mysterious while communicative.

Figure 9: **Narration and Ideological Criticism**

Narrative voice and perspective are aesthetic choices [see figure 8]. Put blatantly, biblical story's omniscient narrator is a literary creation. While omniscient narration masquerades as a "no-eye," objective view, ideological criticism reveals it to be told from a particular world-view's perspective. Recent re-tellings of biblical stories from modern world-views, of course, dramatize this point as they adopt the perspectives of characters within biblical stories [e.g., MacLeish; Miles; and Morrow].

In presenting stories, narrators may blatantly reveal themselves or they may act covertly. That is, narrators may tell or show a story [Booth, Fiction; Genette, 161-85]. **Showing** creates the illusion of a direct presentation of a story. Drama and the reproduction of speeches approximates showing. **Telling** interposes the narrator as a filter between the story and its audience. The classic novel typifies the overt teller (e.g., Fielding or Trollope). Narrative summaries, reports, and comments on characters and events are the most obvious signs of the overt narrator [cf. Chatman, 228-48].

Biblical story combines obtrusive comments with a tendency toward showing. Showing is most obvious in the biblical fondness for direct speech. For example, God's creation (Gen 1), the Exodus plagues (7:8-11:10), and Uriah's murder (2 Sam 11) are all speech-scenes [Alter, Narrative, 178-89].

Further, biblical stories tend toward the **laconic** [cf. Auerbach, 12-13]. Biblical stories seldom describe their heroes' physical appearance. Exceptions, like hairy Esau, simply prove the rule. Said "hairiness" is essential to the story. While "inside views" of characters do appear, they are rare compared to those in the classic novel. In fact, they are often noticeably absent. Thus, the incredibly wrenching story about the sacrifice of Isaac says nothing about Abraham's feelings or thoughts. It narrates only what he does and says (Gen 22).

The narrator does intrude, however, to reveal the divine perspective. Thus, the sacrifice of Isaac combines laconic scene with the introductory, obtrusive comment that God tested Abraham (Gen 22:1). Scenes themselves can function as such comments (cf. the interpretative effect which Job 1-2 has on the rest of that book).

In sum, biblical story narrators are anonymous voices who present laconic stories from the divine perspective. At times, they intrude into their stories to reveal the divine mind.

Narrative Time: Episodic Pace; Prophecy and Typology

Narrative time concerns story's duration and order. **Duration** identifies the relationship of discourse time to story time. Does it take longer to tell than it would to happen or vice versa? Only in the reproduction of speech are discourse and story time equal. With the narration of events, the issue is **pace**. Is the relationship between story and discourse even (e.g., one day = one paragraph) or does the amount of story covered in discourse vary? In most narratives, of course, the relationship varies.

Biblical pace is **episodic**, the discourse moves quickly from one important scene to another. Thus, Exodus passes from Joseph's death to the exodus merely by saying "a new king arose over Egypt, who did not know Joseph." Rapidly sketching Israel's slavery, Moses's charmed life, and Moses' flight to Midian (1-2), Exodus, then, spends as much discourse time on Moses' interview with **Yahweh** (3:1-4:17). The narrative, then, reports in great detail the plague cycle leading to the exodus (5:1-12:41). In short, the narrative moves quickly through generations to pause for and to emphasize God's revelatory actions in **detailed scenes**.

Order also calls attention to differences between discourse and story. Flashforwards or foreshadowings discourse story information in advance of its story-time. Flashbacks withhold the discourse of information until a later propitious moment.

Subsequent story clarifies **flashforwards**. Both the steady gathering of stones in Shirley Jackson's "The Lottery" and John the Baptist's fate (Mk 3:6; 6:14-29) portend ominously. Biblical didacticism, however, often subverts such aesthetic subtleties. Thus, divine and prophetic words guarantee narrative futures. The creative word in Gen 1 is, of course, the most famous example. Similarly, in 1-2 Kings, prophets speak, and the narrative invariably follows. Ahijah tells Jeroboam he will be king over Israel (1 Kings 11:31-39). Though Jeroboam flees for his life to Egypt, Jeroboam becomes king of Israel (12:20). Later, Ahijah predicts the end of Jeroboam's reign (14:7-16). Partial fulfillment is immediate (14:17-20, including a reference to Jeroboam's death). Complete fulfillment, though postponed, comes as certainly (15:27-30). To ensure that the reader remembers, the narrator comments retrospectively upon Ahijah's prediction.

Similarly, when Jesus predicts his death (e.g., Mk 8:31; 9:31; 10:33-34), the gospel cascades to that end. En route, Jesus makes other predictions as well: for example, that a man will provide a colt for Jesus triumphal entry (11:2-8); that a fig tree will wither (11:14); that a man carrying a pot of water will prepare a room for them (14:13-16); that a disciple will betray him (14:18-21); and that the disciples will desert him (14:27-31). Later narratives fulfill each of these and, on occasion, refer retrospectively to the prediction (e.g., 11:20-21; 14:72).

Such retrospects are, of course, **flashbacks**. In literature and film, flashbacks are more common than foreshadowings. Thus, Homer withholds the story of Odysseus' scar until the most affective moment--the time of the nurses' recognition [bk. XIX]. Contemporary detective fiction lives through flashbacks. The film D.O.A. uses flashback memorably by beginning with a man notifying the police of his murder. The remainder of the movie dramatizes the crime he reports.

Figure 10: **Typology and Allegory**

Allegory and typology are **non-literal** readings attributing hidden depths to texts. Typology writes or reads new story in terms of traditional symbols/stories. Allegory reads more creatively harmonizing story with an external philosophy or theology. Thus, ancient Jews and Christians read scripture in terms of Platonic philosophy [cf. Grant and Tracy, 52-62, 83-91]. Allegory is an integral part of traditional readings [cf. chap. 2]. Historical-criticism rejects allegory as part of its rejection of tradition and its creation of a modern reading strategy. It favors *literal* readings. Of course, modern literary-criticisms are more appreciative of non-literal readings of **mythic (symbolic) texts**.

Typology, closely related to allusion and allegory, is a distinctive biblical flashback. In essence, typology assumes that biblical stories are told and should be read in light of one another. Typology

> establishes a connection between two events or persons in such a way that the first signifies not only itself but also the second, while the second involves or fulfills the first. [Auerbach, 73]

The sense that the event, person, or story repeats or fulfills an original suggests a new meaning.

The NT reads the HB typologically. At times, the authors even use the word "type" (e.g., Rom 5:14; 1 Pet 3:21). More often, the actual term is not used, but the intent is clear. Jesus is the new

Moses, Joshua, David, Elijah, and so forth. The church, of course, is the new Israel. In short, Christian writers describe the significance of Christ and the church by reapplying old symbols.

In fact, the entire biblical story-telling tradition lives through this reuse of symbols [see chap. 3]. The result is a forward look, an *eschatological* perspective. The reader expects symbols to reappear and awaits fulfillments.

Not only is typology a perfectly logical reading for the biblical tradition, it also makes perfect mythic sense. After all, myths reveal models (types) forever repeated and renewed. More importantly, typology's logic depends upon and suggests the divine sovereignty ideology. Typology establishes a connection

> between two events which are linked neither temporally or causally--a connection which it is impossible to establish by reason in the horizontal dimension . . . It can be established only if both occurrences are vertically linked to Divine Providence . . . . [Auerbach, 73-74]

Typology, then, gives biblical story a sense of breadth (a continuing tradition) and depth (transcendent sovereignty).

In review, the distinctive biblical manipulations of narrative time--fulfilled prophecy and typology--have several effects. First, they foster and further the divine sovereignty message. They create a sense that a providence beyond the story "calls the shots" and supplies meaningful connections between events. Further, the continuing reuse of symbols and patterns creates a tradition of story-telling. Narratives are part of an interconnected whole. Third, these time manipulations include the mythic community. If important prophecies are narratively unfulfilled--for example, the gospel expectation of Jesus' return--the mythic community itself awaits fulfillment. More generally, myth's types (models) continue to mold members of the myth-ritual community.

Style: Parataxis and Symbolism

Style refers to a work's distinctive artistic expression, its tone, flavor, or feel.   Dominant features of biblical style include repetition, an emphasis on narration, a fondness for speech, laconic scenes, obtrusive narrative comments, episodic pace, and typology. Each contributes to the Bible's sacred feel. In short, the Bible has **a mythic style**.

More concretely, style involves **semantics** (word choice, usage, and meaning) and **syntax** (sentence arrangement). Semantically, biblical stories are *symbolic*. Syntactically, they are *paratactic*.

Parataxis means "a placing alongside."   It refers to the arrangement of sentences (or words) by coordination (with "and," "or," "but," etc.) or juxtaposition, rather than by subordination. That is, parataxis piles sentences together **without subordinating conjunctions** (after, when, because, etc.). Thus, the gospel of Mark connects episode after episode with "and immediately." In fact, in an attempt to write readerly English, translators often obscure the Bible's tendency toward parataxis.

Parataxis is typical of speech (biblical orality) and of unsophisticated writing (cf., e.g., the speech of small children). The Bible's extensive use, however, has sophisticated effects.

First, with the laconic scene, it creates the illusion that biblical narrative merely presents uninterpreted facts. It reports this event, and this, and this, and so forth. The causal interpretations of subordinating (periodic) syntax are absent.

Second and paradoxically, parataxis' juxtapositions demand interpretation. One must supply connections in order to make sense. Interestingly, this sense often defies logic. Parataxis requires one to see matters from *multiple perspectives* as in Prov 26:4-5:

Do not answer fools according to their folly,
   or you will be a fool yourself.
Answer fools according to their folly,
   or they will be wise in their own eyes.

The plague cycle's description of Pharaoh's hardened heart as both his act and that of God is a more famous and more troubling example (Ex 7:8-11:10).

Figure 11: **Symbolic Language**

Philosophers classify the uses of language as cognitive, expressive, performative, and phatic. For most, religious language is expressive (suggesting human emotions or attitudes), not cognitive (conveying empirically testable information). Those who do think that religious language is cognitive understand it to offer information about the sacred, a "supra-empirical" reality. Religious language, then, is inevitably symbolic. The religious wholeheartedly agree. If religious language were not symbolic, it would reduce the transcendent to mere human language, the infinite to the finite. Of course, to believe that the ultimate could be described literally would be nothing less than idolatry [cf. Tillich, Dynamics, 41-54]. It would confine God within human language.

The Bible's **semantics** also differs from that of logical, discursive texts. Like poetry, its symbolic semantics reaches **beyond cognitive significations**. While one can distinguish figurative and *literal* language in the Bible [cf. Caird, Language], even literal biblical speech is always about the transcendent beyond.

Symbolism allows any event to become a hierophany [Eliade, Profane, 11-12]. Thus, Biblical historians find God's judgment in

Israel's destruction (2 Kings 17). Joseph discovers God's purpose in his brothers' ill will (Gen 50:20). Jesus sees the kingdom of God in a farmer sowing and a woman baking. Later readers find Christ's love for the church in the erotic love songs of the Song of Solomon.

The result is a populist style. In symbol, the everyday (love, business, and war) becomes the realm of the divine [cf. Auerbach, 22-23, 31-33].

Narratees and Readers: Persuasion and Conversion

If the narrator is the text's voice, the **narratee** is the text's ear. If the implied author is the author's ethical and aesthetic choices, the **implied reader** is the author's expected audience (or expected effects). If the implied author is the author the reader infers as she reads, the implied reader is the "person" the reader becomes as she reads.

Normally, biblical story's narratee is anonymous. Of course, this anonymity suits ritual discourse well. In that anonymity, the community members can find themselves addressed.

Some narratees, however, are more specific. Prophetic oracles, for example, often speak to specific community members: kings, priests, the elite, and so forth. The NT letters often address specific churches or even individuals (e.g., Philemon; Timothy; Titus). The psalms address God.

These individualized narratees create a gap between narratee and reader. Others also read and hear. Thus, while the psalms have God as their narratee, the community also hears. Again, NT letters addressed to specific individuals are also overheard by the churches to which they belong (e.g., Philemon).

Eventually, time widens these gaps. The canonization of prophetic oracles and NT letters broadens their audience, but not their narratees. As scripture, they become the reading property of the entire community.

The **myth-ritual complex bridges gaps** between narratees and readers by passing on mythic identities from one generation to the next. As a community member, the reader identifies herself as the one addressed. Ritual discourse **imperializes**. It incorporates readers into the community making them the addressees of the biblical myth, stories, and sayings. In short, **the implied reader is a mythic identity foisted upon readers**.

Real readers can, of course, **resist** this process. They may not wish to adopt said identity. Authors, of course, know this and craft differently (become different kinds of implied authors) as they imagine varied responses.

In a **complimentary** relationship, the reader accepts the work's proffered identity easily. In an **incongruent/congruent** situation, persuasion is necessary. Such readers may or may not be convinced. In a **confrontational** scenario, the author deliberately thwarts the reader's expectations. Foregoing persuasion, the author tries to produce a creative tension that will shock the reader into a new perspective, into a conversion to the work's perspective [Torgovnick, 16-18].

Biblical **myths expect complimentary reading**. They speak to believers, to a community sharing a mythic perspective and identity (the Israel of God or Jesus' disciples). They do not argue for the myth. They dramatize it in ritual discourse. Of course, this process continually educates, nurtures, and recreates the mythic-community.

Theodicies, texts justifying myths in the face of chaos, **must convince their readers**. They strive for a congruent relationship by explaining evil in light of the mythic world-view (e.g., Gen 3). Works addressed to readers who fail to understand the consequences of the mythic identity or to those who have *apostasized* also assume an incongruent scenario. Such texts strive for congruence by educating or **reproving**.

Both theodices and reproofs use *rhetoric* to persuade. Biblical rhetoric convinces by appealing to **charisma or tradition**. The former entails an author's appeal to his special, personal charismatic experiences. Prophets (e.g., Isa 6; Ezek 1) and apostles (e.g., 2 Cor 12) use this technique. The attempt to convince by appealing to tradition, the repository of shared values and identity, is more common. Here, authors persuade by recalling and reinterpreting the myth. Hence, prophets repeatedly refer to "the God of the Fathers," the exodus, the covenant, and the law. Later authors enjoyed the luxury of appealing to scripture as well.

Confrontational texts move beyond rational persuasion. Such works must create a new vision, a revelation. Instead of rehearsing the myth, they **employ parable and *metaphor*** [Crossan, Dark, 47-62]. The prophet and the poet juxtapose that which does not seemingly belong in order to create new, revelatory perspectives (metaphor). All flesh is grass. The hated Samaritan is good. The prodigal son is lovingly forgiven. Such images do not persuade rationally. Instead, they entice and capture (or are unsuccessful).

Figure 12: **Texts and Readers**

Complimentary	**Incongruent**	**Confrontational**
Ritual	Rhetoric	Vision
Myth	Theodicy	Irony, Metaphor
Torah	Prophets	Jonah/Job
Gospel	Letters	Parables

The reuse of old symbols is mildly confrontational (e.g., Jer 31:31-34). Irony, the inversion of old symbols and patterns, is more dramatic (e.g., Jesus' <u>Good</u> Samaritan, Mark's dying Christ, and Jonah's disobedient prophet). Both *irony* and metaphor captivate. They seduce one into adopting new perspectives.

Wrenched from its ritual discourse, **the entire Bible stands in a confrontational relationship with a modern reader**. Time has introduced gaps between the narratee and the reader. The Bible can no longer rely on its expected reader. Shared world-views have vanished [see chap. 1]. If the Bible proves effective, moderns must convert to its revelatory, new insights or struggle to align with the text's implied reader.

Summary: The Myth-Ritual Character of Biblical Discourse

If the Bible's story-features are mythic [see chap. 3], its discourse-features are ritualistic. Among ritual's important functions are the creation of the experience of the sacred (the transcendent) and the promotion of a lasting community identity (a tradition). Not surprisingly, many biblical discourse-features suggest either transcendence or tradition.

Transcendence lurks behind orality's dominating other, the "word of God" effect, prophetic and typological manipulations of time, and symbolic semantics. Orality's sociality, the inseparableness of the narratee and the implied reader, and ritual discourse's fundamental imperialism foster **a sense of community**. The drama of ritual discourse, typology, and parataxis encourage communal involvement (interpretation). The Bible's mythic function foists a communal identity upon readers. Finally, orality's repetitiveness and typology (the reuse of symbols and patterns) provides the lineaments of an ongoing interpretative **tradition**.

Review Questions

1. What is ritual's relation to myth?
2. How does the oral Bible differ from a textual Bible?

3. Is the entire Bible mythic?

4. Contrast ancient and modern history.

5. What is an "implied author" and a "word of God" effect?

6. Describe the Bible's distinctive flashforwards and flashbacks. How do they foster biblical ideology and a sense of tradition?

7. What is multi-perspectivism?

8. What does time do to the relationship between narratee and reader? What does the myth-ritual complex do?

9. What kinds of relationships with readers do myth, theodicy, and metaphor have?

10. How do the Bible's discourse-features reflect its ritual quality?

Questions for Reflection

1. Can the Bible be read outside a myth-ritual context? Should it be?

2. How might the electronic age change the Bible's appropriation and content? Have movies adapted the Bible? Have televangelists? Are these modifications appropriate? Why or why not?

3. Compare sociological and literary definitions of myth.

4. Why would the reader wish to distinguish narrative perspective and voice? Are biblical narrators truly omniscient?

5. Distinguish allegory and typology. Are either appropriate for a mythic text?

6. Is "literal" religious language possible?

For Further Reading

For discussions of ritual, see Livingston, 104-35; Doty, Mythography, 72-106; and Turner.

On various discourse-features, see the appropriate listings in Holman and Harmon.

The classic discussion of media is McLuhan. Boomershine,

"Megatrends"; and **idem**, Story, has done significant work with biblical media.

Form criticism was the first scholarly method to investigate the Bible's oral forms. For introductory discussions, see McKnight, What; Hayes, Form; Koch, Growth; and Tucker, Form. For more technical appraisals, see Bultmann, History; Dibelius, Tradition; and Guettgemanns. For more recent discussion of biblical orality, see Kelber, Oral, 1-43; Ong; and Silberman.

Robert Alter, Narrative, provides illuminating examples of biblical story's tendency to repetition, variation, and type-scenes.

For literary discussions of genre, see Dubrow; Hirsch; and Gerhart. Detweiler; Kort; and W. Smith, Scripture, have important discussions of scripture as a genre.

Thompson, 16-49; Aune, NT; Damrosch; and Fisch discuss specific biblical genres in some detail. Most introductions and commentaries consider the genre of individual biblical books.

On ancient history, see Aune, NT, 77-115; and D. A. Russell, Ancient.

Gottwald, "Poetry"; Alter, Poetry; and Kugel discuss biblical poetry.

Chatman, 147-51, describes narratives as communications involving authors, implied authors, and so forth. The classic discussion of the implied author is Booth, Fiction. On narrators, see Chatman, 146-267; Genette, 161-262; Uspensky; and Lanser.

See Petersen, "Point," for an application to one biblical work.

Prince discusses narratees. Iser; and Fish, Artifacts, develop the notion of the implied reader.

For a brief summary of Chatman from the perspective of biblical criticism, see Powell, What. For a sophisticated application to one biblical text, see Culpepper.

For a brief introduction to narrative showing and telling, see

Genette, 161-85.

Genette, 33-160, has the most comprehensive discussion of narrative time. Culpepper applies the concepts helpfully to a biblical text.

On typology, see Frye, Code, 78-101; Grant and Tracy, 28-51; and Fishbane, 350-79.

On symbolism and religious language, see Tillich, Dynamics; and Eliade, "Methodological." For a discussion of biblical figures of speech, see Caird, Language.

Auerbach, Mimesis, 22-23, 31-33, 41, 151; and Sternberg, 48-57, discuss the Bible's populist style.

Torgovnick catalogues the potential relationships between a text (author) and a reader. Crossan, Dark, 47-62, summarizes the potential relationships between a text and "reality."

See Kennedy; Stowers; and Mack and Robbins for a discussion of biblical rhetoric.

INTRODUCTION TO TORAH

The *Septuagint* divided *Torah* into five books. Their English names, as well as the designation "Pentateuch" for the whole, reflect this Greek background. In the HB, the works' titles are their opening words.

Figure 1: **The Books of Torah**	
English	**Hebrew**
Genesis	In the beginning
Exodus	These are the names
Leviticus	And he called
Numbers	In the wilderness
Deuteronomy	These are the words

Torah is **Israel's founding myth** and **defines her as the people of Yahweh** [see figure 3]. Its story is a two-fold *cosmogony*, ordering the world and Israel.

The primeval cosmogony describes the divine ordering of the "natural," historical world in which Israel lives. The creation of Eden and its loss through human disobedience (a *sin theodicy*) dominate the story-line.

In response to that tragedy, God orders Israel through *election* and *covenant*. God promises the fathers land and descendants. Egyptian slavery threatens the

Figure 2: **Outline of Torah**

1. Ordering the cosmos (Gen 1-11)
2. Ordering Israel (Gen 12 - Deut 34)
   a. Election/Promise (Gen 12-50)
   b. Deliverance (Ex 1-18)
   c. Covenant/Cult (Ex 19 - Deut 34)

promise, but God delivers the people to Sinai where he reveals the covenant and the cult. For Torah, that revelation restores Eden.

Figure 3: **Election and Ethnocentrism**

As election threatens to become arrogant *ethnocentrism*, various HB texts warn Israel to **avoid pride**. Thus, the Deuteronomist reminds Israel that her election is from the divine freedom, not her merit (e.g., Deut 8-9). Others understand Israel's election to give her a missionary responsibility to the nations (e.g., Isa 40-55). Finally, much later traditions explain Israel's election through a story of **the nations' failure** (cf. Rom 1). According to one late legend, God offered Torah to everyone, but only Israel accepted it.

Appropriately for myth, God dominates Torah. He creates, chooses, elects, delivers, and reveals. He speaks both the world and Israel into existence. Torah's characteristic style, then, is narrative-engendering speech.

As myth, Torah reaches out imperialistically through both story and ritual. Torah does not simply describe what was, it also defines Israel as God's created, chosen, and delivered people. God's demands (e.g., henotheism and cleanness) symbolize Israel's attachment to God. Further, Torah's cult continues to dramatize the myth and provide access to sacred power for the community. Torah's characters are mythic models of *henotheism* or *apostasy*. Torah, then, continues to challenge its myth-ritual community to live henotheistically.

Not surprisingly, then, Torah is the Jewish scripture **par excellence**. Ancient Jews declared that God revealed the Torah completely at Sinai. Later prophets (Prophets) and scribes (Writings, Talmud) merely transmitted and interpreted this fundamental revelation. Thus, the arrangement and tripartite division of the HB reflect both Torah's mythic superiority and a "prophetic succession" (tradition).

Figure 4: **Civil Religion**

The civil religions of modern nations resemble ancient natural religion myths [cf. Jones and Richey, 3-18; Nisbet, "Civil"; Marsden, Religion, 42-45]. A civil religion is a set of **common beliefs** (e.g., "the American way") enshrining the nation with sacred significance and providing social cohesiveness through a sacred story, symbols, education, and rituals. The United States, for example, has a mythic story of founding fathers, amazing deliverances (the revolution), and the creation of a society with sacred, founding documents (e.g., the Constitution). A sacred calendar memorializes the myth (e.g., Thanksgiving, Independence Day, Presidents' Birthdays, and Memorial Days) [cf. J. Robertson, 9-18]. Interestingly, spokespersons for the American story often bathe it in biblical imagery [cf. Bellah, "Civil"; Bercovitch]. For example, the pilgrimage of Europeans to America becomes an exodus from slavery to the promised land. The Puritan commonwealth becomes a "city set on a hill." The Civil War becomes a divine judgment.

Questions for Reflection

1. Compare the Jewish and Christian understandings of Torah.
2. Compare Israel's natural religion myth with the founding story of the United States.
3. How do people within natural or civil religions avoid arrogance?

CHAPTER 5

THE PRIMEVAL EDEN LOST
Genesis 1-11

Introduction: Relation to Torah

Genesis 1-11 is the story of **God's primeval ordering and that order's loss**. This introductory mythic sketch of the human condition sets the stage for Torah's Eden Restored story.

Content Summary

God creates the world and Eden (Gen 1-2). Almost immediately, **humans lose Eden** by violating God's instructions (Gen 3). Life outside Eden is harsh and violent (Gen 4). A genealogy of long-lived heroes (Gen 5) depicts life's continuance and connects the beginnings with later stories about civilization.

Despite remarkable human fertility and increasing civilization, no one recovers Eden. In fact, increasing human wickedness motivates God to destroy the world with **a flood** (Gen 6-8). After this recurrence of chaos, God begins anew with Noah (9:1-19).

The remaining narrative depicts the world on the eve of Israel's origin (9:20-11:32). Genealogies explain the world's population (10) and Abram's ancestry (11:10-32). Genesis 9:20-28 also provides an advance explanation of Canaan's slaughter. Nevertheless, Eden is still lost. The tower of **Babel** story (11:1-9) reprises Gen 3 on a civilization-wide scale. It criticizes human efforts to reach heaven, a symbol for order-Eden.

Figure 1: **The <u>Enuma Elish</u>** [for text, see Pritchard, 60-72]

The Mesopotamian creation myth begins with a **theogony**. Apsu and Tiamat, the primeval pair, produce the other gods. When these newly created gods disturb Apsu, he plots their destruction, but the wise Ea discovers the plan and kills Apsu preemptively. Tiamat, then, rules the gods tyrannically. Eventually, **Marduk** defies her. Catching her in a net and ordering the winds to blow her fiery breath back into her, he punctures the puffed-up goddess with an arrow.

Then, Marduk creates by splitting Tiamat like a shell-fish to form the firmament and the earth separating a watery chaos. Other gods become astral objects [IV.135-46; V]. Finally, he creates a "savage":

Blood I will mass and cause bones to be.
I will establish a savage, 'man' shall be his name. . . .
He shall be charged with the service of the gods
That they might be at ease! [VI.5-8]

The epic ends with a description of the building of Marduk's temple (in Babylon) and a long hymn of praise to Marduk.

Both Gen 1 and the <u>Enuma Elish</u> assume a three-level cosmology. Both begin with a watery chaos and build to the creation of humans. Both are national epics. Genesis 1, however, makes a **more forceful statement about God's sovereignty**. It has no theogony and no god-war. Genesis 1 also portrays humans as **vice-regents** with God, rather than as mere waiters.

Genre

Genesis 1-11 is a **myth**. It describes the world's founding and significant, precedent-setting actions (e.g., marriage, sex, agriculture, civilization, arts, and nations-language). Religiously, it summarizes the human condition and provides *etiologies* for rituals like the sabbath.

In Gen 1-11, God is constantly present. He takes center stage as story-actor (Gen 1-3) or effector (Gen 4; 6-9; 11). The human characters are mythic heroes. As such, they enjoy far greater powers (naming the animals, frightening God, and scaling the heavens) and stature (Gen 5:1-6:4) than the norm.

Figure 2: **The <u>Adapa Myth</u>** [text in Pritchard, 76-80]

Trying to protect his favorite Adapa from a divine plot, the god Ea warns Adapa not to eat or drink of that which the gods offer. Unknown to Ea, however, the gods had already decided to confer immortality on Adapa. Refusing their bread of life, Adapa remains mortal.

Both Gen 3 and the <u>Adapa Myth</u> connect human mortality with divinely prohibited food. What the <u>Adapa Myth</u> depicts as **cruel fate**, however, Gen 3 portrays as the result of human disobedience (**sin**).

Style

Genesis 1-11 has two distinctive styles. Portions resemble a catalogue (Gen 1; 5; 10). Genesis 1, for example, uses a repeated pattern to tell the creation story:

> And God said, "Let there be . . ." And it was so.
> And God saw that it was good. And there was
> evening and morning . . .

By contrast, Gen 2-4 has a flowing, vivid narrative style.

The respective sections also have differing vocabularies and theological perspectives. In Gen 1, **Elohim** creates, but in Gen 2, **Yahweh** forms humans. **Elohim** returns in Gen 5. The God of Gen 1 is transcendent while the God of Gen 2-3 is immanent.

Figure 3: **Two Creation Accounts**

	Gen 1	**Gen 2**
style	catalogue	story
wording	Elohim	Yahweh
theology	transcendence	immanence
humans	image of God	from ground
setting	watery chaos	desert

The humans of Gen 1 are in the "image of God" while those in Gen 2 are "from the ground."

Such differences make it difficult to read Gen 1-11 as a literary whole. For this reason, most consider Gen 1-11 (and Torah) a composite production [cf. chap. 8; Barton, <u>Reading</u>, 20-29].

Tragic Story Patterns: Eden; Flood; Babel

Genesis 1-11 tells **three Eden Lost stories**. First, God creates the world and a garden in which humans may live well and have dominion (Gen 1-2). When they fail to live under God's authority, God expels humans from **Eden** (Gen 3). Outside Eden, fertility and civilization (dominion) continue, but human wickedness increases. God, then, destroys order a second time with a **flood** (Gen 6-8) which reprises the primeval chaos (1:2). God's covenant with Noah promising a moratorium on floods provides a third ordering (9:1-17). Drunkenness, nakedness, and slavery indicate this lesser Eden's limitations (9:20-27). Finally, humans make a towering assault on heaven. God's response is the third chaos: the confusion of human language (11:1-9).

Loss continues and grows as Eden Lost repeats itself on a worldwide scale in Flood and Babel. Each story and Gen 1-11 itself have a *tragic shape*. Catastrophe swallows promising beginnings.

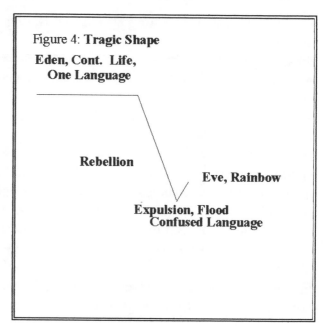

Figure 4: **Tragic Shape**

Eden, Cont. Life, One Language

Rebellion

Eve, Rainbow

Expulsion, Flood Confused Language

Genesis 1-11, however, does not succumb to a tragic vision of life. Loss and alienation are not all. In every loss, some **hope** still glimmers. Thus, despite God's predicted penalty, Eden's fruit-eaters do not die. Instead, Eve becomes the "mother of all living" (cf. 3:20 with 2:17). Although Cain kills his brother, God protectively "marks" Cain, and Cain mysteriously finds a wife. Although wickedness increases, God preserves Noah and his family in the ark. In short, Gen 1-11 asserts God's **creative mercy** even as God defends order catastrophically.

More importantly, Gen 1-11 is not tragic because it merely begins Torah. To Eden Lost, Torah responds with Israel's national epic. Thus, Babel's confused languages give way to Abram's call (12:1-3). In this **comic myth**, then, there are gardens and arks in the midst of chaos.

Plot Conflict: Sin and Melodrama

The sin plotting increases the distance from tragedy. These

humans do not perish because they pursue their characters to absurd limits (as do Prometheus and Hamlet), nor because they struggle against fate (as does Oedipus), nor because they get caught between two rival value systems (as does Antigone). Rather, these victims receive their "just desserts" (cf. 6:5-8). Genesis 1-11, then, is a *melodrama* or morality play, not a tragedy.

God establishes a good (cf. Gen 1), but fragile order. Humans live in a paradise with divinely demarcated boundaries. When Adam and Eve succumb to temptation and eat the forbidden fruit, their expulsion surprises only because it is not "the full extent of the law." Adam and Eve *sin*. In Judeao-Christian thought, sin is an offense against God. It is *faith*'s opposite, the antithesis of loyalty and obedience. In Gen 1-11, humans do not live as creatures of God's good order. They think they can do better by their own devices. They aspire to be God (3:5, 22; cf. 11:6).

```
╔══════════════════════════════════════════════════════╗
║                                                        ║
║  Figure 5: Sin Plotting                                ║
║                                                        ║
║  SENDER  --------->  OBJECT  -----------> RECIPIENTS   ║
║  God                 Eden                 Adam/Eve      ║
║                        ^                               ║
║  HELPER  ---------->  SUBJECT <---------- OPPONENTS    ║
║  faith               God                  sin          ║
║                                                        ║
╚══════════════════════════════════════════════════════╝
```

Babel tells the same tale more nakedly. There is no "moral" offense, only the assault on heaven. By contrast, the Flood moralizes. There, the wicked perish while the righteous have an ark (Gen 6:5-8).

An alternative **holy war** reading makes **the snake** of Gen 3 into Satan, God's apocalyptic foe [see figures 9-10]. This holy war reading is difficult to maintain solely on the basis of Gen 3. The snake is simply not a rival contending with God. Instead, the snake is a mere plot device providing the vehicle for human temptation. In fact, in contrast to other ANE creation stories, nowhere in Gen 1-11 does God establish his order against external opposition (a holy war) [see figure 1].

The order of Genesis deteriorates from within. The recipients reject their gift. That is, Gen 1-11 has a **sin plot**. Of course, one could propose another holy war reading in which the Genesis-humans (not chaos or the snake) contend with God. They wish to and come perilously close to being "like God" (3:5-6, 22-24; 6:1-4; 11:6-9). Traditionally, of course, that has been read as sin. Of course, it could "also be read as actions on the part of a threatened God to keep man from realizing the role which God gives to man in the first creation story" (see 1:28-30) [Thompson, 79]. If so, the story becomes a **"cosmic joke"** in which

> a sly game is being played upon man. God is portrayed as a somewhat deceptive, diabolical figure in relation to man; he sets man up in a situation only to thwart him from realizing what is potentially accessible. God stalemates man, and man seems not to know when he has overstepped his place. [Thompson, 79]

Divine Characters: Sovereign Orderer

Creation and destruction forcefully demonstrate **the divine sovereignty**. Life and death obey his word. The Sovereign establishes and ruthlessly defends his order. Not even his own mandates (fertility and civilization in 1:28) can threaten that order (11:1-9).

For this and other ancient creation stories, **order and Orderer** are unquestionable. At times, however, the order and story have a moral cast. The order is "good" (Gen 1). God gives humans a "paradise." Further, the Eden-ending curses are "justly" related to offense (3:14-19). Similarly, Gen 6:5-8 ethicizes the flood's destruction as a judgment. The whole, nevertheless, resists moral summation. Why does God create? Why does God allow Adam and Eve to live after their death-deserving offense? Why does God prefer Abel to Cain? Why does Ham's offense "justify" Canaan's slavery? In short, this God is the quintessential **Holy**, the life-giving and death-dealing Other beyond human comprehension (cf. Job 38:1-42:6).

Interestingly, the Sovereign's identity is somewhat vague. God appears without introduction in full creative stride [Sternberg, 322-25]. The absolute beginning suggests both the story's ritual discourse and its revelatory quality. First, the Creator needs no introduction because he is the God known and addressed in worship. Second, subsequent story gradually reveals the Creator's identity.

The Creator is the generic **Elohim**, not the specifically Israelite **Yahweh** (1:1). Such nomenclature is, of course, quite appropriate for the maker of heaven and earth, who is hardly a mere national deity. The plural form **Elohim** and the perplexing plural verb forms (in 1:26; 3:22; 11:7) qualify an apparent monotheism. Scholars explain the plurals as references to a divine court or as plurals of majesty (e.g., when a leader refers to himself in the plural by saying "we have done/decided . . .").

The subsequent national epic reveals the vaguely known **Elohim** to be Israel's **Yahweh**. The maker of Israel is none other than the maker of heaven and earth. As appropriate for myth, God is intensely present. In fact, Gen 2-4 portrays an *anthropomorphic* God who walks and talks with humans. By contrast, Gen 1 portrays an aloof, transcendent God [see style]. Humans know him both by the results of his action (a world, confused language) and through the medium of story.

In theological language, God is both **immanent** (Gen 2-4) and **transcendent** (Gen 1; 11). While able to appear in the world, he is separate from it. Even in this most mythic section, then, God is both present and absent.

Figure 6: **Conceptions of God**

The Western religions conceive God as a **personal** being both **transcendent** (other) and **immanent** (approaching or approachable). Such a God transcends the natural, historical order (empirical reality) while active in it.

This conception differs strikingly from both deistic and pantheistic understandings of God. For **deism,** prominent in the West in the seventeenth and eighteenth centuries, God is not active in the world he created. The world is a mechanistic, closed system of natural causes and effects (no miracles). By contrast, **pantheism** understands God to be part of the world (as does polytheism). For the classic Eastern religions, God is so radically immanent that the divine is the only reality. Material reality and individual egos are mere illusion.

Human Characters: Free Creatures

For Gen 1-11, humans are the Sovereign's dependent creatures. Their **finitude** and limitation are clear in their creation "from the ground" (Gen 2:7) and in their mortality (Gen 3:19; "to dust you shall return").

Humans, however, are also **free.** They are made in the **"image of God"** (1:26-27). This image includes or enables the mandate to "have dominion" (1:28). On earth, humans act as God's vice-sovereigns (cf. 2:19-20; 9:1-7).

Divine sovereignty, however, incorporates human dominion. The Sovereign demands faith from his creatures. He does not expect or tolerate rebellion (3:5-6, 22-24; 11:6-9). Human freedom exists, then, only within limits.

Genesis 1-11 makes no attempt to resolve the philosophical conundrum of **determinism and freedom**. It merely asserts in story-form both divine sovereignty and human responsibility. It even satirizes those who would deny their own responsibility by blaming God. God does not excuse the fruit-eaters who pass blame adolescently to "the woman whom you gave" or to the serpent who tricks (3:12-13). All bear responsibility (3:14-19).

For this narrative, divine sovereignty founds human responsibility. Creation founds an order, a space, within which humans are genuinely responsible. Belief in human responsibility is **an optimistic anthropology**. Despite failures, the Sovereign continues to expect faithfulness. If Adam fails, Noah does not. Ultimately, both Adam and Noah symbolize the Sovereign's **demand for faith**.

These story-characters are humans, **not Israelites**. All humans are in the divine image (Gen 1:26-28). The covenant made with Noah (9:1-17) is for all. From Noah's sons come the known world (9:19; 10).

The story's end, however, narrows the story's focus. Abram's genealogy introduces his preferential treatment (11:27-12:3). Presumably, the Sovereign can choose whom he will (cf. 4:4-5) or whom he must for Israel to have a story (national epic) or land (cf. 9:24-27, though this choice is ethicized). This juxtaposition of universality (Gen 1-11) and national epic (11:27-12:3) presents **election** in its rawest, most disturbing form.

Myth: Cosmogony and Theodicy

Genesis 1-11 is a cosmogonic myth. It orders the cosmos in which humans live accounting for creation, human mortality, families, human fertility and struggles, civilization (e.g., agriculture, cities), the ancestry of the nations, and the diversity of human languages. This world, of course, is the world as seen by ancient Israel. That is, this **cosmogony** sets the stage for Israel's own cosmogony.

Genesis 1-11 provides humankind's basic mythic identity: **creatures of God**, dependent but in his image. It also presents a basic demand of **faith**, responsible living within the divinely provided order. Enoch and Noah, both of whom are said to have "walked with God," are positive exemplars (5:22-24; 6:9). In conservative, traditional fashion, the order is the sacred's chief symbol and avenue.

Genesis 1-11 also offers a **theodicy** to explain Eden's loss. Tradition reads Gen 3 as the classic example of the biblical **sin-theodicy**. This theodicy attributes mortality, suffering, evil, and chaos to sin. Chaos is the divine response to human rebellion (3:14-19; 6:5-7). Adam, the flood generation, and the people of Babel typify such rebellion.

ANET: Hierarchy and Science

Genesis 1-11 depicts God's creation and defense of a **rigid, hierarchical order**. Not surprisingly, the story is difficult for democratic and scientific moderns.

The order of Gen 1-11 has **conservative, traditional, and authoritarian** presuppositions. Its cultural code assumes monarchy, patriarchy, and male chauvinism. It prizes the old and rejects the new as dangerous. It does not allow debate. It demands obedience. Its God is the ruthless defender of hierarchical orders.

For **modern egalitarians**, this story is a "cosmic joke" perpetrated by a ludicrous despot. Readers within ancient, traditional societies, however, valued order far more highly. Rebels threatening security-providing orders were culprits. By contrast, moderns value mavericks and **individualists**. For ancients, the order made ethic possible. For moderns, the hierarchical order is the antithesis of "political correctness."

Figure 7: **Albert Camus, <u>The Rebel</u>** [cf. figure 9]

Moderns find identity in rebellion, not obedience:

> . . . rebellion plays the same role as does the "cogito" in the realm of thought . . . . I rebel--therefore we exist. [Camus, <u>Rebel</u>, 22]

That rebellion founds a human world, replacing the "reign of grace by the reign of justice" [Camus, 56]:

> . . . only two possible worlds can exist for the human mind: the sacred (or, to speak in Christian terms, the world of grace) and the world of rebellion. [Camus, 21]

Genesis' cosmogony is equally problematic. The attribution of creation (flood, linguistic diversity, etc.) to divine supernatural activity confounds the modern, scientific perspective. Does Gen 1-11, then, **conflict with modern science?**

The simplest answer is yes. Clearly, the two **envision the world differently.** For Gen 1-11 and most ancient near easterners, the world is a three-layered affair: the heaven above, the earth, and the water beneath the earth (cf. Ex 20:4). Creation forms a dry land in the midst of a watery chaos (1:2, 6-10). A firmament, the solid-underside of heaven (NRSV, "dome"), keeps the watery chaos above from destroying the cosmos. The flood reintroduces this primeval watery chaos (7:11). The firmament rests upon mountains at the edge of the flat earth. The earth rests upon pillars which go down into the watery chaos beneath the earth. Fixed in the firmament, the sun, moon, and stars track back and forth across the sky (1:14-18).

Figure 8: **Gilgamesh Epic** [text in Pritchard, 72-99]

Gilgamesh's search for immortality brings him to **Utnapishtim**, who tells Gilgamesh how he survived the flood. Following Ea's advice, Utnapishtim had built a ship and survived a catastrophe so great that it frightened even the gods. When the flood was over (which was determined by releasing birds), Utnapishtim sacrificed to the gods who granted him immortality in return.

Utnapishtim challenges Gilgamesh to gain the gods' attention by staying awake for seven days. Failing, he searches for a rejuvenating plant. After he obtains the plant from the bottom of a lake, a snake eats it (and sheds its skin) while Gilgamesh sleeps. Failing in his quest, Gilgamesh accepts his mortality and returns home to be a great ruler.

The epic has obvious similarities with Gen 3 and with the **Adapa Myth** [see figure 2]. Utnapishtim's story also resembles Noah's. Of course, the Genesis story has a more sovereign God, who is not frightened by the flood, and a more ethical tone as its flood is a divine judgment on wickedness, rather than a capricious act.

While this world-view corresponds with naked-eye observation, science hardly envisions the world so. More importantly, science's perspective is a **functional atheism**. Thus, science never cites God as a causal explanation. For science, the cosmos is a closed continuum of cause and effect. This perspective, rather than any particular theory like evolution, is the real conflict between biblical myth and science.

Figure 9: **Milton's Satan**

Milton transforms Eden's snake into a Satan who still craves sovereignty even though banished to hell for a failed revolt [from <u>Paradise Lost</u>, I.242-63]:

Is this the region . . that we must change for heaven?
. . . Be it so . . . farthest from him is best . . . .
Here we may reign secure; and, in my choice,
To reign is worth ambition, though in Hell:
Better to reign in Hell than serve in Heaven.

One can, of course, try to avoid the conflict by restricting religion and science to **separate, operational spheres**. Perhaps, religion plays a meaning/value game while science plays a means/methods game. Perhaps, religion should restrict itself to "Who created and why?" while science asks "How does the world work?" Unfortunately, both religion and science are imperialistic systems attempting complete explanation, prediction, and control.

Again, one could avoid conflict by **prioritizing either religion or science**. Thus, one could simply dismiss religion as an antiquarian curiosity whose false answers have gradually fallen before the progress of science. Alternatively, one could force science to bow before an inerrant Bible containing all truth (as do creation scientists).

Such prioritizing affords little help. In the late twentieth century, modern science is inescapable. One simply cannot read biblical literature the same way after Galileo, Darwin, Freud, and Einstein. Nevertheless, late twentieth-century humans also remain religious. Not surprisingly, then, many moderns and post-moderns

question science's hegemony.   Science has brought brilliant technological advances, but valuing science alone has produced attenuated lives ethically, aesthetically, and spiritually impoverished.

Figure 10: **Genesis 3 and Paradise Lost**

Cast into hell [see figure 9], Satan plots to attack God by attacking humans [II.344-86]. Meanwhile, in heaven, the Son offers his own life in order to redeem man [III.203-343]: "So heavenly love shall outdo hellish hate. . ." In Eden, the snake-Satan seduces Eve who has foolishly left Adam's protection. Adam eats for love of Eve, "fondly overcome with female charm" [IX.999]. Despite Eden's loss, an angel (Michael) prophesies Christ's ultimate victory over Satan. In response, Adam praises God:

O goodness infinite, goodness immense!
That all this good of evil shall produce,
. . . . Full of doubt I stand,
Whether I should repent me now of sin
By me done and occasioned, or rejoice
Much more that much more good thereof shall spring;
. . . over wrath grace shall abound. [From XII.469-78]

Milton's epic transforms Gen 3 by placing it in the larger context of Satan's rebellion and fall (based on expansions of Isa 14:12-15; Lk 10:18; and Rev 12:7-12). He also identifies Satan and the snake and makes Satan partially responsible for the fall [I.34; but cf. III.95-134]. More importantly, he connects lost Eden with the story of Christ's incarnation and cross [II.274-343]. In this, Rom 5 is as generative for Milton as Gen 3.

In sum, modern science and Gen 1-11 are in conflict. Ancient humans hardly write with twentieth-century codes. **Dialogue** between the codes **may, however, prove liberating**. Modern science's acknowledged benefits might humble the arrogant religious tendency to proclaim God's final truth. On the other hand, Gen 1-11 may inform modern science that life is more than the sum of materialism, empiricism, and determinism. Gen 1-11, then, may still offer life-enhancing symbols and values.

Review Questions

1. Apply the reading method of chaps. 3-4 to Gen 1-11. List its genre, plot shape, plot conflict, depiction of God, mythic function, and ANE problems.
2. Why is Gen 1-11 a myth?
3. Is Gen 1-11 tragic?
4. Compare sin and holy war readings of Gen 1-11.
5. Is the God of Gen 1-11 moral?
6. Are the humans of Gen 1-11 free?
7. Discuss the possible relationships between Gen 1-11 and modern science.

Suggestions for Alternate Readings and Reflection

1. Does the mandate of 1:28 conflict with the actions in 3:22 and 11:6-7?
2. Who tells the truth in Gen 3 about the relationship between the fruit, power, and death?
3. Is the "sin" reading an anachronistic imposition on Gen 3? How would a structuralist read Gen 1-3? Is mortality the reconciliation of the disparate images of humans in Gen 1:27-28 and 2:7?
4. Feminists object to the hierarchical order in Gen 1-11. Why is Gen 2-4 particularly offensive? Why might Gen 1 be a more palatable story?
5. Advocates of "creation science" want Gen 1 taught as science in the public schools as a scientific alternative to evolution. Is Gen 1 science? Creation scientists often read the six days of Gen 1 as

creative periods separated by eons in order to account for geological evidence. Some read 1:1-2 as a creation, catastrophe, and second creation. In this way, they can find and lose the dinosaurs between 1:1 and 1:2. Is this a literal reading? Why might one read the text so?

6. Compare the conceptions of mortality in Gen 3 and other ANE myths.

7. How does Paradise Lost change Gen 3?

8. Compare Gilgamesh, Camus' rebel, and Milton's Satan.

For Further Reading

For commentaries on Genesis, see Rad, Genesis; Sarna; and Brueggemann, Genesis. The collection of essays in Anderson, Creation in the OT, is also helpful.

For data on sources in Gen 1-11, see Habel.

For various ancient myths resembling episodes in Gen 1-11, see Pritchard; Brandon; and Kramer. For world mythology dealing with the same themes, see Rosenberg; and Eliade, Essential.

Ancient creation stories depict the formation of order from chaos. For discussion, see Eliade, Profane, 20-113; Niditch; and Anderson, Chaos. Heidel, Babylonian, compares Gen 1 with the Enuma Elish in detail.

Heidel, Gilgamesh, compares the Mesopotamian and Israelite flood stories. Damrosch, 88-143, discusses the formation of the Gilgamesh Epic in some detail.

For a reading of Gen. 1-11 as anti-myth, see Schneidau.

On the Bible and tragedy, see Humphreys, Tragic. Frye, Code, 169-98, argues that the Bible is comic in structure. Cf. Josipovici, 42-47, 85-87, 225.

For introductions to theological concepts like God, the image of God, and sin, see the entries in Eliade, ER; Buttrick; Crim;

Metzger and Coogan; and Cross and Livingstone. See also the relevant sections in various OT theologies: Rad; Eichrodt; and Jacob.

Livingston, 242-45; Monk, 179-85; Cox; and Ricoeur, Symbolism, 47-99, are also helpful on sin.

For comparative introductions to divine conceptions, see Livingston, 169-201, or Monk, 126-45.

For the conflict between science and religion/Bible, see Krentz, 10-22; and Alan Richardson, Bible. For a brief review of creation science, see Livingston, 229-30. For more information, see Roland Frye.

CHAPTER 6

THE FOUNDING FATHERS
Genesis 12-50

Introduction: Relation to Torah

Abram's genealogy (11:10-32) connects the cosmogony and the founding fathers' story (Gen 12-50) which begins Israel's Eden Restored story. Abram and Jacob father the people of Israel. More importantly, divine promises (e.g., Gen 12:1-3) and covenants with the fathers foreshadow the land and the covenant which ultimately form Israel as God's people.

Genre: National Epic

On the one hand, the tale of the "founding fathers" belongs to the mythic genre. Its legendary heroes create mythic order (Israel) and perform precedent-setting actions (e.g., circumcision). Jacob, renamed Israel, and his twelve sons are the *eponymous* ancestors of **Israel** and her twelve tribes (47:27-49:28). Further, God still enters the story as actor at propitious moments. This section, then, functions as part of Israel's cosmogonic myth.

On the other hand, the tale resembles the ancient epic, poetic tales depicting peoples' origins or important national heroes [see figure 1]. While Gen 12-50 (and the rest of Torah) is not poetry, it does episodically relate the nationally important tale of the great heroes' divinely-aided quest for a land. With due reservations, then, one may also think of Torah as a non-poetic **epic.**

Figure 1: **Ancient Epics** [cf. chap. 5, figures 1 and 8]

The most famous ancient epics are Homer's Iliad and Odyssey. The Iliad tells the tale of the wrath of Achilles. His honor slighted, he first refuses to fight, but, then, he enters the war to avenge his friend and to defeat Hector and the Trojans. This heroic tale of war and honor has little resemblance to Torah.

Like Torah, however, the Odyssey is the story of a divinely assisted journey to the homeland. Despite Poseidon's opposition, Odysseus returns home from the Trojan War with the aid of Athena. Entering his home disguised as a beggar, Odysseus wins a contest, delivers his long-suffering wife Penelope from incessant suitors, and restores peace to his homeland.

The Aeneid, the major Roman epic, has similar features. It describes Rome's founding by the Trojan hero Aeneas [I.1-11] who arrives at Rome only after receiving divine assistance versus angry gods. En route, the quintessential Roman hero must forego love, queen Dido who "loves him beyond all telling," in order to fulfill dutifully his destiny [IV.468-75]. Arriving in Italy, Aeneas finds himself in a divinely-assisted war, the telling of which strongly resembles the Iliad.

Content Summary: Genealogy and Promise

Genesis 12-50 is the story of the family of Abram (12-27) and Jacob (27-50) and the family's two important sons, Isaac (21-27) and Joseph (37; 39-47; 50). Genealogies connect the whole: Abram begets Isaac, who begets Jacob, who begets the twelve. In fact, the overall style of Gen 12-50 is the **genealogical connection of episodic scenes**. Even minor characters are genealogically defined (e.g., Nahor, Lot, Ishmael, Abram's other sons, and Esau).

Thematically, the **divine promise** unites the various episodes into the father's continuing quest for land and descendants:

> Now the LORD said to Abram, "Go from your country and your kindred and your father's house to the land that I will show you. I will make of you a great nation, and I will bless you and make your name great, so that you will be a blessing." (12:1-2)

The **lack of a son** dominates the Abram episodes. Although God frequently promises descendants (e.g., 13:6; 15:7), none are forthcoming. Abram and his barren wife grow old as he suffers unremitting wanderings, famines, wars, abductions of Sarah (twice), divine visitations, circumcision, and family squabbles. Both Abram and Sarah suggest creative alternatives to the promise (15-17) and doubt the promise's fulfillment (17-18). The divine promise is unrelenting, however. Finally, beyond hope, the promised son is born (21:1-7) to Abram, fittingly renamed Abraham (17:5).

Promise in hand, Abraham loses a son (Ishmael, 21:8-21) and almost loses the promised son in a bizarre **divine test** (22). When Sarah dies, the landless Abraham buys land in which to bury her (23) and sends Eliezer to the ancestral homeland to find Isaac a wife (24).

After Abraham's death (25) and a brief Isaac interlude (26), the story shifts to **the rivalry between Isaac's twins, Esau and Jacob** (25:21-34; 27). Jacob, the younger, procures the elder's birthright and, then, steals the paternal blessing as well. The resulting animosity forces Jacob to leave for the ancestral homeland. En route, God repeats the promises of land and descendants to Jacob while Esau dallies with foreign women (28).

In twenty years of wrangling with his deceitful uncle Laban, Jacob steadily prospers. He gains two wives, eleven sons, and much wealth. Envy forces Jacob to leave Haran and he returns to the (still) promised land. En route, Jacob encounters and makes peace with Laban (31), Esau (32-33), and God (32:22-32). Despite problems in the land (34), a third divine encounter climaxes the Jacob story, reiterates the divine promises, and **transforms Jacob into Israel** (35).

After the birth of the twelfth son (Benjamin) and the death and burial of Rachel and Isaac, the story turns to **Jacob's sons** (37-50). Jacob's preferential treatment of Joseph, Rachel's eldest son, and Joseph's arrogant dreams lead the brothers to sell him into Egyptian slavery. In Egypt, divinely-aided dream interpretations help Joseph rise from slavery through prison to become Pharaoh's second-in-command (39-41).

Meanwhile, famine forces Jacob to send his sons to Egypt. A disguised Joseph gives them food, but he detains a brother to see if they will return with Benjamin (42). Continued famine forces Jacob to risk Benjamin. When the brothers return, Joseph tests them. Charging Benjamin with theft, he attempts to discover if the brothers will leave the new favorite in Egypt (43-44). When the brothers will not, Joseph discloses his identity, and the entire family is reunited in Egypt (45-47).

Near death, Jacob blesses Joseph's sons (48) and his own (49) foreshadowing Israel's history. Jacob dies, and Joseph buries him in the promised, yet not given, land. Although the brothers fear Joseph's revenge, Joseph declares that God used their animosity to deliver Israel (50:20). Genesis ends with Joseph's death and his coffin **awaiting the journey to the promised land** (50:26).

Story Pattern: Quest and Heroes

The story's unifying theme is **the divine promise of descendants and land**. As those promises are not soon forthcoming, the fathers' story is **a quest**. Despite the delay, the story does not have a tragic shape. Instead, its shape is that of an **unfulfilled comedy**, a story of faith and hope before the promise [see figure 2].

The promises of descendants and land have different story-lives.

At first, **barren and lost wives** mock the promise until **miraculous births** occur (21:1-7; 25:21). Jacob, too, has a temporarily barren wife (Rachel), but Leah and the handmaidens are an embarrassment of riches. Even in this plenty, however, the divine involvement is evident (29:31-30:24). Jacob's twelve sons symbolically fulfill the "dust of the earth" and the "stars of heaven" promises (13:16; 15:5). Various genealogical notes (e.g., 25:1-6, 12-18; 36) make Abraham, as promised, the father of nations (17:5). Beginning in barrenness, the story ends with a multitude in Egypt (Gen 50:20; Ex 1:9).

Unfortunately, the Egyptian end leaves the land-promise unfulfilled. Repeated references to this non-fulfillment form a counterpoint to amazing human fertility (e.g., 15:12; 24:7; 26:4). Abraham and Isaac **remain**

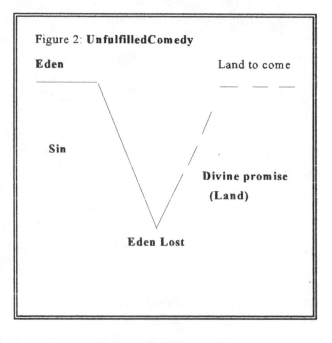

Figure 2: **UnfulfilledComedy**

Eden

Land to come

Sin

Divine promise (Land)

Eden Lost

aliens and sojourners (e.g., 23:4; 26:3). The purchase of land for Sarah's grave (23), the need to send "home" for Isaac's wife (24), and Jacob's purchase of a living-space perilously near Shechem (33:18-35:8) dramatically recall this unfulfilled promise.

The Jacob and Joseph stories foreshadow the future. Although often outside the land in Haran or in Egypt, they are always returning (cf. Gen 28:4; 31:13). Not surprisingly, then, Joseph returns Jacob's body to the land for burial (50:1-14). Strikingly, Genesis ends with Joseph's reminder that God will bring them "to the land that he swore" to the fathers (50:24) and with his body in a moveable "coffin in Egypt" (50:25-26).

Read as a whole, Gen 12-50 has an **unfulfilled quest** pattern. Read separately, however, the Jacob and Joseph stories have heroic shapes [cf. Campbell, Hero, 30, 245-46]. Separated from their families, both surmount difficulties (in Haran or Egypt) to be reunited with their families in better, although tenuous, circumstances.

Plot Conflict: Election and Covenant

Readers can easily read Gen 12-50 as a holy war in which God overcomes various opponents to the promise (Abram's age, barren and lost wives, quarrelsome natives, family squabbles, foreign rulers, famine, attempted fratricide, and coffins in Egypt) In fact, the promise's triumph forms the plot of many episodes in Gen 12-50.

One can also read the fathers' story as a **revelation of the divine promise**. The first major plot moment is God's promise (12:1-3). Connective episodes reveal this promise to one father after another [see figure 3]. The second major plot moment, then, is the *election* **of the promise's recipients**. Given the divine sovereignty ideology, firmly established by Gen 1-11, plot suspense does not turn on whether but on when, how, and to whom God will deliver the promises.

God's promise constructs a relationship with a particular people. Ultimately, the promise takes the form of a *covenant*. A covenant is a formal agreement usually made binding by an oath or ritual (e.g., sacrifice, Gen 15; Ex 24:3-8; circumcision, Gen 17; meal, Ex 24:9-11). The closest modern analogy is the legal contract. In the ANE, some covenants were between equals **(parity)** and some were between a

> **Figure 3: Continuing the Promise**
>
> | Gen | 12:1-3 | Revealed to Abram |
> |---|---|---|
> | | 15 | Covenant, Ab.'s sacrifice |
> | | 17 | Circumcision as symbol |
> | | | Abram > Abraham |
> | | 26:2-5 | Revealed to Isaac |
> | | 28:10-17 | Revealed to Jacob |
> | | 35:9-15 | Jacob > Israel |
> | | 50:24 | Joseph remembers promise |
> | Ex | 6:2-9 | God remembers |
> | | | Revealed to Moses |
> | | 19-40 | Covenant with Israel |

sovereign and his vassal (suzerainty). Obviously, the covenant between God and Abram is a **suzerainty** covenant.

In such, the suzerain imposes obligations on the vassal which he justifies by his past gracious actions for his vassal (cf. Ex 20-23). Genesis 12:1-3 does not fit this model. As it is their initial encounter, neither God nor Abram has a past upon which to mortgage the future. Here, then, the **suzerain-God obligates himself** (but Abram must go). Later, when God and his people have a past, humans will not be so free (e.g., Sinai). Phrased mythically, God acts graciously when humans are outside Eden. After God establishes an Eden, God demands responsible behavior from his vassals.

Divine Characters: The Promiser

As the God of Gen 1-11 spoke the cosmos into existence, the God of Gen 12-50 **speaks (promises) Israel into existence.** The Sovereign's choice of a particular people demarcates him as a **nationalistic deity.** Some story-elements, however, depict a "larger" deity, the "Judge of all the earth" (18:25) who is effective outside the promised land (e.g., 12:1, 17-20;) and is superior to kings, cities (e.g., 12:17-20; 14; 19; 20; 26:1-11), and nations (e.g., 21:13-21; 25:23).

The Promiser demands. Abram must go. Each father must live with mere promise. Dramatically, the life-giver can even demand Isaac's sacrifice (22). Nevertheless, the Holy One is not unreachable. Abraham and God debate Sodom's fate. In fact, Abraham convinces God to commute Sodom's punishment if God finds ten righteous men within the city (18:16-33). Jacob and God are less intimate, but Jacob also negotiates (28:18-22) and wrangles with God successfully (32:22-32).

The Promiser differs from the Orderer of Gen 1-11. Instead of defending order, this God **presses toward a dim future**. Although the promise is unfulfilled, the descendants and the repetitions of the promise demonstrate God's faithfulness.

Interestingly, the Promiser is **not uniformly present**. Some stories have little or no reference to God (e.g., 14:1-16; 34; 36; 38, omit v. 10) while others involve God as a character (18). In general, God's presence gradually decreases [Patrick, God, 22-25]. Thus, while God is a story-actor in the Abraham story, he never appears in the Joseph narrative.

In the Joseph narrative, fraternal envy and chance seem to motivate the

Figure 4: **Providence Conceptions**	
Sacred Direct	**Sacred Indirect**
Abraham Jacob	Joseph

story. Intrusive narrative comments (37:2, 21) and Joseph's speeches (45:4-13; 50:20), however, indicate **God's unseen control**. The growing dependence on characters and dreams (37; 40-41) to reveal the divine purpose clearly distances God (cf. 50:24 with 12:1-3).

By contrast, God is **directly present** in the Abram story.

Divine repetition of the promise and Abram's constant worshiping (e.g., 12:7-8; 13:4, 18; 14:17-24; 15; 17; 20:17; 21:33) make Abram's wanderings a spiritual quest. God speaks to and appears to Abraham (17:22). An anthropomorphic God eats with Abraham, promises him a son, and debates the fate of Sodom and Gomorrah with him (18). Further, the narrator constantly ascribes story-effects to God (the deliverance of Sarah from Pharaoh's harem, the destruction of Sodom and Gomorrah, the birth of Isaac, the procurement of Isaac's wife, and children for Isaac's barren wife).

God's presence, however, is ambiguous. When three men visit Abraham, one gradually becomes the LORD (Gen 18). In Gen 22:11-19, Abraham deals with "the angel of the LORD" who later speaks as the LORD (v. 16). Others have equally equivocal visitations. Hagar twice deals with "the angel of the LORD" (16:7-14; 21:17-21), but both Hagar and the narrator later identify this figure as God. Again, while the narrator describes Jacob's famous night-struggle with a man (32:24-32), Jacob twice describes his opponent as God (32:30; 33:10). The whole, of course, leaves the divine story-actor shrouded in mystery.

Jacob is not as intimate with God as Abraham. Others mediate the divine purpose to Jacob (25:23; 27:27-29; 28:1-4; 30:27-30). God does appear to Jacob, however, in dreams and night visions (28:10-15; 46:2-4) and speaks on two occasions (31:3; 35:1-15). These theophanies (28:10-15; 35:1-15) bookend the Jacob story and transform what often appears to be Jacob's secular family struggle for property into Israel's sacred narrative.

Faithful Abraham

The interval between promise and fulfillment demands faith. Abraham typifies this faith (cf. Rom 4; Jas 2). When God commands Abram to go, Abram does so without remark (Gen 12:1-4). Little is said about Abram's inner state (though see, e.g., 17:17; 18:12). His faith, then, is not an intellectual struggle against doubt but the external, objective matter of **alignment with God**. That is, faith equals practical commitment to the promise. Will he wait for the promise or will he seek other means to realize descendants (Eliezer, Hagar) and the land? His faith is no foregone conclusion. As he wavers (suggesting alternatives to the promise), God perseveres, reiterates the promise, and finally renames him "the father of a multitude" (17:5).

> Descendant-promised fulfilled, God tests Abraham:

> Take your son, your only son Isaac, whom you love,
> and go to the land of Moriah, and offer him there as
> a burnt offering on one of the mountains that I shall
> show you. (22:2)

Again, Abraham merely goes. Throughout the entire scene, the only "inside view" is the narrator's note that the whole is a divine test (22:1). Direct action and speech dominate the story. The few descriptions are essential to the story: Abraham is father; Isaac is his only, beloved son.

Abraham's hopes (revealed by speech, 22:5, 8) are realized by God's provision. Nevertheless, the end jars. Although Isaac lives, no one rejoices (contrast 21:6-8). Instead, the story merely recounts the naming of the place and repeats the promise (22:14-18). The result, of course, emphasizes the divine sovereignty and the demand for faith, not human turmoil.

Elect Jacob

No character earns the promise. God mysteriously selects. Jacob typifies this mystery as God dramatically **chooses the younger** over the elder brother (25:23; cf. 48). This choice contravenes the firstborn's rights (the law of **primogeniture**). Here, Jacob symbolizes Israel, the least of the nations, but still God's chosen (cf. Deut 8-9).

Figure 5: **Kierkegaard's Faithful Abraham**

For Kierkegaard, the sacrifice of Isaac is the premier example of faith as a passionate, absurd act. Kierkegaard modernizes Gen 22 by providing Abraham with "inside views":

> But Abraham said to himself, "I will not conceal from Isaac whither this course leads him." . . . And Abraham's face was fatherliness . . . . But Isaac was unable to understand him . . . . Then for an instant he turned away from him, and when Isaac again saw Abraham's face it was changed, his glance was wild, his form was horror. He seized Isaac by the throat, threw him to the ground, and said, "Stupid boy, dost thou then suppose that I am thy father? I am an idolater. Dost thou suppose that this is God's bidding? No, it is my desire." Then Isaac trembled and cried out in his terror, "O God in heaven, have compassion upon me, God of Abraham, have compassion upon me. If I have no father upon earth, be Thou my father!" But Abraham in a low voice said to himself, "O Lord in heaven, I thank Thee. After all it is better for him to believe that I am a monster, rather than that he should lose faith in Thee." [Fear and Trembling, 27]

For modern readers, the choice surprises because Jacob is **despicable**. He extorts his brother (25:29-34) and tricks his father

(27). For the text, of course, God's prior (25:23) and subsequent (28:10-22) choice, not the dirty dealing, make Jacob the chosen.

Where Abraham obeyed immediately, Jacob bargains shrewdly (e.g., 25:29-34; 28:10-22; 29:15-30; 30:25-43; 31:43-54). Jacob's initial promise-revelation scene, then, is somewhat ambiguous (28:10-22). A reader can understand the scene as a typical covenant ratification (with sacrifice and pledges) or read it as an extortion:

> If God will be with me . . . then the LORD shall be
> my God . . . and of all that you give me I will surely
> give one tenth to you. (28:20-22)

Jacob does, however, ultimately prove faithful. Upon divine command, Jacob leaves first Haran (31:3, 17-18, like Abram in 12:4) and then Shechem (35:1-4). The hostility of those environments does, however, make obedience quite prudent (31:1; 34). Jacob's faith is most apparent, then, when the bargainer foreswears a claim upon his father-in-law's property (implicit in the household gods) and cleaves to the God of the promise (35:1-15). This last promise scene at Bethel, then, clarifies the ambiguity in the first (28:10-22) which it repeats save for the omission of Jacob's bargaining words (28:20-22).

Joseph: The Unlikely Hero

The fathers are unlikely heroes. After all, why should God choose Abram or Jacob? The best example of this well-known **ancient type-character**, however, is Joseph [Scholes and Kellogg, 165-66]. Sold into slavery by jealous brothers, he soon oversees Potiphar's house. Unjustly imprisoned, he soon oversees the prison. Through the ability to interpret dreams and administer, he comes to oversee all of Egypt.

The narrator, of course, attributes Joseph's success to God

(39:2,23) as does Joseph's dramatic rejection of revenge:

> Even though you (the brothers) intended to do harm
> to me, God intended it for good, in order to preserve
> a numerous people . . . (50:20; cf. 45:4-15)

These reflections, of course, dramatize biblical ideology. Joseph does not rise by his own power but by God's.

Figure 6: **Horatio Alger, Jr. and the American Dream**

Horatio Alger, Jr. is synonymous with the **American Dream**, the belief that anyone can attain fame and fortune through hard work [cf. Tebbel, 4-6]. Alger told story after story of poor boys who make good through virtue and hard work [e.g., Ragged Dick]. Like many biblical stories, Alger's tales are melodramas parceling out material rewards. Alger's virtue is, however, Victorian middle-class mores, not **Yahwistic henotheism**. Like biblical heroes, however, Alger's boys rise from poverty only by coming to the attention of a benevolent patron. This patron, of course, is not quite the biblical **deus ex machina**.

Joseph's reflections also testify to his development. In short, Joseph moves from arrogant, naive boasting (35:5-11) to mature responsibility. Like Jacob and Abraham, then, Joseph proves faithful. Not surprisingly, then, his last words recall the divine promise (50:24-25).

This character development is possible because God is distanced from the story [see figure 4]. As a result, character's speech (Joseph's) and even "inside views" (e.g., 37:3, 4, 11) now explain the story's movement.

Even Joseph's brothers change. In the beginning, they are ready to kill or enslave a brother and lie to their father (37). At the story's end, they will not leave a brother in trouble nor take their father's favorite from him. Instead, one of them offers himself in the brother's place (44:18-34). Like Joseph, they have matured.

Figure 7: The Founding Mothers

While women--Sarah, Hagar, Rebekah, Rachel, Leah, Dinah, Tamar--figure prominently in Gen 12-50, the text is **patriarchal and *androcentric*.** Women are shamefully barren or are son-producers (29:31-30:24). Women are vulnerable creatures by means of which males take honor from other males (e.g., 34). Again, women are dangerous creatures and may lead men astray (24; 26:34-35; 28:1-9; 38). In short, women are portrayed from a male point of view.

Even the strong, memorable women escape this dominant perspective only by playing the "father's" game, successfully maneuvering within family politics. Thus, Sarah successfully eliminates Ishmael, her son's rival (21:8-19). Rebekah successfully elevates her favorite son Jacob over the father's favorite Esau (27). Rachel successfully enters the son-bearing contest with Leah (30:1-24). And, Tamar, the wiliest of them all, plays the prostitute in order to bear children in Judah's family (38). Tamar's story dramatizes concisely the patriarchal story-world's perimeters for woman: **whore or son-bearer.**

Myth: The Faithful Elect

These heroes are Adam's mythic opposite. Each father proves faithful. Abraham sacrifices Isaac. Jacob buries the gods. Joseph finds success by relying upon God, rather than himself.

Further, the fathers also oppose Cain's violence. Abram rescues Lot. Esau and Jacob reconcile. Both Joseph and his brothers finally reject violence against the brother.

These founding fathers receive the promise which creates Israel. They model faith, which this section presents as **endurance** (or hope) before the promise is fulfilled. Further, the fathers are the first to circumcise (17), to tithe (28:20-22), and to found important sanctuaries (e.g., 35:1-15). In these cases, the myth founds ritual acts or places.

Genesis 12-50 begins to establish what being Israel means. Here, the mythic identity is **the elect people of the promise**. The promise is the sacred's chief vehicle. As the heroes are carefully genealogically related, race/family is another powerful mythic identifier. The result, of course, is a **natural religion** story. Not surprisingly, then, foreign women pose danger (e.g., 24; 26:34-35; 28:1-9). Further, other genealogies demarcate the world in which Israel lives (e.g., those of the Arabic tribes, Moab, Ammon, and Edom).

ANET: An Elect People

Natural religion disturbs the modern "liberal" reader in a pluralist world. To moderns, racism lurks behind such conceptions. Despite its family orientation, however, Gen 12-50 is not racist. Non-Israelites (e.g., Melchizedek and Hagar) worship and recognize God. Further, God is at times the "Judge of all the earth" (18:25). More importantly, **racism** is an anachronistic interpretation of this ancient text. Genesis 12-50 does not deliberately oppose modern pluralism. It lives among and competes with other natural religions (those of Ishmael and the Arabs and of Esau and the Edomites).

Nonetheless, **election haunts**. The move from the God of the cosmos (Gen 1-11) to the God of Abram and Jacob shocks. Why should the God of the whole earth prefer Abram and, then, Jacob?

Why not Nahor, Lot, Ishmael, Esau, or Laban?

Both the text and later interpreters ethicize the story. Thus, Laban and Esau disqualify themselves by worshiping foreign gods (31:19-35; 35:1-4) and marrying foreign women (28:1-9). In a similar attempt at justification, the later rabbis said that Torah was offered to all nations, but that only Israel accepted it.

Figure 8: **Self-Reliance**

Emerson's famous essay, "Self-Reliance," is a classic example of alienated, modern individualism:

> And truly it demands something godlike in him
> who has cast off the common motives of
> humanity, and has ventured to trust himself for
> a taskmaster. High be his heart, faithful his
> will, clear his sight, that he may in good
> earnest be doctrine, society, law to himself,
> that a simple purpose may be to him as strong
> as iron necessity is to others. [284]
>
> Society everywhere is in conspiracy against the
> manhood of every one of its members. . . . The
> virtue in most request is conformity.
> Self-reliance is its aversion. It loves not
> realities and creators, but names and customs.
> [276]

The contrast with biblical anthropology could not be clearer.

Despite these ethicizations, the problem ultimately turns on the divine sovereignty. God chooses whom he will (Mal 1:2-3). The "Wholly Other" remains beyond human categories.

Not incidentally, the same Holy One demands the horrific sacrifice of Isaac (22). Once again, interpreters scurry to tame the text. Thus, many scholars observe that ancient religions frequently involved child sacrifice (apparently as a fertility rite inducing further progeny; cf. Ex 13:1-16). Genesis 22, then, becomes Israel's dramatic rejection of that horrific custom. More textually, one can observe that God did provide a ram and that the narrator designates the event a "test" (22:1). Nevertheless, here, as with election the "primitive" Holy One at the heart of biblical ideology is difficult to avoid.

Review Questions

1. Apply the reading method of chaps. 3-4 to Gen 12-50. List its genre, plot shape, conflict, depiction of God, mythic function, and ANE problems.

2. Compare Gen 12-50 to ancient epic.

3. What holds Gen 12-50 together as a literary whole?

4. What is the literary and mythic function of the genealogies?

5. What is a covenant?

6. How does the God of Gen 12-50 differ from the God of Gen 1-11?

7. Why are Abraham and Jacob ambiguous? Successful?

8. Why is racism anachronistic as applied to Gen 12-50?

Suggestions for Alternate Readings and Reflection

1. What kind of literary patterns dominate Gen 12-50? Do phrases (e.g., "these are the descendants") or stories recur? What kind of stories occur most often?

2. Are the promise-sections mere repetitions or do they have important variations? Who speaks? To whom? Is there a response?

3. Doublets are similar occurrences (e.g., the delivered wife in 12:10-20; 20; 26:1-11; or the founding of Bethel in 28:10-22; 35:9-15). How might a historian or narrative critic explain doublets?

4. The promise foreshadows the future. How do 15:13-15; 48-49 manipulate narrative time? What is their effect?

5. Genesis 22 is a classic example of biblical story's combination of laconic scene and obtrusive narration. Explain other passages--e.g., 37-38; 43-45--using the showing-telling model [see chap. 4].

6. What is the point of Gen 22?

7. The cultural codes animating Gen 24 and 38 are not those of modern romantic love/comedy. Explain the cultural assumptions behind these passages. Is Gen 29 a romantic love story?

8. Why is God's presence ambiguous in the theophanies of Gen 12-50? Why does God's presence gradually decrease?

9. Feminists find Gen 12-50 offensive. Why? Can any passages support a feminist ideology (e.g., Gen 38)?

For Further Reading

For commentaries on Genesis, see chap. 5.

On ancient epic, see Tillyard, 1-20; Van Seters, Search, 18-31, 224-37; and Damrosch, 37-87. On heroic quests, see Campbell, Hero, 30, 245-46; and Brockway.

On the significance of genealogies, see Wilson, Genealogy.

On election and covenant, see the relevant entries in the various biblical theologies and dictionaries. Eichrodt's theology is organized around the notion of covenant. For ANE covenant materials, see Mendenhall, "Covenant"; **idem**, Law; McCarthy; and Roberts, in Knight and Tucker, 93-94.

On theophany and the divine depiction, see the relevant entries in biblical theologies and dictionaries. Terrien's Elusive is organized around the notion of God's presence. See also Fretheim, Suffering, 79-106. Patrick, God, treats in some detail God's literary depiction.

On faith as commitment, see W. Smith, <u>Meaning</u>, 170-92. On the "objectivity" of faith, goodness, etc., see Monk, 179-83; Pedersen, I-II: 196-212, 358-62, 411-52; and Rad, <u>Wisdom</u>, 77-82, 96-96, 128.

Auerbach, 3-23, has a classic comparison of the characterization techniques involved in Genesis and the <u>Odyssey</u>. Cf. also Alter, <u>Narrative</u>, 114-30, on ambiguous human portrayals.

On the unlikely hero in ancient narrative, see Scholes and Kellogg, 165-66. For exhaustive biblical examples, see Nickelsburg, "Genre," 153-84.

CHAPTER 7

THE EXODUS
Exodus 1-18

Introduction: Relationship to Torah

Exodus is the heart of Israel's national epic. Here, **Yahweh becomes Israel's God**, revealing himself to prophet (3-4) and to people (19-20). These revelations bookend Israel's deliverance from Egyptian slavery (5-15). Exodus, then, **repeats on a national level the promise-covenants and deliverances** of Genesis (miraculous births, saved wives, and delivered sons).

Content Summary: Revelation and Liberation

Exodus sets the stage quickly (1-2). In order to control the threat of a growing Israel, Pharaoh first enslaves Israel and, then, condemns male Israelite babies to death. Ironically, Pharaoh's daughter saves one baby (Moses) from the edict. When Moses matures, he kills an Egyptian for mistreating a Hebrew and, then, flees to the wilderness (Midian).

While Moses is living in Midian as a shepherd, God reveals himself to Moses at the mountain of God in a burning bush (3-4). He **reveals his name** and his intention to deliver Israel and commissions Moses to bring the people to the mountain.

Back in Egypt, Moses and Aaron announce God's program to worshiping Israelites and a recalcitrant Pharaoh who demands "bricks without straw" (4:29-5:19). After a reprise of Moses' commission (5:22-7:7), the battle begins. Ten terrible **divine plagues deliver** Israel (7:8-11:10). Rituals (passover and the firstborn's consecration) surround the final, climactic plague, the death of the Egyptian firstborn (12-13). After Israel leaves, Pharaoh pursues them to the sea where God **parts the waters** for Israel and drowns the pursuing Egyptians (14:21-31). Not surprisingly, Israel celebrates (15:1-21).

Israel, then, proceeds to the mountain (15:22-19:2). On the way, God graciously provides direction, water, manna from heaven, and military defense for an incessantly complaining people.

Style: Salvation and Hierophany

Passing over untold years, Exodus' **episodic** style emphasizes enslavement, revelation, and deliverance. Despite memorable "special effects" (bush, plague, and sea), divine speech dominates. Thus, the opening divine speech forecasts the entire story (3:1-4:23). After the opening

Figure 1: **Narrative Forecasts**	
Divine Speech	**Later Narrative**
to the land (3:8, 17)	Joshua
the exodus (3:10,17)	Ex 12:29-14:31
to the mountain (3:12)	Ex 19-Num 10
assembly (3:16)	Ex 4:29-31
wonders/plagues (3:20)	Ex 7:8-11:10
plunder (3:21-22)	Ex 12:33-36
signs (4:1-9)	Ex 7:8-24
hardened heart (4:21)	Ex 5-14
death of the firstborn (4:23)	Ex 12:29-32

divine speech (which 6:2-7:7 repeats), subsequent narrative is an anti-climactic **fait accompli**.

The story-creating speech resembles the style of Gen 1: "Then God said, let there be . . . and it was so." In the plague cycle, in particular, the basic structure is a staccato-pattern of speech and report: "The LORD said . . . and (it was) as the LORD had said" or "Moses and Aaron did as the LORD commanded" (see 7:8-11:10). These dominating divine speeches give the story a *hierophanic* flavor. Not surprisingly, **the story moves from revelation (3-4) to revelation (19-20).**

Figure 2: **The Plagues**

While divine or Mosaic speech (10:3-6; 11:4-8) forecasts the plague narrative in exact detail, interesting developments do occur. First, the Egyptian magicians eventually fail to copy the divine wonders (8:19-20) and ultimately fall before the plagues themselves (9:11). The Egyptians gradually recognize divine activity and favor the Israelites' release (8:19-20; 9:20; 10:7; 12:33, 36). Second, God begins to protect Israel from the plagues (e.g. 8:20-23; 11-12). Third, the conversations between Pharaoh and Moses about "temporary" release ebb and flow as Moses asks for more and more freedom.

Plague	Forecast	Narrative
water to blood	7:14-19	7:20-24
frogs	8:1-5	8:6-7
gnats	8:16	8:17-19
flies	8:20-23	8:24
plague	9:1-5	9:6-7
boils	9:8-9	9:10-12
hail	9:13-22	9:23-26
locusts	10:3-6, 12	10:13-15
darkness	10:21	10:22-23
death of firstborn	11:1-2, 4-8	12:29-30

Story Pattern: Deus ex Machina and Answered Lament

Exodus begins in chaos. Pharaoh's murderous world is demonic, seemingly devoid of the divine presence (save for 1:17, 20-21).   The horror is so great that later tradition remembers Egypt as the symbol of chaos/death (cf. Hos 11:5).

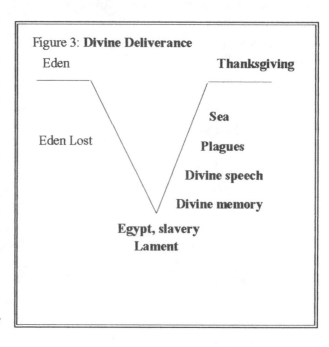

Figure 3: **Divine Deliverance**

Eden

Thanksgiving

Eden Lost

Sea

Plagues

Divine speech

Divine memory

Egypt, slavery
Lament

Moses augurs hope. His mother's ingenuity and a bit of luck delivers him from Pharaoh's edict, but he fails to deliver others (2:11-15). He escapes with his own life alone. As the hero-tale aborts, however, **the divine memory promises deliverance**:

> The Israelites groaned under their slavery, and cried out. Out of the slavery their cry for help rose up to God. God heard their groaning, and God remembered his covenant with Abraham, Isaac, and Jacob. (2:23-24)

The subsequent divine speech-acts are the **deus ex machina** deliverance.   Seen differently, the Exodus story moves from complaint through deliverance to praise (Ex 15:1-21). Interestingly, this pattern is that of the psalmic *lament* (e.g., Ps 3; 13; 22; 44).

Not incidentally, story-**rituals** mimic the story's dangerous transition through chaos to order. Bloody rituals--a horrific, alternative circumcision story (4:24-26; cf. Gen 17); passover and unleavened bread (12:1-28); and the firstborn's consecration (13:1-16)--save life. Further, the continuing re-enactment of the latter two rituals passes on the exodus-story to future generations.

Figure 4: **The Seder**

Jews annually celebrate the Seder in their homes as a memorial of the exodus. A symbolic meal and the questions of the youngest person present relive the exodus:

Why is this night different from all other nights? For on all other nights we eat leaven and unleavened alike, but on this night only unleavened. On all other nights we eat any kind of herbs, but on this night only bitter herbs. On all other nights we do not dip even once, but on this night twice. On all other nights we eat either upright or leaning, but on this night we lean! [Gaster, Passover, 58]

Symbol	**Referent**
matzoh (unleavened bread)	haste of departure
bitter herbs/horseradish	bitterness of slavery
shankbone of lamb	original passover

Plot Conflict: Holy War vs. Pharaoh

Pharaoh's murderous program unwittingly opposes the divine program (cf. 2:23-24) and creates a holy war plot. The opening divine speech defines the conflict and ordains its outcome (3:19-22) [see figure 1]. As a result, the competition is over before it begins.

God is not contending with Pharaoh. He props him up:

> I will harden his heart, so that he will not let the people go. Then you shall say to Pharaoh, "Thus says the LORD: Israel is my firstborn son. I said to you, 'Let my son go that he may worship me.' But you refused to let him go; now I will kill your firstborn son." (4:21-23)

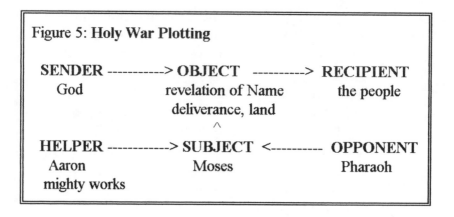

Figure 5: Holy War Plotting

SENDER ----------> OBJECT ----------> RECIPIENT
God   revelation of Name   the people
                deliverance, land

HELPER ----------> SUBJECT <---------- OPPONENT
Aaron   Moses   Pharaoh
mighty works

Pharaoh resists questioning the divine identity ("Who is the LORD, that I should heed him and let Israel go?" 5:2) and increases Israel's burden (bricks "without straw," 5:3-19).

Unimpressed, God asserts that he will reveal himself:

> Say therefore to the Israelites, "I am the LORD, and I will free you . . . . I will be your God. You shall know that I am the LORD your God who has freed you from the Egyptians. I will bring you into the land . . . . I am the LORD."(6:6-8)

> I will harden Pharaoh's heart, and I will multiply my signs and wonders in the land of Egypt . . . . and bring

my people the Israelites, company by company, out of
the land of Egypt by great acts of judgment. The
Egyptians shall know that I am the LORD . . . (7:3-5)

In short, **the holy war becomes a revelation** (which continues at the
mountain, Ex 19-20). Not surprisingly, then, the battle proper--the
plague cycle--follows the speech-engendering style [see figure 2].
Finally, the battle concludes with acclamations recognizing God's
acts (14:25, 31; 15:1-21).

Figure 6: **Exodus, Liberation Theology**

For the oppressed of all ages, the exodus is one of the
most popular biblical stories:

> Reading the Bible with the eyes of the poor is a
> different thing from reading it with a full belly.
> If it is read in the light of the experiences and
> hope of the oppressed, the Bible's
> revolutionary themes--promise, exodus,
> resurrection and spirit--come alive [Moltmann,
> cited in Robert Brown, Unexpected, 19].

The exodus symbolizes the hope that these victims of the
institutional violence of established orders (reigning political,
social, economic structures) will be "free at last." Not
surprisingly, then, they sing,

> Go down, Moses
>   Way down in Egypt land,
> Tell ol' Pharaoh,
>   Let my people go. [D. Brown, Enduring, 128-30]

Characters: God; The Revelation of the Name

The story, then, reveals the name to Moses at the mountain (3-4), to the Egyptians in wonders, and to the people in wonders and at the mountain (19-20). Through this revelation, **Yahweh becomes Israel's God**:

> I am the LORD. I appeared to Abraham, Isaac, and Jacob as God Almighty, but by name 'The LORD' I did not make myself known to them. . . . I will take you as my people, and I will be your God. You shall know that I am the LORD your God, who has freed you from the burdens of the Egyptians. (6:3, 7)

Correspondingly, Israel becomes Yahweh's firstborn (4:22-23; 13:1-16).

This story-God is **a nationalistic liberator**. For his people, he reduces Egyptian order to chaos by plagues and flood (sea). For his people, he slaughters the Egyptian firstborn. For his people, he leaves the Egyptians drowned. Put simply, God separates Israel from the Egyptians (e.g., 8:22-23; 9:4, 19, 26; 10:23; 11:7).

Inclusive elements are, however, present. God does on occasion make provision for non-Israelites (e.g., 9:19-21; 12:48-49). Further, God is the life-demanding Holy, not only for Egypt, but also for Israel (e.g., 13:1-16; 4:24-26). Finally, the story reveals God to be LORD "in this land (Egypt)" (8:22) and throughout the earth (9:16). By his mighty works, God reigns supreme:

> Who is like you, O LORD, among the gods?
> Who is like you, majestic in holiness,
>   awesome in splendor, doing wonders? (15:11; cf. 9:14)

The bloody conflict, however, casts God in nationalistic hues. The combination of sovereignty and nationalism is most obvious, brutal, and **dehumanizing in the hardening of Pharaoh's heart**.

While the story describes this hardening from several perspectives, the story deliberately sets Pharaoh's actions within

Figure 7: **Who Hardens Pharaoh's Heart?**	
God	4:21; 7:3; 9:12; 10:1, 20, 27; 11:10; 14:4, 8
Pharaoh	8:15, 32; 9:34
No agent	7:13, 14, 22; 8:19; 9:7, 35

the divine sovereignty in order to *demythologize* him (4:21; 14:4, 8). That is, the story debunks the Egyptian notion that Pharaoh is divine. For biblical ideology, no god can stand against Yahweh. Like other characters, the demythologized Pharaoh is a mere "human before God." For there to be holy war, then, **Yahweh** must "allow" opposition or even cause it with hardened hearts.

While the nationalistic Liberator is constantly present in mighty works and in speech, most characters know God only **indirectly**. Moses hears God speak. Others know God through Moses' **prophetic** interpretation of the plagues and the sea. The result is a **prophetic conception of providence** in which God is directly present for the prophet and present in the prophet's words for the people.

Characters: Moses, the Reluctant Prophet

Moses, then, is the *prophet* who mediates between God and people:

> When all the people witnessed the thunder and lightning . . . they were afraid . . . and said to Moses, "You speak to us, and we will listen; but do not let God speak to us, or we will die. . . ." Then the people stood at a distance, while Moses drew near to the thick darkness where God was. (Ex 20:18-21)

As mediator, Moses **symbolizes both the sacred and faith**, the proper response to the sovereign.

Moses' career, however, begins with failure and flight. His ill-advised attempt to liberate his people fails. Once empowered by God, however, Moses' career takes a different turn. God must convince the reluctant Moses, however (3:11-4:17; 5:22-7:7). God forces Moses to forego his self-concern. It is **who God is, not who Moses is,** that matters.

Figure 8: **The Reluctant Prophet**

Moses' Objections	**God's Response**
Who am I? (3:11)	I will be with you (3:12)
Your name? (3:13)	I AM WHO I AM (3:14-22)
What about unbelief? (4:1)	Perform these signs (4:2-9)
I cannot speak (4:10)	I will teach you (4:11-12)
Someone else? (4:13)	Aaron (4:14-17)
Why did you send me? (5:22-23)	Repetition of promises (6:2-9)
Why should Pharaoh listen to me? (6:12, 30)	I have made you like God (7:1-7)

Moses learns obedience (e.g., 7:20) and becomes "like God to Pharaoh" (7:1). The plagues begin and end at his word. Upon his command, the sea parts. He mediates the divine wilderness-provisions and the divine word at the mountain. In short, he is the life-giver and the life-demander (cf. 11:4-8).

Moses actualizes this sacred power, however, only as he has faith. The end of his career, like its beginning, vividly demonstrates this point. When he fails to trust, he fails (cf. the enigmatic Num 20:2-13) and dies in the wilderness (Deut 34).

This story makes Moses the **mythic exemplar** of all later prophets (Deut 18:15; cf. Num 12:6-8; Deut 34:10-12). Later prophets are like Moses:

> 1) they have an intimate *charismatic* relationship with God (spirit-possession, visions);
> 2) they **mediate** between God and people
>   a) interceding for the people,
>   b) delivering divine messages, and
>   c) providing access to the sacred; and
> 3) they **symbolize faith**.

Human Characters: Faith and Rebellion

The Exodus-characters are "humans before God." As such, they display either faith or rebellion. If Moses symbolizes faith, Pharaoh symbolizes rebellion. He is little more than the plot function "opposition." Given this type-casting, Pharaoh's conversations with Moses follow a pattern which Israel later recapitulates.

Figure 9: **A Pattern of Opposition**

Pharaoh's Plague Cycle	**Judg 3:7-12**
refusal to recognize God	apostasy
divine plague	foreign oppression
request for deliverance	request for deliverance
Mosaic/divine deliverance	judge delivers
hardening of Pharaoh's heart	new apostasy

Israel, too, can oppose God. The **people vacillate** between faithfulness and rebellion. They initially believe the divine word

(4:31). Opposition makes their faith wane (5:21; 6:9; 14:10-12). Beyond the plague-sea deliverance, the people become more and more recalcitrant. Thus, the people reverse Moses' pattern. Where he moves from doubt to faith, they **move from worship to apostasy**. Not surprisingly, then, they die in the wilderness (Num 14:20-35). Ultimately, the Israelites face the same God that the Egyptians did (cf. Ex 15:26). Election does not efface responsibility.

Myth: The Name and the People

The revelation of the name to Moses and the people creates them as **Yahweh's Israel**. In addition to that basic mythic identity, they are also the people whom God brought out of Egypt (e.g., 12:17; 13:3, 8, 14-16; 19:3-6; 20:2).

Exodus also provides *etiologies* for important Jewish rituals: passover, unleavened bread, and the firstborn's consecration (12-13). Reenacting the sacred time, these rituals "remember" the mythic founding events (12:14; 13:3) and thereby inculcate the young with the community's myth (12:14, 17, 24, 26-27; 13:8, 14). They condense into one act/symbol the myth (12:13; 13:9, 16). Thus, in passover, the people eat a lamb whose blood once protected the Israelites from the death angel. They eat dressed for travel as the story-Israelites once did. By dramatizing the myth, the ritual unites the story-world and the world of the worshiper [see figure 4]. The worshipers become those whom God brought out of Egypt.

ANET: Control Mechanisms

Pharaoh's hardened heart and the miracles are symptoms of the divine sovereignty ideology. Of course, that ideology controls life differently than does modernity's rationalism and individualism.

Natural religion's cultural codes, the divine sovereignty ideology, and the holy war plot explain Pharaoh's hardening. The story demythologizes Pharaoh. The demythologizing does not, however, justify **dehumanizing Pharaoh**.

Figure 10: **Human Freedom** [cf. chap. 6, figure 8]

For Sartre, humans are "condemned to freedom" [see Velasquez, 87-90]. Neither God nor society can determine them. They must create themselves by acting. For Sartre, then, "existence precedes essence." The notion that anyone or anything else can determine humans is an illusion or the deliberate attempt to avoid responsibility. In either case, it is "bad faith." For Sartre, then, humans are not creatures, but creators. The biblical idea that humans exist within divine limits is "bad faith."

For natural religions, the outsider is not truly human. Exodus climaxes with **drowned Egyptians and celebrating Israelites**. While one might defend this perspective in the ancient world, it is indefensible amidst modern pluralism. Today, that attitude inevitably leads to "**redemptive violence**" [cf. Mack, Myth, 368-76; Jewett, Captain]. In favor of Exodus, however, one must note that later story depicts Israel, too, as catastrophically opposed to God.

Pharaoh's demythologizing reflects basic biblical ideology. For the Bible, human responsibility depends upon prior divine actions. **Human freedom exists only within limits**. Pharaoh's hardening is merely a particularly blatant example of that pre-modern anthropology. Modern individualists do not accept such anthropologies. They wish to control their own lives [see figure 10]. For them, Pharaoh is not free, but a divine victim.

Likewise, *miracle* suggests to modern readers a world beyond control. Modern science typically conceives the world as an explicable, closed continuum of natural cause and effect. For that perspective, miracle is a **"violation of natural law"** or an extremely unlikely "statistical improbability."

Not surprisingly, then, some explain biblical miracles like the plagues "naturally." For some, then, the bloody Nile results from bacteria rendering the water red and undrinkable. Fleeing the water, frogs die in droves and, as a result, the insect population increases. Not surprisingly, diseases follow. Plagues seven through nine--thunderstorms, locusts, and darkness (sandstorm)--are clearly natural events. For this viewpoint, the tenth plague is difficult to explain, so it becomes a literary attempt at poetic justice or a mythic etiology for the firstborn's consecration. The sea-crossing is either wind-effect (15:21) or the crossing of a marshy area in which the Egyptian chariots mired (15:25) [cf. Mihelic and Wright, 3:822-824].

Such an explanatory reading obviously has modern appeal. Unfortunately, it has questionable assumptions and effects.

First, it presumes that readers can easily recover history from the story. It mistakenly assumes a one-to-one correspondence between the story-world's characters and events and reality. This interpretation misconstrues the story's genre. Exodus is not history, but myth. Exodus does not merely state what once happened. Rather, it tells the founding story and transmits that mythic identity to subsequent generations through its myth and ritual.

Second, the naturalist reading omits the most important story-character, God. While the wondrous phenomena remain, their biblical causation does not. The result ignores the story's point about the divine sovereignty.

For the Bible, miracles are not "violations of natural law," but *hierophanies*. Miracles reveal in a particularly clear moment the ever-present divine control of the sacred cosmos. They function as **condensed symbols of the divine sovereignty**. The wondrous phenomena, like the burning-bush, are only attention-getting **"special effects."**

Figure 11: **The Ten Commandments**

Cecil B. DeMille's famous movie, televised annually near Passover, dramatically and romantically interprets the exodus. DeMille was famous for spectacles. Not surprisingly, then, he can dramatize the call of Moses and the crossing of the sea to great effect. DeMille's movie differs from the biblical story, however, because of his romantic additions. His additions transform the Exodus story of a divine hero into that of a human hero (Charlton Heston) and give that hero a compelling "love-interest." These emphases noticeably change the story's pace. In contrast to Exodus, then, DeMille's movie plods on for quite some time before the call of Moses in order to establish the hero's background and romantic interest.

Review Questions

1. Apply the reading method of chaps. 3-4 to Ex 1-18. List its genre, plot shape, conflict, depiction of God, mythic function, and ANE problems.
2. Compare the styles of Gen 1 and Ex 1-18.
3. Compare Ex 1-18 to a lament.
4. What is the significance of Ex 5:2 for the plot conflict? What is the significance of 4:21-23 and 14:25, 30-31?
5. How does the story demythologize Pharaoh? Dehumanize him?
6. What is a prophet?
7. What does miracle mean in the biblical story-world? In the modern world?

Suggestions for Alternative Readings and Reflection

1. Read Exodus as a revelation plot.

2. According to form critics, biblical healing stories have three parts: description of the problem, the cure, and an acclamation of God. Compare the Exodus story to this form.

3. Apply the showing-telling model to Ex 3-4.

4. For the ancients, names revealed character (cf. the name changes in Genesis). What does **Yahweh** reveal about the character of Israel's God?

5. Are Pharaoh and Moses honest with one another?

6. Explain the hardening of Pharaoh's heart.

7. Is miracle possible today?

8. For ideological critics, the Exodus story is quite important. Explain how Gen 1-11 and Ex 1-18 might appeal to different socio-economic, political, and religious positions.

9. Compare Cecil B. DeMille's Ten Commandments to Ex 1-18.

For Further Reading

For Exodus commentaries, see Childs, Exodus; Clements, Exodus; and Croatto.

For laments, see chap. 14.

For a summary of various biblical accounts of the plagues (including Ps 78; 105), see Anderson, Understanding, 69-71.

On the Name, see chap. 3.

On Pharaoh's hardened heart, see the commentaries.

On Moses as a "type-prophet," see Blenkinsopp, History, 157-60, 189-90. On Moses more generally, see Rad, Moses.

On miracle, see Richardson, Miracle; Kee, Miracle; and the bibliography in chap. 5 on religion and science.

For critiques of the notion of "redemptive violence" endemic to natural religion and ethical dualism, see Mack, <u>Myth</u>, 368-76; Girard, <u>Violence</u>; **idem**, <u>Scapegoat</u>; and Jewett, <u>Captain</u>. These analyses critique respectively the gospels, myth, and American foreign policy.

CHAPTER 8

SINAI, THE WILDERNESS, AND DEUTERONOMY
Exodus 19 through Deuteronomy 34

Introduction: Relationship to Torah

The Sinai revelation is **Torah's climax**. That revelation completes election and exodus and makes Israel a natural religion people (Ex 19:5-6). Although new apostasies demonstrate this order's ephemerality, covenant renewals offer new Edens (Ex 33-34; Deut).

Content Summary: Covenant and Apostasy

This lengthy section has four scenes: 1) the founding of the *covenant* (Ex 19-24); 2) the founding of the *cult* (Ex 25-40; Lev); 3) the departure from Sinai and wilderness (Num); and 4) the renewed covenant (Num 21-36; Deut).

At the mountain, **God creates Israel as his covenant partner**. In a meteorological theophany, he delivers the **Ten Words** (Ex 19-20). When the people are frightened, God consents to speak to Moses alone in "thick darkness." The subsequent "covenant code" (20:22-23:33) makes various demands and reaffirms the promise (23:20-33). The people's formal acceptance of the covenant concludes this scene (24).

God, then, instructs Moses to found **the cult**, its utensils, and officials (25-31). Meanwhile, Aaron and the people perversely construct and **worship golden calves**. Only Moses' intercession saves the people from destruction (32). After judgments, God renews the covenant in a dramatic appearance to Moses (33-34).

The people, then, properly establish the cult (35-40) [for detail, see myth and ritual]. The divine glory settles on the tabernacle (40), priests and Levites are ordained (Lev 8-10), and the people sacrifice (Num 7:1-9:14).

After necessary preparations (e.g., censuses), the people **depart Sinai** for the land (Num 10). En route, the **people complain** despite God's provision of food and leadership. After Israel arrives at the land's southern border, spies reconnoiter the land. The spies' report leads the people to doubt their ability to take the land and to threaten to stone their faithful leaders (Num 13). Once again, Moses' intercession averts the people's destruction (cf. Ex 32-34), but God judges terribly. He condemns the faithless generation to **wandering** and death **in the wilderness** (Num 14:27-33). The people, then, make an unsuccessful attempt on the land (14:39-45).

Despite apostasies (e.g., 21:4-9; 25) and the death of Miriam and Aaron, God brings the people through several military victories to **the land's border** (21-24; 25; 31). There, Moses prepares the people for entry into the land by taking a census (26) and dealing with property issues (27; 32-36).

There, Moses also delivers his **farewell address,** three separate sermons demanding *henotheism* (Deut 1-4; 5-28; 29-30). The first expounds the theme through a historical review of the journey from the mountain. The last forecasts future apostasy, destruction, and repentance. The middle sermon is a lengthy collection of legal materials which stresses centralized worship (e.g., 12). A covenant ratification ceremony (26:16-19; 27-28) with curses for apostasy (27) and blessings for obedience (28) concludes the sermon.

Moses (and God), then, appoints Joshua as his successor (31; cf. Num 27:12-23), praises God, blesses the people (Deut 32-33), and dies (34).

Genre: Covenant and Demand

While story continues, divine speeches at Sinai and a series of Mosaic sermons dominate this section. The speeches are not sustained, logical argument. Instead, they are **sayings-catalogues** (often having unifying themes: e.g., cleanness, Lev 11-15; holiness, Lev 19-26). Their real connection resides in their divine or Mosaic source. These significant speakers make these sayings foundational. They are **the mythic speech which founds Israel as Yahweh's vassal.**

Figure 1: **Hittite Suzerainty Treaty** [cf. Mendenhall, <u>Law</u>]

Hittite Suzerainty Treaty	**Biblical Parallels**
Identification of the suzerain	"I am the LORD your God" (Ex 20:2)
Suzerain's benefits	"Who brought you out of Egypt" (Ex 20:2)
Stipulations (no other suzerains)	(Ex 20:3-23:19) Henotheism
Public presentation/reading	(Ex 24; Renewals in Deut 26-28; Josh 24)
Gods who witness	No clear parallel
Blessings and curses	(Deut 26:11-28:68)

The sayings, then, are **gifts of mythic identity**:

> Now therefore, if you obey my voice and keep my covenant, you shall be my treasured possession out of all the peoples. Indeed, the whole earth is mine, but you shall be for me a priestly kingdom and a holy nation. (Ex 19:5-6)

Today you have obtained the LORD's agreement: to
be your God; and for you to walk in his ways . . . and
to obey him. Today the LORD has obtained your
agreement: to be his treasured people, as he promised
you . . . (Deut 26:17-18)

Figure 2: **Law as Gift or Restriction?**

Modern individualists resent external authorities [cf.
chap. 7, figure 10]. Nietzsche's call for different ethics for
the strong and the weak (the herd), Freud's understanding of
civilization and religion as neurosis, and Emerson's call to
self-reliance are sophisticated examples of such hostility to
authority. The attitude is also evident in voter apathy,
hostility to the Internal Revenue Service, and in the "they
can't tell me" response to seatbelt regulations. The constantly
repeated movie plot in which a lone hero saves a troubled
society from evil or inept authorities (government, law
officials, bureaucracy, corporate business) raises the attitude
to the mythic level. In that cultural context, virtually bereft of
language justifying social responsibility [see Bellah, Habits],
law can be nothing more than external restriction of human
freedom.

Scholars often call these sayings "**law**," a possible translation
of the Hebrew "Torah." Where law connotes restrictions for
moderns, however, Israel understood God's demands as gifts of
identity and life. By concretizing the covenant and transmitting the
sacred (by the cult), the sayings create a sacred order in which
humans can live well (cf. e.g., Deut 27-28). Not surprisingly, Israel
celebrates these demands:

Your decrees are my delight,
they are my counselors. (Ps 119:24)

I will never forget your precepts,
for by them you have given me life. (119:93)
Your word is a lamp to my feet
and a light to my path. (119:105)
With open mouth I pant,
because I long for your commandments. (119:131)

Style: Apodictic and Conditional

The covenant demands come in both apodictic and conditional forms [cf. Alt, 101-71]. **Apodictic** sayings are absolute demands with an authoritative tone like "Thou shalt not kill" (most of the Ten Commandments, Ex 20:10-17; cf. 21:12, 15-17; 22:18-20, 21-22, 28-31; 23:1-3, 6-9). From a Greek verb, "to point," apodictic prescribes **the limits of action**.

Conditional sayings ("if . . . then . . .") apply apodictic to **specific cases**. In the process, case law limits apodictic. For example, does "you shall not kill" cover unintentional acts, acts of war, or capital punishment? The endless possibilities boggle the mind as does ever-growing case law [see figure 8].

Case law defines liabilities, sets penalties, and prescribes remedies (cf. the numerous examples in Ex 20:22-23:33). The most famous penalty is the "law of retaliation" (**lex talionis**):

If any harm follows, then you shall give life for life,
eye for eye, tooth for tooth, hand for hand, foot for
foot, burn for burn, wound for wound, stripe for
stripe. (Ex 21:23-25)

Seemingly harsh, the regulation actually limits vengeance (cf. Ex 21:18, 22, 26-28; 22:1-17). The prescribed penalties and remedies keep society from degenerating into the war of "all against all." They

assume what White calls "the fiction of relief," i.e.,

that damages received from legal action somehow make right the situation and reintegrate "the juridical order of society" which has been disturbed. [Thompson, 147]

In terms of the covenant, **apodictic demarcates the limits of the biosphere in which humans may safely live.** They provide warnings that chaos lies a h e a d . Rephrased, they say "if you kill or steal, then death, violence, and chaos lie ahead." The community of t r u s t deteriorates. When such

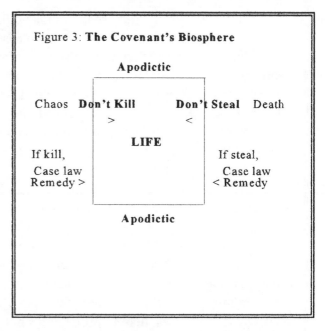

Figure 3: **The Covenant's Biosphere**

Apodictic

Chaos **Don't Kill** **Don't Steal** Death

> <

LIFE

If kill,   If steal,
Case law   Case law
Remedy >   < Remedy

Apodictic

offenses occur, the **case law repairs the damaged order** [cf. Thompson, 148].

The covenant demands **apply only within the covenant**. Outside the biosphere, there is only chaos and death. Thus, "thou shalt not kill" applies to covenant-partners, but not to Canaanites. Put bluntly, it does not prevent "the only good Canaanite is a dead Canaanite" attitude [see chap. 9]. Further, "thou shalt not kill" does not apply to fellow-Israelites if they have damaged the biosphere. Capital punishment may be the necessary remedy (cf. Ex 21:12-17, 23, 29; 22:18-20).

The demands **create and maintain the covenant**. These

traditional, mythic sayings call their hearers to be Israel. Often, they include motivations (mythic verities or consequences) to keep the covenant.

Figure 4: **The Ten Commandments and Cultural Context**

In ancient Israel, "thou shalt not kill" did not apply to war or capital punishment. Modern individualism demands a more inclusive reading. Patriarchy also restricted the commandments. Thus, "thou shalt not commit adultery" prohibited offenses against other Israelite males (a woman's father or husband; cf. Lev 18:6-17) in order to create a society safe from vengeance. Women were protected only as they were attached to protected men. Of course, modern egalitarians are appalled.

By contrast, other commandments, like the prohibitions against graven images and profaning the name of the Lord, are too cultic for modern world-views. Such commandments protect the divine sovereignty from religious arrogance. That is, they deny that mere possession of divine artifacts or magical use of the divine name will control the deity. As modernity does not share this respect for the divine sovereignty, it reduces them to prohibitions against foul language or religious art work.

Some **motivations** rely on the covenant God's identity as jealous (Ex 20:5), holy (Lev 19), or gracious to Israel (Ex 20:2):

> For I am the LORD your God; sanctify yourselves therefore, and be holy, for I am holy. . . . For I am the LORD who brought you up from the land of Egypt, to be your God; and you shall be holy, for I am holy. (Lev 11:44-45)

Other motivations call the people to actualize their mythic identity:

> You shall not wrong or oppress a resident alien, for
> you were aliens in the land of Egypt. (Ex 22:21; cf.
> 23:9)

Consequential motivations are also quite frequent (e.g., Ex 20:5, 7; 21:12; 21:15-17; Lev 18:3-5, 28):

> Honor your father and mother so that your days may
> be long in the land that the LORD your God is giving
> you. (Ex 20:12)

Deuteronomy (e.g., 27-28), in particular, often motivates by referring to the **curses and blessings** which accompany apostasy and obedience respectively. The consequential motivations, of course, have *ontological good* notions.

Figure 5: **Hammurabi's Law Code** [text in Pritchard, 163-80]

Israel's law codes have many ancient parallels [see Pritchard, 159-223]. The most famous is that of Hammurabi. Like Moses, Hammurabi receives the demands from a god (Shamash) which make the "good life" possible. They establish justice and the people's welfare [Pritchard, 165, 178]. Although some of the individual laws resemble Torah statutes, Hammurabi's code regulates a far more complex society with far more socio-economic distinctions [cf. Pritchard, 175]. Thus, while Hammurabi's code ends with curses and blessings resembling Deuteronomy [178-80], the rhetoric addresses fellow kings, not the common person.

Style: Composite

The motivations reveal that **law is a conversation**, rather than a set system of rules. That is, it is **an ongoing activity**, rather than an objective reality [White, "Rhetoric," 298-318]. Not surprisingly, then, the covenant demands have **seams** indicating their production over a period of time.

Figure 6: **Seams in Torah**

1) variant vocabularies, styles, and theologies
   a) Cf. Gen 1:1-2:4a; 5 with 2:4b-4:26
   b) Cf. the theology of Ex 24:9-11 with 33:17-34:18 and Deut 34:10
2) doublets, "stories told twice"
   a) Cf. Gen 12:10-20; 20:1-18; 26:6-11
   b) Cf. Moses' two calls in Ex 2:23-4:17 and 6:2-7:7
   c) Cf. the various decalogues (Ex 20:1-17; 34:10-28; Deut 5:6-21)
3) variant etiologies
   a) Circumcision (Gen 17:9-14; Ex 4:24-26; Josh 5:2-9)
   b) Levites (Ex 28:1-5; 32:25-29; Num 25:10-13)
4) anachronisms
   a) References to Moab as "Beyond the Jordan" (Deut 1:1)
   b) References to the king (Deut 17:14-20)
   c) Various references to life in the land

The text itself acknowledges this point. First, God speaks to the whole people (Ex 20). Then, God speaks to Moses in a dark cloud (the Covenant Code). Then, God speaks to Moses on the mountain (Ex 25-31). Then, God speaks to Moses from the tabernacle (Leviticus). Then, bypassing oracles in the wilderness, Moses speaks to the people in Moab (Deuteronomy).

These various speeches do not fit together neatly. Even a cursory reading reveals seams. The "Covenant Code" interrupts the narrative flow between Ex 20:21 and 24:1. Leviticus 8-10 connects to Ex 25-40, rather than to Lev 1-7. The date of Num 9:1-14 connects with that of Ex 40:17, rather than with that of Num 1:1. Deuteronomy 27 is a story about Moses in the third person which interrupts the first-person Mosaic sermon contained in Deut 5-28. Any reading could easily multiply examples.

Figure 7: **Narrative Connections**

Editors have made deliberate attempts to connect the seams. Thus, the text connects the three versions of the decalogue (Ex 20:1-7; 34:11-28; and Deut 5:6-21) by presenting the first as the initial revelation (Ex 20), the second as necessitated by the people's apostasy (Ex 34), and the third as a Mosaic reminder (Deut 5). Similarly, Moses' two calls become an initial call and its renewal.

The sayings also occur in **multiple and varied versions**. There are three versions of the Ten Commandments (Ex 20:1-17; 34:10-28; Deut 5:6-21) and several festal calendar lists (Ex 23:10-19; 34:18-26; Lev 23; Deut 16:1-17). Further, Deut 12-26 revises earlier materials in light of a new demand for centralized worship.

Apparently, the community lived with, applied, and reworked the covenant demands over centuries. Not surprisingly, many believe that Sinai-Deuteronomy contains several law codes [see figure 8]. Once the Torah text was "fixed" and additions were no longer possible, oral traditions continued applications. Eventually, that oral tradition was itself codified as *Mishnah* and then as *Talmud* [see figure 9].

Figure 8: **Law Codes and Written Sources**

In Torah, scholars identify law codes from different cultures and times:

1) the Ten Commandments (Ex 20:1-17);
2) the (agrarian) Covenant Code (Ex 20:22-23:33);
3) the (priestly) Holiness Code (Lev 19-26); and
4) the (monarchical) Deuteronomic Code (Deut 12-26).

Many scholars explain Torah's seams [see figure 6] and these law codes through a tradition history. That tradition began with oral materials and passed through four written sources before culminating in Torah itself [see Anderson, Understanding, 158, 452-54]. Scholars call the first source the **Yahwist** and date it to the David-Solomon kingdom which it describes as the fulfillment of the promises to Abraham. The **Elohist** came from the northern kingdom and retells the Moses-Sinai story to provide a myth for that kingdom. The **Deuteronomist** (Deut 12-26?) came from the late seventh century, was intimately related to Josiah's reform (2 Kings 22), and provided the theological basis (obey and prosper) for the Deuteronomic history [see chap. 9]. The **Priestly** materials, from the exilic period, give special attention to the cult (holiness, cleanness, and separation) and produced Torah's "final form."

The material's composite nature puzzles modern readers. Perhaps, narrative integrity was not a concern for ancients who may simply have wished to collect all the available sources. After all, most ancients would not read Torah as a whole. Perhaps, the ancients understood Torah's sayings as an anthology arranged thematically or with "catch-words."

Figure 9: **The Mishnah** [Danby's translation]

With Torah an established text, the rabbis created oral traditions updating and interpreting Torah's sayings. The *Mishnah* compiles these traditions (ca. 200 CE) in six divisions: 1) seeds, 2) feasts, 3) women, 4) damages, 5) holy matters, and 6) cleanness. These sections are anthologies connecting sayings by authority, theme, or "catch-words." The **Mishnah** records incredibly specific rabbinic decisions and debates:

> A tailor should not go out with his needle [on Friday] near to nightfall lest he forget and 'go out'; nor should a scrivener [go out then] with his pen; nor should a man search his clothes [for fleas] or read by lamplight. Rightly have they said: A schoolmaster may look when the children are reading but he himself may not read. In like manner a man that has a flux may not eat with a woman that has a flux, since it lends occasion to transgression [Shabbath, 1.3].

The **Mishnah** extends priestly legislation to the laity, so almost one-fourth of the work deals with "cleanness." In this tradition, these rabbis sincerely discharged the responsibility they believed was theirs as Moses' successors: "Be deliberate in judgement, raise up many disciples, and make a fence around the Law" (Pirke Aboth, 1.1).

Narrator: Soliloquy; Prophet; Priest

While the biblical-story narrator remains, he recedes behind characters' speech. The narrator introduces either God (e.g., Ex 20:22; 25:1; Lev 1:1) or Moses (e.g., Deut 1:1-5; 4:44-49; 29:1-2) who, then, speak at length in dramatic *soliloquies*. The result is an absent-narrator or a **character-narrator effect**. The narrator returns, however, to introduce new speakers or to describe responses to divine speech (e.g., Ex 24; 35-40; Lev 16:34; 24:23; Num 1:17-47). In short, the narrator frames the speech-catalogues. Not incidentally, Torah as a whole provides a story-frame for these speeches.

The absent narrator of the speech-catalogues creates the impression that a character (God or Moses) speaks directly to the narratee--reader. The speech-catalogues, then, appear to be the direct, **unmediated divine word**. They are **Torah par excellence**.

Despite this rhetorical effect, the divine voice remains that of a character in a narrator's story. Even at its most direct, the divine voice is mediated. The notion of unmediated divine speech is an **aesthetic illusion**.

Further, the story-God's voice gradually becomes more distant. While the opening divine Sinai-word is to the people directly (Ex 20:1-17), the people, then, request a **speech-mediator**:

"You (Moses) speak to us, and we will listen; but do not let God speak to us, or we will die. . . ." Then the people stood at a distance, while Moses drew near to the thick darkness where God was. (Ex 20:18-21)

Thereafter, God speaks only to Moses in the cloud, from the mountain, or from the tabernacle. Moses, then, mediates the word. In Deuteronomy, the divine character-voice recedes completely behind his prophet's.

As myth, of course, the speech-catalogues provide for continuing mediators: either *prophets* or *priests*. Thus, God commissions Joshua to succeed Moses (Num 27:18-23; Deut

34:14-15, 23); and Moses anticipates a continuing succession of prophets for the people (Deut 18:15). The story also establishes the *cult*, the continuing vehicle of the sacred [see myth].

Figure 10: **Yom Kippur**

Yom Kippur climaxes Judaism's fall holy days, the "Ten Days of Repentance" extending from **Rosh Hashanah** (New Year) to **Yom Kippur** (the Day of Atonement). According to tradition, God sits in judgment during this ten-day period and decides human destinies for the next year. **Yom Kippur** is the last opportunity for repentance before God's decisions.

According to Lev 16, only on this holiest day did the high priest enter the Holy of Holies to sprinkle the blood of a bull and a goat in atonement for the people's sins. The priest also confessed the people's sins while laying his hands upon another goat before releasing it into the wilderness. This ancient ritual clearly intends to expel contagious impurities from the community. For contemporary Judaism, the ritual is a psychological, introspective process of self-scrutiny called the "affliction of the soul." Various liturgical rituals, including the reading of Jonah (a story of repentance), lead up to the climactic "closing of the gate" symbolizing the last chance for repentance [see Gaster, Festivals, 135-86].

The **priests** are the divinely appointed cult officials (Ex 28-29; Lev 8-10; Num 17; 20:22-29; 25:10-13). The divine selection is the priestly equivalent of the prophetic call. It establishes a priestly dynasty flowing from Aaron. Other priestly claimants are subordinated (the rest of the Levites, Num 3-4; 8) or ruthlessly deposed (Lev 10; Num 16-17).

The priests **preside over the cult**. They are the "holiest" of the holy people and mediate the Holy's benefits to the people. They offer the sacrifices and so forth. Perhaps, most importantly, the high priest enters the holiest place on the Day of Atonement to make atonement for the people (Lev 16) [see figure 10]. In addition to their cultic acts, the priests continue the "divine voice." They mediate God's blessing:

> The LORD bless you and keep you;
> the LORD make his face to shine upon you
>   and be gracious to you;
> the LORD lift up his countenance upon you,
>   and give you peace. (Num 6:24-26)

They define God's continuing demands:

> You (Aaron) are to distinguish between the holy and the common, and between the unclean and the clean; and you are to teach the people of Israel all the statutes that the LORD has spoken to them through Moses. (Lev 10:10-11)

They are also the traditional, institutional source for new oracles. Their breastplate of judgment contains the Urim and Thummin (Ex 28:15-30), the sacred lots cast by the priest to determine God's judgment (cf. Deut 33:8; cf. 1 Sam 14:41-42).

Narrative Time: Myth and Pace

The cult makes the aesthetic illusion of direct divine speech a mythic reality. Here, the divine demand addresses the community member of each successive generation. Thus, quite graphically, Moses addresses the second-wilderness generation as if they were the Sinai-generation:

> The LORD our God made a covenant with us at

Horeb. Not with our ancestors did the LORD make this covenant, but with us, who are all of us here alive today. (Deut 5:2-3)

The covenant demands belong to mythic or cultic time [cf. Eliade, Profane, 68-70]. In the myth's rehearsal and the cult's performance, the present and the founding time merge. Thus, the sacrificer presenting the first fruits (Deut 26:1-5) merges his story with that of the ancestors:

> A wandering Aramean was my ancestor; he went down into Egypt and lived there as an alien, few in number, and there he became a great nation, mighty and populous. When the Egyptians treated us harshly and afflicted us . . . we cried to the LORD . . . The LORD brought us out of Egypt . . . and he brought us into this place and gave us this land . . . . So now I bring the first of the fruit of the ground that you, O LORD, have given me. (Deut 26:6-10)

Of course, Moses' hearers are neither the exodus generation nor land-possessors. The sayings-catalogues reach beyond the text to incorporate future generations.

Deuteronomy is particularly adept at this imperialism. In addition to frequent covenant renewal stories (5:2-3; 26:16-19; 31:10-11; cf. Ex 32-34; Josh 23-24), Deuteronomy foreshadows the mythic community's future of apostasies, judgments, and repentances (29-30). In this way, it predicts the myth's repetition in history [cf. chaps. 9, 11].

Not surprisingly, Torah's narrative pace emphasizes these mythically important sayings. Not only do they make up the bulk of Torah, the concentrated speech-scenes also slow Torah's frantic pace to a stand-still. Time stops while God and Moses speak. The people remain at the mountain or in the plain of Moab. The land waits. In pace, as well as mythic time, the covenant-demands last forever.

Story Pattern and Plot Conflict: Covenant and Apostasy

Sinai's narrative "pause," like a television commercial, provides the word from the sponsor which is the story's **raison d'etre.** The **founding of covenant and cult** (i.e., Israel) finally **restores Eden.** Covenant and cult provide a s a c r e d biosphere in which Israel may live long and prosper [see figure 3].

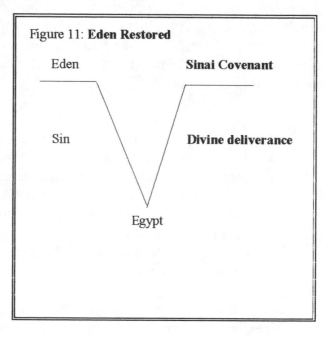

Figure 11: **Eden Restored**

Eden

Sinai Covenant

Sin

Divine deliverance

Egypt

The fact that this Eden arrives before (outside) the land emphasizes the divine sovereignty. Revelation is the narrative climax, not the land. In typical Torah fashion, divine speech comes first and guarantees subsequent narrative **(revelation plot).** Further, the wilderness setting is appropriate for myth which belongs to a primeval time different from that of any story-hearers. The wilderness also dramatically symbolizes the chaos which forever surrounds mythic orders. Finally, the setting propitiously suits mythic continuance. Whether the hearers inhabit the land or not, they can still be Israel, the people created by divine promise and demand.

Unfortunately, a tragic, **sin plot** attends Sinai's revelation. The people apostasize at the mountain (the golden calf, Ex 32-34) and at the promised land's border (Num 13-14; cf. 20-21; 25). Not surprisingly, divine judgments kill thousands and leave the people wandering in the wilderness with plagues, fire, leprosy, military defeats, earthquakes, and snakes. Strikingly, Israel faces the same God that the Egyptians did (cf. Ex 15:26). Ephemeral Eden is lost as it arrives. In short, **Israel's founding story repeats the general human story** [see myth].

Nevertheless, the **story continues**. Once again, Eden Lost is not story's end. At every apostasy, Moses intercedes for the people, and a long-suffering God renews the covenant (cf. Ex 32-34; Num 13-14). The renewed covenant gives renewed opportunities. Will new story-characters live the covenant or apostasize? Deuteronomy's Mosaic sermons open this story to include later members of the mythic community [see mythic identity].

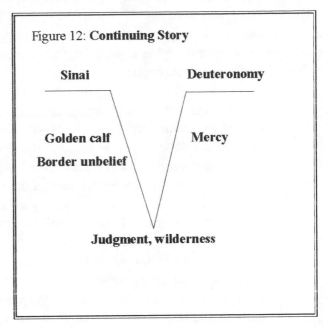

Figure 12: **Continuing Story**

Sinai   Deuteronomy

Golden calf   Mercy
Border unbelief

Judgment, wilderness

Divine Character: Jealous, Long-suffering Yahweh

At Sinai, **Yahweh becomes Israel's Holy Sovereign**. This Sovereign speaks Israel into existence and specifies the contours of her continuing identity and existence. Without Yahweh, there is no Israel. Not surprisingly, this nationalistic Orderer is **jealous** of his vassals' affections (Ex 20:2-3; Deut 6:4-5) and judges those who dare to align themselves with other deities (Ex 32-34). In fact, Deuteronomy reads Israel's entire history in terms of this jealousy. They have (1-4) and will (29-30) suffer when they worship other gods (cf. Judg; 2 Kings).

Figure 13: **The Social Contract Myth**

Torah is the divine revelation of Israel's social structure in covenant and cult. This society is a sacred entity (biosphere) given from above. By contrast, most moderns perceive society to be a human product [e.g., Berger, Canopy, 3-51]. Thus, liberalism has replaced the revelation myth with the myth of the "social contract":

> Wherever any form of government apart from
> the merest tyranny exists, reflection on the
> basis of the State cannot but lead to the notion
> that, in one sense or another, it is based on the
> consent . . . of its members. . . . Add the desire
> to find actual justification for a theory in facts,
> and . . . this doctrine of consent will inevitably
> be given a historical setting. . . . the State will
> be represented as having arisen, in some
> remote age, out of a compact or, in the more
> legal phrase, contract between two or more
> parties. The only class that will be able to resist
> the doctrine is that which maintains the divine
> rights of kings, and holds that all existing
> governments were imposed on the people by
> the direct interposition of God. [Cole, xxi-xxii]

Israel's repeated, horrible destructions explain the popular notion that the OT God is a harsh, wrathful God (often juxtaposed to the NT God of mercy). This story's continuance beyond apostasy to renewed covenants is, however, powerful rhetoric for an altogether different view:

> The LORD, the LORD, a God merciful and gracious, slow to anger, and abounding in steadfast love and faithfulness, keeping steadfast love for the thousandth generation, forgiving iniquity and transgression and sin, yet by no means clearing the guilty, but visiting the iniquity of the parents upon the children and the children's children, to the third and fourth generation. (Ex 34:6-7; cf. Num 14:17-19)

Despite horrible plagues and wilderness wanderings, Torah presents God as loving, **merciful**, and gracious. God elects a weak, undeserving people (Deut 4:38; 7:1, 7-8), cares for them as parents care for their children (Deut 1:31; 8:5; 14-15), and provides for society's lowliest members (the alien, the poor, the widow, and the orphan; Ex 22:21-27). He is a compassionate God (Ex 22:27). Even the divine demands intend the people's well-being (Deut 4:40; 5:29; 6:24).

The cult, of course, symbolizes the Holy One's **accessibility** and graciousness (see particularly, Ex 19:10, 12, 21, 23; Lev 11:44-45; 19). Further, God appears directly to found the covenant and cult (Ex 19-20; 24; 40). Throughout, God's glory, his visible manifestation, dwells upon the tabernacle or leads the people's journey (cf. Ex 40:34-38; Num 9:15-23).

God, however, also recedes behind mediators (prophet, priest, and cult), so the conception of providence shifts from direct to **institutional**. Gradually, God is known not directly but mediately (cf. Deut 34:10) [see myth-ritual]. Put differently, the foundation of the cult, like the sin-theodicy and the two-ways ethic, rationalizes and ethicizes the Holy. **The cult tames** (institutionalizes) the Holy's primitive, mysterious power.

Figure 14: **Deconstructing the Cult**

As a religious bureaucracy, the cult rationalizes the Holy providing safe access to this power. Ironically, this domesticated Holy is quite far from the basic religious experience of terrifying power. Not surprisingly, then, charismatic and mystic experiences of the Holy randomly punctuate institutional religion.

Torah, of course, attempts to avoid the cultic emasculation of the Holy. For Torah, only God can reveal ways of access. Further, the commandments forbidding graven images and profaning the name proscribe religious arrogance. They reject the presumption that one can control God's actions magically. In short, Torah must ironically claim that its cult does not contain nor control the Holy.

Human Characters: Israel's Mythic Identity

Torah reveals Israel to be God's covenant partner. Not surprisingly, the Sovereign expects henotheistic faith from his vassals (e.g., Ex 20:2-3; Deut 6:4-5). The Sovereign also demands that his vassals treat each other fairly and compassionately. Leviticus 19:18 renders the concern pithily: "you shall love your neighbor as yourself." In short, the people are to actualize their mythic identity and become like their Holy God who "executes justice for the orphan and widow":

> You shall also love the stranger, for you were strangers in the land of Egypt. (Deut 10:18-19; cf. Ex 22:21-27; 23:6-7)

> When you reap the harvest of your land, you shall not reap to the very edges of your field . . . you shall leave them for the poor and the alien: I am the LORD your

God. (Lev 19:9-10)

For I am the LORD your God; sanctify yourselves
therefore, and be holy, for I am holy. (Lev 11:44; cf.
19)

Figure 15: **Deconstructing Ethnocentrism**

Torah founds Israel as a natural religion. As such, it is
inherently nationalistic; nevertheless, certain elements rebuke
any ethnocentric complacency. Most importantly, Israel
faces the same judging God that the Egyptians did (cf. Ex
15:26). As Israel tells her story, then, she depicts her loss of
Eden at Sinai and at the land's border. Thus, Israel's
founding story twice recapitulates Gen 3. Ironically, then,
Israel's ethnocentric myth suggests that she is only a specific
instance of what is true generally of humans (Adam).

Various characters incarnate faithfulness (Ex 35-40) or
apostasy (Ex 32; Num 13-14). The speech-catalogues depict these
opposed lifestyles as the "**two-ways**," obedience which leads to life
or apostasy which leads to death (cf. Ex 23:20-33; Lev 26; Deut 28).
The story's repetition of covenant and apostasy, the
speech-catalogues' imperialism, and the cult indicate that these "two-
ways" remain open as mythic possibilities. As myth, Torah is not
merely about the primeval past. Its community can still "choose
life":

See, I have set before you today life and prosperity,
death and adversity. If you obey . . . then you shall
live and become numerous, and the LORD your God
will bless you in the land that you are entering to
possess. But if your heart turns away and you do not
hear, but are led astray to bow down to other gods and

serve them, I declare to you today that you shall
perish; you shall not live long in the land that you are
crossing the Jordan to possess. . . . Choose life . . .
(Deut 30:15-19)

Of course, the way of death also provides the community with a
sin-theodicy not unlike Gen 3. In fact, the Sinai-Wilderness story
repeats the general, human story of Gen 3 in Israel [see figure 15].

Myth and Ritual: The Sacred Bureaucracy; Gift and Demand

The *cult*, the sacred's *bureaucracy*, provides safe access to
the Holy. The cult also orders life.

The **sacred calendar** unites ordinary time with mythic, sacred time. The festivals memorialize and repeat the founding time anew. They also prevent time from being an undifferentiated succession of days. They punctuate,

Figure 16: **Sacred Bureaucracy**
1) sacred **places and utensils** (tabernacle, ark, etc.) (Ex 25-27)
2) sacred **people** (priests, high priest, Levites) (Ex 28-29; Lev 8-10; Num 3-4; 8)
3) sacred **calendar** (sabbath, passover, first fruits, pentecost, new year, day of atonement, booths) (Ex 23:10-19; 34:18-26; Lev 23)
4) sacred **acts** (observe calendar, sacrifice (Lev 1-7), purity, diet (Lev 11-15), and special vows)

order, and rejuvenate life. Life is lived from sabbath to sabbath, from
passover to passover.

Cultic paraphernalia orders space.   Symbols of divine

presence--the tabernacle and ark--center Israelite space. Thus, the tabernacle stands at the center of the wilderness camp (Num 2). The tabernacle itself is divided into three spheres of increasing holiness: the court, the sanctuary, and the holy of holies where the ark resides (Ex 26-27). As one enters the tabernacle, then, one gradually approaches the Holy. Not surprisingly, values increase as one draws nearer to God. The court has bronze implements, but only gold will do in the sanctuary. Further, the holy of holies is so intense that the high priest enters only once a year on the Day of Atonement [see figure 10].

The cult orders **people** as well. First, of course, God's election of Israel separates her from the nations. Then, God chooses Levites, priests, and a high priest from within Israel to serve as God's special officials (Ex 13; 28-29; Lev 8-10; Num 3-4; 8). Other Israelites may also become increasingly holy for specific occasions like worship (festival or sacrifices) or special vows (Nazirites, Num 6; holy war soldiers, Deut 20).

To approach the Holy, one must be holy. God makes Israel holy by choosing her as his people (Ex 19:3-6). Israel, then, graciously becomes holy by **association** (cf. Lev 19). **Holiness is contagious**.

Separating holiness, however, also **demands**. Israel must be different from the other nations (Lev 18). The increasing value of the tabernacle utensils as one approaches the Holy and the elaborate requirements made upon those who are aligned most closely with God (the priests) symbolize holiness' demand. Thus, God requires the Levites in return for the deliverance of Israel's firstborn (Ex 11-13). Further, the cult demands the sacrifice of the best as the **basic act of worship** (Lev 1-7). **Sacrifice** reciprocates God's gift in thankfulness for (thanksgiving offerings) and in maintenance of the relationship (sin, guilt, atonement).

The separating demand is also evident in the symbol of *cleanness.* Cleanness specifies acts done in the right time and place.

It carefully observes cultic patterns. In short, cleanness separates. The unclean destroys separations and boundaries. It is "dirt," something out of place [cf. Douglas, Purity].

Figure 17: **A Separate Peace**

For Torah, evil is not wholly outside the community. The community itself apostasizes and needs purification rituals to maintain its order. Similarly, John Knowles' story of a New England prep school during World War II knows no separate peace. Instead, the narrator (Gene) jealously destroys his friend Finny. At the novel's climax, Finny finally admits Gene's malice. Years later, after Finny's death and burial, Gene returns to bury part of himself and to find some peace. Like Torah's biosphere, then, A Separate Peace knows only fragile, internally threatened order.

Like the cult generally, cleanness legislation orders the world. Thus, the dietary regulations follow and respect the divine ordering of fish of the sea, birds of the air, and beasts of the field (cf. Gen 1). **Clean animals** stay in the proper place, move as they should, and eat the proper things. Thus, clean (edible) water animals have fins and scales (no shrimp). Clean birds fly. Clean animals also reflect Israel's pastoral background: animals which chew the cud have cloven hoofs (no pigs; cf. Lev 11:2-8).

Living cleanly and observing the cult make one an Israelite. The cult transmits Israel's mythic identity from generation to generation. Its acts are condensed symbols of "Israeliteness." The cult, then, establishes a continuing connection with the founding time.

ANET: Closed, Traditional Society and Contagion

Torah's world-view is that of **a closed, traditional society**. Such societies carefully regulate **boundaries**:

> Just as the social body is concerned about its boundaries (frontiers, city walls, gates), so too the physical body is the object of concern as to its surface (skin, hair, clothing) and orifices (eyes, mouth, genitals, anus). What crosses the frontier, the city walls, and the door of the house is of great concern: strangers are always suspect. What flakes off the body surface and what pours from its orifices are comparably of great concern. All of these substances are matter which is out of place and so dangerous, even unclean. [Neyrey, "Unclean," 77]

Unless the AIDs epidemic has revived them, such attitudes are foreign to modernity. Modernity simply does not have the clearly defined boundaries and group identities of traditional societies [see figure 4; Malina, Anthropology, 14-15].

Further, the concern for separation and cleanness reflects *ontological* conceptions about holiness and *goodness*. For this perspective, the holy is a power with obvious, **material consequences**. Thus, obedience brings life, peace, and prosperity. Disobedience brings death, war, and economic disaster (the "two-ways").

Further, holiness and uncleanness are **contagious**. One becomes holy by association with God. One becomes unclean by association with the unclean (foods, bodily emissions, the dead, and outsiders). Not incidentally, the divine command to slaughter the land's inhabitants intends to prevent apostasy's contagion (e.g., Deut 7:1-6). The inhabitants must die or they will be a "snare" unto Israel (e.g., Ex 23:23-33).

The entire cult, as well as representative acts, depends upon effective contagion. Why else does one lay hands on the sacrificial animal or the priest? Why else can one offer an animal instead of one's own life? This objective and contagious notion of holiness is, of course, radically different from modernity's subjective, psychological understanding of guilt, sin, goodness, and holiness.

Figure 18: **The Picture of Dorian Gray**

Where Torah has objective, contagious notions of good, evil, holiness, and impurity, modernity depicts such matters as subjective, **psychological states**. Good, evil, holiness, and guilt (note the change from impurity) have become matters of conscience or intention (cf. Kant's "the only thing good is the good will"). Modern people still want external objectivity on these points, however. They want "murder to out" (cf. detective fiction; Poe, "The Tell-Tale Heart").

Oscar Wilde's famous The Picture of Dorian Gray dramatizes this modern tension (the desire for melodrama). In the fantastic story, Dorian Gray's hidden portrait shows the effects of his growing cruelty and debauchery (subjective evil), while he still appears young and innocent. Ultimately, Dorian destroys the portrait attempting to destroy his conscience. When he stabs the portrait, the portrait becomes young, Gray becomes old, and he dies (objective evil).

Review Questions

1. Apply the reading method of chaps. 3-4 to the Sinai-Wilderness material. List its genre, plot shape, conflict, depiction of God, mythic function, and ANE problems.

2. Name the four scenes in this story.

3. How does the covenant resemble a Hittite suzerainty treaty?

4. Are the sayings laws?

5. Are the sayings-catalogues universal?

6. What motivates the keeping of the covenant demands?

7. Why do scholars find the sayings-catalogues composite?

8. How is the style of this material similar to Gen 1?

9. What aesthetic, stylistic choices facilitate the impression that the covenant demands are on-going and contemporary? What story-content facilitates the impression that the mythic identity continues from one generation to the next?

10. Compare this story to that of Gen 3. What is the theological significance of this similarity?

11. Is the God of the Sinai-Wilderness material long-suffering?

12. What is institutional providence?

13. What are the two ways of Israel's mythic identity?

14. How does the cult order life? How does it transmit mythic identity?

15. What does it mean to say that holiness is contagious?

16. What is a closed, traditional society?

Suggestions for Alternate Reading and Reflection

1. Sometimes Christians apologetically describe Christianity as a religion of grace in contrast to Judaism as a religion of law. Is this an appropriate distinction? Does the Torah story contain grace?

2. Do contemporary Jews and Christians observe the covenant-demands?

3. Are the Ten Commandments nationalistic or universalistic? Are the Ten Commandments individual or societal directives? Is it possible to follow the Ten Commandments?

4. Compare Mt 5:21-30 with Ex 20:13-14. How does Matthew's reading alter the Exodus sayings? Does Matthew's reading respect the sayings' cultural code? Which reading is more modern?

5. Are sin and uncleanness the same notions? What is a sin of the "high hand" (cf. Num 15:27-30)? Does the sacrificial system (Lev

4-7) cover intentional sins? What does this suggest about the ability to keep Torah?

6. How does the similarity of the Sinai-Wilderness story to Gen 3 suggest the deconstruction of Israel's natural religion myth?

7. How does the bureaucratizing of the Holy deconstruct it?

8. Compare the covenant to a "social contract."

9. Why might there be three versions of the Ten Commandments (Ex 20:1-17; 34:10-28; Deut 5:2-9) in the Sinai-Wilderness material?

10. Contrast ancient and modern notions of goodness and evil.

11. Contrast the **Mishnah**'s interpretation of the HB with that of the NT.

12. Why do modern people resent law?

For Further Reading

On the significance of Torah for Judaism, see Neusner, <u>Way</u>; and E. Sanders, <u>Palestinian</u>.

For commentaries on Deuteronomy, see Rad, <u>Deuteronomy</u>; and Weinfeld.

On the covenant in antiquity, see the bibliography in chap. 6. On the covenant-society, see J. P. M. Walsh.

On law, see Patrick, <u>OT Law</u>.
On apodictic and conditional law, see Alt, 101-71.
On law as conversation or rhetoric, see Thompson, 145-49; James White, <u>Legal</u>; and **idem**, "Rhetoric."
On the Ten Commandments, see Childs, <u>Exodus</u>, 384-439; Harrelson; and Stamm and Andrew. The text's enumeration follows the Protestant listing. With reference to the Ex 20 list, Judaism names v. 2 as the first commandment while vv. 3-4 become the second. Catholicism makes vv. 3-4 the first commandment and divides v. 17 into two commandments. Protestants read v. 3 as the first commandment.

On the composite nature of Torah, see most introductions to the HB; Friedman; DeVries; and Campbell and O'Brien. For attempts to read Torah as an integral whole, see Childs, OT as Scripture; and Mann.

For a translation of the Mishnah, see Danby.

For ritual, see the bibliography in chap. 4.

For discussions of Israel's cult; see Flanders, Crapps, and Smith, 181-90; Ringgren, Israelite; and Pedersen. For discussions of contemporary Jewish ritual, see Gaster, Passover.

For holiness and ritual, see Gammie, Holy, 9-44.

For sacred space and time, see Eliade, Profane, 20-113.

On cleanness and order, see Douglas, Purity; and **idem**, Natural; Neyrey, "Unclean"; and Neusner, Purity. For a more philosophical view, see Ricoeur, Symbolism.

For comparisons of closed and open societies, see Malina, Anthropology, 13-65.

On divine revelation as a social sanction, see Livingston, 311-24; Johnstone, 27-32.

INTRODUCTION TO THE PROPHETS

Late Jewish tradition divided the Prophets into two sections: the **Former Prophets** and the **Latter Prophets**. The Former Prophets include Joshua, Judges, Samuel, and Kings (the latter two were considered one book). The Latter Prophets include Isaiah, Jeremiah, Ezekiel, and twelve smaller prophetic books. While the Former and the Latter Prophets differ in literary form, they share a mythic function. They **transmit Torah's mythic identity** to the later community.

The Former Prophets

The Former Prophets are **ancient history**. In fact, later Bibles (e.g., the LXX or Vulgate) often group these works together with others in a "history" section including Ruth, 1-2 Chronicles, Ezra, Nehemiah, Esther, Tobit, and Judith.

As ancient history, the Former Prophets' ideological perspective differs radically from that of modern histories [see chap. 4, genre]. In particular, this ideological starting point is the Torah myth. As the Former Prophets tell Israel's history, they assume that Israel belongs to God and that he controls her fate. The Former Prophets further understand that fate according to **the Deuteronomist's "two-ways"** ideology. Thus, Israel's life or death depends respectively upon her faith or apostasy. For the Former Prophets, Israel's entire history dramatizes this two-ways and individual characters provide models of **faith** (e.g., Joshua, the prophets, David) or **apostasy** (e.g., Achan, Solomon, Jeroboam, Manasseh, Israel).

This perspective allows the Former Prophets to present Israel's tragic loss of the land (the exile) as a **sin-theodicy**. Various divine deliverances do, however, complicate and retard this simple apostasy story. God mercifully delivers the people from oppressors (judges and kings) and offers opportunities to repent (the prophets). These elements

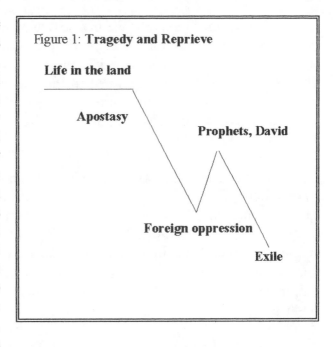

Figure 1: **Tragedy and Reprieve**

Life in the land

Apostasy

Prophets, David

Foreign oppression

Exile

and the formation of the Davidic Kingdom provide temporary reprieves on "**the road to ruin**."

The theodicy, of course, maintains meaning in the face of chaos. The exile as divine judgment means that the people **still belong to Yahweh**, not to foreign imperialism. Further, the repeated divine mercies allow hope even in exile (cf. Deut 30; 1 Kings 8). The Former Prophets do not, however, relate that tale.

The Latter Prophets

The Latter Prophets are fifteen books of oracles. Ancient Hebrew texts contained the fifteen prophets on four scrolls: Isaiah, Jeremiah, Ezekiel, and the Twelve. Because of this difference in length, tradition refers to the first three as the **major prophets** and the final twelve as the **minor prophets** (Hosea, Joel, Amos, Obadiah, Jonah, Micah, Nahum, Habakkuk, Zephaniah, Haggai, Zechariah, and Malachi).

The dominant genre is the **oracle**, the announcement of an imminent divine action for a specific historical occasion. For the prophets, God is about to act **either to judge or to save** his people. The prophetic God is not confined to the cult or to the mythic tradition. Instead, he is a part of current political, military events. As a result, the prophetic oracles tell a **new divine story** about God's present acts. The myth is now.

Textualization adapts the prophetic myth. It removes the oracles from their specific historical occasion and relegates them to the past. Thus, they become part of the mythic tradition and can in ritual call people to **repent** (judgment oracles) or to **hope** (salvation oracles). Further, the editing of many of the books into sections of first judgment and then salvation oracles creates a **salvation through judgment** story. This story corroborates the Former Prophets' sin-theodicy response to the exile and imagines a future beyond exile.

Later Christian use of the prophets also removes the prophets from their historical and ritual context. In Christian readings, the oracles become divine foreshadowings of or predictions of God's salvific acts in Jesus Christ and the church (e.g., the use of Isa 7:14 in Mt. 1:23). That is, they are attached to a new myth (to the gospel rather than Torah).

Questions for Reflection

1. What are the mythic functions of the prophets?
2. Compare Jewish and Christian understandings of the prophets.

CHAPTER 9

LIFE IN THE LAND
Joshua and Judges

Introduction: Relationship to Torah

Torah and the *Former Prophets* have intimate connections. First, the Former Prophets follow the "two-ways" ideology so closely that scholars often refer to them as the *Deuteronomic History*. In addition, Moses' third sermon (Deut 29-30) foreshadows the Former Prophets' tragic story. Second, Joshua finally realizes the promise of the land (Gen 12; etc.). This connection between Joshua and Torah leads some to join Joshua to the Torah as a *Hexateuch*.

Content Summary: Land and Apostasy

Following divine instructions (1:1-9), Joshua leads the faithful people into the land (contrast Josh 2 with Num 13). The people cross the Jordan River on dry ground and enter the land as if enacting a ritual (a monument, circumcision, and passover).

The ritual aura continues as Israel defeats Jericho with parade, shout, music, and the ritual sacrifice of the city's inhabitants (save for Rahab and her family in 6:21-25). When an Israelite (Achan) keeps some of the devoted goods as spoil, his disobedience leads to **military defeat** at Ai. When Joshua uncovers the sin, the people stone the culprit and his entire family. The purified Israel, then, slaughters the inhabitants of Ai (8:24-29). In fact, only the crafty Gibeonites (9) escape Israel's murderous advance "because the LORD **God of Israel fought for Israel**" (10:40-42; cf. 11:10-23).

184

The land in hand, Joshua **allots the land** to the tribes by lot (13-21; note how prominently Judah and Joseph figure). Despite Israel's success, native remnants remain as portents of future disaster (15:63; cf. 13:13; 16:10; 17:12-13; Judg 1:19, 21, 27-35; 2:1-3).

Joshua ends with a final sermon exhorting the people to keep the henotheistic, *xenophobic* covenant (23:12-16). The people, of course, formally accept this reprised Deuteronomic covenant (24:16-28).

Judges describes Israel's life in the land as a **repeated cycle of apostasy and deliverance**. After Israel commits apostasy (2:1-4; 3:1-6), God allows a foreign nation to oppress her. When Israel repents, God raises up a hero (judge) to deliver her. When the judge dies, Israel commits apostasy again (cf. 2:8-19; 3:7-12). Judges names twelve such heroes (cf. the number of tribes), but tells stories of only six.

Figure 1: **Judges** (with stories)

Othniel (3:7-11)
Ehud   (3:12-30)
Deborah (4:1-5:31)
Gideon (6:1-8:35)
Jephthah (10:6-12:7)
Samson (13:1-16:31)

The story is quite dismal. Judges ends in desperate, apostate days (at least, non-centralized worship, 17-18; cf. Josh 22) and in intra-tribal strife (19-21).

Genre: Deuteronomistic History

Torah is Israel's founding myth. The Former Prophets hand on that tradition. They read and write Israel's history in the land from the perspective of Torah's world-view. In particular, this history dramatizes the Deuteronomic "two-ways" perspective. The Former Prophets, then, are a *Deuteronomic History*. Continued theophanies and miracles are, of course, wholly appropriate for this genre which may have mythic (e.g., Josh 6; 10), miraculous (Judg 4-8), or realistic atmospheres (Josh 22; Judg 17-21).

Story Pattern and Plot Conflict: The Land Given and Lost

Joshua realizes the divine **promise of the land** and restores Eden. The Judges' cycle of apostasy-judgment repeatedly disturbs this Eden, but God's heroes repeatedly restore the land and give the people new chances.

The gift of the land and the judges' reclamation projects are **holy war plots**. Jericho falls to a ritual procession (Josh 6). Divine panic, hailstorms, and an arrested sun determine the battle against the five kings (10:9-14; cf. Judg 4:12-16).

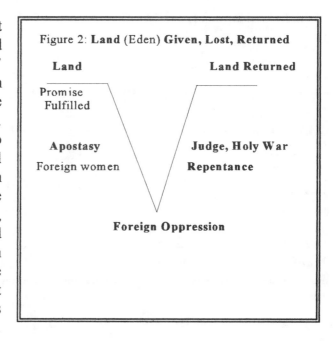

Figure 2: **Land (Eden) Given, Lost, Returned**

The Lord's spirit empowers the heroes' military victories (e.g., Judg 3:10; 11:29; 14:19). Battles precede according to divine instructions (e.g., Josh 6; 8; Judg 4; 7). Clearly, God fights for his people and gives Israel the land (e.g., Josh 24:12-13).

For the ancients, war was a **ritual act**. Soldiers, often untrained amateurs, were "priests" temporarily consecrated to divine service. War began with worship, purifications, and with priestly, prophetic, or divine blessings and instructions. A successful *holy war* ended in thanksgiving ceremonies with the thankful people **devoting** spoils to God. Humans were **banned** from participating in these spoils (Josh 6:17-7:26). In fact, Deuteronomic legislation places all the land's "living" under the ban (e.g., Deut 20:16-18).

Figure 3: **Holy War Legislation**

Deuteronomic Legislation	**Conquest Examples**
ritual purifications (23:9-14)	Josh 3:5; 5:2-12; 7:13
priestly blessing (20:1-3)	Josh 6:6-7; 8:3-8
certain troops released (20:5-9)	Judg 7:2-8
offer of peace/slavery to enemy (20:10-11)	Josh 9; 11:19-20;
death of enemy males, spoil regulations (20:12-18)	Josh 6:17-21, 24; 8:26-29; 10:20-43; 11:8-23
rejection of wanton destruction of natural resources (20:19-20)	no instance

Achan's disastrous violation of the ban (Josh 7:10-15) symbolizes Israel's laxity. Ultimately, Israel fails to slaughter the enemy. For the xenophobic Deuteronomist, the failure to remove the land's inhabitants leads directly to the apostasy cycle of Judges (cf. Josh 23:12-16; Judg 3:1-5). As a result, a sin plot dominates Judges.

Figure 4: **Holy War and Sin Plots**

	SENDER ------>	OBJECT ----->	RECIPIENTS
Holy War	God	the land	his people
Sin	God	the land	his people

	HELPERS ----->	SUBJECT <----	OPPONENTS
Holy War	judges, miracles	God	foreigners
Sin	foreigners	God	his people

Figure 5: **A Woman to Blame**

The text's *xenophobic* equation of foreign women and apostasy reflects the world-view of a patriarchal, closed society. It also superficially resembles argumentative males from Adam ("the woman that you gave") to the present who claim "that somewhere there's a woman to blame" [from Jimmy Buffett, "Margarittaville"]. The text, however, actually has an altogether different rhetoric. It does not blame the women. Like Eden's snake and fruit, women are **only vehicles** for Israel's apostasy. Such characterization offends modernity, but it does make it impossible for Israel to evade responsibility for her own sin. Further, if the modern reader screams at Samson, "Beware Delilah!" [cf. audiences at horror-movies who cry out, "Don't open that door!"], the text has led the reader to accept its **rhetoric of repentance**. The reader can, then, sing with Jimmy Buffett: "It could be my fault . . . I know its my own damned fault."

Divine Character: Holy Warrior

The God of Joshua and Judges is a nationalistic, Holy Warrior. As a result, outsiders are divine opponents or tools. The notion that other nations have their own gods only slightly mitigates this **ethnocentrism** (cf. Judg 11:24).

Figure 6: **Canaanite Religion**

The religion of the land's inhabitants (Canaanites) explained seasonal **fertility** through a myth of Baal's death and resurrection (cf. the Greek Demeter and Persephone). When Baal fell victim to Mot, the god of death, the crops grew again only when Baal's consort Astarte (cf. Ishtar and Isis) rescued him [for texts, see Pritchard, 129-55]. Canaanite ritual mimicked this pair's sacred marriage with rituals involving sacred prostitutes. Apparently, the rituals were a form of **sympathetic magic** presuming that proper ritual activity would induce acts in the "real world" (cf. voodoo).

As the settlement of the land involved Israel's transformation to an agricultural society, Canaanite religion must have been quite tempting. Israel knew **Yahweh** to be a war-god, but his agricultural prowess was an unproven commodity. Of course, the Deuteronomist rejects Israelite involvement with Baal as a violation of **Yahweh**'s henotheistic demands. For that historian, the prophets led a minority **Yahweh**-alone movement while most of Israel combined **Yahwism** and the local fertility religions.

The Warrior is also the God of tradition. He promised and now delivers the land. Further, he is the **jealous** God of the Mosaic covenant who judges those who deviate from henotheism (e.g., Josh 1:1-9; 23-24). The repeated apostasy-cycle, however, creates a portrait of God as **longsuffering**:

"Did I not deliver you from the Egyptians . . . . Yet you have abandoned me and worshiped other gods; therefore I will deliver you no more. Go and cry to the gods whom you have chosen; let them deliver you in the time of your distress." And the Israelites said to the LORD, "We have sinned; do to us whatever seems good to you; but deliver us this day!" So they put away the foreign gods from among them and worshiped the LORD; and he could no longer bear to see Israel suffer. (Judg 10:11-16; cf. Ex 34:6-7)

Figure 7: **Divinely Empowered Heroes**

Like Judges, Homer's Iliad has divinely empowered heroes who win military engagements with divine support [e.g., I.510-530]. The beginning of the climactic battle is typical:

> In turn Zeus who gathers the clouds spoke . . . .
> all you others go down, wherever you may go
> among the Achaians and Trojans and give help
> to either side, as your own pleasure directs you.
> . . . and the gods went down to enter the
> fighting, with purposes opposed. Hera went to
> the assembled ships with Pallas Athene . . . .
> But Ares of the shining helm went over to the
> Trojans . . . [XX.19-40]

Unlike Homer's contending gods, of course, Judges' **Yahweh** has no rivals with whom to contend.

God is present in *charismatic* leaders like Joshua, Deborah, and Gideon. Thus, God promises Joshua to be with him as he was with Moses (Josh 1:5). Further, God empowers the judges with his spirit for war (e.g., 3:10; 11:29; 14:19).

Nevertheless, the mythic period is over. God speaks to Joshua directly and through Moses (e.g., Josh 20:2). Now, even the prophet has a mediator! Joshua hands on a prophetic tradition which distances God while making him known institutionally in the Mosaic Torah (institutional providence).

Although the judges are charismatics, the story does not often describe their interactions with God. Jephthah's vow and Samson's plaintive prayer are incredibly one-sided communications (Judg 11:30-31; 16:28-30). Only Gideon converses with God like Moses (6-7). Theophanies are rare (though see 2:1-5; 6-7; 10:11-14). Typically, the narrator, rather than characters, explains God's story-involvement (see 2:6-3:6; 10:16). In Judges, then, God is known in the heroes' charismatic actions, rather than in their speech. God is known **institutionally in holy war and in war prophet** (e.g., Deborah).

Human Characters: Deuteronomic Mythic Identity

Joshua and Judges **recast myth as history**. Their characters incarnate the Deuteronomic "two-ways" mythic identity and serve as mythic models. Joshua, his generation, and the judges choose to serve God. Achan and the Judges' people are faithless respectively in holy war and in henotheism. The faithful live at peace in the land. The apostate suffer oppression.

Apostasy's disastrous judgments present a sin-theodicy. If the Sinai-Wilderness narrative extends the mythic identity of Gen 3 to Israel, Joshua and Judges extend that same mythic identity into the land and into history.

The story presents this **theodicy** in a **pedagogical**, rather than retributive, fashion. God takes no delight in Israel's suffering (Judg

10:16). Further, God gives the people over to oppressors so that he may have them back. **Oppression teaches** them to return to God. As those who repent (cf. Deut 30:1-10; 1 Kings 8:27-53), they may provide models for apostate readers. Their characterization, then, creates a **rhetoric of repentance**.

Joshua and the Judges: War Prophets and Unlikely Heroes

The leaders succeed and replicate Moses. Joshua's appointment dramatizes his **Mosaic succession** (cf. Num 27:18-23; Deut 31:7-8; Josh 1:1-9). Like Moses, Joshua is a prophet. He has an immediate, charismatic relationship with God (e.g., Num 27:18; Deut 34:9; Josh 1:1-9; 3:7-8; 4:1-3; 6:1-5). As a result, he mediates between God and the people (cf. Josh 7 with Ex 32-34 and Num 13-14).

Unlike Moses, however, Joshua has a predecessor. Joshua, then, is the first in a line of institutional or **traditional prophets**. He passes on not only what he receives immediately from God, but also what he has received from Moses:

> And there, in the presence of the Israelites, Joshua
> wrote on the stones a copy of the law of Moses . . . .
> And afterward he read all the words of the law,
> blessings and curses . . . (Josh 8:32, 34).

From his commission (Josh 1:1-9) to his last words (23-24), then, Joshua calls the people to Mosaic henotheism (i.e., symbolizes faith).

Of the judges, Gideon most resembles Moses. Like Moses, Gideon is a reluctant hero whom God must persuade to his task with various signs (including the famous fleece, Judg 6:11-26; 36-40). Further, his henotheistic stand against Baal symbolizes Mosaic faith more clearly than any other judge (6:25-32). He calls Israel to be God's peculiar, separate people (cf. the anti-king bias in 8:22-23; 9).

Figure 8: **Women Warriors**

Charisma knows no gender boundaries. Deborah is the judge, not Barak, and Jael strikes the climactic, holy war blow (4:17-22). Nevertheless, these women warriors live in an *androcentric*, patriarchal world, so their status and victory surprises (4:9). These women warriors debunk male pride and highlight male (sexual) weaknesses (cf. Samson). As a result, one can read them as a deliberate subversion of cultural *patriarchy* (a feminist reading) or read a character's speech (Judg 4:9; Jdt 8:33) as an ironic deconstruction of the text's own standards. Such readings, however, minimize the text's rhetoric in favor of more modern ideologies. For the text, these heroines do not serve to advance modern feminism. Instead, these surprising, unlikely heroines (like the heroes) demonstrate the text's divine sovereignty ideology (cf. the apocryphal Judith).

In addition to their traditional Mosaic character, the heroes are also *charismatics*:

> The spirit of the LORD came upon him, and he judged Israel; he went out to war, and the LORD gave Cushan-rishathaim of Aram into his hand . . . (3:10; cf. 11:29)

That is, the judges are enthused. Filled with the divine, they enjoy military success (cf. Deut 31:3-6; Josh 6; 10-11) [see figure 7]. The judges, then, are war prophets who **embody the divine Warrior**. Charismatic military success defines the judges. Divine election, not their character, is important. Any, even prophetess and outlaw, can serve.

Even the Herculean Samson has great strength only when aligned with God. Dedicated by his parents as a "nazirite," Samson abstains from the fruit of the vine, razors, and corpses to symbolize his commitment to God (cf. Num 6; Judg 13:3-5). Although the vow is not prominent early, it dominates the story's end. Samson's long hair symbolizes his alignment with God (16:15-23). Shaved, Samson weakens for "the LORD had left him" (16:20). Not surprisingly, Samson winds up "eyeless in Gaza." His powers return only with his realignment with God (16:28) when "the hair of his head began to grow again . . ." (16:22).

Figure 9: **Iphigenia and Jephthah's Daughter**

In Aeschylus' Agamemnon, Agamemnon sacrifices his daughter (Iphigenia) to pacify an angry deity (Artemis) and gain success against Troy. His wife Clytemnestra murders him in vengeance upon his return from Troy. In Euripides' Iphigenia at Tauris , Artemis rescues Iphigenia by substituting a deer for her (cf. Gen 22). Compared to these stories and Gen 22, Jephthah's sacrifice troubles (Judg 11:29-40). Unlike Gen 22 and Agamemnon, it is not divinely motivated. Unlike Gen 22 and Iphigenia, it does not involve a divine rescue. Unlike Agamemnon, it does not trace the horrible consequences of the act. In short, it is the most morally laconic of these stories.

In addition to charisma, an **unlikely hero pattern** portrays the judges as divine agents (cf. 2:16-18). The Gideon story, for example, brings divine salvation through the weakest and least (6:15). In that story, God twice dramatically reduces Gideon's troops so that all will know that the victory is God's (7:1-8).

Deborah's deliverance is equally unlikely. After all, she is a heroine (war prophetess) in a patriarchal text [see figure 8]. She announces holy war and celebrates God's victory (5:1, 12; cf. Ex 15:21). Barak depends upon her for divine guidance. He does not have the spirit. Tellingly, a woman (Jael) strikes the decisive blow. Clearly, divine agency is at work (cf. Judg 4:15; 5:4-5).

Jephthah, too, is an unlikely hero (11:1-12:7). Ostracized by his family and reduced to banditry, he returns to champion his people at their request (11:6-11) and with divine empowerment (11:29). Little more than a outlaw, he serves God's purpose. Like Samson, however, Jephthah seems unaware of the divine presence. Despite the spirit's presence, he makes an unnecessary and unfortunate vow (11:30-31, 34-40).

Figure 10: **The Natural**

In Bernard Malamud's The Natural, a mysterious, seductive woman shoots Roy Hobbs (the natural) snatching his athletic career from him. Fifteen years later, Roy is a rookie sensation on a last-place team. When another seductress (Memo Paris) infatuates him, he falls into a slump. He returns to his natural form only when another mysterious woman (Iris) inspires him to be a hero. When he gorges himself at a party, Roy misses the end of the season. Released from bed to play in the playoff game, he throws the game for a bribe. The book ends with a boy imploring Roy, "Say it ain't true, Roy" (cf. Shoeless Joe Jackson).

Incidentally, the movie adaptation, starring Robert Redford, transforms Roy into a hero. In the movie, Roy overcomes Memo's poisoning (note the change from gluttony), rejects the bribe, and wins the game and Iris. While the movie destroys the hero's similarity to Samson, it retains a "vehicular" view of women.

Of the judges, only the Herculean Samson seems a likely hero. Surprisingly, then, Samson is Judges' most obvious failure. He alone suffers defeat (16:21-25). Instead of delivering his people, he brings greater trouble (15:9-13). After his death, the Philistine threat remains (1 Sam 4-6). In fact, Samson's tribe, Dan, ultimately migrated to the north to escape Philistine pressure (18). While noble, the penultimate line of his story contrasts with the report of successful battles in Joshua:

> So those he killed at his death were more than those
> he had killed during his life. (16:30)

Samson's tragic story is a powerful lesson for Israel (cf. Achan). Like Israel, he forgets his vows and repeatedly fails with foreign women (who symbolize apostasy; cf. Josh 23:12-16; Judg 3:5-6). But, like Israel, too, in the midst of suffering he remembers the source of his strength and returns to God (16:28).

ANET: Slaughtered Innocents

Joshua and Judges are bloody tales of imperialistic wars. Innocents are slaughtered everywhere.

For modern readers, war is not a holy ritual. Soldiers are not holy amateurs. The ban and devotion do not make modern, economic sense. The notion that ritual offenses contagiously debilitate is nonsense.

Achan's stoning is not so troublesome. After all, he has broken the rules. His family's stoning appalls, however. Modern individualism simply does not understand how one person's sin or righteousness effects another. Ancients, however, assumed such **contagion**. One's acts, particularly those of representative figures (fathers, priests, kings), can influence another. The entire cultic system depends upon the notion [see chap. 8]. Thus, God visits iniquity upon the third and fourth generations (Ex 34:7). Israel, then, must carefully remove all of Achan's contagion.

Further, the text understands Israel as a corporate entity, not as a group of independent individuals. The death of the wilderness generation does not prevent Israel from occupying the land. Thus, the death of thirty-six innocent soldiers is the logical consequence of Achan's sin. Wicked Israel cannot prosper. The stoning of Achan's family removes the debilitating contagion. Then, Israel proceeds to victory (Josh 7-8).

Figure 11: **Lebensraum ("Living Space") and the Other**

The Israelites moved into a land already occupied. According to their own traditions, they conducted a genocidal war to gain "living space." Peaceful co-existence was not an option. The inhabitants of the land were simply too **other**.

Similarly, Europeans immigrated to the Americas and displaced the natives. The Europeans, of course, justified their actions by appealing both to their **manifest destiny** and to the natives' otherness (savages, barbarians, red men). By the end of the nineteenth century, the European immigrants had reduced the native population to impoverished, disenfranchised remnants.

Until recently, Americans read this mythically as good's displacement of evil [e.g., in Westerns like the Howard Hughes trilogy starring John Wayne]. An increasingly pluralistic society has had difficulty maintaining that mythic security. Not surprisingly, a backlash has created a new popular myth of the good Indian and the bad settlers [cf. the recent movie, Geronimo]. Both perspectives, of course, are mythic simplifications reducing history's complexities to *ethical dualism* (us and the other).

Like Achan's family, **Jephthah's daughter** is a dependent, secondary character in a patriarchal society. Her father determines her life and death. Like Achan's family, Jephthah's daughter is a holy war casualty [see figure 9].

Apparently unaware of his spiritual empowerment (11:29), Jephthah makes an ill-considered vow. Given that vow, both Jephthah and his daughter act nobly. Neither attempts to evade the horrible oath (11:35-36). Like Abraham, Jephthah fulfills his religious duty. Unfortunately, no ram saves the daughter. Such notions of honor and religious duty are, of course, utterly foreign to the modern liberal. Fortunately, the modern reader may note that God did not demand the vow and that the Bible ultimately anathematizes child-sacrifice (Jer 7:31; Mic 6:6-8; Ps 106:37).

Figure 12: **Religious Attitudes Toward War**

Western religious groups have taken three different attitudes toward war: 1) **pacifism** (e.g., Christianity before Constantine); 2) **just war** (e.g., Augustine); and 3) the **crusade** (e.g., Joshua, the Crusades, and Islamic **jihad**) [Bainton, 14-15]. Pacifism withdraws from the world. The crusade attempts to dominate the world. The **just war** position requires critical interaction with the world. According to classical thinkers, for a war to be just, it must be **properly authorized** (by the state); have a **just cause and goal** (greater justice and peace); be **waged justly** (no atrocities); and have the reasonable expectation of reaching a **greater good** (procure more benefits than appeasement would) [cf. Bainton, 33-43].

The deaths of Achan's family and Jephthah's daughter pale beside Israel's slaughter of the land's inhabitants. Vilely, the text presents this violence as divinely mandated (e.g., Deut 7-9; 11; 20). Of course, various texts rationalize the slaughter [see figure 13].

The rationalizations, of course, reflect a **xenophobic, natural religion** for whom outsiders are humans only if they become part of

Israel (e.g., Rahab and the Gibeonites). Typically, outsiders are merely obstacles preventing imperialistic Israel from her living-space (cf. Josh 11:23). Not surprisingly, then, one can slaughter

> Figure 13: **Rationalizing Genocide**
>
> Texts explain Israel's occupation of Canaan as the result of the following:
>
> 1) an **ancestral curse** upon Ham/Canaan (Gen 9:22-27);
> 2) a divine **judgment** upon wickedness (Deut 9:1-6; Lev 18:24-28);
> 3) an attempt to **prevent** Israel from learning apostasy (Deut 20:17); and
> 4) God's **promise** to the ancestors (Deut 9:1-6).

outsiders with divine approval. Judges is slightly more moderate. It does not demand slaughter, but it does demand that Israel remain aloof [see figure 5]. Clearly, a closed, traditional society is trying to protect itself (or explain its disaster) [cf. chap. 8].

Unfortunately, such attitudes still persist [see figure 12]. Though modern intellectuals and politicians debate the justice of particular wars, "our side" is almost invariably the "just side" [see figure 14].

Fortunately, the Bible's own reflections ultimately deconstruct holy war. The divine sovereignty ideology will not brook any national pride as its rival (cf. Deut 9:5-6; chap. 8, figure 15]. Thus, the biblical story constantly makes even Israel stand before the "Judge of the whole earth." If Israel is a divine scourge in Joshua, she is the victim of other scourges in Judges and Kings.

Figure 14: **"The War Prayer"**

In Mark Twain's "The War Prayer," an aged stranger arrives at a patriotic church service to fulfill prayers for military victory if the worshipers can stand the results their prayers imply:

> O Lord our God, help us to tear their soldiers to
> bloody shreds with our shells; help us to cover
> their smiling fields with the pale forms of their
> patriot dead; help us to drown the thunder of
> their guns with the shrieks of the wounded,
> writhing in pain; help us to lay waste their
> humble homes with a hurricane of fire; help us
> to wring the hearts of their unoffending
> widows with unavailing grief; help us to turn
> them out roofless with their little children to
> wander unfriended the wastes of their
> desolated land in rags and hunger . . . . for our
> sakes who adore Thee, Lord . . . blight their
> lives . . . . We ask it, in the spirit of love . . .
> [220-21]

Review Questions

1. Apply the reading method of chaps. 3-4 to Joshua-Judges. List its genre, plot shape, conflict, depiction of God, mythic function, and ANE problems.

2. How does ancient history differ from modern [see chap. 4]? In what ways are Joshua and Judges similar to Deuteronomy?

3. Compare the story pattern and plot conflict of Joshua-Judges to that of the Sinai-Wilderness materials.

4. What is a holy war? What is the ban?

5. How are the judges unlikely heroes?

6. Why does God order the slaughter of the land's inhabitants and of Achan's family?

Figure 15: **Ruth (A Woman's Perspective?)**

In Ruth, an Israelite widow (Naomi) recovers male protection. Naomi and her foreign daughter-in-law (Ruth) return to Israel where Naomi plans (2) and Ruth executes (3) Boaz's seduction. After gaining the approval of a nearer kinsmen, Boaz marries Ruth who bears him a son (4:1-13). Thus, barren Naomi gains a son (4:13-17).

The barren woman fulfilled, like other such stories, assumes patriarchal codes (including the custom of levirate marriage; cf. Deut 25:5-10; Gen 38). This story does, however, follow the women's perspective, plight, and celebration. These women are not mere vehicles, but Boaz is.

Interestingly, Ruth is also less xenophobic than Joshua-Judges. Like Rahab, Ruth is included in Israel and her son (Obed) is one of David's ancestors. Ruth is not, however, completely open to outsiders. The Moabitess must become part of Israel, and, despite the work's name, the story is far more concerned with the Israelite Naomi (her barrenness and son, 4:14-17) than the Moabite Ruth.

Suggestions for Alternate Reading and Reflection

1. How do Josh 1:1-9 and 23-24 provide closure for the book? How do they connect Joshua to Deuteronomy and to the Former Prophets?

2. Compare Josh 11:20 with the "hardening" of Pharaoh's heart.

3. Compare Josh 13-21 with the Genesis genealogies in terms of literary and mythic function.

4. What is the point of Josh 22 and Judg 17-18? Do they have any relation to Deut 12?

5. Compare Joshua's covenant renewal (23-24) with the founding

of the covenant (Ex 19-20; 24). Who speaks? How is God portrayed? Is Joshua's covenant more focused (in terms of demands)?

6. Do the stories of the judges entertain as well as exhort? What features might be entertaining? Is there suspense? Is there comedy? Can you find any macabre, sexual, or scatological humor in the Ehud tale (3:12-30)? Does the Samson story have elements of low comedy (slapstick)?

7. Compare the sacrifice of Jephthah's daughter and that of Isaac (Gen 22). Who initiates the action? Who speaks? Does the Jephthah story differ from Gen 22 in narration (showing and telling)? What is the narrator's perspective on Jephthah's sacrifice? Why is the narrator's perspective clearer in Gen 22? Who is nobler: Abraham, Isaac, Jephthah, or the daughter?

8. Compare the characterization of women in the Deborah story (Judg 4-5), Judith, Ruth, and the Samson story (Judg 13-16). Are any palatable to modern feminism?

9. What is the genre of Judith and Ruth? Is it similar to that of the stories of the judges? Compare fiction and *legend*.

10. Compare the holy war ideology in Joshua-Judges with Hitler's imperialistic desire for German **Lebensraum**. With European settlement of the Americas.

11. What is the relationship of religion and violence? Does violence ever have religious sanction? Is violence ever justifiable religiously? Do some violent acts offend more than others? Which is less offensive: the death of the Egyptian firstborn (and/or the drowning of the Egyptians) or the slaughter of the land's inhabitants? The sacrifice of Isaac or of Jephthah's daughter?

For Further Reading

On the Deuteronomic History, see Cross, Canaanite, 274-89; Ackroyd, "Historical," 300-05; Noth, Deuteronomistic; and Weinfeld.

On war in Israel, see Ringgren, Israelite, 53-54; Pope,

"Devoted," in Buttrick, 1:838-39; Rad, Der heilige; and Lind.   On God as Holy Warrior and the slaughter command, see G. Ernest Wright, Deuteronomy, 2:327-28, 390-92.

On war prophets, see Blenkinsopp, History, 61-68.

On religion and violence, see Bainton; Girard, Violence; and **idem**, Scapegoat.

On the Baal cults, see Anderson, Understanding, 184-93; Pritchard, 129-55; Albright, Yahweh; Cross, Canaanite; and Mark Smith.

On the religion of agrarian empires, see Ellwood, 41-42, 52-60; and Bellah, "Evolution," 24-35.

On charisma, see Weber, Theory, 358; Parrinder, "Charisma," in Eliade, ER, 3:218-22; and Wilson, Prophecy, 21-134.

On Judith, see Nickelsburg, Jewish, 105-09.

On Ruth, see Rauber; Hals; Niditch, "Legends"; and Sasson.

CHAPTER 10

THE COMING OF THE KING
1-2 Samuel

Introduction: Relationship to the Former Prophets

In Judges, the apostasy cycle threatens the people's future in the land. Samuel postpones the loss of the land through the new story of the coming of the king.

Genre: Realistic, Ancient History

Samuel is an ancient history which unabashedly depicts the monarchy's establishment as a divine act. It is **propaganda for the Davidic dynasty**, not a modern, scholarly research report detailing as objectively as possible "what really happened" [cf. chap. 4, genre]. Nevertheless, modern scholars judge portions of 1-2 Samuel (e.g., the "Succession Narrative" in 2 Sam 9-20) to be *realistic* history.

They do so because the Deuteronomic perspective (which dominates Judges and Kings) is far less obvious here (though see 1 Sam 8-12). Further, in this story, God is only indirectly involved [see God]. As a result, the story is **less pedantic** and more natural. Human emotions, ambitions, and purposes appear to move the story (Saul's jealousy, David's ambition and lust, palace intrigues). Of course, as this is **biblical realism** [see chap. 3, atmosphere], narrative comments reveal the divine control hidden behind this human world (e.g., 1 Sam 16; 2 Sam 7; 12).

Story Content: The Coming of the King

First Samuel begins with the story of Samuel's miraculous birth (1-3). Despite this auspicious beginning, leaders (Eli's sons) oppress God's people. Further, the Philistines successfully campaign against Israel, and Israel loses the ark of the covenant (4-5). After God restores the ark (5-6) and Samuel defeats the Philistines (7), the **people demand a king** (8:5).

At this point, one story strand describes **the king as apostasy** (8:7; cf. 8:20; 10:17-27; Judg 8-9) and details the monarchy's future horrors (8:9-18; 12; cf. Deut 17:14-20). Another strand, however, presents Saul as a charismatic holy war prophet, not unlike Samuel (9:1-10:16; 11). Several holy war indiscretions (13-15), however, move Saul away from Samuel and God (e.g., 15:35). Not surprisingly, God chooses and empowers a new king, David (16).

The second half of 1 Samuel (17-31) describes **Saul's fall and David's inexorable rise** (cf. 16:13-14). Not surprisingly, the jealous, fearful Saul attempts to kill David personally (18:10-11; 19:8-10), through his family and servants (19:1-17), and through the Philistines (18:17-29). These attempts are, of course, against the Lord's anointed. David, by contrast, twice refuses to raise his hand against the Lord's anointed (24; 26). While Saul struggles to save his lost kingdom, David, the king "after God's own heart" (13:14), waits calmly for God.

First Samuel ends in **disaster**. Facing holy war without prophet and God (28:6), Saul seeks divine revelation illegitimately. That message, however, forecasts the Philistines' victory over Saul and Israel (28:15-19). First Samuel, thus, begins and ends with a Philistine victory. Meanwhile, David becomes an outlaw (25) and a Philistine vassal (27; 29).

Second Samuel opens with **a dirge** (1:17-27). Israel is broken, defeated, and divided. **David becomes king over Judah**, but one of Saul's sons rules Israel from exile. Quickly, however, treason and assassination dispatch Saul's son (2-4) and bring David to the throne (5). Impressive military victories (5:7-15; 8; 10-13; 21:15-22) and political and religious centralization (5:6-16; 6-7) solidify David's reign. More importantly, a prophet announces that **God has promised David an everlasting dynasty**. Thus, divine legitimizations (1 Sam 16 and 2 Sam 7:8-16) enclose David's reign.

The story, however, is hardly over. The **identity of David's son-successor** is not yet disclosed. Further, indiscretions embroil David in **family and political turmoil**.

Impregnating Bathsheba, David murders her husband Uriah to cover up the sin (11). When the prophet Nathan accuses David, he repents; nevertheless, the child dies and David's family begins to trouble him (12) [see God]. After a family triangle involving rape and murder (13), David's son Absalom gathers an army of malcontents and drives David from Jerusalem (15-16). Clever intelligence (17) and David's army (18) save his kingdom, but not his son (cf. 18:33-19:8). Restoration programs, then, fan tribal animosity into a new revolt (19-20). Once again, however, the army preserves David's kingdom. In addition to these wars, David also faces famine (21) and plague (24).

David, however, successfully navigates these troubles through his continuing relationship with God (see 12; 24). In contrast to Saul's suicide, David's story ends with praise (22), remembrance of the divine promise (23), and repentance (24). The story ends, however, with David's **succession undecided** (see 1 Kings 1-2). He has lost son after son to divine judgment, to fratricidal murder, and to revolt.

Story Pattern: The Davidic Order

The story of David and his dynasty resembles ancient hero quests. Separated from his family by the divine choice (1 Sam 16),

David goes through a series of trials (1 Sam 17-31) before establishing himself and his dynasty as Israel's new order (2 Sam 7). The story, of course, is no mere secular hero tale. God's choices bookend David (1 Sam 16; 2 Sam 7). Further, the

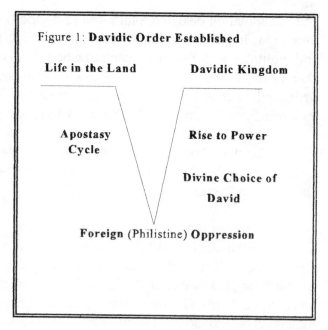

Figure 1: **Davidic Order Established**

Life in the Land   **Davidic Kingdom**

Apostasy Cycle   **Rise to Power**

Divine Choice of David

Foreign (Philistine) **Oppression**

lengthy Samuel preface (1 Sam 1-16) connects both Saul and David to earlier story. That connection and the divine election make the kingdom a new Eden.

Plot Conflict: The Legitimacy of the King

The story's major conflict concerns the king's theological and political legitimacy. Theologically, **is the king apostasy** (1 Sam 8; 12) **or is the king a divine gift** (1 Sam 16; 2 Sam 7)? Politically, is Saul or David the legitimate king? Which son will succeed David? Stories with such conflicts are **myth wars** [see chap. 3, plot conflict]. They identify God's designated agents.

Despite its apostate beginnings (1 Sam 8-15), **God's election** of David and his dynasty settles the monarchy's theological legitimacy (1 Sam 16; 2 Sam 7). David's political legitimacy (over Saul) depends on the juxtaposition of his positive portrayal (spirit, faith) with Saul's negative portrayal (evil spirit, estranged from God).

Other than the allusive "Jedidiah," the identity of David's successor is little more than the fact that Solomon is the last son left standing when the horrors of David's troubles pass (though see 1 Kings 1-11).

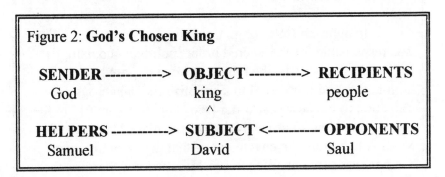

Figure 2: **God's Chosen King**

Myth: **Chartering the Davidic State**

Samuel is the founding story chartering the Davidic state (cf. Torah). As such, it provides a new mythic identity for Israel. Now, the people are **the people of the king**.

Here, the king is the sacred's vehicle. The king acts as holy warrior, as prophet (1 Sam 10:9-13; 11:6; 16:13), and as a priest (2 Sam 6:12-19; 7; 1 Kings 8:1-9:9). In particular, however, the king as king bestows sacred benefits of peace (1 Sam 11:13; 2 Sam 7:10-11), justice (2 Sam 23:3-4), and righteousness:

> His authority shall grow continually,
>   and there shall be endless peace
> for the throne of David and his kingdom.
> He will establish and uphold it with justice and with
>   righteousness from this time onward and forevermore.
>   (Isa 9:7)

The king **administers God's order**, a sacred biosphere. As a result, the king represents God, and some texts even name him "**the son of**

God" (2 Sam 7:14; cf. Isa 9:6; Ps 2; 89; etc.).

Figure 3: **Sacred Kings**

In agrarian states (e.g., Canaanite city-states), the king was responsible for the sacred order (political and natural). In New Year festivals, the king was often deposed, humiliated, and reinvested to symbolize the dangerous transition to the new year/order [see chap. 9, figure 6]. In the Babylonian New Year Festival, the king played the role of Marduk in a dramatic enactment of that god's victory over Tiamat/chaos [see chap. 5, figure 1]. The king-Marduk, then, made a dramatic procession to a temple where a sacred-marriage took place (fertility ritual) [see Livingston, 123-25]. While Israel probably did not have such a ritual, she did have enthronement ceremonies which similarly stressed the king's responsibilities for order (cf. e.g., Ps 2; 47; 93; 96-99).

In the ANE, then, the king was a supra-human person. In ritual and formal address, the king was "the son of God" (e.g., Ps 2:7; 89:26-27) or even god (cf. Ps 45:6) [for examples, see Ringgren, Religions, 37-39, 101-02, 170-72]. Israelite monotheism probably understood such language in terms of adoption. For other ancient states (e.g., Egypt), the king was actually divine.

This king myth dramatically changes Israel's story. This myth justifies a state "like the other nations," rather than a "covenant-people" organized tribally and charismatically. This new myth stands **in tension with Torah** because it has a different understanding of God and the people. In the Hexateuch, God overthrows kings to bring his people from slavery to land. In the land, God establishes a tribal covenant-people led by temporary charismatics. By contrast, in 1-2 Samuel, God establishes a permanent, hierarchical kingdom which threatens to become oppressive (cf. 1 Sam 8:10-18).

Figure 4: **Liberals vs. Conservatives**

The Bible contains stories celebrating God's liberation of his people from oppressive kings (e.g., the exodus) and stories celebrating the establishment of hierarchical orders (e.g., creation, Sinai, and David). Despite the claims of recent egalitarians, then, the Bible is not uniformly for the disenfranchised and oppressed [see chap. 7, figure 6]. In fact, the Bible is not wholly in support of any modern ideology, conservative or progressive.

Selective readings which argue otherwise miss the necessary interplay between **tradition and reform** which is the warp and woof of religion. Living religions thrive on the conflict between institution (established myth-ritual complex) and charisma (prophetic or mystic insight-imagination). Lasting religion requires both the priest to superintend tradition and the prophet to create new metaphors.

One should be wary, then, of a conservative or liberal Bible. Biblical literature and its reading is inexorably contextual. Created and read in situations of exile and frustration, the Bible is for the poor and oppressed. In natural religion settings, it is for the successful and the hierarchical status quo.

Not surprisingly, then, 1-2 Samuel only gradually legitimizes the king. Slowly, the story shows David to be God's choice and the man "after God's own heart" (charisma, faith). To this end, the story bears **structural similarities to the earlier traditions**.

Like the Hexateuch, the David story begins with **election and promise**. In fact, David is **a new Abraham**. As God promised Abraham land, descendants, and a blessing, he now promises David a place (rest), a house (dynasty), and a great name (cf. Gen 12:1-3 with 2 Sam 7:8-16).

Further, like all previous leaders, David stands **under the divine demand**. He (and all other kings) stands constantly under divine (prophetic) critique (2 Sam 12; 21; cf. 1 Sam 13-15). Further, despite "everlasting" promises, the Deuteronomic two-ways clearly conditionalizes this promise (1 Sam 12:14-15; 1 Kings 2:1-4):

> Then the LORD will establish his word that he spoke concerning me: "If your heirs take heed to their way, to walk before me in faithfulness with all their heart and soul, there shall not fail you a successor on the throne of Israel." (1 Kings 2:4)

This condition connects the king to the land myth intimately and subjects the quite mortal king to Israel's true divine Sovereign. The king comes and goes at the divine pleasure.

Divine Character: The Hidden Sovereign

This nationalistic Orderer is not as obvious a part of the story as previous orderers (cf. creation and Sinai). The narrator does, however, often comment on divine activity.

Figure 5: **Narrative Reports about God's Story-Involvement**

1 Sam 1:5; 2:12, 17, 21, 25, 26; 3:1-14, 19, 21; 5-6; 7:10, 13; 8:7-9, 22; 9:15, 17; 10:10, 22; 11:6, 7; 12:18; 14:23; 15:10-11, 35; 16:1-3, 7, 12, 13-14, 23; 18:10, 12, 15, 28; 19:9, 20-23; 23:14; 25:38; 26:12; 2 Sam 5:10; 6:7; 7:1; 8:6, 14; 11:27-12:1; 12:15, 24-25; 17:14; 23:10, 12; 24:1, 15-17, 25

Figure 6: **Narrative Engendering Speech**

Reference	Speaker	Announcement
	1 Samuel	
2:27-36	man of God	judgment on Eli's house
3:10-14	Samuel	judgment on Eli's house
3:19-4:1	Samuel	general oracles
8:6-18	Samuel	oppressive kings
9:6	Samuel	truth of his oracles
9:15-17	Samuel	Saul to be king
10:1-8	Samuel	signs for Saul
11:6-7	Saul?	holy war
12:14-25	Samuel	two-ways
13:13-14	Samuel	end of Saul's kingdom
14:6-12	Jonathan?	holy war
15:1-3	Samuel	holy war
15:10, 17-31	Samuel	rejection of Saul
16:1-13	Samuel	David as king
17:45-47	David?	holy war
22:5	Gad	flight from Saul
28:15-19	Samuel	Saul's defeat and reject
	2 Samuel	
7:4-16	Nathan	Davidic dynasty
12:7-14	Nathan	Domestic troubling
12:25	Nathan	Jedidah
23:1-7	David	Everlasting dynasty
24:11-19	Gad	Judgment on David

Prophetic speech also indicates God's involvement. In fact, prophetic speech engenders ensuing narrative (as divine speech did in Genesis and Exodus) [see figure 6]. At least, half of these speeches belong to Samuel who dominates 1 Sam 1-16. This section, then, has a **prophetic conception of providence**. Only Samuel knows and reveals God's purposes (cf. 3:14; 28).

In fact, both Saul and David know their election only through Samuel (1 Sam 9-11; 16). Unlike previous rulers, then, the king depends upon another (the prophet) far more than previous heroes have (though cf. the priestly, 1 Sam 23:10-12; 30:7-8; and prophetic David, 2 Sam 24).

In the Saul story, God is more **horribly indirect**. He refuses to answer Saul (28:6) and harries him with an evil spirit (16:14-23; 18:10; 19:9; 19:20-23?). God becomes Saul's tormenter (16:15) and enemy (28:16). Terribly, God is **both absent yet malevolently present**.

Figure 7: **Tragedy and the Bible**

On several occasions, biblical literature comes quite close to *tragedy*. Many characters (e.g., Adam, Israel, and Saul) have glorious beginnings, swift reversals, and **horrible ends**. Their fall, however, is not according to some **error in judgment** as Aristotle's classic discussion of tragedy prescribes [see his Poetics]. Instead, these stories are *melodramas*, in which the hero receives his just desserts.

Both tragedy and biblical melodrama (sin plots) defend order by excluding the fallen hero. Tragic rhetoric aims at inducing pity and fear. Biblical rhetoric aims at inducing **repentance**, at aligning the reader with the story-God. Biblical story, then, typically moves from tragedy to a **larger divine comedy**. Stories do not end with Adam outside Eden or Saul slain on Gilboa. They press on to new Edens and new kings.

In the **realistic Succession Narrative** (2 Sam 9-20), God is less clearly involved. Human ambitions and machinations dominate. Narrative comments are strikingly rare (but see 17:14). When David seemingly escapes unscathed from his murder of Uriah, however, the narrator comments tellingly: "But the thing that David had done displeased the LORD, and the LORD sent Nathan to David" (2 Sam 11:27-12:1).

This rare revelation into the divine mind suddenly sets David's story in the context of the divine sovereignty. Nathan's subsequent oracle (12:7-14) engenders narrative and provides subsequent narrative a sacred heading or context (as 1 Sam 16 does for 17-31).

Figure 8: **Nathan's Oracle**

2 Sam 12:7-14	**Later Narrative**
constant warfare	revolts (15-20)
domestic troubles	rape, murder, revolt (13-19)
wives to another	to Absalom (16:22)
death of child	12:18
Jedidiah	1 Kings 1-2

God's provision of a Davidic successor remains allusively hidden, however. Although Nathan names Bathsheba's second son "Jedidiah," "the beloved of the LORD" (2 Sam 12:24-25), the nature of God's favor is not clear. Is he beloved because, unlike his brother, he survived, or does "beloved" mark him as David's successor?

Later, Nathan and Bathsheba conspire to put Jedidiah-Solomon on the throne. Their plot depends upon Adonijah's hasty, offensive assumption of kingly status and upon David's (unnarrated) promise that Solomon would have the throne. Not even Nathan refers to "Jedidiah." Only the defeated Adonijah refers to Solomon's enthronement as God's act:

> You know that the kingdom was mine, and that all
> Israel expected me to reign; however, the kingdom

> has turned about and become my brother's, for it was
> his from the LORD. (1 Kings 2:15)

God's sovereignty, then, is hidden behind the machinations. Only later story makes it transparent (1 Kings 3-11).

Figure 9: **Depicting Sacred Providence**

Direct	**Prophetic**	Institutional	**Indirect**	**Estranged**
	Moses, Samuel		Joseph, David	Saul
		Judges		

Human Characters: Samuel, The Prophetic King-Maker

Samuel is a judge (cf. the typical judge-cycle in 1 Sam 7:2-17). In fact, he is Samson's successful "double." His birth story (with barren mother, prayer, and nazirite vow) strikingly resembles Samson's (Judg 13). Unlike Samson, however, he keeps his nazirite vow and is successful against the Philistines.

Except for 7:10-11, Samuel is involved in war only as its prophet (cf. Deborah). Thus, he offers sacrifice (7:9; 13:8-14; 15:32-33), intercedes (7:5, 9), and provides prophetic oracles (15:1-3; 28:15-19). As a prophet, Samuel has an intimate relationship with God (3:1-4:1). He provides people and kings with God's oracles [see figure 6]. He represents God. To reject Samuel is to reject God (8:7; 13; 15). He makes kings for God (9-10; 16). Samuel also symbols faith. Thus, his last testament calls the people to the Deuteronomic two-ways (12).

Samuel, however, is a **new kind of prophet** (cf. 9:9). With the monarchy, the prophet no longer dominates the story (or the civil order). The king story leaves the prophet on the periphery. Now, the prophet appears only to proclaim oracles which do, however, reveal the story's meaning (cf. 2 Sam 7; 12; 24). The prophetic appearances, then, are theophanies.

Saul: The Rejected King

Saul, too, is a **charismatic war prophet** (1 Sam 9-11). The spirit possesses him (10:6, 10-13; 11:6; 19:23-24) empowering him to military success (11:6-15). Saul, however, comes to a bad end. He dies alone, cut off from Samuel (9:15-17; 11:7) and God (28). Without divine support, Saul loses to the Philistines and dies a suicide (31).

While this story-shape resembles *tragedy* [see figure 7], it is only a part of a larger comedy, the establishment of the divine monarchy. After 1 Sam 16, David is the story center. To make the story tragic, one would have to isolate Saul from his larger context [see Humphreys, "Tragedy"]. Further, the story is not tragic because the *melodrama* traces Saul's fall to his sin. Saul's sins are holy war offenses. He usurps Samuel's priestly prerogative (13), fails to fulfill a vow (14; contrast Jephthah), and fails to observe the ban (15; cf. Achan). Such violations are, of course, suicidal presumption for holy warriors. Not surprisingly, both prophet and the Holy Warrior desert Saul (15; 28). Saul becomes non-elect:

> For rebellion is no less a sin than divination,
>   and stubbornness is like iniquity and idolatry.
> Because you have rejected the word of the LORD,
>   he has also rejected you from being king. (15:23)

The subsequent loss of the spirit, the troubling evil spirit (16:13-16), sealed heavens (28), defeat, and suicide (31) are anti-climactic.

Figure 10: **King Arthur**

In the English-speaking world, Arthur is the legendary "once and future king." Arthur is an unlikely hero who takes a sword from a stone and, thereby, ascends to the throne. Although he unites England and defends her from external aggression, his court is beset by adultery, murder, and intrigue (cf. the story of Lancelot and Guinevere, Arthur's wife). While this story has some formal similarity to that of David, **chivalric codes** dominate the Arthurian legends: the knightly quest for purity (Galahad), the struggle against temptation, the nobility of lords and ladies, and courtly love.

This world-view is not present in the David story. One can hardly imagine David and Bathsheba struggling against temptation or taking holy orders. Further, unlike David, Arthur is a noble character above the fray and above evil. In particular, he cannot see "evil" (the relationship of Guinevere and Lancelot). Arthur is finally mortally wounded in battle. The sword is returned to the lake; a barge carries Arthur away to Avalon; and Lancelot and Guinevere take holy orders. Despite this end, of course, the hope of a new "Arthur" continues [see figure 11].

David: Once, and Future King

David is **Saul's opposite**. David is not presumptuous, but faithful and repentant. David is not rejected, but eternally chosen.

While Saul is an imposing, kingly figure (9:2), even David's father (Jesse) cannot imagine that David would be king (16:1-13). Later, he is not thought "fit" for battle by family, by Saul, or by his opponent Goliath (17). Ominously, he cannot wear the protective armor. David's unlikeliness, however, bespeaks the true divine hero:

This very day the LORD will deliver you into my hand . . . so that all the earth may know that there is a God in Israel, and that all this assembly may know that God does not save by sword and spear; for the battle is the LORD's . . . (17:46-47)

Figure 11: **The Messiah**

When reigning kings fell below the Davidic standard and when new kings were enthroned (cf. the enthronement psalms and oracles), "David" augured a hopeful future. When crisis threatened the kingdom and when the kingdom fell, some turned these hopes into the promise of a new king (e.g., Isa 2:1-4; 9:2-7; 11:1-9). Scholars refer to such hopes as **messianic** expectation. The **Messiah** is literally the "anointed one." In the HB itself, the term always refers to a present ruler (or official), not to a future hope. Some later interpreters, however, read various OT passages as messianic (e.g., Ps 2; 2 Sam 7; Isa 7; 9; 11; Zech 9).

Messianic interpretations are prominent in Christianity (Messiah appears only twice in the Mishnah). **Christos** is, of course, the Greek form of the Hebrew Messiah. Jesus the Christ is, then, Jesus the Messiah, the expected future king [cf. Handel's famous musical]. NT References to son of David and son of God are, of course, also messianic. When Christianity moved into the Greek-speaking world, however, Christ became a part of Jesus' name.

Even after Goliath, David remains an **unlikely hero** because Saul remains on the throne. David, however, remains faithful. He relies upon God and becomes king against impossible odds. Harried by Saul (27:1), forced into the wilderness, reduced to an outlaw existence (25), relegated to Philistine servitude (27; 29), and facing rival claimants to the throne (2 Sam 1-4), David rises to the throne. His rejection of violence against Saul symbolizes his **faith**:

"Do not destroy him; for who can raise his hand against the LORD's anointed, and be guiltless?" David said, "As the LORD lives, the LORD will strike him down; or his day will come to die; or he will go down into battle and perish. The LORD forbid that I should raise my hand against the LORD's anointed . . ." (1 Sam 26:9-11; cf. 24:6-7, 9-15)

David waits (cf. 2 Sam 1-4).

As king, David is faithful, despite **his sins**. Convinced of sin, he **repents** and entrusts himself to God's judgment and mercy (2 Sam 12; 24). Not surprisingly, then, he is the king "after God's own heart" (1 Sam 13:14). He is God's own king (16:1). In fact, he becomes the "once, and future king." God establishes his dynasty (2 Sam 7:4-16; 23:1-7). Further, he becomes **the standard** by which later kings are judged [see chap. 11]. When the kingdom fails, he becomes a symbol for **a new king**.

ANET: Davidic Propaganda

Modern readers may see Saul's fall and David's rise as little more than Davidic propaganda. After all, Saul's offenses are petty ritualistic matters compared to David's heinous offenses (adultery and murder). Further, both Saul and David repent. Of course, Saul's repentance goes unheeded, while David's is accepted (cf. 1 Sam 15:24-31; 2 Sam 12:13).

A modern novelist might add clarifying "inside views" which would justify the different fates of Saul and David. Biblical story's "showing" characterization does not work in this way [see chap. 4, narrator]. For biblical style and ideology, **election** is a sufficient explanation of David's success and Saul's failure.

The story, however, rationalizes Saul's fall (and, hence, David's rise) with **holy war ideology**. Saul's indiscretions (1 Sam

13-15) dramatize his rebellion (15:23). He attempts to stand alone, without Samuel and God. In a holy war context, this is presumptuous folly and meets a deserved end. By contrast, David remains a man of faith. Despite prophetic promises of kingship, he will not raise his hand against the Lord's anointed. He waits upon God [see David].

Review Questions

1. Apply the reading method of chaps. 3-4 to 1-2 Samuel. List its genre, plot shape, conflict, depiction of God, mythic function, and ANE problems.

2. Is 1-2 Samuel better history than Judges? Why or why not?

3. Is the king apostasy or divine gift? What passages support each position? What settles the issue?

4. How does the king myth change Israel's story?

5. How does 1-2 Samuel reconcile the David and land stories?

6. Describe the conception of providence in the Saul story and in the story of David's succession. What is the literary function of Nathan's oracle in 2 Sam 12:7-14?

7. How does Samuel differ from earlier prophets?

8. Is Saul a tragic figure?

9. How does the text rationalize the divine preference for David?

10. How is David the "future king"?

Suggestions for Alternate Reading and Reflection

1. Compare Samuel (1 Sam 2-7) to Samson (Judg 13-16). What biblical patterns do both stories use?

2. How does 1 Sam 4-6 demonstrate that the Philistine victory is not a divine defeat? How does 1 Sam 28-31 indicate that the last victory is not a divine defeat?

3. What is the "Deuteronomic" interpretation of the king (see Deut 17:14-20; 1 Sam 8:9-18; 12)?

4. How are Samuel, Saul, and David like the judges? How do they differ?

5. Compare Saul's holy war indiscretions to the depiction of Achan (Josh 7) and Jephthah (Judg 11-12). Do their depictions make it easier to understand Saul's rejection?

6. Contrast Saul's end in 1 Sam 28 and 31 with that of David in 2 Sam 23-24.

7. Is David a divine choice or an astute politician (cf. 1 Sam 23-25; 26-27; 29-30; 2 Sam 1-4)?

8. How does the Davidic monarchy compare to ANE monarchies?

9. Was pre-monarchical Israel an egalitarian society?

10. Compare the Bible and tragedy.

11. Why did Israel develop a messianic hope? Did all Israelites (or Jews) have such a hope?

For Further Reading

For commentaries on 1-2 Samuel, see Hertzberg; and McCarter.

On ancient history, see chap. 4 and the bibliography there; Aune, NT, 77-115; Veyne, 5-15; Miller and Hayes, 54-79; Harvey, The Historian, 14-19; and Van Seters, Search.

On the different attitudes to the monarchy and possible literary sources, see Birch.

On David and Abraham as important characters for the Yahwist, see Humphreys, Crisis, 78-88; Brueggemann, "Yahwist"; Clements, Abraham; and Van Seters, Abraham. If the hypothesis were correct, the Yahwist's propaganda for David would resemble Eusebius' legitimation of Constantine's empire.

On the Messiah, see Jenni; Rivkin; Mowinckel, He; Horsley and Hanson, 88-134; and Charlesworth, Messiah. For relevant texts from late Judaism and early Christianity, see Nickelsburg and Stone, 161-201.

On kings and sacred orders, see Ellwood, 41-42, 57-60;

Bellah, "Evolution"; Szikszai; Humphreys, <u>Crisis</u>, 60-72; Ringgren, <u>Israelite</u>, 220-38; **idem**; <u>Religions</u>, 36-42, 99-107, 169-73; Mowinckel, <u>He</u>, 21-95; and J. P. M. Walsh, 1-32.

On Samuel the prophet, see Blenkinsopp, <u>History</u>, 60, 64-66.

On Saul and tragedy, see Humphreys, "Tragedy"; **idem**, <u>Tragic</u>, 23-66.

CHAPTER 11

THE KINGDOM
1-2 Kings

Relationship to the Former Prophets

In 1-2 Kings, the Deuteronomic two-ways perspective stands in judgment of the kings. When **the kings apostasize**, the land and the kingdom are lost. The king story, then, only temporarily saves the land story from its forecast end (cf. Deut 29-30). This double loss gives the Former Prophets a tragic shape.

Content: The Road to Ruin

Although Solomon succeeds David through palace intrigue (1-2), his visions, wisdom, and prosperity (3-4) identify him as David's promised heir (cf. 8:15-26 with 2 Sam 7). After Solomon builds a temple for God (5-9), he also **builds foreign sanctuaries for his many wives** (11:1-8). God, then, takes Israel from the family of David, leaving them only Judah and Benjamin (12).

Israel apostasizes immediately (12:19, 25-33). Jeroboam, her first king, builds questionable worship-centers, so prophets predict the demise of king, family, and Israel (13-14). The road to ruin, however, is long. Many kings separate the prophetic threat and its fulfillment.

In Israel, the war between the Omride dynasty and the prophets is a definitive moment. Ahab, Omri's son, and Jezebel, Ahab's Tyrian wife, sponsor the worship of Baal (16:29-33). Elijah, **Yahweh's prophet**, responds with a drought and a fertility contest between **Yahweh** and Baal (17-18). When **Yahweh** wins, Elijah has to flee Jezebel's wrath. At the wilderness mountain, **Yahweh** commissions Elijah to appoint successors for himself and Ahab (19).

When Jezebel has an Israelite murdered to acquire a vineyard for Ahab, Elijah consigns Ahab and Jezebel to carrion-dogs. Ahab's **repentance postpones ruin** yet again (21). Nevertheless, as prophetically predicted, Ahab does soon die despite his best efforts at security (22).

When Elijah vanishes, Elisha succeeds him as prophet, miracle-worker, and anti-Omride (2 Kings 2-8). Fulfilling Elijah's commission, Elisha appoints Jehu king (8:7-15; 9). Jehu's bloody revolution finally dispatches Jezebel, temporarily ousts Baal, founds Jehu's dynasty in Israel, and leads to bloody revolutions in Judah as well (10-12).

Despite the **prophetic revolution**, apostasy continues. After Jehu's dynasty ends (15:9-12), Israel catapults toward ruin. Her succession of short-lived kings ends with the **Assyrian conquest** (17). Interestingly, this end is primarily Deuteronomic comment, not "objective" report.

Ominously, Judah and her wicked king Ahaz are also apostate (16; a foreign altar). Judah, however, does not fall. Instead, Hezekiah's faith and repentance leads to miraculous deliverances (18-20). The Babylonians are already on the scene, however (20:12-19); and the apostasy of the next king (Manasseh) condemns Judah to Babylonian imperialism (21).

Josiah's reforms, following the dictates of a recently found book of Moses (22-23; Deuteronomy?), postpone disaster. Nevertheless, a series of kings falls to Egypt (23:31-37) and, then, Babylon (24-25). Babylon twice deports citizens and, on the second occasion, **destroys Jerusalem and the temple**. The narrator reports painfully: "So Judah went into exile out of its land" (25:21). As Kings ends, survivors flee to Egypt (25:22-26), and the remaining Davidic descendant remains in Babylonian custody (25:27-30).

Genre and Style: Catalogues and Morals

Kings, like the rest of the Former Prophets, belongs to the genre of **ancient history**. Not surprisingly, given these generic conventions, Kings is both realistic and moralistic.

Figure 1: **Ancient, Moralistic Histories**

Herodotus' The History (or The Persian Wars) explains the enmity between the Persians and the Greeks [1.1-5]. Herodotus has a moral. Humans should beware **hubris** (cf. Greek tragedies) and resign themselves to their fate. As a result, a repetitive, tragic pattern dominates his history. Kings who ignore wise counsel and oracles against arrogant imperialism come to bad ends [e.g., Croesus, 1. 53-54, 73, 86-87, 91; Cyrus, 1.207; Xerxes, 7-9].
Thucydides' History of the Peloponnesian War foregoes divine interventions in favor of a more modern, objective report [cf. his famous description of the plague, 2.48-53]. He also foregoes moralism in favor of a **Realpolitik** (cf. Machiavelli). For Thucydides, Athens lost her empire because of bad leadership, bad advice, and a failure of nerve. not because of fate or sin.   Athens failed to defend her empire wisely and without pity [e.g., 2.63; 3:37, 40].

Even though each king is not a Deuteronomic model, Kings catalogues each king (e.g., 1 Kings 16; 2 Kings 15) according to a set formula:

1) ancestry, age, date (according to opposing king);
2) story elements;
3) Deuteronomic evaluation; and
4) dismissal: length of reign, reference to annals, "slept with the fathers," succeeded by . . . .

This cataloguing and the citation of additional sources of information (e.g., 1 Kings 11:41; 14:19, 29) creates an **impression of accuracy**.

Figure 2: **Plutarch's Models of Virtue**

Plutarch, the most famous ancient biographer, wrote a series of parallel lives comparing famous Greeks and Romans. Each of the lives sets out the essentials of birth, family, education, career, and significance; but the real matter is the hero's character: for example, Antony's vain ambition, Brutus' tragedy, or the Roman military virtues of Fabius and Marcellus. Like the Deuteronomist, Plutarch highlights their characters in order to inculcate virtue:

> . . . a man ought to apply his intellectual
> perception to such objects as . . . are apt to . . .
> allure it to its own proper good and advantage.
> Such objects we find in the acts of virtue,
> which also produce in the minds of mere
> readers about them an emulation and eagerness
> that may lead them on to imitation. . . . And so
> we have thought fit to spend our time and pains
> in the writing of the lives of famous persons. . .
> [Pericles, 1]

At the same time, Kings **moralizes**. Kings writes Deuteronomic history, so those who obey prosper and those who disobey perish. Lengthy commentaries spell out this perspective in great detail (e.g., 1 Kings 9:3-9; 11:9-13; 2 Kings 17:7-20; cf. Deut 29-30). The narrator also offers an evaluation of each king (except for Shallum, 2 Kings 15:13-16; and Athaliah, 2 Kings 11:1-20) [see figures 3, 4].

Kings has two clear mythic models, the evil, apostate king Jeroboam and the **good king David** who has become the *apotheosized* standard of virtue (cf. 1 Kings 15:5). Good kings are like David and they worship in Jerusalem alone (cf. Deut 12).

From this Judean perspective, all Israelite kings are bad. **Jeroboam, the first king, is the mythic model of vice** because he built alternate sanctuaries (1 Kings 12:26-33). The narrator condemns these sanctuaries as Baal worship and because they are like Sinai's golden calf (Ex 32). Other Israelite kings continue Jeroboam's "sin" (cf. 2 Kings 17:21-23). Despite this blanket condemnation, the narrator does observe that some are noticeably worse or better than the apostate norm because they respectively **encourage or purge Baal worship**.

Figure 3: **Evaluating Israelite Kings**	
Jeroboam	The apostate who is the reason for Israel's destruction (1 Kings 12:26-14:16)
The Norm	". . . walking in the way of Jeroboam"
Worse	Encouraged Baalism Omri (1 Kings 16:25-26) Ahab (16:30-33; 21:25-26) Ahaziah (22:52-53)
Not So Bad	Purged Baalism Jehoram (2 Kings 3:2-3) Jehu (10:28-31)

The bad Judean kings also follow Jeroboam's model or that of the nations. They, too, are idolatrous. The **apostate Manasseh** is the epitome of Judean evil and the scapegoat for the exile (2 Kings 21:2-9). The honorable Judean kings are **like David**. They worship **Yahweh** alone, but they are not perfect because they do not centralize worship in Jerusalem. They allow the "high places," local cult centers, to remain. Only Hezekiah and Josiah are like David at his best. They both sponsor **major reforms**. In fact, Josiah "undoes" Jeroboam's sin by destroying his altar (2 Kings 23:15-20) and holding a

Figure 4: **Evaluating Judean Kings**

David	The ideal standard Hezekiah (2 Kings 18:3-7) Josiah (22:1-23:30)
Honorable	Leave high places Asa, Jehoshaphat, Jehoash, Amaziah, Jothan
Bad	Walked in ways of nations, Israel, Rehoboah, Abijam, Jehoram, Ahaziah, Ahaz, Amon, Jehoahaz, Jehoiakim, Jehoiachin, Zedekiah
Manasseh	The apostate, reason for exile (2 Kings 21:2-9)

national (including Israel) passover (23:21-23). Hezekiah, Josiah, and David are the Deuteronomic models of faith.

Style/Time: Narrative Engendering Speech

Various reliable characters enunciate the Deuteronomic two-ways which controls Kings' narrative: David (2:1-4), God (3:14; 6:11-13; 9:3-9; 11:11-13), Solomon (8:22-61), and a prophet (11:31-39). Kings also reports prophetic oracles which engender ensuing narrative. Only false prophets predict events which do not come to pass (1 Kings 13:18; 22:19-28; cf. Deut 18:21-22).

Figure 5: **Narrative-Engendering Speech in 1 Kings**

Prophecy	Fulfillment in 1-2 Kings
Division of kingdom (11:11-39)	1.12:15-20
Josiah to destroy Jeroboam's altar (13:2-3)	2.23:15-18
Death of prophet (13:21-22)	1.13:24-26
End of Jeroboam's house (14:71-4)	1.15:28-30
Death of Jeroboam's child (14:12-13)	1.14:17
Exile of Israel (14:15-16)	2.17:5-23
Baasha's house destroyed (16:2-4)	1.16:9-13
Death of firstborn of Jericho's builder (Josh 6:26)	1.16:34
Drought (17:1)	1.17:7
Cornucopia of meal/oil (17:14)	1.17:16
Rain and fire (18:1, 23-24, 41)	1.18:38, 45
Hazael anointed king (19:15)	2.8:15
Jehu anointed king (19:16)	2.9:13
Elisha as Elijah's successor (19:16)	1.19:19-2 2.2:15
Bloody revolt of Jehu/Elisha (19:17)	2.9-10
Ahab's victory (20:13-14)	1.20:21
Aramean attack (20:22)	1.20:26
Victory over Arameans (20:28)	1.20:29-30
Death of disobedient prophet (20:36)	1.20:36
Death of king (Ahab, 20:42)	1.22:34-38
Death of Jezebel (21:23)	2.9:33-27
Death of Ahab (22:17, 28)	1.22:34-38

Not even the most ingenious human efforts can prevent the fulfillment of a genuine prophecy (e.g., 1 Kings 11:40; 22:30-38). **Only repentance postpones** (1 Kings 21:27-29) or **changes the prophetic word** (2 Kings 20:1-6).

Figure 6: **Narrative-Engendering Speech in 2 Kings**

Prophecy	Fulfillment
Death of Ahaziah (1:4, 6, 16)	1:17
Fire from heaven (1:10, 12)	1:10, 12
Water without rain (3:16-17)	3:20
Victory over Moab (3:18-19)	3:24-25
Birth of son to barren (4:16)	4:17
Cure of Naaman's leprosy (5:10)	5:14
Warnings about war (6:9-10)	6:11-13
End of Aramean siege of Samaria (7:1)	7:16
Death of disbelieving captain (7:2)	7:17-20
Seven-year famine (8:1)	8:2-3
Hazael to be king of Aram (8:13)	8:15
Jehu to be king of Israel (9:3, 6)	9:13
Death of Ahab's house (9:7-10)	9:24-28; 10:1-14, 17
Death of Jezebel (9:10)	9:33-37
Jehu's four-king dynasty (10:30)	15:10-12
Three victories over Aram (13:19)	13:25
Extension of Israel's boundaries (14:25)	14:25
End of Assyrian siege of Jerusalem and death of their king (19:6-7, 20-31)	19:35-37
Hezekiah's recovery (20:1-7)	20:12-21
Shadow retreats (20:9-10)	20:11
Babylonians to spoil Judah (20:16-18)	24:13-16
Exile for Manasseh's sins (21:10-15)	24:2-4
Deuteronomic curses postponed beyond Josiah's day (22:15-20)	23:30-31
Exile (23:27)	24-25

Pattern and Plot Conflict: Tragic Shape and Sin-Theodicy

Kings depicts the **tragic loss** of the monarchy and the land in exile.

Solomon's glorious beginning intensifies the pathos. His **idyllic reign** fulfills the prophetic promise to David (2 Sam 7:13-14). He builds the house for God. The temple's dedication recalls the tabernacle's glory (cf. 1 Kings 8-9 with Ex 40). Theophanies mark the event (6:11-12; 8:10-11; 9:2-9). Solomon, promised son and temple-builder, is the ideal king wisely administering a prosperous kingdom (his wisdom, 3:5-28; 4:29-34; 5:12; 10:1-13; peace and prosperity, 4:24-25; 5:12; 10) [see figure 9].

The two-ways refrain repeatedly punctuates this idyllic report rather ominously (2:1-4; 3:14; 6:11-13; 8:22-61; 9:3-9; 11:11-13). Kings conditionalizes David's everlasting promise (cf. 2 Sam 7:15-16):

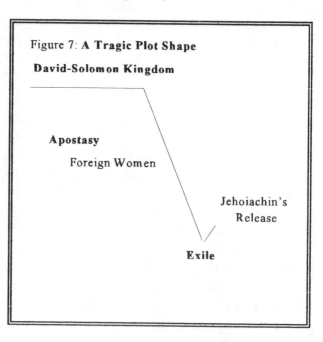

Figure 7: **A Tragic Plot Shape**

David-Solomon Kingdom

Apostasy

Foreign Women

Jehoiachin's
Release

Exile

If your heirs take heed to their way, to walk before me
in faithfulness with all their heart and with all their
soul, there shall not fail you a successor on the throne
of Israel. (1 Kings 2:4)

Solomon's apostasy turns the plot toward Israel's "road to ruin." The report that "Solomon loved many women" (11:1) symbolizes his apostasy. That comment contrasts dramatically with "Solomon loved the LORD" (3:3). From that point, Solomon's fortunes, and those of the kingdom, change with terrible swiftness. Divine troubling begins immediately (11:14-40) and culminates in the kingdom's division (11:11-13).

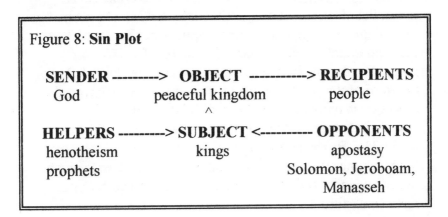

Figure 8: **Sin Plot**

SENDER ---------> OBJECT -----------> RECIPIENTS
God   peaceful kingdom   people
                     ^
HELPERS ---------> SUBJECT <---------- OPPONENTS
henotheism   kings   apostasy
prophets   Solomon, Jeroboam,
                                       Manasseh

Solomon's story is that of Kings in microcosm. He is a mythic model, a symbol, of the entire story (cf. Samson). That story is, of course, **a sin plot**. **Three major apostasies** explain the major losses. First, Solomon's apostasy leads to the kingdom's division (1 Kings 11:11-13). Second, Jeroboam's apostasy leads to Israel's destruction (2 Kings 17:7-20). Third, Manasseh's apostasy leads to the exile (21:1-18; 23:26-27).

The Davidic dynasty's loss of Israel follows quickly upon Solomon's apostasy. The judgments of the apostasy of Jeroboam and Judah do not follow so quickly. As Kings is realistic history [see genre], Israel and Judah continue for some time. The continuance also suits Kings' moralism. It demonstrates the divine longsuffering, the prophets' functions, and the story's rhetoric.

Figure 9: **Plato's Ideal King**

Kings' evaluation of kings by an ideal standard was not unusual in antiquity. The most famous discussion of the ideal king is, of course, Plato's discussion of the philosopher-king who is "a friend of truth, justice, courage, and self-control" [The Republic, 6:487]. For Plato, without such kings, the ideal, just state is impossible [5.473]. As such individuals are rare, Plato spends some time discussing how the state might create (educate) its rulers [bks. 6-7]. In particular, the philosopher-king must have the "knowledge of the form of the good" which is "the end of all endeavor, the object on which every heart is set" [Plato explains the knowledge of the good with the famous allegory of the cave, 6.507-21]. By the knowledge of the good, the philosopher-king becomes the guardian of that which is right and valuable in society and avoids the temptation of lesser goods (e.g., fame or wealth).

Divine Character: The Jealous, Longsuffering Judge

The God of Kings is a nationalistic, longsuffering Judge (cf. Judg 10:10-16) who jealously demands **henotheism**. The only sin of note is apostasy, the worship of gods other than Yahweh or worship in places other than Jerusalem. The Judge, however, remains faithful to his promise to David:

> Yet for the sake of your father David I will not do it (division of the kingdom) in your lifetime; I will tear it out of the hand of your son. I will not, however, tear away the entire kingdom; I will give one tribe to your son, for the sake of my servant David and for the sake of Jerusalem, which I have chosen. (1 Kings

11:12-13; cf. 11:32, 34-36, 39)

The Judge passes judgment slowly. He is **longsuffering** (or merciful) (cf. 1 Kings 15:4; 2 Kings 8:19; 19:34; 20:6). Further, on several occasions, **repentance defers judgment** (e.g., 1 Kings 21:27-29; 2 Kings 20:1-6; 22:18-20).

God appears directly during the temple-building era as a legitimating presence (1 Kings 3:5-14; 6:11-14; 8:10-11; 9:1-9). For most of the story, however, God is present only in the voices of the narrator and the prophet(s). These "voices" transform political-military imperialism into God's judgment on apostasy (e.g., 2 Kings 17:7-23; 24:3-4, 20). Narrator and prophets speak with one voice (a **prophetic providence**). As a result, the narrator addresses the narratee-reader as the prophet does the story-characters.

Prophets: Divine Representatives

The prophets know God and his purposes intimately through visions and the spirit (e.g., visions, 1 Kings 19:4-18; 22:19-23; 2 Kings 6:17; and spirit, 1 Kings 18:26-29; 22:24; 2 Kings 2:9, 14-18; 3:15). The prophets are **powerful figures**. At Isaiah's word, the Assyrians depart and the sun retreats (2 Kings 19:1-20:11). Like the primitive holy, the prophets give (1 Kings 17:17-24; 2 Kings 4:18-37; 13:21) and take away life (1 Kings 13:20-32; 2 Kings 1:9-16; 2:23-25). The Elijah-Elisha section is particularly replete with such miracles. Not surprisingly, as miracle-workers, the prophets resemble (repeat?) Moses [see figure 10].

The prophetic **oracles reveal the divine purposes** and control. Even kings stand beneath this higher Sovereign. Thus, the prophets make (e.g., Jeroboam, Hazael, and Jehu) and unmake (e.g., Solomon, Jeroboam, Baasha, Ahab, Ahaziah, and Ben-hadad) kings according to the divine will.

The story of Naboth's vineyard (1 Kings 21) illustrates God's rule. Jezebel knows no higher authority than the king and has Naboth murdered so that Ahab can possess the vineyard. When the dastardly deed is done, however, Elijah appears out of nowhere, yet from God, to pronounce the true Sovereign's judgment.

Figure 10: **Elijah-Elisha Miracles**

Elijah	**Elisha**
(1 Kings 17-19; 2 Kings 1-2)	(2 Kings 2-7; 13)
Drought	Cross Jordan dry-shod
Divine provisions	Purification of water
Cornucopia	Death of small boys
Resurrection	Water in wadi
End of drought	Supply of oil for widow
Fire from heaven	Child for barren
Horeb theophany	Resurrection
Cross Jordan dry-shod	Purification of stew
Whirlwind into heaven	Feed a hundred with few loaves
	Cure of Naman's leprosy
	Impute leprosy to Gehazi
	Floating axe head
	Sight and blindness

The prophet **incarnates God's sovereignty and demand**. Not surprisingly, then, the prophets call the people to henotheistic faith (Deuteronomistic obedience; e.g., 1 Kings 11:38; 18:20-39). After apostasy ("on the road to ruin"), this demand becomes a call to repentance. Thus, Elijah demands single-minded devotion to God:

> How long will you go limping with different opinions? If the LORD is God, follow him; but if Baal, then follow him. (1 Kings 19:21)

The Deuteronomic prophet **ruthlessly opposes Baal**, even sponsoring bloody pogroms against his worship (1 Kings 18:40; 2 Kings 8-10).

Paradoxically, the prophets are both **traditional and innovative**. Their Mosaic character, Deuteronomic message, and opposition to Baal mark them as conservatives. They retard Kings' tragic movement pulling the kingdom back from disaster. Their call to repentance makes them "speed bumps" on "the road to ruin." At the same time, they innovate. Their oracles depict a God constantly working in and with the people. As such, their oracles and revolutionary acts sketch out new futures for the people [see chap. 12].

Figure 11: **Rome's Destruction of the Temple**

In The Jewish War, the Jewish historian Josephus describes the destruction of the Jewish temple by the Romans as the result of sin (second temple, 70 CE). For Josephus, however, it is not the Jewish people who are to blame. It is only a few criminal rebels who did not know that God had gone over to the Romans [1.1-30; 2.345-401; 5.362-419]. Further, unlike Kings, Josephus did not write to inculcate henotheism. Instead, he wrote to create a working relationship with the Romans.

The Gospel of Luke describes the same destruction as the result of sin and unheeded prophets. For Luke, of course, the rejected prophet in question is Jesus (cf. 13:33-35; 19:41-44; 23:26-31). Thus, Luke's aim is not Deuteronomic henotheism, but faith in Jesus (e.g., Acts 2:37-39).

Myth: Sin-Theodicy

The garden and the wilderness present the sin-theodicy for

humanity and Israel respectively in a mythic form. Judges applies that theodicy to Israel's history, to her life in the land. Kings uses the same theodicy to explain the end of history, the exile.

Kings relentlessly subjects seemingly secular political and military events to the Deuteronomic perspective. By so doing, it transforms an all too common and realistic story into a moral tale (a melodrama). It **transforms fate into meaning**. It does not insure happiness, but it does rescue a sense of order. The Deuteronomic moralist transforms exile and Babylonian imperialism into the divine purpose. Paradoxically, this meaning comforts, rather than terrorizes. God's longsuffering hands are preferable to the Babylonians' (cf. 2 Sam 24:11-14).

Obviously, the sin-theodicy **continues the faith**. It takes God "off the hook." He did not fail to protect the people from their enemies. He used their enemies against them. God is both sovereign and just. The successful sin-theodicy allows **Yahwism** to continue.

Further, it **suggests a future for the people**. Although they are apostate (their mythic identity), they remain the Lord's. The Deuteronomist calls his audience, like his prophets call the characters, to repentance. Readers who accept the Deuteronomist's moralism--the explanation of the exile as God's just judgment on apostasy--find themselves called to henotheism (including centralized worship) and repentance. The sin-theodicy, then, advances a **rhetoric of repentance**.

The exile is a horrific end. It returns the people symbolically (in Babylon) and literally (2 Kings 25:26) to Egypt. Terribly, the end reverses the exodus deliverance (cf. Jer 44). For the Deuteronomist, however, the apostate people remain connected to God. Therefore, the Deuteronomist expects a future beyond judgment:

> If they sin against you . . . so that they are carried
> away captive to the land of the enemy . . . yet if they
> come to their senses . . . and plead with you in the

land of the captors, saying "We have sinned, and have done wrong; we have acted wickedly" . . . then hear in heaven . . . and forgive your people . . . (from 1 Kings 8:46-53; cf. Deut 30:1-10)

Figure 12: **Lincoln's "Second Inaugural Address"**

The sin-theodicy did not vanish with antiquity. Thus, Lincoln describes the Civil War as a divine judgment on slavery:

> If we shall suppose that American Slavery is one of those offences . . . He now wills to remove, and that He gives to both North and South, this terrible war, as the woe due to those by whom the offence came, shall we discern therein any departure from those divine attributes which the believers in a Living God always ascribe to Him? . . . Yet, if God wills that it continue, until all the wealth piled by the bondman's two hundred and fifty years of unrequited toil shall be sunk, and until every drop of blood drawn with the lash, shall be paid by another drawn with the sword, as was said three thousand years ago, so still it must be said "the judgments of the Lord are true and righteous altogether." [in Hollinger and Capper, 1:392-93]

In light of this "salvation beyond judgment" motif [see chap. 12], Kings' end may offer some hope. The final coda states that Jehoiachin has been released from prison (2 Kings 25:27-30). That remark may be a dismal comment on the Davidic dynasty's subjugation to Babylon or a subtle suggestion that the Davidic promise continues.

Figure 13: **Macbeth and <u>Crime and Punishment</u>**

Modern versions of the sin-theodicy often trace its psychological toll (e.g., guilt). In Shakespeare's <u>Macbeth,</u> the title character murders the king to usurp his throne. While no one determines Macbeth's guilt, the murder still has horrific consequences. The couple has terrible visions [e.g., III.iv], and Lady Macbeth slowly goes mad, walking in her sleep, washing her hands, and chanting "Out, damned spot!" [V.i.39]. Macbeth searches in vain for some "oblivious antidote" to "pluck from the memory a rooted sorrow" [from V.iii]. As no cure is forthcoming, the Macbeths die horribly.

Dostoevski's <u>Crime and Punishment</u> is more redemptive. Raskolnikov, a poor student, decides to exhibit his extraordinariness by murdering an old pawnbroker. The crime, however, hurtles him into a delirium of fear, guilt, and illness. As his delirium increases, he meets two characters who represent different solutions. Sonia, the holy fool, typifies confession and redemptive suffering while the dissolute Svidrigailov symbolizes increasing alienation and suicide. Raskolnikov opts for confession, drinks the cup of suffering, and is resurrected with Sonia in/by love (note that the raising of Lazarus figures twice in the novel's last half).

ANET: The Weaknesses of the Sin-Theodicy

Taking God "off the hook" puts humans "on the hook." For moderns, the sin-theodicy fatally **erodes self-confidence**, induces excessive guilt, asserts guilt facilely, and enervates attempts at reform. As a result, contemporary versions of the sin-theodicy are often unconvincing and offensive. For example, Tammy Faye's assertion that hurricane Hugo was God's judgment on Charlotte for the persecution of Jim Bakker convinced few. Fundamentalists who define AIDs as God's judgment on homosexuality leave most moderns aghast.

Of course, both of these examples differ in an important fashion from Kings' sin-theodicy. In each case, they describe **someone else's misfortune** as "God's will." These theodices are not empathetic. By contrast, Kings describes the disaster of its own people. Kings does not inflict, but suffers the "will of God."

Figure 14: **Tell-Tale Hearts**

Like the sin-theodicy, detective fiction reflects the human desire for justice (a meaningful order). People want others to receive their "just desserts." Of course, contemporary fiction sees that end as the result of the workings of human conscience or of clever detective work, not as divine intervention. In short, detective fiction "naturalizes" justice.

In Poe's "The Tell-Tale Heart," the objective denouement still remains. In the haunting tale, a murderer hears the beating of his victim's heart whom he has left under the floorboards until he is driven to confess his murder.

In the recent movie, <u>Presumed Innocent</u> (based on the novel by Scott Turow), all objectivity is gone. A woman murders her husband's lover. The police (and the audience) suspect the husband. The husband is accused and tried, but acquitted. As the movie ends, he finds and cleans the murder weapon in his basement. Neither he nor his wife are free, however. His voice-over ends the movie: "There is justice." Unlike Shakespeare, Dostoevski, and Poe, Turow's justice is purely psychological effect. No confession or external punishment remains.

The sin-theodicy's major obstacle today, of course, is the **demise of the divine sovereignty** ideology. Moderns see disasters like the exile as imperialism or human evil, not as a divine judgment. The result is the end of traditional faith and the construction of different theodicies. Thus, instead of a Deuteronomic moralist, the Holocaust has haunting reporters like Elie Wiesel. His recollection of his thoughts as he watched a young boy hang is emblematic:

> Behind me, I heard the same man asking: "Where is God now?" And I heard a voice within me answer him: "Where is He? Here He is--He is hanging here on this gallows." That night the soup tasted of corpses. [Wiesel, Night, 76]

While this sounds like the end of faith (the Holocaust ended many traditional faiths including liberalism), Wiesel and others actually construct a theodicy more palatable to modernity. That is, they call for ethical human action, for defense of the weak, and for reform. In short, they repeat over and over, "Never Again!" Rejecting Kings' reliance upon divine intervention, they **call for dialogue and democracy**. Instead of attempting to placate and obey God, they educate humans in virtue. For them, a sin-theodicy would merely enervate necessary human action [cf. chap. 5, figure 7].

Review Questions

1. Apply the reading method of chaps. 3-4 to Kings. List its genre, plot shape, conflict, depiction of God, mythic function, and ANE problems.
2. What three apostasies and judgments dominate Kings?
3. What makes Kings a moralistic history?
4. Why does the story continue beyond apostasy? Why is repentance an important motif in Kings? Who repents? What is a "rhetoric of repentance"?
5. In what ways are the prophets traditional figures? Innovators?
6. What are the strengths of the sin-theodicy? The weaknesses?

With what do moderns like Wiesel replace the sin-theodicy?

Suggestions for Alternate Reading and Reflection

1. Compare the atmosphere and conception of providence in the Succession Narrative (2 Sam 9-20) and Solomon's reign (1 Kings 3-9). Why does the conception of providence change? What purpose does it serve?

2. According to the Deuteronomist, what are the characteristics of a false prophet (cf. Deut 13:1-5; 18:15-22)? What do 1 Kings 13 and 22 add to this depiction? What is God's relationship to false prophecy?

3. How is Solomon a symbolic figure? What symbolic significance does he have compared to David (cf. 2 Sam 7:13-14), to ANE sacral kings (cf. 1 Kings 3-4), and to Samson?

4. How does Kings resolve the tension between the divine promise to David (2 Sam 7) and the Deuteronomic two-ways moralism?

5. In what ways does the Deuteronomic view of the king challenge ANE sacral king concepts?

6. The Deuteronomist reads the first Babylonian invasion (2 Kings 24:2-4) as God's judgment on Judah/Manasseh's sins. The description in 2 Kings 25 of the fall of Jerusalem and the temple is remarkably free of comment. Why? Does 24:20 point backward or forward?

7. What does it mean to say that the end of Kings reverses the Exodus story? What does Jer 44 add to this story? How do these two passages' characterizations compare to the people's characterization in the wilderness story.

8. Is 2 Kings 25:27-30 dismal or hopeful? How does Deut 30:1-10 suggest hope for the apostates?

9. Compare Wiesel's position to that of the Deuteronomist. Is it more or less optimistic? Is it more or less fatalistic? Is it more or less noble (heroic)?

10. Compare the rhetorical goals of Kings with those of Herodotus, Thucydides, Josephus, and Luke. How do Plutarch's models differ from those in Kings?

11. How do modern sin-theodicies differ from that of Kings?

For Further Reading

For a commentary on Kings, see R. Nelson.

On the Deuteronomic history, see the references in chap. 9.

On ancient history generally, see the references in chaps. 4 and 9. For an introductory treatment of the historians, see also Michael Grant, Historians. For more depth, see Bury; and Fornara.

For a discussion of the relationship of a possible Deuteronomic school and the Latter Prophets, see Blenkinsopp, History, 188-93.

CHAPTER 12

GOD'S NEW ACTS
The Latter Prophets

Introduction: Relationship to Torah and the Former Prophets

The prophets connect later generations with the founding time and Moses, the founding prophet. They **transmit Torah's mythic identity** and demands. Jewish tradition divides the prophets into the Former Prophets, the history from Joshua through 2 Kings [see chaps. 9-11], and the Latter Prophets, **fifteen books of prophetic oracles**. Tradition further divides these books by length into three major (one scroll each in antiquity) and twelve minor prophets (all on one scroll).

Figure 1: **The Latter Prophets**

Major	**Minor** ("The Twelve")	
Isaiah	Hosea	Nahum
Jeremiah	Joel	Habakkuk
Ezekiel	Amos	Zephaniah
	Obadiah	Haggai
	Jonah	Zechariah
	Micah	Malachi

In the Former Prophets, the prophet is a story-character representing the divine perspective and contending with competing authorities (e.g., the kings or foreign deities). In the Latter Prophets, the prophet is the narrative voice. Simplistically, then, the Former Prophets contain **stories about prophets** while the Latter Prophets contain **their sayings**.

Content Summary: God's New Acts

For the Latter Prophets, **God's definitive acts lie in the immediate future**, rather than in the mythic past:

> Do not remember the former things,
>   or consider the things of old.
> I (God) am about to do a new thing . . . (Isa 43:19-19a)

The turn to the future challenges the past's authority; nonetheless, the prophet is not free from tradition. Sharing the world-view of a mythic community, the prophet depicts God's new acts in that myth's symbols as a coming holy war, a new exodus, a new king, a new covenant, or a new temple [see figure 3]. Put concisely, the prophet describes the new in terms of past divine acts.

Ironically, then, the prophet is simultaneously **innovator and traditionalist**. Prophetic oracles give the present meaning by serving as an interpretative juncture uniting the mythic tradition and the future.

Genre: Judgment and Salvation Oracles

While the books of the Latter Prophets contain story (see media), they are primarily collections of sayings addressed either to God or to humans [see Westermann, Basic]. The former reports the prophets' converse with God and includes praise (e.g., Am 4:13; 5:8-9; 9:5-6; Mic 7:18-20; Zeph 3:14-20), lament (e.g., Jer 11:18-12:6; 15:10-21; Joel 1:19-20), confession of faith (Jon 2:2-9; Hab 3), request (Mic 7:14-20), and dialogue (Hab 1:2-2:5).

Most of the sayings, however, are addressed to humans. The core of prophetic speech is **an oracle announcing an imminent divine act.** The oracles are **occasional**. They are from a specific prophet to a specific audience at a specific moment. In fact, titles locate prophetic works and books in specific historical moments (for example, this is "the word which Amos saw during the reign of . . ., two years before the earthquake," Am 1:1-2).

At times, a prophetic story sets the scene for a prophecy. In Isa 7, for example, in the context of the Syrio-Ephraimitic war, Isaiah calls King Ahaz to trust in God, rather than to entangle himself in political alliances with Israel and Syria. As inducement, Isaiah offers Ahaz an oracle of comfort indicating God's imminent deliverance:

> Look, the young woman is with child and shall bear
> a son, and shall name him Immanuel. . . . For before
> the child knows how to refuse the evil and choose the
> good, the land before whose two kings (Israel and
> Syria) you are in dread will be deserted. (7:14-16)

Their occasional nature distinguishes the prophetic from Mosaic sayings. Torah belongs to the eternal present of myth and ritual while prophetic sayings **apply a mythic world-view** to a specific moment. Further, as mythic speech, Torah's demands come from the primeval past (tradition). By contrast, the oracle challenges the present in light of its immediate future.

The oracles predict either **disaster or good fortune**. With the former, the prophet announces an impending disaster as a divine **judgment or punishment** of the addressee: for example,

> Thus says the LORD:
> For three transgressions of Judah
>   and for four, I will not revoke the punishment;
> because they have rejected the law of the LORD,
>   and have not kept his statutes,
> but they have been led astray by the same lies
>   after which their ancestors walked.
> So I will send a fire on Judah,
>   and it shall devour the strongholds of Jerusalem. (Am 2:4-5)

For the slaughter and violence done to your brother Jacob

> shame shall cover you,
> and you shall be cut off forever. (Ob 10)
> As you have done, it shall be done to you;
> your deeds shall return on your own head. (Ob 15b)

Often, as in these examples, the oracle also contains an **accusation**, a reason for the coming punishment. While the prophets are incredibly creative fault-finders, one can categorize their accusations as **offenses against God or against their fellows** (including neighboring nations). Probably, the prophetic tradition included a "catalogue" of

---

Figure 2: Prophetic Accusations

Offenses against God
   Religious apostasy (Hosea;
     Zephaniah; Jeremiah; Ezekiel)
   Political apostasy (Isaiah;
     Zephaniah; Jeremiah)
   Ritual offenses (Haggai; Zechariah;
     Third Isaiah; Malachi; Ezekiel)

Offenses against fellows
   Domestic social injustice
     (Amos; Micah)
   War crimes (Nahum; Obadiah)

---

offenses which an individual prophet could apply to any audience. As a result, most prophetic books include a wide range of similar accusations; nevertheless, individual prophets do have recognizable, dominant criticisms.

As God's "strange work" of judgment (Isa 28:21), the prophets predict the onset of war, famine (Am 8), drought (Jer 15:2-4), earthquake (Hab 2:6), locusts (Joel), and so forth. **War-siege imagery** occurs most frequently. On occasion, the prophets predict the arrival of a specific foreign invader as the instrument of the divine displeasure (Hosea, Micah, and Isaiah name Assyria; Habakkuk, Jeremiah, and Ezekiel name Babylon):

> Ah, Assyria, the rod of my anger--
>> the club in their hands is my fury!
> Against a godless nation I send him,
>> and against the people of my wrath I command him,
> to take spoil and seize plunder,
>> and to tread them down like the mire of the streets.
> (Isa 10:5-6; cf Jer. 22:6-7)

As the real destroyer is God, some oracles simply announce God's impending arrival, "**the Day of Yahweh**" [cf. Rad, Message, 95-99]:

> The great day of the LORD is near,
>> near and hastening fast;
> the sound of the day of the LORD is bitter,
>> the warrior cries aloud there.
> That day will be a day of wrath,
>> a day of distress and anguish,
> a day of ruin and devastation,
>> a day of darkness and gloom
> a day of clouds and thick darkness
>> a day of trumpet blast and battle cry
> against the fortified cities
>> and against the lofty battlements.
> I will bring such distress upon people
>> that they shall walk like the blind;
>> because they have sinned against the LORD . . .
> (Zeph 1:14-17; cf. Am 5; Nah 2; etc.)

The imagery of cloud, darkness, and fire recalls theophany as well as war (cf. Ex 19:16; Ps 18:7-5). For the prophets, then, war and other **disastrous realities are divine theophanies**:

> Therefore thus I will do to you, O Israel;
>> because I will do this to you,
>> prepare to meet your God, O Israel!
> (Am 4:12; cf. Joel 3:13-14)

The prophet describes disaster not only by depicting empirical disasters as judgmental theophanies, but also by **reversing revered mythic traditions**. For example, instead of fighting for Israel on the "day," now God engages in holy war against Israel (cf. Am 5:18-20). Instead of exodus, the prophet describes new enslavements (e.g., Hos 11:5). Instead of Zion's exaltation, the prophet predicts its razing (e.g., Mic 3:9-12; Jer 7). Instead of election, the prophet announces God's renunciation of the people (e.g., Hos 1:8).

But, the prophets are not merely doom-sayers. They also announce good fortune as divine salvation. As judgment reverses past myths, **salvation restores those old mythic realities**. As with disaster, prophetic salvation is essentially **God's presence**:

Figure 3: **Imagining Salvation**	
Symbol	**Prophet**
New exodus	Hosea; Second Isaiah
New covenant	Jeremiah
New temple	Ezekiel
New David	Isaiah; Micah; Haggai
New creation	Second Isaiah
New Eden	Ezekiel

> A voice cries out:
> "In the wilderness prepare the way of the LORD,
>   make straight in the desert a highway for our God.
> Get you up to a high mountain,
>   O Zion, herald of good tidings . . .
> say to the cities of Judah,
>   "Here is your God!"
> See the LORD comes with might,
>   and his arm rules for him;
> his reward is with him,
>   and his recompense before him." (Isa 40:3, 9-10)

As with disaster, divine salvation can employ agents:

> I have aroused Cyrus in righteousness,
>   and I will make all his paths straight;
> he shall build my city and set my exiles free . . .
>   (Isa 45:13; cf. 44:28)

> But you, O Bethlehem of Ephrathah,
>   who are one of the little clans of Judah,
> from you shall come forth for me,
>   one who is to rule in Israel . . . . (Mic 5:2)

> It is too light a thing that you should be my servant
>   to raise up the tribes of Jacob
>   and to restore the survivors of Israel;
> I will give you as a light to the nations,
>   that my salvation may reach to the ends of the earth.
>   (Isa 49:6)

Unlike the judgment oracles, salvation oracles do not have accusations. They are not the result of human merit or demerit. Their reason is **the divine honor** (e.g., Isa 41:20; 45:6-7; 48:9-11; Ezek 20:22, 40-44; 36:22-32; cf. the similar theme in the exodus story) or God's **legendary mercy** (e.g., Hos 11:8-9). The latter is so well-known and so constant that the prophet Jonah caustically remarks that God cannot be trusted to destroy (4:2; cf. Ex 34:6-7). Nevertheless, God's **salvation surprises**. It is as beyond human ken as the reanimation of a valley of dry bones (Ezek 37:1-14) or a shoot rising from a dead stump (Isa 11:1; Jer 23:5; Zech 3:8; etc.).

Narrator: Charismatic Voices

The use of messenger formulas ("Thus says the LORD") and the use of first-person pronouns (the "divine-I") in oracles constitute an **audacious claim to speak for God**. This direct assertion differs from biblical story's subtlety. Story's "word of God" effect depends upon the implication that its anonymous human voice tells the tale from the divine perspective [see chap. 4, narrator]. Only Torah-sayings compare to the prophets' more direct claim to speak for God [see chap. 8, narrator].

Figure 4: **Ancient Prophets**

Prophecy is a cross-cultural phenomenon [see Wilson, Prophecy, 21-134]. Ancient Mari, in particular, had prophets who resemble Israel's in form, content, and function. Blenkinsopp's description of the standard pattern of ecstatic prophecy in Northern Mesopotamia and Syria makes this clear:

> These intermediaries were generally, but not invariably, **associated with sanctuaries** where they **pronounced oracles** accompanied by sacrificial rituals. Their revelations were generally, but not invariably, supportive of the ruler and his political and military undertakings. One of their principal functions was to further these undertakings by pronouncing **the curse on foreign enemies.** [History, 59; emphasis added]

Prophetic speech arises from the prophets' personal religious experiences. They have seen visions (e.g., Isa 6; Ezek 1-3; Am 1:1) or been possessed by the divine. Such possession is a specialized form of *charismatic* religious experience. The possessed are both ecstatic and enthused. As **ecstatics**, the prophets "stand outside" themselves. They enter a trance either spontaneously or through some technique (e.g., the use of drugs, fasting, blood-letting, music, etc.; cf. the Baal prophets in 1 Kings 17). As **enthused**, the prophets "have a god within." Not surprisingly, such individuals often act dramatically, if not grotesquely [cf. Crapanzano; I. M. Lewis].

Put concisely, the prophets are **overwhelmed by God** (e.g., Jer 20:7-13). God so dominates the prophets' experience that everything else is devalued. The prophets live continually in the sacred. The normal world and ordinary existence are far from them. Thus, the prophets do not see disaster or good fortune, but the divine arrival.

This intimacy with the divine, rather than institutional office, appoints, supports, and justifies the prophets. That intimacy also alienates the prophets from their fellows (cf. Jer 11:18-12:6). They do not live in their world. They are **channels for the sacred**.

Narratee and Rhetoric: Poetry and Demand

Unfortunately, the prophets' private religious experiences hardly publicly guarantee their claims. While Torah's divine authority is a mythic given for the community, the prophets' similar claims to divine authority do not receive such a respectful, obedient hearing. Standing in an incongruent relationship with their audiences, the prophets have to **win acceptance** [see chap. 4, narratee]. The prophets persuade their audiences to share their esoteric visions and often unpopular messages by relying on personal experiences, mythic traditions, and poetry.

Ironically, the prophets' **private religious experiences** are some evidence for their claims. Recognizable charismatic activity gains the prophets a hearing (e.g., 1 Sam 9:9-13). So, too, do dramatic **symbolic acts** which enact the prophets' messages (e.g., Hosea's marriage, Hos 1-3; Isaiah's nakedness, Isa 20; and Ezekiel's haircut, Ezek 5). Further, prophets also report their visions in order to substantiate their "call" (e.g., Isa 6; Jer 1; Ezek 1-3).

Prophets also rely on **common mythic traditions** in order to persuade. For example, foreign nation oracles resemble the curses of ancient holy war prophets and find a receptive audience in Israelite nationalism (e.g., Obadiah; Nahum). Cultic sayings borrow persuasiveness from the myth-ritual complex (laments; thanksgivings). Prophetic critique itself eventually creates a tradition which gives subsequent prophets a hearing (cf. Jer 26). In the same way, fulfilled prophecies, like those concerning the exile, substantiate later prophetic claims (cf. the power of fulfilled prophecy in Isa 36-39; Jer 52; Deut 13; 18).

Prophetic innovation, however, often requires **the reversal of mythic givens**:

> You only have I known of all the families of the earth;
> therefore I will punish you for all your iniquities.
>
> Are you not like the Ethiopians to me,
>   O people of Israel? says the LORD.
> Did I not bring Israel up from the land of Egypt,
>   and the Philistines from Caphtor
>   and the Arameans from Kir? (Am 3:2; 9:7)

While this twist on popular election surprises (cf. Jer 7), the notion that the Holy Warrior will now fight against Israel may be even more startling (e.g., Am 5; Zeph 1). The proud do not expect judgment and the hopeless do not expect salvation.

The prophets' worlds differ strikingly from those of their contemporaries. The prophets imagine alternatives that others do not consider:

> It is the vocation of the prophet to keep alive the ministry of imagination, to keep on conjuring and proposing alternative futures to the single one the king (the powers that be) wants to urge as the only thinkable one.
>
> The practice of imagination is a subversive activity not because it yields concrete acts of defiance (which it may) but because it keeps the present provisional

and refuses to absolutize it. [Brueggemann, Imagination, 45, 119, n. 1]

Such alternatives require more than mere rhetorical persuasion. Prophetic oracles must capture their audience's attention and minds. In this, **poetry** avails more than logic.

Figure 5: **Magical Words**

Antiquity understood **words as objective parts of reality**, not mere labels. This assumption is the basis of the idea that knowledge of a deity's name will allow the worshiper to procure benefits from the deity simply by using his name according to prescribed rituals. Words, then, are realities with demonstrable effects. Blessings and curses respectively improve and weaken those who are their objects (cf. Num 22-24; Deut 26-30). Further, once spoken, words cannot be recalled (cf. Gen 27:30-40).

The ancients understood prophecy similarly (cf. narrative-engendering speech). Thus the prophets' oracles would actually bring about either judgment or salvation. Two features of Israelite prophecy, however, **condition this magical view**. First, Israelite prophets were rhetoricians, not mere predictors [see figure 6]. Second, the HB's divine sovereignty ideology means that God's future is not determined even by God's past acts or words. The biblical God can repent. That conviction is, of course, a major premise in the Jonah story (Jon 3:9-4:3) in which God's mercy irks a doom prophet.

The prophets' evocative poetic symbols and use of parallelism interpret empirical events (Am 1:2b) as divine acts (Am 1:2a):

> The LORD roars from Zion,
>> and utters his voice from Jerusalem;
> the pastures of the shepherds wither
>> and the top of Carmel dries up. (Am 1:2)

The oracle quickly transforms reality into *hierophany* [cf. Alter, Poetry, 146]. Antithetical parallelisms, of course, can capture the prophetic visions of dramatic divine reversal. Thus, two brief lines-- "you are like Gilead" but "I will make you a desert" (Jer 22:6)-- suffice to move from legendary fertility to waste.

Rhetorically, prophetic poetry creates the prophets' religious experiences for the audience. The poetic oracle intends to **trap the audience** [cf. Alter, Poetry, 139-44]. Like David before Nathan's parable (2 Sam 12), the prophetic audience finds itself embroiled in the prophetic world.

Figure 6: **Divination**

Prophecy and divination are closely related. Israelites went to prophets, as Greeks went to Delphi, and inquired concerning the divine will (cf. 1 Kings 22). In this, the prophet resembles the priest who wields the Urim and Thummin (Ex 28:15-30; 1 Sam 14:41-42) and the witch at Endor (1 Sam 28). Israelite tradition, however, does not remember the classical prophets as diviners. Their messages do not come at request. Of course, the tradition may have reduced the prophets' foretelling role out of respect for the divine sovereignty [see figure 5] and in order to portray them as **unheeded preachers of repentance**. For the tradition which uses them to explain the exile and to call the community to repent [see myth], the prophets are **more rhetoricians (preachers) than predictors (diviners)**.

The poetic oracle **demands decision**. Oracles of judgment

demand repentance. Salvation oracles inspire hope. In short, the oracles call the audience to align with the prophets' God regardless of the powers-that-be.

Some prophets, however, may have been merely "doom" sayers (Amos? Micah?). They may have expected their word to have a "magical" effect. Nonetheless, tradition remembers the prophets as **preachers of repentance**, although largely unheeded ones (2 Kings 17; Jer 25; Am 2; Isa 6:9-12). Even though repentance is unlikely, tradition understands the prophets as "warners," **not just as predictors** (cf. Ezek 2-3).

Media: Prophetic Books; Orality and Texuality

The prophets' occasional oral oracles have come down to posterity as sacred texts [see figure 8; appendix 1]. Textualization (and *canonization*) dramatically changes the prophetic oracles. The charismatic becomes **institutional**. The occasional becomes **general**. The poetic is interspersed with prose. Originally short, independent oracles are expanded and read in connection with other oracles. The oracle becomes **part of an anthology** of oracle and story.

Oral oracles confronted their auditors with a crisis of decision. By contrast, readers of the prophetic anthologies receive material stamped with institutional approval. Only the "true," reliable spokespersons for God remain. As such, the community can no longer reject the prophetic words. Like Torah, they are part of the community's myth. The prophets have become **Mosaic tradents** (cf. Deut 13; 18).

Textualization makes the prophetic oracles artifacts. The myth-ritual community, then, has to revive the oracles for its present through generalization or re-oracling.

Generalization uncovers a "principle" of continuing

significance. One might, for example, simply assert that a prophetic oracle reveals God's **modus operandi**. Quite generally, for example, the prophets show God to be the just judge who condemns the oppressor and liberates the oppressed.

Re-oracling transfers past oracles to new occasions. For example, Matthew applies Isa 7:14 to Jesus' birth. Isaiah's oracle promises Ahaz deliverance from his enemies during the Syrio-Ephraimitic War. Eight hundred years later, Matthew's re-oracling transforms the words into a prophecy of Jesus' virgin birth (Mt 1:23 relies on the *Septuagint*). Such re-oraclings are characteristic of early Christianity's reading of the prophets (and of the HB).

Before the formation of a standardized prophetic text, one could contemporize simply by adding words, phrases, or new oracles to the collection. Thus, even a cursory reading of Isaiah, for example, reveals **several different prophetic moments**. Broadly speaking, Isa 1-39 addresses the eighth century Assyrian crisis, Isa 40-55 the sixth century Babylonian crisis, and Isa 56-66 the late sixth/early fifth century restoration. Further, different symbols and themes dominate each of these sections.

Actually, the matter is even more complex. Isaiah 36-39 duplicates material from 2 Kings 18-20 and differs in style and message from the judgment oracles in Isa 1-39. Instead of destruction, Isa. 36-39 narrates Jerusalem's miraculous deliverance. Isaiah 13-27 also has a

Figure 7: **Rewriting Isaiah**	
Isa 1-12; 28-31	8th cent. judgment oracles
Isa 36-39	Exilic adaptation of story
Isa 13-23	Exilic adaptation of foreign nation oracles
Isa 40-55	Exilic salvation oracles
Isa 56-66	Restoration oracles
Isa 24-27	5th- 3rd cent. additions

different "feel." Isaiah 13-23 is a series of foreign nation oracles pronouncing judgment upon Judah's enemies. As Babylon figures more prominently than Assyria, the material seems to reflect that later crisis. Isaiah 24-27 cosmocizes prophetic material in a fashion similar to post-exilic *apocalyptic*. The exaltation of Zion (2:2-4) and David (9:2-7; 11:1-9) themes are also typical of the post-exilic era.

In sum, then, the Isaiah material has been reworked several times. Like Torah, then, the prophets provide a tradition of re-reading and application along with their original materials.

Figure 8: **The Formation of the Prophetic Books**

The prophets' relationships to their books resembles Moses relationship to Torah. Although some (post-exilic) prophets may have written their books, in general, the prophetic books are community products. Between the original oral oracle and textualization stand several "contemporizing" moments:

1. 8th - 5th cent. oral oracles
2. Additions to Israel's prophets applying the message to Judah (during Hezekiah's reign?)
3. Additions reflecting the Deuteronomic reform (late 7th cent.)
4. Deuteronomic, exilic reinterpretation (Deuteronomic corpus of prophets?)
5. Post-exilic additions concerning Zion's exaltation
6. Apocalyptic additions
7. Oracles seen as "fixed" corpus (2nd cent.; Sirach)

Textualization also adds **stories about the prophets**. This material is often (but not always) a third-person prose report in contrast to the oracles' first-person poetry. The story elements include titles (and dates for individual oracles in some prophets like Ezekiel), vision reports (e.g., Isa 6; Ezek 1-3), symbolic actions (e.g., Isa 20; Jer 13; 27-28; Ezek 4; 5; 12; Hos 1; 3), references to fulfilled prophecy (Isa 36-39; Jer 27-29; 52), and stories about prophetic conflict (Am 7:10-17; Isa 7; Jer 26-44; Jon).

These stories have two important functions. First, the titles and dates attach the oracles to a specific occasion. Second, the other story elements substantiate the prophetic message. Symbolic acts dramatize the prophetic message. Visions and fulfilled prophecy buttress the prophets' divine authority. Finally, conflict stories legitimate the prophets by displaying their character and integrity under fire.

The Structure of Prophetic Books [see appendix 1]

Editors connected independent oracles into an anthology using various techniques. Theme and word connections are evident, for example, in series of "woe" (Hab 2:6-20; Isa 5:8-24), "king" (Jer 21:-23:8), or "prophetic" (Jer 23:9-40) oracles. Such thematic connections easily expand into "generic" groupings of foreign nation oracles (Am 1-2), various judgment oracles (Am 3-6), and vision reports (Am 7-9). Mini-collections of foreign nation oracles are, in fact, quite common. Finally, some oracles are chronologically ordered (e.g., Ezekiel, Haggai, and Zechariah). In fact, the Latter Prophets' corpus itself represents a rough chronology or succession of prophets (co-joined with an ordering by length, i.e., the distinction between major and minor prophets).

However, the most pervasive structural patterns are **cultic forms** and a **salvation through judgment pattern**.

Laments (e.g., Jer 11:18-12:6; 15:10-21; 17:14-18; 18:18-23; 20:7-18) and thanksgivings (Isa 12; 49; 55; Jon 2:2-9) appear frequently. Some prophetic books climax in such forms. Micah ends with praise of the delivering God (7:8-20). Zephaniah ends with a call to humility and a celebration of God's enthronement (3). Such endings structure these whole books. They transform judgment oracles into penitential texts which serve as **myth-ritual preparation for God's delivering presence**.

Third Isaiah (56-66) works similarly. That prophet explains that the people's sins have prevented the realization of the hopes of Isa 40-55. Third Isaiah, then, calls the people to repent. Thus, the very center of Third Isaiah is a call to repentance (Isa 59) which leads to Zion's long awaited exaltation (60-62). Lest one miss the point, a second cry for divine help (63-64) leads yet again to Zion's exaltation (65-66). Similarly, on the occasion of a locust plague (1:2-7; 2:1-11), Joel calls Israel to repent (1:8-14; 2:12-17) as preparation for God's deliverance (2:18-27; 2:28-3:21).

By contrast, Habukkuk is a divine consultation on justice. Instead of repentance, the dialogue leads to a call to faith (2:2b-5). Thus, Habakkuk leads the community through lament to faith. Habakkuk, thus, climaxes with a thanksgiving psalm praising God, the deliverer. Foreign nation oracles (e.g., Obadiah; Nahum) offer hope more simply. Their ritual curses upon the enemy lead to the enemy's destruction and Zion's exaltation.

The joining of the nations' destruction with Israel's salvation creates the second structural

Figure 9: **Salvation Through Judgment**

	Judgment		Salvation
	Israel	Nations	
Isa	1-12	13-23	40-55
Jer	1-25	46-51	30-31
Ezek	1-24	25-32	33-48
Joel	1:2-2:11	2:12-3:21	
Am	1-9	1-2	9:11-15
		Obadiah	
		Nahum	

pattern--one of **salvation through judgment**. Typically, the pattern is 1) Israel's judgment; 2) the nations' judgment; and 3) Israel's salvation. Although this pattern does not always appear completely, it occurs so often that it appears to be the structural pattern behind the prophetic corpus, or **the implied prophetic story**. That implied pattern is, of course, the "mythic-v" of Eden Lost and Eden Restored.

Plot Conflict: Sin and Holy War

The judgment oracles have a sin-plot. The people's sins--religious/political apostasy, ritual offenses, and social injustice--disrupt the people's peaceful mythic order. The prophets, their oracles, and God's coming judgment are God's HELPERS. They urge the people to realign with God.

By contrast, the salvation oracles have a holy war plot. When the divine punishment concludes, God restores his people's fortunes by plucking them from the

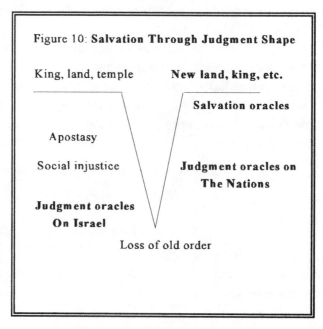

Figure 10: **Salvation Through Judgment Shape**

King, land, temple   **New land, king, etc.**

Salvation oracles

Apostasy

Social injustice   **Judgment oracles on The Nations**

Judgment oracles On Israel

Loss of old order

nations' hands. The nations are no longer God's HELPERS but, like Pharaoh, become God's OPPONENTS. Numerous unlikely heroes--foreign kings, revived Davidic kings, and the prophets--assist God's deliverance.

```
┌─────────────────────────────────────────────────────────────┐
│   Figure 11: Sin and Holy War Plots                         │
│                                                              │
│           SENDER ------> OBJECT --------> RECIPIENTS        │
│   Judge   God          mythic order          people        │
│   Save    God          restored order        people        │
│                             ^                                │
│           HELPERS ------> SUBJECT <------- OPPONENTS        │
│   Judge  prophet, nations    God             sinful        │
│   Save   unlikely heroes     God             nations       │
└─────────────────────────────────────────────────────────────┘
```

Mythic Identity: People Before the Coming God

The prophetic oracles locate (or identify) their hearers mythically. Before the coming God, the prophet depicts the people as **those to be judged or those to be saved**. Thus, the prophet defines his audience as against ("not my people") or with ("my people") God. The sinful think themselves secure, but the prophet sees them sliding toward destruction, death, and disaster. Those in chaos think themselves without hope, but the prophet poetically imagines them delivered by God's coming salvation.

The oracle **orients the hearer to a mythic future**. Textualized, the oracle becomes an artifact of the mythic tradition, but several factors allow the prophets to maintain their mythic futurity. The prophetic tradition creates the impression that judgment-salvation is a **continuing, repeating pattern** or God's **modus operandi** [see media].

Ritual use also asserts futurity. In the cult, judgment oracles become **calls to repentance**. Salvation oracles become **calls to hope**. Lament and assurance materials become calls to faith. In short, the cultic audience's mythic location replicates that of the original audience. Through myth-ritual, the cultic audience becomes the prophetic narratee.

Even as texts, then, the prophets offer a **new myth**. That which defines life and mythic identity is **the coming God**. The prophets refuse the traditional myth-ritual God. Their God is frighteningly new. His important acts are now.

This newness leads the prophets to "**mythologize history**" [Thompson, 193]. In history, the prophet sees God. The prophet's poetry imagines the imperialistic designs of Assyria and Babylon, the rise and fall of nations small and great, and various economic disasters as God's purposive activity. For the prophets, **history is theophany**.

Myth: Theodicy and Succession

As a corpus, the Latter Prophets (like the Former Prophets) provides a sin-theodicy for the exile. In fact, the exile validated the prophetic judgment oracles (though see Jer 44).

The prophets' salvation through judgment pattern, however, surpasses punishment. God's judgment is part of a continuing relationship with his people. Of course, this **educative notion** requires corporate assumptions. Israel spans the disasters. Individuals do not.

The Latter Prophets also produce **alternatives to the sin-theodicy**. Habakkuk, for example, considers the people's suffering the result of temporary injustice, rather than sin. As a result, Habakkuk counsels **submission** to (faith in) God's overwhelming sovereignty:

> If it seems to tarry, wait for it;
>   it will surely come, it will not delay.
> Look at the proud!
>   Their spirit is not right in them,

but the righteous shall live by faith. (Hab 2:3-4)

For Second Isaiah, suffering has a **redemptive** purpose. The "servant" suffers, not for his own sins, but for those of others:

> But he was wounded for our transgressions,
>   crushed for our iniquities;
> upon him was the punishment that made us whole,
>   and by his bruises we are healed. (Isa 53:5)

Finally, the foreign nation oracles proclaim that **God will soon redress current injustices**. In the imminent future, God will bring the proud and lofty low and exalt Zion (e.g., Nahum; Obadiah).

Ironically, the prophetic texts came to have a function within the myth-ritual complex. Their occasional voice applies and hands on the Mosaic Torah to later generations. Ironically, then, the prophets became traditionalists. The charismatics were transformed into institutional men [see figure 12].

Divine Character: The Holy and Ethical Monotheism

God is overwhelmingly present to the prophets in vision and charisma. The prophets know the primitive Holy One. Prophetic explanations of judgment, however, rationalize that basic experience. God's working of weal and woe becomes explicable. This trend also creates lofty **ethical compendiums**:

> With what shall I come before the LORD,
> and bow myself before God on high? . . .
> He has told you, O mortal, what is good;
>   and what does the LORD require of you
> but to do justice, and to love kindness,
>   and to walk humbly with your God? (Mic 6:6, 8)

Thus says the LORD of hosts: Render true judgments,

show kindness and mercy to one another; do not oppress the widow, the orphan, the alien, or the poor; and do not devise evil in your hearts against one another. (Zech 7:9-10)

The prophetic God dominates history. The Holy One decides the fate of Israel and the nations. Assyria and Babylon are but divine tools who do his will whether wittingly or unwittingly. This emphasis eventually leads to **monotheism** (cf. Isa 40-55). If God controls the nations, their gods are as nothing.

Figure 12: **True and False Prophecy**

While replete with prophetic conflict (e.g., 1 Kings 22; Jer 26-28; Am 7:10-17), biblical story offers no clear criteria by which one may discriminate true and false prophets. Its clearest statements **define true prophets as Mosaic and as accurate predictors** (Deut 13; 18). Neither criteria is incredibly helpful when an oracle demands an immediate decision. Mosaic prophets disagree and one can hardly wait for one to be proved correct in order to act appropriately. In short, these criteria are helpful only after the fact. More importantly, they are institutional criteria. In essence, they **define as true those prophets accepted by the later institution**. Not incidentally, institutions are happy only with "dead," or "textualized" prophets. Thus, the standard party line in both Judaism and Christianity presents prophecy as a thing of the past succeeded by a scribal, priestly tradition.

Despite monotheism, nationalism survived. For most prophets, Israel remains the chosen (but see Am 9:7). Nevertheless, the reduction of Israel to foreign nation status before God (e.g., Am 1-2) is an impressive assertion of God's universal justice. Others dare to envision Israel as a missionary to the nations (Second Isaiah's servant; Jonah) or a world in which all nations worship God (e.g.,

Zeph 3:9). This **missionary monotheism** is quite an advance over *ethnocentrism*; nevertheless, it continues supremacy notions. The servant does not dialogue. Israel's Torah remains the only truth. More horribly, the world-worship scenario often requires a slaughter of the nations (e.g., Zech 14).

While God is intensely present for the prophets, God remains an ambiguous, mediated presence for the audience (i.e., prophetic providence). The movements of Assyria and Babylon are quite clear. Those of God are not. **The world is secular and meaningless until the prophet speaks**. It is the prophetic word which makes God present.

Human Characters

Surprisingly, despite the personality (non-anonymity) of the prophetic oracles, humans are relatively unimportant characters. God is the only true story-character. Others pale before the dominating divine presence. The prophetic audience is reduced to humans before God. Likewise, the nations become mere divine tools. Only the prophet rivals God. The prophet, however, is merely the divine story's voice. The **prophet is** little more than **his message**.

ANET: Prophets and Liberalism

The prophetic God is the awesome Holy beyond control whose works are "strange' (e.g., Am 3:6; Isa 28:21; 45:7). Modern and traditional Gods are tamer. For the modern, the prophetic God is barbaric, capricious, and demonic. Moderns prefer more rational, ethical versions of the deity. The prophets are foreign to modernity. They violate its liberal assumptions about reason, tolerance, and the separation of religion from political affairs.

The prophets are **not rational men, but mystics,**

charismatics, visionaries, and poets. Such styles are foreign to an institutional, bureaucratic age accustomed to careful, articulated social planning. Such styles are foreign to newspaper and textbook readers. For institutional humans, the prophets are **fanatical lunatics**. They are as dangerous as the God they oracle. They do not come with the proper institutional approval. Moderns are bemused by their charismatic claims.

Figure 13: **Prophecy Today**

Despite the closing of the Hebrew prophetic canon, other religious groups since have also had their prophets (e.g., Jesus, Muhammed, Joseph Smith, and David Koresh). In modern society, possession is psychologically and morally questionable, so only the marginal claim it (e.g., David Koresh). By contrast, divination remains respectable. The daily paper carries a horoscope and syndicated columns by people like Jeanne Dixon. Not too long ago, a presidential family had their own astrologer. Periodically, television programs air on ancient prophecies or on the ever popular Nostradamus, a sixteenth-century French doctor fascinated with astrology, magic, and the occult. Nostradamus wrote a series of obscure prophecies anticipating history to the end of the world. His continuing relevance depends upon scribal ingenuity which can interpret, for example, the following obscure passage as a reference to the Kennedy assassinations:

> The great man will be struck down in the day
> by a thunderbolt. An evil deed, foretold by the
> bearer of a petition. According to the
> prediction another falls at night time. Conflict
> at Reims, London, and pestilence in Tuscany.
> [Cheetham, 33]

Further, the prophets are **intolerant**. They are uncompromising, audaciously arrogant, and offensive. On the basis of their claim to divine authority, they demand decision. Modernity prefers dialogue and compromise. Moderns are unaccustomed to prophetic directness and steadfastness.

Figure 14: **Social Justice**

Recent quests for social justice continue the prophetic tradition of social critique. Most recent (nineteenth and twentieth-century) programs, however, grow out of philosophical liberalism's rationalism [see ANET] and individualism. Recent reformers, then, have emphasized the individual to a degree impossible for the ancients. The prophet's concern was always Israel, the entire people of God. More importantly, the recent activist programs assume the human perfectability of the social world. By contrast, the prophet did not expect to reform the world. Rather, the prophet expected God to come. Alignment with this coming God, not social tinkering, is the way to life. Nonetheless, the prophets' impressive ethical compendiums [see divine character] remain grist for modern social activism (e.g., the Social Gospel and the Civil Rights movments), however, disparate their philosophical assumptions.

Finally, the prophets' religion is not confined to the myth-ritual context. Their God acts in the present. On this basis, they **offer social and political advice**. For example, in the face of a pressing military situation, Isaiah's military advice is faith, rather than political-military alliances (cf. Jer 21; 37-38):

> Alas for those who go down to Egypt for help
>   and who rely on horses,
> who trust in chariots because they are many

> and in horsemen because they are very strong,
> but do not look to the Holy One of Israel
>   or consult the LORD!
> The Egyptians are human, and not God;
>   their horses are flesh, not spirit. (Isa 31:1, 3)

Such advice scarcely impresses modern politicians. Modern religion is a private affair, so such advice is **unrealistic fantasy**. Moderns prefer to trust military budgets of "horses of flesh" or "bombs of nuclear fire" [cf. Corbett].

Review Questions

1. Apply the reading method of chaps. 3-4 to the Latter Prophets. List their genre, plot shape, conflict, depiction of God, mythic function, and ANE problems.
2. How do the Latter Prophets differ from the Former?
3. How is the prophet an innovator and a traditionalist?
4. What is the essence of the judgment and the salvation oracle?
5. What forms indicate that the prophets claim to speak for God? What is the basis of their claim?
6. How do the prophets convince their audience?
7. How does textualization effect the prophetic oracle?
8. What kinds of stories about the prophets do the Latter Prophets contain? What is the function of these stories?
9. What is the implied story behind the Latter Prophets?
10. How does the prophets' conception of God combine primitive and sophisticated elements?
11. How do the prophets differ from modern liberalism?

Suggestions for Alternate Reading and Reflection

1. Compare the prophetic oracles to the Torah sayings.
2. What causes judgment? What causes salvation?
3. Why do the prophets use poetry?

4. What does "the prophets mythologize history" mean?

5. Are the prophets diviners? Compare the Hebrew prophets to Nostradamus.

6. Are the prophetic oracles magical?

7. How do mythic communities appropriate prophecy?

8. What is ironic about the institutionalization of prophecy? Can one "deconstruct" the prophets?

9. Are the prophets ethnocentric nationalists or universalists?

10. Why do modern liberals revere the prophets?

11. How does one distinguish a true from a false prophet?

For Further Reading

For historical treatments of the Latter Prophets, see the various introductions; Bible dictionaries; Newsome, Prophets; and Blenkinsopp, History. These works also provide bibliographic assistance in terms of commentaries on the individual prophets. For literary appraisals, see the various articles in Alter and Kermode.

On the prophets and tradition, see Rad, Message, 89-94; Clements, Prophecy, and Tucker, "Prophecy," 331-35.

On additions to and transmission of the prophetic books, see Blenkinsopp, History.

On prophetic speech forms, see Westermann, Basic.

On prophetic poetry, see Alter, Poetry.

For the connection between the prophet's person and his message, see Heschel, 2:1-11, 87-103; Fretheim, Suffering, 149-66.

On the social location of the prophet, see J. Williams, "Social"; Wilson, Prophecy; and Overholt.

On ecstasy, see Blenkinsopp, History, 42-46; Wilson, Prophecy, 21-134; and Tucker, "Prophecy," 350-54.

On true and false prophecy, see Blenkinsopp, <u>History</u>, 184-88; Crenshaw, <u>Prophetic</u>, 13-22, 110; **idem**, "Prophecy, false"; Tucker, "Prophecy," 354-56.

INTRODUCTION TO THE WRITINGS

The third section of the HB, the Writings, includes eleven books with **little apparent literary connection**. Their literary diversity is evident in the Septuagint ordering which distributes these works throughout its fourfold generic arrangement of the HB. Ruth, Esther, Ezra-Nehemiah, and 1-2 Chronicles are part of the history section (with the Former Prophets). Psalms, Job, Proverbs, Ecclesiastes and Song of Songs are the poetry section. Lamentations and Daniel are part of the prophets (with the Latter Prophets).

```
┌─────────────────────────────────────┐
│                                     │
│  Figure 1: The Writings             │
│                                     │
│  Psalms          Job                │
│  Proverbs        Ruth               │
│  Song of Songs   Ecclesiastes       │
│  Lamentations    Esther             │
│  Daniel          Ezra-Nehemiah      │
│  1-2 Chronicles                     │
│                                     │
└─────────────────────────────────────┘
```

The HB considers the Writings a single unit because its books have a common mythic function. The Writings (the scribes) **transmit, as do the prophets, the basic Torah revelation** to new ages. While some works may predate the exile, the Writings provide world-views suitable to the post-exilic period.

Thus, the Chronicler's History and the Psalms construe Israel as a worshiping community. To this end, **the Chronicler** (1-2 Chronicles, Ezra, and Nehemiah) presents Israel's history in terms of the temple established, lost, and found. For the Chronicler, the temple is the sacred's chief symbol and the center of Israel's mythic identity.

Psalms is an anthology of cultic songs. It provides mythic models for basic religious conversation with forms for praise and petition. The psalms teach Israel to have faith regardless of her mythic position. In order, she praises. In chaos, she petitions.

Apocalyptic understands Israel differently as a sectarian community of righteous sufferers. Fortunately, for these victims, apocalyptic visions depict the imminent end of this evil age and the arrival of a divine age of justice in which the oppressed rule.

Wisdom (Proverbs, Job, and Ecclesiastes) offers yet another mythic identity. For its optimistic world-view, the wise can learn the prudent path to success, to a prosperous life in harmony with the divinely created natural and social order. As the wise/good do not always prosper, some texts reflect upon the basic assumptions of the wisdom world-view (Job; Ecclesiastes).

In summary, then, the Writings are a miscellaneous collection of books both literarily and mythically.

CHAPTER 13

THE TEMPLE HISTORY
1-2 Chronicles, Ezra, Nehemiah

Introduction: Revising and Extending the Former Prophets

Chronicles, Ezra, and Nehemiah are a **biblical history** quite similar to the Former Prophets. Chronicles, however, presents a revised story of David and Judah from a **different mythic perspective** than that of the Former Prophets (extolling the temple, rather than the monarchy). It also places that story in a **larger context** extending the story backward to Adam (through genealogies) and forward into the restoration with the addition of Ezra-Nehemiah. Not surprisingly, then, Jerome titled the work "the chronicle of the whole of sacred history."

Content Summary: The Temple Story

After lengthy genealogies, the Chronicler's story focuses on David's preparations for the temple. He takes Jerusalem (1 Chr 11:4-9), moves the ark to Jerusalem (13-16), purchases land for the temple (21), prepares for the temple (17; 22-26), organizes the Levites (15-16; 23-26), and appoints Solomon to build the temple (28-29). David, then, is **the mythic founder of the temple**, not the ambiguous warrior-king of 1-2 Samuel.

For the Chronicler, only the temple kingdom is legitimate, so it **treats the apostate Northern Kingdom sparingly** and critically. Even the North's fall happens "off-stage" (cf. 2 Chr 30:9). Not surprisingly, the Chronicler criticizes Southern kings who align with the North (e.g., 19:1-3; 20:35-37; 25:6-13) and who follow Northern apostasies (e.g., 21:6; 22:3-4; 28:2). The rebellious Northerners refuse invitations to legitimate worship services (30:11) and reject a post-judgment call to repent (30:9-10).

The Chronicler's portrayal of the legitimate cultic monarchy (J u d a h) **concentrates on cultic activities**. Even wars become grand cultic events (20). The important kings are those who reform the temple cultus and organize the Levites like Asa (15), Jehoshaphat (17; 19-20), Hezekiah (29-32), and Josiah (34-35). However, bad kings, unfaithful priests, and unrepentant people increase "until the wrath of the LORD against his people became so great that there was no remedy" (36:16). **The exile**, then, occurs.

> **Figure 1: The Temple Story**
>
> 1) Pre-temple genealogies (1 Chr 1-10)
> 2) Founding the David-Solomon Temple
>   (1 Chr 11-29; 2 Chr 1-9)
> 3) The Temple Kingdom (2 Chr 10-36)
> 4) The Second Temple (Ezra-Nehemiah)

After exile, exiles return (Ezra 1-2) and **rebuild the temple** with Persian support (3-6). Various cultic ceremonies mark the rebuilding stages (3:10-13; 6:16-22; cf. 1 Chr 13-16; 2 Chr 2-7). Although there are Davidic figures (Sheshbazzar, Zerubbabel, and Nehemiah), the king is noticeably absent. Priests (e.g., Ezra), Levites, and governors (e.g., Nehemiah) now play the major roles.

The remainder of Ezra-Nehemiah describes **life in the restored temple society** under Persian rule. The story depicts both the reformation of the society along Torah lines (Ezra 7-10; Neh 8-9; cf. 2 Chr 34:14-35:19) and the political-economic solidification of the community (Neh 1-7; 10-13). Not surprisingly, cultic ceremonies mark important reform stages (Ezra 9-10; Neh 8-9; 12:27-47).

Story Shape and Conflict: Temple Lost and Restored

With the Ezra-Nehemiah material, the Chronicler's history is a **story of two temples**. This story has two notable features, its completeness and its peculiar **deus ex machina**.

For the biblical tradition, this story is notably **complete**. Torah, the Former Prophets, and the Latter

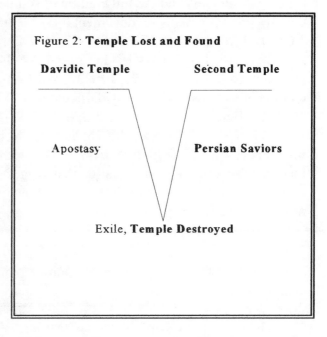

Figure 2: **Temple Lost and Found**

Davidic Temple   Second Temple

Apostasy   **Persian Saviors**

Exile, **Temple Destroyed**

Prophets end with hope, not fulfillment. When Ezra-Nehemiah are included with Chronicles, however, the story depicts a good order in which humans can live well [see myth].

This emphasis on human responsibility and action has a striking corollary in the **Persian saviors**. Typically, biblical story depicts miraculous deliverances from chaos (cf. Ezek 37). For the Chronicler's history, however, it is the "God in Cyrus" who restores the temple society (2 Chr 36:22-23; Ezra 1:1-4). Other Persian emperors also lend their support (Darius, Ezra 6:1-12; Artaxerxes, 7:11-26; Neh 1:1-2:8). Each subsequent emperor properly respects and defends God, his house, and his law. A stress on God's intervening hand, in answer to prayer, appears only in Neh 1:1-2:8. By contrast, it is Cyrus' previous decree which moves Darius. The result is an incredibly realistic story.

Figure 3: **Documentary Style**

The Chronicler's history includes numerous lists (often genealogies) and the full citation of sources and, thereby, creates a realistic (documentary) style. **Lists** include 1 Chr 12:1-40; 15:4-10, 17-24; 23:3-27:34; 2 Chr 17:14-18; 21:2-3; 31:2-3, 11-15; Ezra 1:9-11; 2:2-64; 8:1-14, 24-28; 10:18-44; Neh 3:1-32; 7:7-66; 10:1-27; and 11:3-36. The citation of sources includes **royal documents** (2 Chr 36:22-23; Ezra 1:1-4; 4:17-23; 6:3-5, 6-12; 7:11-26), **letters** (2 Chr 2:11-16; 21:12-15; Ezra 4:8-16; 5:16-17; Neh 6:2-9), and **memoirs** (Ezra 7:27-9:15; Neh 1:1-7:5; 11:1-13:31). The memoirs use a first-person narration that suggests the narrator-character was part of the story he now reports and now offers a documentary report.

The lengthy Chronicler has numerous plot conflicts. The founding of the temple is a mythic revelation. The story of the first temple's loss is a **sin plot** [see myth]. The story of the temple's restoration is an unusual **holy war** in which the foreign rulers act for God against descendants of the first temple

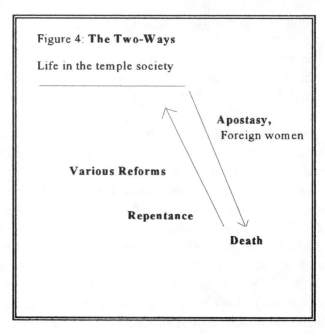

Figure 4: **The Two-Ways**

Life in the temple society

Apostasy, Foreign women

Various Reforms

Repentance

Death

society (the Samaritans).

The various reform/ repentance stories, which are the story's major plot movement, present a conservative version of **the two-ways teaching**. Where cultic apostasy leads to disaster, cultic propriety and reform lead to the good life or to the restoration of the good temple society. In particular, the reforms of Hezekiah, Josiah, Ezra, and Nehemiah pull the community back from the brink of disaster.

Divine Character: Cultic Presence

Although the Persians are the primary agents in the temple's restoration, God remains the true sovereign. Cyrus owes his position to God (2 Chr 36:23). The Davidic monarch, too, is a viceregent subject to God and Torah (1 Chr 11:2; 17:7, 14; 29:22; 2 Chr 6:5-6).

The Sovereign manipulates history to create a temple society. This emphasis on a divinely given order gives the Chronicler's history a **traditional, conservative** flavor. Not surprisingly, legitimacy and community boundaries are major concerns. The exclusion of the North (2 Chr), the Samaritans, and foreign women (Ezra-Nehemiah) from the temple society gives this story-God an extremely **nationalistic**, if not racist, cast. As befits a *natural religion*, foreigners are important only as they impinge upon God's community. Pious foreign monarchs are, however, apparently quite acceptable (e.g., Ezra 6:1-12; 7:11-27; cf. Dan 1-6; Esther).

During the temple's mythic founding time, the conception of providence is direct. Repeatedly, the narrator says that the Lord gave David victories. David converses with God (1 Chr 14:10); nevertheless, David typically has intermediaries between himself and God (cf. 21, prophets; Satan and an angel). Notably, David institutes religious offices (the Levites) to stand between God and Israel (15:13; cf. 13).

The theophany in the Chronicler is, of course, the filling of the temple (2 Chr 5:13-14; 7:1-3). Thereafter, **the temple symbolizes God's presence with the people**. This temple focus creates the Chronicler's distinctive **institutional conception of providence**. For the Chronicler, God blesses the people through the temple (and the king) and the people worship him there. Even passover, a family festival, becomes a temple festival (2 Chr 30; 35). Even military victories come ritually, when the priests blow the trumpets (2 Chr 13:14-15), when kings pray (14:11-12; 20:5-12; 32:20-22; cf. Neh 1-2), and when Levites sing praises to God (2 Chr 20:21-22):

> As they began to sing and praise, the LORD set an ambush against the Ammonites . . . so that they were routed. When Judah came . . . they were corpses lying on the ground; no one had escaped. (20:22, 24)

When God's activity becomes more indirect in Ezra-Nehemiah (but see Ezra 1:1-5; 7:6; Neh 2:8), worship activities still punctuate the narrative (e.g., Ezra 2:68-70; 3:1-6, 10-13; 6:16-22; 8:21-23; 9:1-10:15). In short, God continues to be known institutionally in temple, temple leadership, and Torah (Neh 8-10).

David: Cult Founder

For the Chronicler, David is **the mythic founder** (cf. Torah's Moses). He receives the covenant promises (1 Chr 17) and the founding plans (1 Chr 28:19). He founds the cult. Not surprisingly, he is both prophet and priest. David and some subsequent descendants receive the divine word directly (1 Chr 22; 28; 2 Chr 1:7-13; 7:11-22) and, like prophets, deliver it to others (1 Chr 22; 28; 2 Chr 13:4-12). Second Chronicles 29:25 specifically locates David with the prophets:

> He stationed the Levites in the house of the LORD
> with cymbals, harps, and lyres, according to the

> commandment of David and of Gad the king's seer
> and of the prophet Nathan, for the commandment was
> from the LORD through the prophets.

David also wears priestly garments (1 Chr15:27), offers sacrifices, and blesses the people (16:2). What is acceptable for the cult-founder David, however, is hardly acceptable for later kings (cf. 2 Chr 26:16-20).

This cultic figure hardly resembles Samuel's warrior king. As important features of the Samuel story simply do not appear, the Chronicler's David is **purified**. Of the questionable materials, Chronicles keeps only the census-sin (21; cf. 2 Sam 24). Even that story, however, becomes the occasion for the selection of the future temple's location (22:1). In summary, then, the monarchy's founder (1-2 Sam) has become the founder of the temple:

Figure 5: The Holy David

Chronicles does not include the following items which appear in the Former Prophets:

Saul's reign;
the hostilities between Saul and David;
David's outlaw period;
David's alignment with the Philistines;
David's affair with Bathsheba;
the revolts of Absalom and Sheba; and
Solomon's palace intrigue.

> ... the king and hero at the head of his companions in
> arms has become the singer and master of ceremonies
> at the head of a swarm of priests and Levites; his
> clearly cut figure has become a feeble holy picture,
> seen through a cloud of incense. [Wellhausen, cited in
> Rad, Theology, 1:350]

Other Kings

Chronicles' **temple-David standard** omits the Northern kings from the story. They are in rebellion and worship goat demons (2 Chr 10:19; 11:15). Not surprisingly, the Chronicler rebukes Southern kings who align themselves with the North (19:1-3; 20:35-37; 25:6-13). The favored kings are **those who reform the temple or organize the Levites** in a fashion similar to David (Asa, Jehoshaphat, Hezekiah, and Josiah).

Davidic descendants appear even in the restoration (see 1 Chr 3). Sheshbazzar, prince of Judah (Ezra 1:8), and Zerubbabel, son of Shealtiel (2-6), are Davidic descendants. For Haggai, Zerubbabel is **messianic** (Hag 2:20-23; Zech 3:8; 6:9-15). In Chronicles, Zerubbabel plays a more minor role. Whether or not Chronicles hoped for the restored Davidic kingdom, **the cult takes priority**. Thus, the note of hope at the end of 2 Chronicles stresses the rebuilt temple, while the hope at the end of 2 Kings stresses the freed Davidic king (cf. 2 Chr 36:22-23 with 2 Kings 25:27-30). There is, however, something faintly Davidic about Ezra-Nehemiah's reorganization (particularly Neh 12).

Levites

Levites are **subordinate cultic officials**. According to tradition, the tribe of Levi was dedicated to God's service in place of Israel's firstborn (Ex 13:1-16; Num 3; 8). Within the tribe of Levi, Aaron and his descendants are the superior cultic officials, the priests and the high priest (Ex 28; Lev 8-10; Num 20:22-29). For Chronicles, the Levites remain minor officials (cf. 1 Chr 23:28-32).

Chronicles does, however, frequently discuss the Levites' organization (1 Chr 15-16; 24) and duties. The Levites have charge of the temple vessels, assist the priests, carry the ark, teach the law, administer justice, praise God with music, and participate in reform programs. In addition, individual Levites act as prophets (1 Chr 15:5;

2 Chr 20:14) and scribes (1 Chr 24:6; 2 Chr 34:13).

Chronicles also increases the Levites' presence in the story (e.g., 1 Chr 13-16; 2 Chr 20; 23). In the Deuteronomic parallels, the Levites do not even appear. In 1 Chr 13-16, David brings the ark to Jerusalem (cf. 2 Sam 6). The first attempt is unsuccessful (13). On the second attempt, David entrusts the task to the Levites who safely conduct the ark (15:2, 12-13). David also appoints Levites to remain "as ministers before the ark of the LORD, to invoke, to thank, and to praise the LORD, the God of Israel" (16:4).

Later, David organizes Levites into the **temple singers and musicians** (25). Their praise brings God to act for military victory (e.g., 2 Chr 20:19-24). Similarly, the Levites are the violent agents in Chronicles' version of Jehoida's coup (cf. 2 Chr 23 with 2 Kings 11:4-20).

In fact, the Levites figure so prominently in Chronicles that some have suggested that the Chronicler was himself a Levite or intended to upgrade their status as their numbers/interest dwindled (Ezra 2:36-58; 8:15-20).

Priests and Prophets

Chronicles criticizes the Levites mildly (2 Chr 24:5; 30:15). By contrast, it roundly criticizes the priests (2 Chr 29:34; 30:3, 15; 36:14; Ezra 10:18; Neh 9:34; 13:28-29). Most importantly, their unfaithfulness leads to the temple's destruction (2 Chr 36:14). Despite the criticisms, some of the more important heroes are priests including Jehoida (2 Chr 22-23), Azariah (26:16-20), Jeshua (Ezra 2-6), and Ezra (Ezra 7-10; Neh 8-10).

The prophet also figures in Chronicles (e.g., Nathan, Micaiah, and Jeremiah) and the unheeded prophets still partly account for the exile. Further, Chronicles refers several times to collections of prophetic material (e.g., 1 Chr 29:19; 2 Chr 9:29; 12:15; 26:22;

33:19). On the whole, however, the prophets are less important here than in the Former Prophets. Elijah appears in the story only as the author of a letter (2 Chr 21:12-15). Isaiah plays a minimal role in 2 Chr 32 as compared to his place in the parallel 2 Kings 18:13-20:21. Not surprisingly, on occasion, the Levites replace the prophets (cf. 2 Chr 34:30 with 2 Kings 23:2).

Ezra: The Second Moses

Ezra is the leading priest of the restoration. With Persian support, Ezra leads a **Torah reform** (Ezra 7-10; Neh 8-10) not unlike Josiah's earlier reform (2 Kings 22-23; 2 Chr 34-35). In both instances, Torah's re-revelation elicits confession (Ezra 9; Neh 9), an oracle of salvation/comfort (Neh 8:9-12), public reading and commitment (Neh 8:1-8; 9:38-10:39), reformation or vows (Ezra 10:16-44), and a religious festival (Neh 8:13-18). Where the Josiah reform purged the worship of false gods, the Ezra-Nehemiah reform separates the people from their **foreign wives** (cf. the Deuteronomic notion that foreign women equal apostasy).

Nehemiah: The Successful Courtier

Whereas Ezra is a religious official, Nehemiah is a courtier, a political figure. His distinctive achievement is the political-economic reform of the post-exilic community symbolized dramatically by the **rebuilding of the city's walls**. This act and the **exclusion of foreign women** create an adversarial relationship with Jerusalem's neighbors. Nehemiah successfully presents the move, however, as non-threatening to Persia.

Nehemiah's memoirs (note the first person narration in Neh 1-7) create a realistic atmosphere. Nonetheless, various speeches invoke and celebrate the divine presence. Thus, Nehemiah's story begins with a prayer beseeching God's assistance (1:4-11; 2:4, 8) and ends with a recognition of God's assistance (12:27-43). Further, during the conflict, there are numerous confessions of faith in God (2:20; 4:14, 20) and prayers for assistance (4:4-5, 9; 6:9, 14; three of the four are "curses"). Despite his Persian allegiances, then, Nehemiah remains a biblical hero.

Figure 6: **Successful Courtiers** (Dan 1-6)

The Chronicler imagines a working relationship between an exclusive Jewish temple state and the Persian empire and success for individual Jews within that empire. Thus, Nehemiah is a successful courtier (cf. Joseph and Mordecai). In Dan 1-6, Daniel and the three young men are similar figures. Unlike Nehemiah and Joseph, however, these young men maintain exclusive Jewish rituals (dietary regulations) and refuse to participate in idolatry. Despite their exile (life outside the land), they maintain an exclusive Jewish identity. Their difference brings them to danger, to the attention of foreign kings. God repeatedly saves them, however, by providing them solutions to impossible mysteries (2; 4; 5) and by delivering them from penalties for keeping Jewish rituals (3; 6). Strikingly, God's miraculous acts, which destroy the heroes' lesser rivals, also bring the foreign king to acknowledge God. Like Joseph, then, these heroes succeed in foreign lands and against hostile powers.

Myth: Chartering the Cultic Community

Chronicles offers both a temple founding myth (the story of David and Solomon) and a subsequent temple history. In mythic terms, then, Chronicles charters the temple state [cf. Rad, Theology, 1:347]. Even when the monarchy ends, then, Israel continues:

Israel came back from exile, not as a nation, but as a

religious community. . . . The Chronicler's intention, however, is to show that this profound change in Israel's life was not just a response to the political vicissitudes of the period. Rather, it was a return to the charter of Judaism handed down from David. [Anderson, Understanding, 515]

Figure 7: **"Church" and State**

In a ***natural religion***, "church" and state are part of the same power structure. In post-exilic Judaism, that situation no longer existed. The temple-state was under the control of foreign, political powers. The religious community had to decide to support or to oppose that power. Chronicles represents qualified support of the foreign powers [see shape and conflict]. By contrast, ***apocalyptic*** rejects the state [cf. chap. 15]. These disparate positions are not uncommon. They resemble Troeltsch's famous distinction between churches and sects [cf. Niebuhr, Christ]. "Churches" assume that God works through both the religious community and the surrounding culture (cf. Chronicles). "Sects" assume that culture is radically evil and that the religious community must work apart from and against culture (cf. apocalyptic).

The **temple** spans the different political situations. It remains the sacred's chief vehicle and provides continuity with the founding time:

The history of the nation was not just a series of isolated acts of God in the past; it was centered rather in a continuous institution manned by lineal descendants of those who served in the times of Moses and David, the ongoing family or church of God. There were, of course, times when this organism malfunctioned because of the epidemics of sin.

[Illness] could be avoided . . . by the maintenance of a healthy rapport with the Lord which in turn could be accomplished only through purity of worship in a living institutional milieu. [J. Myers, lxxiii]

Figure 8: **Eusebius**: Chartering the Constantinian Empire

Like Chronicles, Eusebius' Ecclesiastical History describes the triumph of a religious community over the vicissitudes of history. Despite Jewish opposition, state persecution, and internal controversies, God has granted the apostolic church peace under Constantine. This emperor is no less than the second Abraham and divine servant making an idyllic golden age present:

> . . . the mighty victor Constantine, pre-eminent
> in very virtue that true religion can confer . . .
> won back their own eastern lands and reunited
> the Roman Empire into a single whole,
> bringing it all under their peaceful sway . . . .
> Men had now lost all fear . . . day after day they
> kept dazzling festival; light was everywhere,
> and men who had once dared not look up
> greeted each other with smiling faces and
> shining eyes. . . . [from 10.9.7]

Notably, Chronicles is not nearly so satisfied with the Persians.

The **Torah**, which animates the reforms of Josiah (2 Chr 34-35) and Ezra (Neh 8-10), provides further mythic identity and continuity. Ezra and Nehemiah reform the restored community in harmony with their understanding of Torah in order to insure the community's legitimacy. For the reform, Torah **separates Israel** from its neighbors (cf. Neh 9:2; 10:28). The practical consequence is the **expulsion of the foreign wives** who are understood yet again as a conduit for apostasy (Ezra 9-10; Neh 10:28-32; 13:23-27; cf. 2 Chr 8:11). This exclusion pushes the Chronicler's earlier concerns for legitimacy (the South vs. the North and exiles vs. Samaritans) to new extremes. This community is racially, as well as ritually, distinct. Race has become a mythic identifier.

Figure 9: **Openness to Foreigners** (Ruth and Jonah)

Despite the prominent biblical notion that foreign women equal apostasy, **Ruth** presents a Moabite woman positively. She is the means of Naomi's fertility and the ancestress of David (4:13-17)! This foreign woman is faithful. Even more remarkably, **Jonah** imagines God sending a reluctant prophet to hated Assyria to save them from destruction (contrast Nahum; cf. Second Isaiah's suffering servant). Wisdom literature is even more open to outsiders [cf. chap. 16]. Thus, one could array biblical texts on a spectrum from openness to outsiders (universalism) to their exclusion.

Universalism	**Mission**	**Natural Religion**	**Exclusion**
Wisdom	Jonah	Torah	Ezra-Neh.
	2nd Isaiah	Former Prophets	Apocalyptic

ANET: An Exclusive State

Chronicles offers a conservative, exclusionary, establishment theology (though contrast 2 Chr 6:22-23; 30:5). While patriarchy and nationalism are frequent problems for the biblical reader, Ezra-

Nehemiah's dramatic exclusion of foreign women is particularly offensive [but cf. figure 9].

While moderns cannot admire this **exclusionary myth**, they can appreciate the problems facing Chronicles. The exile had destroyed the old natural religion and set the Jews loose in a sea of foreign powers. Without the luxury of isolation, how was Chronicles to maintain Israel's mythic identity?

Figure 10: **Esther**, Fantasies of Violent Revenge

Esther describes the salvation of the Jews through the courageous acts of the queen and Mordecai. The evil Haman plots the royal extermination of the Jews in an attempt to be rid of his rival courtier, Mordecai. Mordecai convinces Esther to risk her life to act for her people (4). Esther puts Haman in a fatally compromising position through two banquets (5; 7) so that Haman, rather poetically, hangs on the gallows he has prepared for Mordecai (7:10). In the denouement, the king elevates Mordecai to Haman's old position and allows the Jews to kill their enemies with impunity on the day they were slated to be killed. The festival of Purim still celebrates Esther's topsy-turvy reversal and its fantasy of violent revenge.

Apart from its apocryphal additions, Esther is remarkably secular. God does not appear in the text and Esther is the most prominent actor, the chief agent of the people's deliverance. Human wits, luck, and violence turn the tide in this secular holy war.

Chronicles responds by chartering a **modified natural religion**, a temple state under Persian hegemony. As the Persians tolerate and support the Jews' ancestral traditions, being good (Jewishly) still equals having it good. Chronicles' exclusive temple-Torah myth accepts this new situation and strives to maintain Jewish identity through an exclusive cultic community.

Still, the cost to foreign women and children rightly troubles the modern. Even modified natural religions **do not mix well with pluralism**. Exclusionary myths are costly in the modern world.

Myth: A Rationalistic Theodicy

The Former Prophets paint retribution broadly. Kings sin and Israel and Judah fall. In striking contrast, Chronicles' kings reap the fruits of their own deeds immediately. This view requires the explanation of seeming anomalies. Thus, Chronicles explains the evil Manasseh's long reign by describing his repentance (2 Chr 33:12-19; cf. The Prayer of Manasseh). Similarly, Chronicles uncovers a decisive disobedience to explain the good Josiah's tragic death (35:22-24). Although these rationalizations strain credulity, they do allow a **simple moral rhetoric**. Each king becomes a mythic model of virtue, vice, or repentance (e.g., Rehoboam and Manasseh).

The addition of **Satan** to the story of David's census-sin (1 Chr 21:1) is another rationalization. In 2 Sam 24:1, an angry Lord incites David. That understanding is acceptable given the basic Holy One who both creates and destroys. Rationalizations of the divine, however, make such acts morally questionable. The Chronicler avoids the quandary by having an adversary tempt. At the heart of such rationalizations, however, lies an inchoate dualism presuming a good god and an evil god. Monotheism, of course, cannot abide such dualism.

Review Questions

1. Apply the reading method of chaps. 3-4 to Chronicles. List its genre, plot shape, conflict, depiction of God, mythic function, and ANE problems.

2. Compare Chronicles to the Former Prophets.

3. Compare the David of the two histories.

4. What is unusual about Chronicles' **deus ex machina**?

5. What is an institutional or cultic providence? Do any other biblical texts have similar conceptions? What provides mythic succession for Chronicles?

6. What is a Levite?

7. Identify "Mosaic" elements and figures in Chronicles.

8. Why might one describe Chronicles as reactionary?

9. How does Chronicles rationalize theodicy?

Suggestions for Alternative Reading and Reflection

1. Do different historical occasions explain the differences between Chronicles and the Former Prophets?

2. Scholars have often associated the Former Prophets with a prophetic school and Chronicles with a levitical or priestly school. What features of the two narratives support such hypotheses?

3. Why is it anachronistic to accuse natural religion texts of nationalism and racism? Is it anachronistic to accuse Chronicles of such?

4. Compare the theories of church and state in Chronicles and apocalyptic. Which perspective do the "successful courtier" stories most resemble? How do Ruth and Jonah compare?

5. Compare the attitudes toward the state in Ezra-Nehemiah, 2 Samuel, and Eusebius.

6. Compare the Esther story literarily and mythically to Exodus.

7. What is most unusual about the Esther story? How do the apocryphal additions to Esther deal with the problem?

For Further Reading

For commentary on Chronicles, see J. Myers.

For discussions of the unity of the Chronicler's history, see

Ackroyd, "Historical," 305-10; Freedman, 436-42; Japhet, 5:531-32; and Newsome, "Toward."

For reflection on the canonical placement of the works, see Talmon, "Ezra," 318; Eissfeldt, 531; Pfeiffer, "Ezra," 2:216; and Japhet, 5:517-18.

For discussion of the historical order of Ezra and Nehemiah, see Bright, History, 392-403; Miller, "Israelite," 17-19; and Anderson, Understanding, 524-27.

For discussion of Chronicles' David, see Freedman, 440-42; Newsome, "Toward," 213-17; Stinespring; and Ackroyd, "History," 510-13. For the treatment of Solomon, see Braun.

For a discussion of the Levites, see Abba; and J. Myers, xxxix, lxviii-lxxi.

For discussion of the restoration period and its literature, see Ackroyd, Exile; Nickelsburg and Stone; and Nickelsburg, Jewish.

For bibliography and introduction to Ruth, Esther, and Dan 1-6, see Niditch, "Legends"; Humphreys, "Life-style"; **idem**, "Esther"; and Niditch and Doran. See also the bibliographies in chaps. 9 and 15. It was once a scholarly commonplace that Ruth and Jonah were written to contest the exclusiveness of Ezra-Nehemiah. Today, that position is taken less often and with less certainty. See Niditch, "Legends," 454; and Blenkinsopp, History, 270-73.

CHAPTER 14

ISRAEL'S PRAISE
The Psalms

Introduction: Israel's Songs of Praise

Psalms is the **temple's hymnal**, the worshiping community's songs of praise. In the Psalms, Israel praises God in and from every conceivable human situation. In fact, the entire book moves toward praise. Each of its first four sections (1-41; 42-72; 73-89; 90-106) ends with a doxology. The last section (107-50) ends with five **Hallelujah** ("praise the Lord") psalms.

Media: Music and Worship

Numerous psalms refer to **temple singing**. While the scores are no longer extant, various titles indicate that some psalms were songs (18; 46), pilgrim songs (120-34), or songs accompanied by a stringed instrument (fifty-seven psalms). Other headings name the tune which should accompany the psalm (cf. 9; 22; 56-59; 75) [cf. Werner; Mowinckel, Psalms, 2:207-17].

In the temple, the psalms **accompanied sacrifice and procession**. Leaders or a choir sung the psalm while instruments (strings, flutes, drums) marked the time. The congregation responded with refrains (Ps 136) or ritual shouts (amen, hallelujah, for ever and ever).

Although various psalms seem appropriate for certain occasions, the psalms are remarkably resilient and flexible. In most cases, they are not bound to specific contexts by explicit historical and personal references. Rather, they reflect **typical, basic human**

conditions. As a result, the psalms are still read, prayed, and sung (cf. 46; 100) in worship.

Figure 1: **Occasions for Psalms**

Some scholars have related specific psalms to specific worship settings like a fall festival reaffirming the monarchy's social-cosmic order [cf. Mowinckel, Psalms] or a fall festival renewing the covenant [cf. Weiser]. Regardless of the merit of those proposals, certain types of psalms clearly belong to different worship settings [see genre]. Thus, hymns seem well suited to communal celebrations (the festivals) recalling God's provision of good orders and salvation. By contrast, the communal laments belong to penitential rites responding to national crises like war or famine (cf. 1 Kings 21:9, 12; Jer 36:9; Joel 1:14). Individual laments, of course, belong to individual situations of distress. Thanksgivings respond to divine deliverances from crises. In addition, the Talmud cites the following times as appropriate for certain psalms [cf. Cronbach; EJ, 13:1322-25]:

24	Sunday	135	Passover
48	Monday	81	New Moon
82	Tuesday	120-34	Tabernacles
94	Wednesday	136	Festive days
81	Thursday	113-18	Pilgrim songs
93	Friday		
92	Sabbath		

Genre and Form: Praise and Petition

At an abstract level, there are two human emotions, **pleasure and pain**. Not surprisingly, the language of worship reflects those two basic situations. The psalms, then, address God with praise and petition. Thus, scholars often categorize the psalms as **hymns and laments** [Westermann, Praise, 15-35].

Figure 2: **Psalms Distinguished by Content**
       [cf. Anderson, Out, 159-67]

Royal	2; 18; 20; 21; 45; 72; 89; 101; 110; 132; 144
Enthronement	24; 29; 47; 93; 95-99
Zion	46; 48; 76; 84; 87; 122
Torah	1; 19:7-14; 119
Wisdom	1; 36; 37; 49; 73; 78; 112; 127; 128; 133
Salvation hist.	78; 105; 106; 135; 136
Penitential	6; 32; 38; 51; 102; 130; 143
Confidence	11; 16; 23; 27:1-6; 62; 63; 91; 121; 125; 131
Imprecatory	35; 59; 69; 70; 109; 137; 140

In its simplest form, the **hymn** (e.g., 8; 19; 33; 100; 103-04; 145; 146-48) calls the community to worship (100:1-2), cites the reason for which God should be praised (100:3), and concludes with a renewed call to praise, a doxology (100:4-5).

Hymns **celebrate God as the source of life and meaning** for the worshiper. The hymns praise the God who creates the world and Israel (the salvation history and the Zion psalms) or who reigns as king (enthronement and royal psalms).

Thanksgivings praise God for a specific deliverance (e.g., 32; 34; 92; 107; 116; 118; 124; 138). The thanksgiving expands the reason for God's praise into a **"before-after" story** depicting the worshiper's pitiful condition (18:4-5; 116:3), the cry for help (18:6; 116:4), and God's deliverance (18:7-19; 116:5-9). That deliverance story is, of course, quite familiar. Not only is it the standard testimonial pattern (whether religious, AA, or Weight-Watchers), it is also the typical biblical **deus ex machina** pattern.

> Figure 3: **Popular Music**
>
> Praise and petition are not unique to the psalms. That primal language grows out of the general human condition of pleasure and pain, of expansion and limitation. Even popular music reflects these emotions. It either celebrates (extols love/the lover) or complains (laments the loss of love/the lover). The popular joke about country western music makes this very point: "What do you get if you play country western music backwards? You sober up and get your dog, truck, and lover back." The similarity is, of course, only in emotional situation. There is a decided difference between the object of the psalm's devotion (the Creator) and that of popular music (a creature) as well as a difference in media between religious worship and commercial radio (or TV).

While the hymn defines and celebrates mythic identities, the thanksgiving reaffirms mythic identities challenged by chaos and anomie. While the thanksgiving celebrates past deliverances, the lament requests such deliverances (e.g., 3; 4; 12; 22; 31; 39; 42-44; 57; 71; 77; 80; 85; 90; 94; 139).

The **lament** is speech "out of the depths," during "the eclipse of God" [Buber, cited in Anderson, Understanding, 552]. In formal terms, it invokes God (13:1; 22:1-5), petitions (13:2-4; 22:6-21), and praises (13:6; 22:22-31). The **petition** is, of course, the centerpiece. It usually includes complaint (13:1-2; 22:6-18), confession of faith (13:5; 22:21), and the request for deliverance (13:3-4; 22:19-21).

The laments **complain** about all manner of troubles including national enemies, drought, famine, plague, sickness, persecution, and guilt. Part of the language may merely be a formal, poetic attempt to depict the affect of distress [see poetry]. Clearly, the crucial problem is **God's absence or inaction** (e.g., 6:3; 13:1; 79:5). About this, the psalmists complain bitterly and provocatively: "Why do you cast us off?"; "Why do you sleep?"; "How long shall I cry for help, and you will not hear?"

Figure 4: **Song of Songs** (or Canticles)

Canticles is a striking collection of **erotic love poems** which may have been sung in taverns or as wedding songs. The songs are a dialogue between a woman (most often) and a man. They extol the virtues and pains of desire and love (cf. 1:2; 4:9; 5:2): "for love is as strong as death, passion fierce as the grave" (8:6b). This praise of sensuality and of the creature (cf. 4; 5; 7) has given many biblical readers pause. Why does the canon include such hymns?

Ideologically, the answer lies in the Hebraic conception of the created order's goodness (cf. Gen 1). Israelite natural religion has a **sacramental** view of the world which expresses itself in notions of the ontological good. Life, including sex and sensuality, is the realm of the sacred. Later Western religion views the world more ambiguously and prizes **asceticism** and life after death. Readers with such assumptions often read Canticles **allegorically** as a story of God's love for Israel, Jesus' love for the church, or the mystic's quest for the beatific vision.

The complaints strive to **provoke God's action**: "Hear and return, O LORD!" (e.g., 13:3a; 22:19; 79:8). To this end, the psalmist appeals to God's honor/mercy (e.g., 79:10-12; 25:16; 55:18; 83) or to his own innocence (e.g., 5; 7; 26; 44:17-22) or repentance (the penitential psalms). That is, the lament makes rhetorical appeals to traditional mythic identities (Ps 22:4-5; 44:1-8; 89:49-51). In trouble, the psalmist **scurries to worship**, a status which is questioned only by death (e.g., 6:5; 30:9; 88:10-11; 115:17; 119:175).

Despite the provocative complaints, the lament is **an act of faith**. It turns to the only one who can deliver. In fact, the lament form itself **moves dramatically from complaint to praise**. Possibly, a cultic official offered an oracle of salvation to the worshiper which assisted this abrupt shift (that is, between the complaint/request and the praise). If so, the oracles have been lost (but see 12:5; 55:12). Regardless, the lament remains even without the oracle an incredibly **practical, ritual** *theodicy*. It inculcates faith even in "the depths."

Figure 5: **Lamentations**

Lamentations is a collection of **dirges** (funeral songs) lamenting the **Babylonian destruction of Jerusalem**. The first four chapters are also alphabetic acrostics, each with twenty-two stanzas (one for each letter of the Hebrew alphabet). Like the lament psalms, Lamentations moves dramatically from despair to hope:

> But this I call to mind,
>   and therefore I have hope:
> The steadfast love of the LORD never ceases,
>   his mercies never come to an end;
> they are new every morning;
>   great is your faithfulness. (Lam 3:21-22)

Ideologically, however, Lamentations is closer to the Former Prophets' sin-theodicy than to the Psalms' laments (e.g., 1:5-10, 18, 22; 4:13-17; 5:7, 16). Further, like the Latter Prophets, Lamentations hopes for a liberation destroying the enemy (e.g., 1:21-22; 3:64-66; 4:21-22).

Style: Conventional, Archetypal Poetry

The symbols of the psalms depict all of life in its relationship to God [see human character]. This worship language transforms every empirical condition, even chaos, by **conversationally uniting it with the sacred**.

Interestingly, Psalms does this with a "formal monotony" [Quell, cited in Ringgren, Faith, 19]. In addition to recurring structural forms [see genre], the same words and phrases appear repeatedly. It is as if the psalmist has **a stock of phrases** to rely upon to depict God's protection (shield, buckler, tower, fortress, wing, canopy, booth, shade, etc.) or the problems of life (ravening beasts, serpents, arrows, burning coals, pestilence, etc.). The result is an "archetypal," mythic tone [Alter, "Characteristics," 617]. These **metaphors are traditional**, not innovative.

In short, the psalms are the **highly stylized language and emotions of worship**. Worship uses conventional, expected images to conform the individual worshiper to the community and its mythic tradition. It establishes mythic models, identities, and world-views. Worship also uses stock images for practical reasons:

> For a text that is to be chanted by pilgrims in procession on their way up the temple mount, or recited by a supplicant at the altar or by someone recovered from grave illness offering a thanksgiving sacrifice, you don't want a lot of fancy footwork in the imagery and the syntax; you want, in fact, an eloquent rehearsal of traditional materials and even traditional ways of ordering those materials in a certain sequence. [Alter, Poetry, 112]

Finally, the conventional language **universalizes** the psalms. The psalmist using traditional form and language places himself in the common, rather than the individual, lot. Thus, the psalm becomes the language of the mythic community. Through this archetypal language, the worshiper becomes **the typical member of the community**.

As ancient Hebrew poetry, the psalms use **parallelism**, an arrangement of words and sounds to repeat, intensify, balance, contrast, or advance the thought/affect from one line to the next [see chap. 4, genre]. In synonymous parallelism, the second line repeats or intensifies the first. In antithetical parallelism, the lines contrast. In synthetic parallelism, the second line advances the first. Psalm 24:1-6 illustrates synonymous (cf. 34:13; 103:3, 9-10) and synthetic parallelism (cf. 14:2):

> The earth is the LORD's and all that is in it,
>> the world and those who live in it;   (synon.)
> for he has founded it on the seas,
>> and established it on the rivers.   (synon.)
> Who shall ascend the hill of the LORD?
>> And who shall stand in his holy place?   (synon.)
> Those who have clean hands and pure hearts,
>> who do not lift up their souls to what is false,
>> and do not swear deceitfully.   (synth.)
> They will receive blessing from the LORD,
>> and vindication from the God of their salvation. (synon.)
> Such is the company of those who seek him,
>> who seek the face of the God of Jacob.   (synon.)

Psalm 25:3 (cf. 1:6) illustrates antithetical:

> Do not let those who wait for you be put to shame;
>> let them be ashamed who are wantonly treacherous.

Of course, parallelism can become more complex. For example, parallelism can be complete, in which case every term in line one has a complement in the second line, or incomplete. Incomplete parallelism can occur with or without compensation. Without compensation, the second line is shorter than the first. With compensation, a term from the first line has no parallel, but expansion of another term or additions make the second line equal in length to the first. Gottwald's translation of Ps 103:3, 7-10 indicates complete parallelism and incomplete with compensation ["Poetry," 831-32]. The hyphens connect words which are translations of one Hebrew word:

> The-forgiver of-all-our-iniquities
>> The-healer of-all-our-diseases (complete)
>
> He-made-known his-ways to-Moses
>> to-the-sons of-Israel his-deeds (compensation)
>
> Compassionate and-gracious is-Yahweh
>> Slow to-anger and-abundant-in-mercy (compensation)
>
> Not-forever does-he-contend
>> And-not-perpetually is-he-angry (complete)
>
> Not according-to-our-sins does-he-deal with-us
>> And-not according-to-our-iniquities does-he-reward-us.
>> (complete)

Obviously, the potential for variation is endless.

Parallelism is hardly simple. It does not merely repeat or contrast ideas. Rather, it intensifies and builds images (or stories) [see Alter, Poetry, 27-84]:

> If something is broken in the first verset, it is smashed or shattered in the second verset; if a city is destroyed in the first verset, it is turned into a heap of rubble in the second. A general term in the first half of the line is typically followed by a specific instance of the general category in the second half; or again, a literal statement in the first verset becomes a metaphor or hyperbole in the second. . . . What this means to us as readers of biblical poetry is that instead of listening to an imagined drumbeat of repetitions, we need constantly to look for something new happening from one part of the line to the next. [Alter, "Characteristics," 615-16]

Narrator: God's Word and Israel's Answer

The psalms' narrator is uniquely human. Other biblical texts offer the direct (Torah) or indirect (biblical story) divine voice. By contrast, the psalms are "**Israel's Answer**."

As the biblical text concerns God's relationship with Israel (and/or humans), it would be woefully incomplete mythically if it did not dramatize the human side of the conversation. The psalms are **paradigmatic conversations with God**. They provide the **prototypes** of praise and petition. They teach the community to talk with God. In the psalms, then, the community knows itself as the Israel of the Lord (cf. the "we" psalms; e.g., 44; 60; 65; 67; 74; 79; 80; 85; 90; 124; 137).

This archetypal voice is not so evident in the "I" psalms which make up the bulk of the Psalter (e.g., 3-7; 13; 18; 22-23; 51). Sometimes the "I" is clearly a **religious functionary** who instructs the community (e.g., 1; 127; 133), who calls the community to worship (e.g., 107; 118; 124; 134; 136; 147-50), who blesses the community (128), or who speaks a divine word to the people (e.g., 75:2-5; 82; 91:11-12; 132:11-18). Again, contents or titles often identify the "I" as a **king** (seventy-three titles associate psalms with David).

These speakers are, of course, clearly **representative**. They speak for the people. Generally, the virtual absence of historical and personal details makes it possible for almost anyone in the community to make the psalm his own. The "I," then, is typical [see style].

What is truly striking about the pronouns in the psalms is their fluctuation. A "we" speaks and then a "divine I" speaks (75). An "I" speaks to Israel about God and then directly to God (135). God is both "mine" and "ours" in numerous psalms. The different speakers and addresses baffle without the realization that the psalms create a community's conversation with God, with itself, and with individual members.

When the psalms become part of the sacred canon, the human voice becomes divine. That is, psalms **become scripture** as well as prayer. How, then, does Israel's praise become God's word?

The problem is, of course, only one of degree. After all, the entire Bible speaks with and contains the human voice. Praise and petition are present in numerous biblical books, particularly in the prophets. Likewise, the psalms contain some "divine speech." Further, the psalms do **function mythically** [see media, myth]. They are the **words of worship** in which the sacred, mythic order becomes a living reality. Finally, like Torah and the Prophets, the psalms **demand and instruct**. Not surprisingly, then, Ps 1 transforms the entire Psalter into a meditation on the way of life [cf. Childs, Scripture, 513-14].

Story Shape, Plot Conflict, and Mythic Location

The lament and thanksgiving psalms recreate the familiar biblical story of the divine deliverance [cf. Brueggemann, "From," 13-19; Westermann, Praise, 259-80].

The lament cries to God "out of the depths" (Ps 130:1). It faithfully **locates the afflicted before God** even while in distress. The lament cries out for divine action, for God to engage in holy war for the worshiper (cf. the imprecatory psalms). It does not explain the worshiper's experience of evil (though see 37; 49; 73). It struggles with it practically. The lament reads the distress as an **opportunity for faith**, as a situation of "potential transformation" [Brueggemann, "From," 4, 8].

The thanksgiving celebrates the transformation. Thus, while its story resembles the lament, its form resembles the hymn. Those who have lived through chaos celebrate reestablished order.

The hymns are less story-like. They reveal, rehearse, and **celebrate the mythic identities and established order** of the mythic tradition.

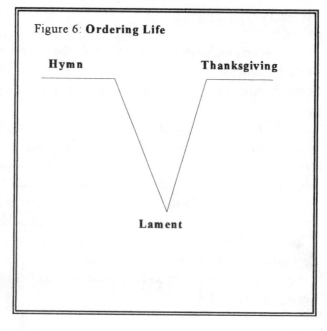

Figure 6: **Ordering Life**

Hymn

Thanksgiving

Lament

Together, the psalms **construct life** ordering it in story form. They provide a pattern (hymn, lament, thanksgiving) by which the worshiper can make sense of life [cf. Brueggemann, "Psalms," 5-10]. Through the psalms, worshipers **apply mythic labels to experience and locate themselves**.

Divine Character: Worship's Conversation-Partner

God is the cult's center, the sacred which provides life and meaning. He is "the good," which makes life possible and worthwhile:

> O give thanks to the LORD, for he is good,
> for his steadfast love endures forever.
> (136:1; cf. 106; 107; 118; Ex 34:6-7)

Not surprisingly, access to this God is terribly important. The psalms provide such access. God is the one to whom humans speak in praise (22:3) and petition (130:1). He is **Israel's dialogue partner** present in the cult (**institutional providence**). In fact, the psalms themselves **make God present**. Even the laments which bewail God's absence/inactivity (e.g., Ps 22:1-2; 42:9-10; 89:46) are bridges to God's redeeming presence. They connect the empirical reality of distress with the desired salvation through a cultic psalm which makes God institutionally present.

Humans: The Basic Mythic Identity

As finite, dependent creatures, humans desperately need the God who establishes the orders of life (hymns, thanksgivings) and delivers from the depths of chaos (the laments). Humans **with God** have the benefits of life. Humans **apart from God** for whatever reason do not [cf. chap. 3,

Figure 7: **Ethical Dualism**	
With God	**Apart From God**
life	death
order	chaos
good	evil
light	darkness
health	sickness
righteousness	sin and guilt
community	alienation
land, temple	exile
praise	no praise

human]. The psalms express this fundamental dichotomy (*ethical dualism*) with a stock-pile [see style] of symbols [cf. Thompson, 58].

God's gracious gift of order--creation, Sinai, king, or Zion--enables humans to live "with God." Cultic piety, including the singing/praying of the psalms, provides continuing access to these benefits. God is "enthroned on the praises of Israel," and Israel receives life in praise. Only in death is there no praise (e.g., 6:6; 30:9; 88:10; 115:17). Thus, for Psalms, "praise becomes the most elementary token of 'being alive' that exists" [Rad, Theology, 1:370].

When the empirical realities of life do not cohere with this basic ethical dualism (or mythic realities), the psalms struggle to realign them. The lament does this subjectively by moving the worshiper from complaint to praise. It also seeks to do it empirically by bringing sacred power into action in life. The psalms seek a **practical theodicy** [see lament]. They implore God's presence (cf. Job) which would, of course, banish death and return the goods of life.

Myth: Ritual Functions [cf. media]

The psalms dramatize the community's myth. Through ritual, they facilitate participation in the sacred, rehearse mythic identities, and order the world [see chap. 4, drama].

The psalms **make the sacred present**. They create conversational access to God. The hymns and thanksgivings acknowledge sacred benefits. The laments pursue them.

The psalms **foster mythic identities**. Through the psalms, the community and individuals remember who they are and publicly display their commitment. Most importantly, through the psalms, the community knows itself as God's conversational partner. The psalms educate the community. They teach them how to talk to God, to praise and petition.

Finally, the psalms **order life**. They locate the worshiper in the community (as a typical member). The typical psalm forms also construct life according to a mythic pattern [see story shape]. They teach one how to live the life of faith both in order (praise) and in chaos (lament).

Figure 8: **Confessions**

Augustine's famous autobiography, Confessions, is a conversation with God echoing the language of the psalms (it cites them at length). While its length far exceeds the psalms, its form is not unlike a thanksgiving. It invokes God in praise, tells the "before-after" story of Augustine's conversion, and then closes in praise. Further, Augustine's world-view resembles the psalms' myth at crucial points:

> Nevertheless, to praise you is the desire of
> man, a little piece of your creation. You stir
> man to take pleasure in praising you, because
> you have made us for yourself, and our heart is
> restless until it rests in you. [1.1]

Clearly, this God resembles the psalms' sacred good upon whom humans depend for their well-being. Augustine's understanding of the good, religious life differs from that of the psalms, however. Living in frustrated, alienated late antiquity, Augustine's religion takes the form of an individualistic flight from the world [cf. bk. 10]. Thus, compared to the psalms, Augustine's confessions are more introspective [cf. the famous pear story in bk. 2], and his fears of the flesh/world are far greater. In short, Augustine is a neo-Platonic ascetic, not a member of a natural religion with ontological conceptions of the good.

ANET: Natural Religion Hymns

The psalms' "formal monotony" fosters their **continuing relevance**. So, too, does their wide range of emotion and situation (order or chaos):

> ... the Psalter is the book of all saints; and everyone,
> in whatever situation he may be, finds in that situation
> psalms and words that fit his case, that suit him as if
> they were put there just for his sake, so that he could
> not put it better himself, or find or wish for anything
> better. [Luther, cited in Miller, Interpreting, 19-20]

Thus, the psalms have a strikingly "human" quality.

The psalms, however, are also strikingly **religious**. That religiosity distances the psalms from the modern secular world. The psalms depict life "before God." By contrast, moderns speak of good and bad fortune.

Figure 9: **"Song of Myself"**

Walt Whitman's "Song of Myself" expresses a world-view quite different from the psalms' notion that life is "before God." For Whitman and other moderns, the self is sufficient unto itself:

I celebrate myself, and sing myself . . . [1]

Walt Whitman, a kosmos . . .
Divine am I inside and out, and I make holy
    whatever I touch or am touch'd from,
The scent of these arm-pits aroma finer than prayer,
This head more than churches, bibles, and all creeds.
[24]

Not surprisingly, the two myths face distress differently. The psalms see chaos as an opportunity for faith, as a time to importune God. By contrast, moderns see distress as cruel fate or as an imposition from "the system" and as a time to implement some ideologically-based reform program. A modern revision of Ps 23:4

illustrates the differences:

> Even though I walk through the darkest valley,
>> I fear no evil
> for you [God] are with me . . . (ancient)

> Though I walk through the valley of the shadow of death,
>> I will fear no evil
> for I am the baddest S.O.B. in town! (modern)

While the secular modern may smile or sneer at this paraphrase, the psalmist would find it unspeakable hubris.

Finally, the natural religion expressed in the psalms distances them from modernity (cf. the royal and Zion psalms). To modernity, the perspective is ethnocentric. The imprecatory psalms are particularly offensive (35; 59; 69; 70; 109; 137; 140):

> Happy shall they be who take your little ones
>> and dash them against the rock! (137:9)

At best, these psalms express a nationalistic understanding of justice. At worst, they are pure hate.

Review Questions

1. Apply the reading method of chaps. 3-4 to Psalms. List its genre, plot shape, conflict, depiction of God, mythic function, and ANE problems.
2. Compare the form of the thanksgiving and the lament.
3. Why do the psalms use stereotypical forms and symbols?
4. What is parallelism?
5. Compare the narrator of the psalms to the biblical story narrator.
6. What kind of pattern do the psalms provide for life?
7. What kind of mythic functions do the psalms perform?

Suggestions for Alternate Reading and Reflection

1. How does the ancient use of the psalms [see media] differ from modern religious music?

2. What is the most basic form of religious speech? How are the psalms related to such speech?

3. Compare the form of the thanksgiving to that of modern testimonials and commercials.

4. How does the lament's theodicy differ from that of the Former Prophets?

5. Why do the prophets and Job use more striking images than the psalms [see chaps. 12; 16]?

6. Are the psalms really scripture?

7. What conception of providence do the psalms have? What other biblical books have similar conceptions?

8. How does the Song of Solomon differ from the typical hymn? What technique did both Jews and Christians use to give the Song more obvious religious significance? Is the Song religious without such an interpretation? Should it be in the canon?

9. How do the world-views of the "poems" of Augustine and Whitman compare to that of the psalms?

For Further Reading

For recent scholarly appraisals of the psalms, see Gerstenberger; and Miller, Interpreting.

On the music of the psalms, see Werner; Mowinckel, Psalms, 2:207-17; and EJ, 13:1319-22.

On conjectures about the psalms use in early worship, see Clements, Hundred, 84-88; Mowinckel, Psalms; Weiser, 35-52.

On the use of the psalms in later Jewish worship, see Greenstein, 42-43; EJ, 13:1322-26; and Cronbach. For use in Christian worship, see Anderson, Out, 3-4, 58; and Miller, Interpreting, 18-21.

On psalm forms, see Gunkel, Psalms; Anderson, Out; and Westermann, Praise.

On the poetry of the psalms, see Alter, "Characteristics"; **idem**, Poetry; Gottwald, "Poetry"; Hrushovski; and Kugel.

On metaphor, see Caird, Language, 152-59; and Lakoff and Johnson, 139-58. On rhythm, see Gottwald, "Poetry," 834; Alter, Poetry, 6-9; Hrushovski, 1201-02; and Kugel, 171-203.

For comparisons of the lament-thanksgiving story and biblical story, see Brueggemann, "From"; Westermann, Praise, 259-80; and Anderson, Out, 31-36.

On the Psalms as mythic locators and as hermeneutic for life, see Brueggemann, "From"; and **idem**, "Psalms."

On ethical dualism and mythic location in the psalms, see Thompson, 58; and Rad, Theology, 1:369-91.

On ritual, see the bibliography in chap. 4.

On the problem of natural religion in the psalms, see Brueggemann, Praying, 67-80; and Anderson, Out, 60-66.

CHAPTER 15

THE APOCALYPTIC NEW AGE
Daniel 7-12

Relationship to the Prophets

Several sections of the Latter Prophets are apocalyptic or contain apocalyptic elements (e.g., Isa 24-27; Zech 12; 14; Joel). In fact, apocalyptic (e.g., Dan 7-12) is similar to prophecy. Both deal with God's "new." Apocalyptic, however, **conceives the new more radically**. The prophetic new is an extension of God's presence and action in contemporary politics and history. For apocalyptic, however, the present is an evil world devoid of God, so a more radical transformation is necessary. Where prophecy looks forward to a new day (era), apocalyptic looks forward to a **new world**.

Apocalyptic also differs formally from prophecy. It is a **scribal phenomenon**, rather than an oral oracle. Apocalyptic is a series of complex vision reports and commentaries on earlier texts.

Content Summary: The New Age

Daniel 7-12 reports a vision of another world. For apocalyptic, God's presence and rule is not immediately obvious in the present evil world. Natural and supernatural forces of evil control the world and the righteous (God's people) suffer. The times become worse and worse as the deteriorating metal statue (Dan 2), the pretentious "little horn" (7-8), and unprecedented anguish (12:1) indicate. Fortunately, however, God will soon intervene and dramatically destroy the powers of this world (cf. Dan 2:35, 44-45; 7:9-18). Then, God and the righteous will reign in a glorious new age (7:27; 12:2-3). Apocalyptic, then, is an **eschatological dualism**, a

story of the present evil age and the glorious age to come.

Genre: The Apocalypse, Vision Reports

Apocalyptic is an adjective describing this **two-ages perspective** or groups/literature permeated by that perspective. By contrast, apocalypse is a genre designation of revelatory literature or vision reports. Not incidentally, apocalypse transliterates a Greek word meaning "unveiling" or "revelation." This explains the title of the final NT book:

> The Revelation of Jesus Christ, which God gave him
> to show his servants what soon must take place; and
> he made it known by sending his angel to his servant
> John. (Rev 1:1)

As that title illustrates, an apocalypse is a divine revelation through a mediator to a seer concerning future events. Daniel 7-12 has a similar structure. Daniel has "night visions" (7:1-2) about the future which an angel interprets (7:16-18; cf. Zech 1:7-6:15).

The central vision (e.g., Dan 7:2-14; Rev 1:12-16) has an elaborate setting

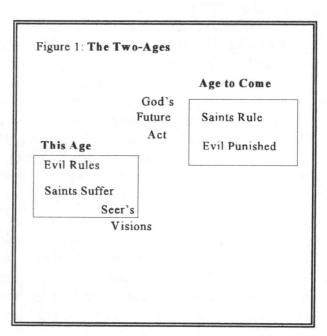

Figure 1: **The Two-Ages**

This Age — Evil Rules, Saints Suffer, Seer's Visions

God's Future Act

Age to Come — Saints Rule, Evil Punished

describing the seer's state either as lying in bed dreaming (Dan 7:1) or as in the spirit on the Lord's day (Rev 1:9-10). Both core visions also include a supernatural interpretation provided by an angel (Dan 7:15-27) or the Lord (Rev 1:17-20). The interpretation in Daniel involves a question-and-answer session between seer and angelic interpreter (a discourse cycle).

Figure 2: **Jewish Apocalyptic**

Apocalyptic was a prominent genre from the second century BCE to the second century CE. The most famous such material is the **Dead Sea Scrolls** from Qumran. That community so expected God's imminent, violent intervention that they withdrew to the desert to avoid the evil world (including the Jewish temple and priesthood). One of their more famous literary remains is the War Scroll. That text provides holy war directions for the upcoming war between the children of light (the Qumran community) and the children of darkness.

Scholars usually date most apocalyptic texts to two **moments of crisis** during this era, the **Maccabean Revolt** against the Seleucid ruler Antiochus Epiphanes ca. 167-164 BCE or the various Jewish revolts against Rome culminating in the **Jewish War** of 66-70 CE. The synoptic apocalypses, portions of Revelation, 2 Baruch, and 4 Ezra stem from the latter crisis. **Daniel**, portions of 1 Enoch (e.g., 83-90), Jubilees, and the Testament of Moses reflect the former.

The vision reports in Daniel and Revelation are historical. They describe the **world's progress to its end** and the arrival of God's new world. Other apocalypses (e.g., 2 Enoch) describe the seer's **other-worldly journeys** where he learns the workings of heaven (e.g., 1 En 72-82; Rev 4) or tours the places of punishment/reward (e.g., 2 Enoch).

In both cases, the revelation of the other world encourages the audience to live in conformity with that world, rather than the present evil world. Thus, if Daniel dates from the time of Antiochus Epiphanes' second-century persecution of the Jews (cf. 1 Macc 1-6), the visions encourage its recipients to maintain their Jewish faith by predicting the imminent divine destruction of the arrogant "little horn" (e.g., Dan 7:8, 20-27).

Figure 3: **The Divine Comedy**

Dante's The Divine Comedy is the classic Western example of a seer's otherworldly journey to the places of reward/punishment. It is, of course, also a classic medieval statement of sin and redemption. In the company of Virgil (human reason), Dante first journeys downward through hell (Inferno). The trip is an ethical valuation of sin as one moves from a bad (opportunism) to the worst sin (treachery). At the bottom of hell lies the greatest traitor, Satan. Each sin is punished poetically so that cold-hearted traitors, for example, are entombed in ice. Dante and Virgil then climb up the mountain of Purgatory (Purgatorio) purifying themselves of the seven great medieval vices and returning to Eden (the human condition before sin). Purified, Dante then meets Beatrice (divine revelation) who leads him through the heavenly spheres to the vision of God himself at the center of the redeemed (Paradiso). Despite the various hierarchies of sin and redemption, a fundamental ethical dualism remains. Those in hell prefer something or someone else to God. Those in heaven find peace in the divine will.

Style and Atmosphere: Ironic Worlds and Mythical Symbolism

Apocalypse creates a mythical world in which no reader has ever lived. The bestial kingdoms, talking horns, defeat of evil, and resurrections of Dan 7-12 are "fantastic." Apocalyptic does not represent reality. It offers **a window on another reality**.

Not surprisingly, then, apocalyptic language is **symbolic**. It is **expressive**, rather than referential [cf. Caird, Language, 260-71]. That is, apocalyptic symbols are more about the creation of certain attitudes--faith, endurance, worship--than they are about portraying a particular historical figure in bestial "drag." Thus, although de-codings of apocalyptic symbols as contemporary figures are perennially popular, such identifications are not apocalyptic's focus. In fact, apocalyptic so concentrates on the other world that it lacks precision in its cryptic speech about this world [cf. Russell, Apocalyptic, 25].

Nonetheless, apocalyptic does offers its own referential self-interpretations. Thus, Dan 7:15-18 defines the hybrid beasts of 7:2-14 as four kingdoms (human being = saints?). The scholarly conclusion that the "little horn" is Antiochus Epiphanes (as above) breathes the same **allegorical** air. Even "correct de-codings," however, rob the symbol of much of its **evocative power**.

The prophets mythologized historical events interpreting drought, war, and so forth as God's acts. The seer adds yet another symbolic level by casting the world's kingdoms and rulers as mythical animals (Dan 7-8) and finally as demons (Rev 12-13; 20). For the seer, the earthly situation reflects a larger supernatural world/conflict (Dan 10:12-14, 20-21). While Daniel does not "demonize," later apocalypses depict their opponents as Satan (e.g., Rev 12-13; 20).

"Satan" **symbolizes a radical experience of evil**. Human sin cannot account for an evil so intense that it seems a part of the fundamental structures of existence. Such evil seems imposed from without by fate, Satan, institutions/bureaucracy, multi-national corporations, and so forth. Further, such radical evil does not match any recognizable schema of retribution. The good, not the evil, suffer. The world has become ironic, a topsy-turvy, demonic place where **chaos reigns**.

Figure 4: **Zoroastrianism**

Zoroastrianism was the religion of ancient Persia (7th cent. BCE) founded by the seer Zoroaster (also called Zarathustra). It imagines the world as the realm of a continuing conflict between good and evil in which the god of light (Ahura Mazda) is constantly challenged by an evil spirit (Angra Mainyu). Ultimately, of course, Ahura Mazda triumphs. Not surprisingly, many scholars think that this eschatological dualism was one source for Jewish apocalyptic.

Apocalyptic uses **combat symbolism** to explain this ironic world. The symbols stem from ANE creation myths [see chap. 5, figure 1] which explain creation as a divine defeat of opposing, often dragon-like, powers (cf. Ps 74:13-14, 17; Job 7:12; 26:12-13, 41; Isa 51:9). Apocalyptic simply transfers this mythic struggle to the future:

> On that day the LORD with his cruel and great and strong sword will punish Leviathan the fleeing serpent, Leviathan the twisting serpent, and he will kill the dragon that is in the sea. (Isa 27:1; cf. Rev 20:2-3)

Of course, the notion that the Divine Warrior will someday defeat evil oppressors is also a familiar part of the Hebrew tradition. It animates the prophets' foreign nation oracles, the **Day of Yahweh** concept, and holy war ideology.

Figure 5: **Non-Dualistic Religions**

In contrast to Western religion, Eastern religion tends to non-dualism. Advaita **Hinduism** is the extreme example. For that religion, **the only reality is Brahman**. The notion that any reality exists independently of or other than Brahman, including the empirical world and the individual person, is nothing other than illusion (maya). There is, then, no great past, present, or future conflict between good and evil. All simply is. Hindu myth and ritual (the yogas) intend to illumine one and to bring one to mystic absorption in Brahman.

Ancient **Stoicism** is a similar monistic determinism. The world-order is a cart behind which one can walk or be drug. It is not good or evil. It simply is. The philosopher learns to accept the unchangeable apathetically.

Taoism's two life-forces, the yin (feminine, dark, destructive) and the yang (masculine, light, creative), seem more dualistic. Taoism does not, however, understand these principles to be in conflict. Rather, they are the ebb and flow of life. The good and successful life harmonizes the yin and yang of life.

Apocalyptic **does not array its symbols logically or sequentially**. Instead, it offers revolving, juxtaposed visions which cover the same material with different imagery or from different perspectives. Thus, Daniel's successive visions **repeat the same story**. Kingdoms succeed kingdoms. The different metals of Dan 2 and the different animals of Dan 7 represent passing powers which become less worthy and more bestial. Finally, a particularly wicked ruler oppresses God's people (the "little horn" of Dan 7-8 and the mighty king of Dan 10-12). Of course, **God,** represented by the stone cut by no human hand (Dan 2), the Son of man (Dan 7), and Michael (Dan 10-12), ultimately dispatches that ruler and **establishes his own**

kingdom.

Figure 6: **Pseudonymity**

For moderns, authorship is an economic matter carefully protected by individual authors, copyright laws, and publishing firms. The quest for individual achievement and economic success has led to extensive regulations about the use of another's work. By contrast, in antiquity, "authorship" covered a **broad spectrum** including texts dictated by, requested by, written for, and written "as if" by an individual author as well as works written by a disciple and forgeries [so Barr, NT, 71].

As Daniel is accurate about the mid-second century and inaccurate about the Babylonian and Persian periods, most scholars date the text to the second century. The ascription to the exilic Daniel, then, is an example of writing "as if." The pseudonymity is essentially a **claim to authority and antiquity**.

Narrator: Fictional Perspectives

The apocalyptic vision reports tend to be **first-person**. Unlike the equally identifiable prophetic narrator, however, the apocalyptic narrator is most often a "literary fiction" (though see Revelation). The apocalypses are **pseudonymous**.

In the case of Daniel, an author writing during the reign of Antiochus Epiphanes (2nd century BCE) adopts the fictional perspective of the exilic Daniel [cf. Collins, Imagination, 13-14; Eissfeldt, 520-22].   Other apocalypses cloak themselves in the **authority of** other **ancient worthies**--Ezra, Enoch, and so forth--as their fictional narrators. To account for the text's rather late appearance, Daniel claims the book was "sealed" until the appropriate moment (e.g., Dan 8:26; 12:4, 9).

Figure 7: **1-2 Maccabees**

For the HB, history ends with Ezra-Nehemiah. Like the works of Josephus, 1-2 Maccabees extend that history by continuing the style and mythic purpose of **biblical history** well into the second temple period. First and Second Maccabees are separate versions of the **Maccabean revolt**. First Maccabees describes the founding of the Hasmonean kingdom as the response to Antiochus Epiphanes. By contrast, 2 Maccabees deals primarily with Judas Maccabeus. Whereas 1 Maccabees is concerned with the Hasmonean kingdom, 2 Maccabees is more concerned with the temple. Judas' restoration of the temple is 2 Maccabees' climax. Interestingly, 2 Maccabees is also far more supernatural (non-realistic) than is 1 Maccabees.

With a historical apocalypse, like Daniel, this ante-dating **presents history** (from exile to Antiochus Epiphanes) **as prophecy**. Such successful "prediction" bestows authority upon the seer and lends credibility to Daniel's genuine predictions (from its writing to the end). More importantly, the "successful" predictions indicate that a hidden **God sets the times** of lesser powers (including the hateful Antiochus Epiphanes).

Story Pattern: A War of Myths

Daniel reflects the demise of **natural**, traditional **religions** in the face of the world empires of Babylon, Persia, Greece, and later Rome. Quite appropriately, then, Daniel's fictional narrator speaks from the **exile**, the event which ended Israel's natural religion.

The empires destroyed the traditional, unified system of political and religious power. Sometimes, as with Antiochus Epiphanes, the empires also deliberately outlawed the old religions. For those clinging to the traditional conceptions of goodness, **faith brought suffering**, rather than prosperity.

Daniel's visions and stories, then, a r e **propaganda for Jewish natural religion**. They imagine God's restoration of the religious tradition. The new age will restore the e q u a t i o n between being good and p r o s p e r i t y. Despite apocalyptic's future bent, then, it is ironically **reactionary**. Its fantasy of the reestablishment of Israelite natural religion wishes to do away with its "modern," pluralistic world.

Figure 8: **Apocalyptic's Comic Fantasy**

Old, natural religion
Good prosper

New natural religion
Saints rule

God's coming

Holy War

Bestial kingdoms, "little horn"
Saints suffer

Daniel's visions do, however, imagine a world "other" than that of the seemingly omnipotent, often oppressive world empires. Daniel relativizes the pretensions of the "little horn." Daniel's apocalypse offers hope to the alienated. In a world lacking theophanic clarity, apocalyptic depicts the situation of the suffering as temporary. The present tragedy is only the beginning of a divine comedy to come.

Seen so, Daniel is a **war of myths**. Competing world-views (value systems) confront one another. What the empire sees as order, the apocalyptic seer interprets as a temporary chaos.

Plot Conflict: The Final Holy War

Daniel's visions plot this war of myths as a **holy war**. They depict the divine conflict with the earth's kingdoms and with supernatural powers (Dan 10:12-14, 20-21). They envision the revelation of the true sovereign's identity.

The **similarity with the exodus** is striking. Once again, a foreign ruler oppresses God's people. Unwittingly, this opponent opposes the

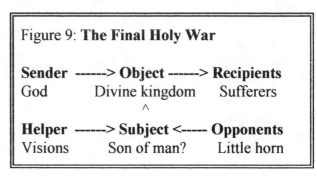

Figure 9: **The Final Holy War**

Sender ------> **Object** ------> **Recipients**
God   Divine kingdom   Sufferers
                      ^
Helper ------> **Subject** <----- **Opponents**
Visions   Son of man?   Little horn

divine program. Once again, God's opponent is hardly a genuine rival. The apocalyptic vision predicts the enemy's rise and fall. God allows the kingdoms and the "little horn" a little time. Of course, God defeats the upstart sovereign by establishing his natural religion. Daniel's visions and their publication are a preliminary stage in God's victory.

Divine Character: The Hidden Sovereign

In the radically evil world of the "little horn," **God is hidden**. He is not known in current events or institutions. In Dan 7-12, even the temple, the institutional vehicle of the sacred, is "desolate" (8:11-14). For apocalyptic, God is **known only in visions**.

Despite visions, God remains distant. The apocalyptic seer,

unlike his prophetic counterpart, requires supernatural aid to understand his visions. Angelic interpretations of the visions are, of course, quite appropriate to apocalyptic's scribal medium. So, too, is the frequent intra-textual commentary. In Dan 9, for example, the angel interprets Jeremiah's "seventy years" of exile (Jer 25:11) as seventy weeks of years, that is, four hundred ninety years of foreign oppression (Dan 9:24-27).

Figure 10: **Apocalyptic Conceptions of Providence**			
Direct	**Prophetic**	**Indirect**	**Hidden**
Gen 1-3	Exodus	Joseph	Little horn's time
Age to Come			**This Age**

The visions, of course, depict **God's future presence** (e.g., Rev 21-22) and conceive the divine providence quite mythically (cf. Gen 1-3). Ironically, then, apocalyptic begins with the unparalleled absence of God (chaos) and imagines his future, unparalleled presence.

For the seer, the absent but future God is the "Most High," the ultimate sovereign. He is also the Judge of both the living and the dead (Dan 12:2-4, 13). The apocalyptic God **raises the dead** to recompense their deeds. While natural religion needs no life beyond for retributive justice, apocalyptic's demonic world does. Not surprisingly, then, the HB's first clear references to a life beyond appear in apocalyptic. Those references are to the "resurrection of the dead," not to the immortality of the soul. For the HB, nothing about the human condition requires the life beyond. It is only the divine justice which makes resurrection necessary. Resurrection, then, is a typically biblical **deus ex machina** (cf. Ezek 37).

Finally, the apocalyptic deity is **nationalistic**. Apocalyptic envisions the restoration of Israel's natural religion. Interestingly, that reactionary hope does not differ substantively from the imperial myth which it challenges. It merely wishes to change the name of the ruling class. By contrast, the tales in Dan 1-6 imagine the conversion, rather than the annihilation, of the opposing sovereign (2:46-48; 3:28-30; 4:34-37; 6:25-27).

Figure 11: **Sects**

Sects are counter-culture groups who feel themselves alienated from the larger society of which they are a part. While all sects have this basic similarity, they differ in particulars. Bryan Wilson has recently devised an elaborate typology of sects to explain the **differing kinds of responses** "colonials" take to imperial power [see his Magic, 18-31]. Some sects develop a myth-ritual system designed to change their perception of the unchanged world or to await God's conversion of them individually. Others attempt to change the world by withdrawing, by reforming the world, by reconstructing the world, or by revolting (either human or divine violence). Daniel reflects the latter kind of sect.

Human Characters: Ethical Dualism

For apocalyptic's *ethical dualism*, one community is good, the children of light/God, and the other is evil, the children of darkness/beasts/the devil.

The elect belong to the Most High. As evil powers are in charge of this age, the elect suffer because of their alignment with the hidden God. They are **the oppressed righteous**. The visions of judgment and reversal both comfort the oppressed and warn them to remain faithful.

Everyone outside this *ethnocentric* community (the nations) is evil. Such an understanding, of course, dehumanizes the outsider. Not surprisingly, then, the nations are beasts or demons. Ultimately, they perish.

Myth: Future Recompense

The apocalyptic community is a sect, an alienated minority in the midst of this present evil age. The sect protests against the dominant imperial world-view and suffers because evil powers currently reign. Ironically, then, the community's righteous suffering becomes a **mark of its election**.

Fortunately, the suffering is only temporary. The apocalyptic vision locates the sect in the time immediately **before the divine reversal** which will right the world. Although the sect lives in chaos, the community knows the coming divine end.

Vision and hope, then, transform the present evil age. It is one thing to live under the "little horn." It is altogether different to live under the soon-to-be-deposed "little horn." Apocalyptic, then, **envisions a future melodrama** in which both the evil and the good will receive their just desserts (cf. Dan 12:2-3).

ANET: Violent, Gothic Escapism

For the modern reader, apocalyptic is a weird, grotesque conglomeration of mystical symbols. These symbols strike the prosaic, literalistic modern world as cartoonish. Combining the cartoon balloons (symbolism) with visions, angels, and demons produces a **gothic supernaturalism** altogether perplexing to the modern rationalist. Not surprisingly, modern readers rush to decode apocalyptic.

Further, apocalyptic's message of an ultimate sovereignty

which determines all comes close to a **denial of human responsibility**. While the limiting of the empires' times comforts the alienated, it raises the question of whether or not their, or any human, actions have any ultimate meaning. The externalization of evil--to bestial empires or demons--also enervates human action. In a world of warring gods, what is a mere human to do? The apocalypse, of course, answers with a call to faith.

Figure 12: **Western (Action) Movies**

Daniel's visions **externalize evil**. The apocalyptic community is innocent. Not surprisingly, then, the apocalyptic remedy envisions the violent annihilation of the evil outside the community. Even here, the apocalyptic community remains innocent because the annihilation is the work of an **external divine agent**.

Such ideas continue today. Thus, in the classic western Shane, a mysterious stranger arrives at the home of a farming family residing in a peaceful valley. Unfortunately, ranchers with corrupt henchmen threaten the peaceful family. The family cannot settle their problems; however, the mysterious stranger ultimately rides into town, kills the bad guys, and leaves town as mysteriously as he has arrived. Here, too, is the innocent community which remains innocent while its problems are solved by a stranger who violently destroys some corrupt society, bureaucracy, or nation. Almost all action movies enact in one form or another this **fantasy of innocent violence**.

From a modern perspective, that response smacks of a **quietism** bordering on fatalism. While a defensible posture for an alienated, disenfranchised minority in an ancient empire, it sounds like an **escapist fantasy** to the modern world.

Finally, apocalyptic is **ethnocentric** by modern standards. Only one community is privy to the esoteric visions and the beneficiaries of the imagined divine reversal. Further, apocalyptic is a reactionary desire to return to a natural religion situation. That desire is naive or malicious in the modern pluralistic world. It does not truly transform the hierarchical oppression of domination against which it inveighs. It is a religious imperialism which **merely wishes to change the name of the ruler**.

Figure 13: **Apocalypse at the Movies**

In contrast to apocalyptic hope, recent movies imagine **horrible new ages**. They represent technology run amuck (e.g., Terminator 2), the aftermath of nuclear war (e.g., the Mad Max series), the result of environmental suicide (e.g., Waterworld), and so forth. Put concisely, their vision is no good news. According to Bernard Scott, these disparate visions demonstrate "the price paid for the loss of transcendence. Without transcendence there is no relief from a continuing hell" [Hollywood, 199-200].

Hope remains in these modern apocalypses in the hero's innocent violence (the Western transposed to the future as in Star Wars) or in the creation of some new, fragile **mini-society** (the couple of Blade Runner or the children of Mad Max Beyond Thunderdome) [see Scott, Hollywood, 200-01].

Further, this imperialism proceeds from an ethical dualism with a frighteningly innocent, **external conception of evil**. It locates evil entirely outside the elect community. This lack of self-examination or protestation of self-righteousness is a "myth of innocence" which all too often leads to redemptive notions of violence delighting itself in the death of the wicked [see Mack, 353-76].

Despite its dangers, however, apocalyptic offers abiding value. Like prophecy, its chief importance is its ability to offer **imaginative alternatives to the current world-order** (myth) in light of its experience of a transcendent reality. Whether or not its imagination is truly "alternative" is, of course, the crucial question. Does it offer change or merely exchange (of the ruling powers)?

Review Questions

1. Apply the reading method of chaps. 3-4 to apocalyptic. List its genre, plot shape, conflict, depiction of God, mythic function, and ANE problems.
2. Compare apocalyptic to prophecy.
3. Explain apocalyptic's eschatological dualism.
4. Why is the apocalyptic world ironic?
5. Why did the seers write pseudonymously?
6. What is apocalyptic's relationship to natural religion?
7. What kind of sects write apocalypses?
8. Why is apocalyptic dangerous in the modern world?

Suggestions for Alternate Reading and Reflection

1. Compare apocalyptic to poetry.
2. Does the scribal nature of the apocalyptic vision reports impugn their integrity as actual reports? That is, are they reports of actual visions or scribal creations? What might a deconstructionist say about the incongruity between vision and report?
3. What contents do the apocalyptic visions typically have?
4. What does it mean to interpret apocalyptic allegorically? Why are readers prone to read apocalyptic allegorically?
5. Does apocalyptic pseudonymity mean that the seer was lying?
6. Why is the notion of resurrection more appropriate to biblical ideology than an immortal soul?
7. Is anything in modern, popular culture guilty of apocalyptic's innocent violence?

8. How do visions of the end in modern cinema differ from ancient apocalyptic?

9. Compare apocalyptic to ANE mythology.

10. Is apocalyptic biblical? That is, do any features of apocalyptic threaten general biblical ideology or does apocalyptic carry biblical ideology to extremes at any points?

For Further Reading

For general introductions to apocalyptic, see Koch, Rediscovery; Russell, Apocalyptic; and J. Collins, Imagination.

Prominent non-canonical examples of apocalyptic are 1 Enoch, 2 Enoch, 2 Baruch, 4 Ezra, and the Testament of Abraham. For translations, see Charles; and Charlesworth, Pseudepigrapha. For introductory discussions, see Koch, Rediscovery; J. Collins, Imagination; and Nickelsburg, Jewish Literature.

For a discussion of the genre of apocalypse, see J. Collins, Apocalypse; Hellholm; A. Collins, Early; and Aune, NT, 226-52.

On apocalyptic symbolism, see Caird, Language, 260-71.

For discussions of the influences on apocalyptic (including prophecy, royal cult, ANE myth, wisdom, Persian dualism, and Hellenistic syncretism), see Hanson, "Apocalyptic," 476-80; J. Collins, "Apocalyptic," 347-56; and **idem**, Imagination, 11-28.

For a discussion of ancient pseudonymity, see Barr, NT, 69-71; and Meade.

For a discussion of sects, see Bryan Wilson, Magic.

On the potential danger in myths of innocence like that of apocalyptic, see Mack, 353-76; Jewett and Lawrence; and Jewett, Captain.

On the relevance of apocalyptic, see Russell, <u>Apocalyptic</u>; and Rowley, <u>Relevance</u>.

CHAPTER 16

WISDOM LITERATURE

Relationship to the HB

Compared to other sections of the HB, the wisdom literature is quite distinctive. It has no obvious commitment to Israel's sacred traditions, and it is strikingly **optimistic about humanity**.

Content and Myth: Trusting God's Order and Humans

Wisdom is a **pragmatic attempt to master life**, an "art of steering," or a tradition about "the way the world wags" [Zimmerli, 317]. Essentially, it is a search for a good, meaningful life. It does, however, proceed from specific assumptions about the nature of the world and humanity.

Wisdom's ultimate metaphysical foundation is the notion that the **world is God's good creation** (e.g., Prov 3:19-20; 8:22-31; Job 38-41; Eccl 3:11; 12:1). This belief leads the sages to trust the world as a sacred order. For the sages, order means that actions have **definable consequences** which the wise know and accept:

> Train children in the right way,
>   and when old, they will not stray.
> Whoever sows injustice will reap calamity,
>   and the rod of anger will fail.
> Folly is bound up in the heart of a boy,
>   but the rod of discipline drives it far away.
>   (Prov 22:6, 8, 15)

Figure 1: **Varieties of Religious Experience**

According to William James, humans have two types of religious experience, the healthy-minded and the sick-souled [see Varieties]. The first is typical of the congenitally happy person, the essential optimist for whom all of life is good. The religion of such persons is a sense of union with the divine (e.g., natural religion, Eastern religion, and mysticisms). Healthy-minded religious persons, like Pelagius, depict religion in terms of human ethical responsibility. By contrast, the sick-souled are morbid and pessimistic. As life is evil or broken for them, their religion is a quest for redemption or liberation (e.g., Western religion). In the West, Augustine's theology of divine grace and human sin is the classic statement of the sick-souled position.

The two types of religious experience are not merely a matter of personal psychology. They are also a **myth war**. For the healthy-minded, humans live in a **divinely given order** (e.g., Eden, Sinai, Deuteronomy, or wisdom). For the sick-souled, humans live **in chaos** and in need of a **deus ex machina** liberation (e.g., Exodus, Second Isaiah, or apocalyptic).

Wisdom optimistically **trusts humans**. The sages believe that humans are educable, so they create and transmit proverbs, generalizing the community's experience, to pass on their experiential insights. The proverbs assert "that life is like this" and invite others to join the wisdom conversation and search. Inductive, experiential knowledge is, of course, contextual knowledge; so wisdom is, in one sense, **the search for the proper time** (cf. Prov 25:11; Eccl 3:1-8) [see Rad, Wisdom, 138-42].

Trusting humans leads wisdom to emphasize reason, rather than revelation. At least, its epistemological starting point is anthropocentric, rather than theocentric. For wisdom, humans do not need a new revelation delivering them from chaos. Rather, they need to learn to live in God's good order.

Nonetheless, wisdom is thoroughly religious. After all, the order is divinely given. Wisdom's trust in humanity, then, does not diminish transcendence. The human search for wisdom is the search to understand an unimpeachable **order transcending human** manipulation:

> The human mind plans the way,
>   but the LORD directs the steps.
> Sometimes there is a way that seems to be right,
>   but in the end it is the way of death.
> The horse is made ready for the day of battle,
>   but the victory belongs to the LORD.
> (Prov 16:9, 25; 21:31)

Not surprisingly, then, the sages can easily describe wisdom as "the fear of the LORD" (Prov 1:7; 9:10; 15:33; Ps 111:10; Job 28:28) or as a divine gift (cf. Job 28) [cf. Rad, Wisdom, 54-69].

For the sages, wisdom identifies the path to the good life (e.g., Eccl 1:3; 2:22-26). Put simply, **the good life is the result of living in harmony with the divine order**. The emphasis on order creates a traditional and conservative ethic **prizing propriety and decorum**. The good life is a **life of self-control** (of prudence, diligence, humility, and temperance) which carefully acknowledges human limits. Its vices are symptoms of a lack of self-control (laziness, drunkenness, adultery, harlotry, and gossip). Wisdom's concerns, then, are the places where limits are challenged and boundaries are crossed (women, wine, food, and speech) [cf. Crenshaw, OTW, 19-20].

For wisdom, the good is **ontological**. It imagines the good in this-worldly, materialistic terms as health, wealth, honor, progeny, longevity, and remembrance. Although speculative wisdom can challenge the assumptions (cf. Job), the wise typically expect to **live**

long and prosper. Conversely, fools perish. Wisdom, then, is life.

Figure 2: **Wisdom and Deuteronomy**

The notion that wisdom/goodness will ultimately be rewarded and that folly/evil will ultimately be punished is quite common. It appears in ANE wisdom, Hebrew apocalyptic, Greek philosophy, Hindu karma, traditional Christian thought, and modern educational and entrepreneurial enterprises. The biblical ideology closest to wisdom at this point is Deuteronomic theology. Wisdom's understanding is, however, clearly distinctive. While Deuteronomic thought understands the good life to follow obedience to specific **divine commands**, wisdom sees the good life as a quest for wisdom. Further, for wisdom, the act-consequence relationship is part of the natural order. By contrast for Deuteronomy, blessing and curse are specific **divine judgments** on obedience and apostasy.

Genre and Style: Practical and Speculative Wisdom

Wisdom texts are of various types. Proverbs is a collection of maxims. Job is a poetic story. Ecclesiastes is a series of random musings. Proverbs is conservative, practical, didactic, and optimistic. Ecclesiastes and Job are critical, radical, speculative, individualistic, and pessimistic. In fact, wisdom falls into two broad categories, **prudential, practical advice** (Prov 10-31) or **speculative investigation** (Job, Ecclesiastes). While the former sketches the practical path to a good life, the latter muses about the possibility of the good life.

The Proverb

The basic wisdom genre is the proverb, a sub-class of the Hebrew **meshalim** (sing. form, **mashal**) which refers broadly to figurative language. At heart, **the proverb compares**:

> A word fitly spoken
>> is like apples of gold in a setting of silver. (Prov 25:11)
> Wisdom is a fountain of life to one who has it,
>> but folly is the punishment of fools. (Prov 16:22)

In contrast to other comparisons, the proverb is a short, **pithy sentence** expressing a culture's traditional common sense:

> A fool and his money are soon parted.
> A penny saved is a penny earned.

Often, proverbs do not compare explicitly. Instead, they **provoke thought** by tying together disparate parts of life such as fire, drink, loose women, salt, speech, laziness, door hinges, ants, and industry. At times, the comparison lies in the connection of traditional wisdom to a specific situation. At heart, wisdom demands applying the right wisdom to the right situation at the right time.

Whereas popular proverbs are remarkably terse, the proverbs in the book of Proverbs have the formal parallel structure of **Hebrew poetry** [cf. Alter, Poetry, 171-73; Scott, Way, 59-63]. This style concretizes and fosters the wisdom world-view. Synthetic parallelism sets out the "act-consequence" relationship succinctly (Prov 22:6). Antithetical parallelism dramatically polarizes the ways of wisdom and folly (Prov 10:1; 15:7):

> Train children in the right way,
>> and when old, they will not stray. (Prov 22:6)
> A wise child makes a glad father,
>> but a foolish child is a mother's grief. (10:1)
> Better is a dinner of vegetables where love is

than a fatted ox and hatred with it. (15:7)

Figure 3: **Wisdom's Media**

Some scholars think that Israel's wisdom reflects a school medium. The direct evidence for schools, however, is late (Sir 51:1-12). References to teachers (Prov 13:14; Eccl 12:9), literacy, and the court's need for scribes and officials supply indirect evidence. It is quite likely, however, that wisdom had various contexts such as the **clan, court, and school** as Israel moved through her various stages of socio-political development [so Crenshaw, OTW, 56-57, 93-99].

Of course, wisdom's character would shift appropriately with its context. In particular, **the wisdom of times of stability is more optimistic than that of times of crisis** [see Crenshaw, "Wisdom," 370; cf. Rad, Wisdom, 237-39]. Israel's basic wisdom world-view might then have come from Israel's natural religion period. Challenges (e.g., Job and Ecclesiastes) to that conventional wisdom would then arise as the nation suffered crises calling into question or ending natural religion and its ontological good notions (e.g., the exile). Similarly, challenge might also arise as the individual became more and more important. Presumably, only growing ideas about individualism would support Job's quest for justice or explain Ecclesiastes' obsession with death. By way of contrast, D-theology and most of the prophets settle such issues at a social level.

As poetry, the proverbs use condensed, symbolic language. Like the psalms, the proverbs are **formal, monotonous poetry**. Most often, they **cluster images antithetically** posing the straight way against the crooked, riches against poverty, life against death, honey against bitterness, and so forth [cf. Alter, Poetry, 170-71]. These metaphors are not shocking, new insights. They **socialize**. Of course, this style is entirely appropriate for pedagogical material.

In addition to proverbs (most of 10-29), Proverbs contains **instruction** (roughly 1-9; 22:17-24:22; 31:1-9). While the proverbs kindle reflection and train judgment, the instructions demand obedience [McKane, Proverbs, vi, 3; Scott, Way, 52]. That instructional tone is particularly obvious in the book's opening words:

> For learning about wisdom and instruction
>   for understanding words of insight,
> for gaining instruction in wise dealing,
>   righteousness, justice, and equity;
> to teach shrewdness to the simple,
>   knowledge and prudence to the young--
> Let the wise also hear and gain in learning,
>   and the discerning acquire skill,
> to understand a proverb and a figure,
>   the words of the wise and their riddles. (Prov 1:1-6)

Throughout the opening section (1-9), a father (1:10-19; 2:1-22; 4:1-27; etc.) or wisdom personified (1:20-33; 8; 9) commends wisdom. Quite strikingly, the section's conclusion graphically parallels the invitations of Lady Wisdom and Dame Folly (9:1-6, 13-18).

The introduction also creates a **religious context** for the secular proverbs in the anthology by subordinating wisdom to the "fear of the Lord":

> The fear of the LORD is the beginning of knowledge;
>   fools despise wisdom and instruction. (1:7; cf. 9:10)

This fear is, of course, roughly synonymous with faith, commitment, obedience, or even religion [cf. Rad, Wisdom, 65-69]. Not surprisingly, in such a context, personified wisdom is life and creation itself (cf. 8).

Ecclesiastes' Skeptical Reflections

Ecclesiastes is an open notebook containing a sage's reflections upon wisdom. Ecclesiastes quotes (e.g., 7:1-14; 4:9-12; 10:2-11:6), reviews, and questions proverbs [Gordis, 95-108]. If the proverbs offer a "try it and see" philosophy, Ecclesiastes concludes that they do not work and offers another teaching in their place (4:17-5:8; 7:9-14; 10:1-6; etc.).

Two refrains dominate Ecclesiastes' musings. "Vanity and a chase after wind" is prominent in 1:12-6:9 while "not find out/who can find out" occurs often in 6:10-11:6 [Wright, "Riddle," 252-58]. Throughout, Ecclesiastes struggles with one question and repeats a simple, practical answer: "What do people gain from all their toil?" "There is nothing better for mortals than to eat and drink, and find enjoyment in their toil" (cf. 2:24; 3:12-15, 22; 5:17-19; 9:7-10; 11:8-12:7).

Ecclesiastes' tone is somber and depressing. Its rambling style matches its message about **the futility of it all**. In such a work, non-progressive repetitiveness, contradictions, and uncertainties are not surprising. Some sections are, however, so contradictory that they are generally regarded as orthodox glosses (e.g., 3:17; 7:18; 8:12-13; 11:9b; 12:9-14) [Crenshaw, OTW, 146].

Job: Prose, Poetry, Lament, and Dispute

Broadly speaking, Job encloses a poetic dialogue (3-42:6) in a prose framework (1-2; 42:7-17). The prose sets the stage for the poetic drama and resolves its tensions.

The introductory prose poses a difficult question, **"Does Job serve God for naught?"** Its answer is that Job is disinterestedly righteous. He does not expect the goods of life for his piety (2:10).

Surprisingly, however, the dramatic poetry reopens the

question. The poetry's Job is quite demanding. If this is his life, he would rather die (3). This Job does not clearly serve God for naught. He begins a **lament** (cf. 29-31) which would rectify his situation.

```
┌─────────────────────────────────────────────────────────────┐
│                                                             │
│   Figure 4: Job's Structure                                 │
│                                                             │
│     1-2      Prose introduction with rapid shifts between   │
│              Job's trials and the heavenly court which      │
│              decides his fate                               │
│                                                             │
│   3:1-42:6  Poetic dialogue including:                      │
│             3; 29-31    Job's curses and oath of innocence  │
│             4-27; 32-37 Dialogues with friends in which Job │
│                         maintains innocence and they try to │
│                         bring him to repentance             │
│             38:1-42:6   The whirlwind and Job's repentance  │
│                                                             │
│    42:7-17  Prose conclusion restoring Job's prosperity     │
│                                                             │
└─────────────────────────────────────────────────────────────┘
```

Amidst Job's complaint, however, is a lengthy dramatic **dialogue with his friends** (4-27; 32-37). Job's friends represent conventional wisdom and assume that goodness brings goods. They agree with the adversary that no one serves God for naught. They presume, then, that Job's fate is the result of a secret sin. As a result, they struggle to **bring him to repentance** which will end his suffering (4:8; cf. 8:6-7; 11:13-20; 22:21-30; Josh 7:1). They presume his repentance will restore his fortunes. In this, they work for Job.

Their sympathy and concern for Job deteriorate, however, as the dialogue progresses. Ultimately, if Job will not repent, they will have none of him. If Job or their conventional wisdom must go, let it be Job. Job's world is too disconcerting.

Figure 5: **The Whirlwind**

The whirlwind is a blatant assertion of the divine sovereignty over the creature. For some readers, God rejects human concerns for **theodicy** and bluntly puts Job in his place. After all, despite human narcissism, the world is amoral; and **humans are insignificant** [Tsevat; Greenberg; 298-99; Alter, Poetry, 104-06]. Others try to avoid what appears to them to be little more than a divine bully. For them, then, the whirlwind is an act of gracious condescension in which the Creator deigns to speak to his creature. Rejecting Job's presumptuous criticism, God changes the question of theodicy to **the question of piety**, the issue of life before the Sovereign [cf. Otto, 79-80; Terrien, Job, 236-39; Rad, Wisdom, 224-36].

Job's own experiences challenge the wisdom world-view. He knows that he **suffers innocently** (e.g., 9:21; 27:2, 4-6; 23:10-12). He refuses, however, to leave the matter there. Fearfully (9), he **seeks God** (and life). To this end, he offers a ritualized oath of innocence (29-31). He calls down curses upon himself if he lies when he says that he suffers innocently:

> Oh, that I had one to hear me!
>   (Here is my signature! let the Almighty answer me!)
>   Oh, that I had the indictment written by my adversary!
> Surely I would carry it on my shoulder;
>   I would bind it on me like a crown;
> I would give him an account of all my steps;
>   like a prince I would approach him. (31:35-37)

In short, Job wants to know why he suffers. He wants an answer to the riddle of his life. Clearly, he does not assume that one should serve God for naught.

Figure 6: **Repentance and Rebels**

Many modern readers want Job to stand up to the
divine bully. It is unlikely, however, that the ancients with
traditional, hierarchical world-views could imagine or
celebrate such rebels. The closest analogy is the ancient hero
who accepts divine superiority but **tricks the divine** into
bestowing some boon (e.g., Utnapishtim or Prometheus). One
can read Job's repentance in this fashion as an insincere trick.
As Job cannot defeat God or hold him to account, he can
regain the goods of life by **placating this petulant deity**. If
so, Job's repentance humors God [cf. Williams, "You,"
231-55; Robertson, "Book," 467-68].

Most, of course, read Job's repentance as a genuinely
religious act. If so, Job repents his protested righteousness
and his attempt to foist human standards upon the divine. He
accepts divine transcendence and human finitude.
Foreswearing hubris, he becomes a man of faith or a man in
quest of faith/myth. More literarily, of course, Job's
repentance affirmatively answers the adversary's question.

Job's oath elicits responses from Elihu (32-37) and the
whirlwind (38-42:6). While the somewhat comic Elihu repeats the
friends' themes, he also anticipates the theophany's theme of **human
finitude** (e.g., 33:12-14) **before the Creator's overwhelming power**
(e.g., 34:13-15; 36:26-37:24):

> Those who have sense will say to me,
>   and the wise who hear me will say,
> "Job speaks without knowledge
>   his words are without insight." (cf. God's speech)
> Would that Job were tried to the limit,
>   because his answers are those of the wicked.
> For he adds rebellion to his sin; (cf. the friends' themes)

he claps his hands among us.
and multiplies his words against God. (34:34-37)

The **theophanic whirlwind** categorically refuses Job's right to question the divine sovereignty. Job does not have the requisite power or wisdom to contend with God. Not surprisingly, then, the whirlwind does not answer Job. It **refuses his questions**. Of course, the reader already knows that the adversary's question is the definitive one for the story. With his argument invalidated, Job sensibly withdraws:

Therefore I have uttered what I did not understand,
   things too wonderful for me, which I did not know. . . .
therefore I despise myself,
   and repent in dust and ashes. (42:3bc, 6)

Ironically, **Job repents** just as the friends have wished. That repentance harmonizes the poetry with 2:10. Once again, Job serves God for naught.

Instead of a philosophical theodicy, then, Job offers a humbling theophany and the Bible's most innovative, striking poetry [see Alter, Poetry, 76-83, 190-92]:

Job's first poem is a powerful, evocative, authentic expression of man's essential, virtually ineluctable egotism: the anguished speaker has seen, so he feels, all too much, and he wants to see nothing at all, to be enveloped in the blackness of the womb/tomb . . . . In direct contrast to all this withdrawal inward and turning out of lights, God's poem is a demonstration of the energizing power of panoramic vision. Instead of the death wish, it affirms from line to line the splendor and vastness of life . . . . When the world is seen here through God's eyes, each item is invoked for its own sake, each existing thing having its own intrinsic and often strange beauty. [96-97]

That is, the whirlwind rejects Job's narcissism and calls him beyond himself to God and his splendid creation.

Thereafter, the prose epilogue is anticlimactic. The return of prosperity satisfies conventional wisdom and the desire for a happy ending, but it leaves the answer to the adversary out of focus.

Narrator/Implied Reader: Job's Dramatic Confrontation

While its prose has a typical biblical narrator, the poetry in Job is a **dramatic dialogue**. The narrator, then, is absent except for occasional introductions of speakers (e.g., 3:1; 4:1; 6:1; cf. the Torah sayings). As the narrator recedes, the narrative standards become less certain. Without clear narrative statements, how does the reader know which character speaks for the text's narrative standards?

Fortunately, the prose supplies an interpretative frame for the poetry. Within the poetry, **repetition and stage presence** (length and quality of speeches) provide interpretative clues. Not incidentally, Job, friends, and whirlwind reiterate the message of human finitude and the Creator's sovereignty.

The poetry **confronts** the (implied) reader. It creates a poetic experience, not rational persuasion. The poetry strives to bring the reader to see life newly. To that end, it utilizes innovative metaphors and vivid images. Even the introductory prose is shocking and parabolically provoking.

Proverbs and Ecclesiastes: Traditional and Individual Voices

Popular proverbs use the voice of communal common sense, or **traditional wisdom**. The book of Proverbs filters this traditional wisdom through the individual, authoritative voices of a father (e.g., 1:10-19; 2:1-22; 4:1-27), personified wisdom (e.g., 1:22-33; 8:4-36), or a mother (31:2-9). Editorial work has further ascribed mini-anthologies to the legendary wise including Solomon (1:1; 10:1; 25:1), the wise (1:6?; 22:17; 24:23), Agur (30:1), and Lemuel (31:1). Traditional wisdom, of course, finds **willing listeners**. Proverbs, then, instructs. It has no need to convert "fools."

Figure 7: **Existentialism**

For modern existentialism, the world is a theater of the absurd in which humans must carve out limited meanings under the horrible specter of death. While Ecclesiastes inhabits a similarly opaque, threatened world, Ecclesiastes remains certain that the world has a hidden, divine meaning. Unfortunately, humans cannot uncover that meaning. Rather, they must simply accept their fate ("lot"). Ecclesiastes, then, counsels a submission far from existentialist rebellion. Unlike existentialism, Ecclesiastes lives without denying either death or God.

Ecclesiastes has a far more individualized narrator. The personal voice is, of course, necessary for the **confessional**, autobiographical style of one who has **tried wisdom and found it wanting** (e.g., 1:12-2:26). Not surprisingly, Ecclesiastes does not expect a ready reception. To gain a hearing, the text utilizes the artifice of Solomonic authorship. If any Hebrew tried wisdom and wealth, it would be the legendary Solomon. Nonetheless, editorial additions indicate that later readers still found Ecclesiastes dissonant. The additions place Ecclesiastes' critique within the communal context of wisdom (1:1-2a; 12:8-14). That frame both legitimizes and reduces Ecclesiastes' challenge.

Story Pattern and Conflict: Wisdom's Two-Ways

Proverbs reveals the character, way, and results of wisdom.

Its description of wisdom also sets out the way of folly through antithetical parallelism. Thus, Proverbs has two potential stories, the **way of the wise and the way of the fool**. The wise live in harmony with the created order and, thus, live well. By contrast, fools ignore the order and perish. Their story is an incipient tragedy.

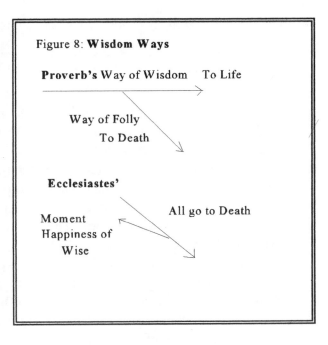

Figure 8: **Wisdom Ways**

Proverb's Way of Wisdom   To Life

Way of Folly
To Death

Ecclesiastes'

Moment
Happiness of
Wise

All go to Death

By contrast, Ecclesiastes knows only the way of death (e.g., 2:12-17; 3:20; 9:2-6). For Ecclesiastes, every **life is tragic**. Thus, wisdom does not truly profit (1:18; 2:15; 8:16-17). Ecclesiastes, then, cannot counsel wisdom. Instead, it recommends the enjoyment of whatever **momentary happiness** might interrupt the inexorable path to death:

> Go, eat your bread with enjoyment, and drink your wine with a merry heart; for God has long ago approved what you do. Let your garments always be white; do not let oil be lacking on your head. Enjoy life with the wife whom you love, all the days of your vain life that are given you under the sun, because that is your portion in life . . . . Whatever your hand finds to do, do so with your might; for there is no work or thought or knowledge or wisdom in Sheol, to

which you are going. (9:7-10; cf. 6:18)

Given its horror of death, this courageous counsel is all that remains.

Figure 9: **Ethical Systems**

Ethical theorists sometimes divide ethical systems into deontological and teleological approaches. Deontology is a rule-based approach. One has a clearly defined duty or responsibility to follow (cf. Deuteronomic thought, Stoicism, and Hinduism). Teleology is a **goal-based approach to ethic**. Having adopted a goal, one acts in order to achieve that goal (e.g., wisdom's good life). The most common goals are happiness (Aristotle) or pleasure (Epicurus). As long as one does not understand hedonism (an ethical system with pleasure as its goal) in terms of short-term sensuality, one might even describe wisdom as a **hedonistic ethic**. At least, like Epicurus, wisdom sought to minimize pain and maximize pleasure through a life of self-control.

Story Pattern and Conflict: Job's Deus Ex Machina

Two cross-conflicts dominate Job, the adversary's question about disinterested righteousness and Job's quest for God.

In the first conflict, God allows Job to suffer to test **the nature of his piety**. Does Job serve God "for naught" (for God himself) or for the goods that Job receives from this piety? Notably, God trusts Job. The story is a holy war plot, a cosmic contest between the adversary and God in which Job is an unknowing pawn.

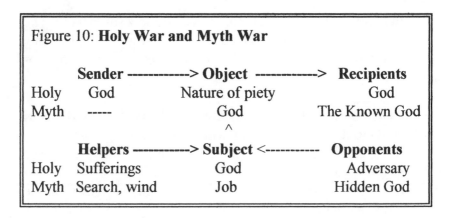

Figure 10: **Holy War and Myth War**

	Sender ------------>	**Object** ------------>	**Recipients**
Holy	God	Nature of piety	God
Myth	-----	God	The Known God

	Helpers ------------>	**Subject** <------------	**Opponents**
Holy	Sufferings	God	Adversary
Myth	Search, wind	Job	Hidden God

Ignorant of the heavenly wager, the dialogue partners of the dramatic poetry try to align Job's piety/sin and material conditions far too neatly. More importantly, their wisdom world-view threatens to answer negatively the adversary's question. Neither Job nor the friends appear to serve God for naught. The **deus ex machina** whirlwind, however, brings about Job's repentance and resolves the adversary's question. Job now serves God "for naught."

The poetic drama contains the second conflict in which Job **seeks God** in the midst of his

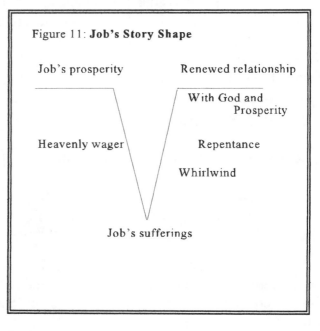

Figure 11: **Job's Story Shape**

Job's prosperity

Renewed relationship

With God and Prosperity

Heavenly wager

Repentance

Whirlwind

Job's sufferings

inexplicable sufferings. For conventional wisdom, God is known in order and prosperity. Where, then, is God in Job's sufferings? The friends say that this experience is judgment. Job himself knows only God's mysterious absence. Job, however, dares to seek a God "for him" (9:13).

The conflict, then, is a myth war with **rival conceptions of God**. Is God a God of order in which all suffering comes from wickedness, or are God and life more mysterious? Finally, Job wins through the hidden and conventional God to find the God of the whirlwind. In this climax, although Job must acknowledge the divine sovereignty, he finds the relationship with God that he seeks (42:5). The prose epilogue conventionalizes and clarifies. Of course, Job prospers again.

Divine Character: The Hidden Creator

In general, the God of the wisdom traditions is a **universal, indirect Orderer**. He is equally available to all (universal) as he is known primarily through reflection on the orders that humans confront (indirect) and as he provides the order in which all live. This universal, indirect Orderer contrasts strikingly with the national God of biblical story.

Figure 12: **Nationalism and Universalism**			
Reactionary	**Natural Religion**	**Mission**	**Universalism**
Apocalyptic	Torah	Jonah	Gen 1-11
Ezra-Nehemiah	Prophets	Second Isa	Wisdom

Ecclesiastes, of course, is not so optimistic. For Ecclesiastes, humans are so finite that they cannot know God or the order of life. God is completely hidden and the world is **opaque**, confining, damning:

I have seen the business that God has given to
everyone to be busy with. He has made everything
suitable for its time . . . . yet they cannot find out
what God has done . . . . God has done this, so that all
should stand in awe before him. (3:10-11, 14)

Job, too, knows the hidden God and the meaningless world,
but he refuses to accept his alienation and God's remoteness. Job
searches relentlessly for God. In the whirlwind, Job directly
confronts the deity. Although this God terrifies (terrorizes?), he is for
Job to the extent that he speaks with him. Finally, Job finds a God
directly present.

Figure 13: **Imagining Providence**

Direct	**Prophetic**	**Cultic**	**Cultural**	**Hidden**
Whirlwind	Torah	Psalms	Wisdom	Sufferings
	Prophets	Chronicles		Ecclesiastes

While Ecclesiastes retains a belief in the divine sovereignty,
the divine benevolence has become suspect:

All this I laid to heart, examining it all, how the
righteous and the wise and their deeds are in the hand
of God; whether it is love or hate one does not know.
(9:1)

Death is all encompassing. It creates a gulf between humans and
God which renders trust impossible and leaves only fear (3:14; 5:7;
8:12-13).

Job, too, knows terror before the absolute sovereign who

cavalierly wagers Job's life and, then, bullies Job into repentance while refusing to accommodate human judgment. By human standards, God is irresponsible. He accounts to no one. In short, for Job, as for Ecclesiastes, God is the terrifying Holy beyond rationalized and conventional securities.

Figure 14: **Deism**

Deism, the fruit of the interaction between the Western religious traditions and modern science, conceives God as the absent creator of a mechanistic world operating according to a closed system of natural causes and effects. That conception, of course, renders miracles impossible and petitionary prayer ludicrous.

While wisdom's God of the world order resembles this God, the wisdom world is mysterious, not mechanistic. Thus, God may, on the odd occasion, intervene in the wisdom world (e.g., Job's whirlwind; Prov 21:30-31). As a result, the wisdom God is more sovereign, but less transcendent than the deist God.

Myth 2: Trusting Humans

Wisdom is fundamentally **optimistic about humans**. For conventional wisdom and Proverbs, humans can know and do the good (or wisdom). That, of course, is the very basis of wisdom's two-ways teaching. Unlike the Deuteronomic two-ways, however, this ideology is not primarily a theodicy. The proverbs do not seek to account for the ills of life after the fact. Rather, they are a practical program designed to achieve the best possible life. They **educate for success**.

Figure 15: **ANE Wisdom**

HB wisdom resembles other ANE wisdom as a
comparison of Prov 22:17-24:12 with the Egyptian
"Instruction of Amen-em-opet" demonstrates [see Crenshaw ,
OTW, 220-22:

> Never make friends with an angry man
> nor keep company with a bad-tempered one.
> (Prov 22:24)
> Do not associate to thyself the heated man,
> Nor visit him for conversation. (Amen. 11:13-14)

> Do not move the ancient boundary-stone
> which your forefathers set up. (Prov 22:28)
> Do not carry off the landmark at the boundaries of the
> arable land . . . (Amen. 7:12)

The closest parallels to Israel's speculative wisdom are
in Sumeria. Some describe "I Will Praise the Lord of
Wisdom" as a Babylonian Job. That story's noble hero loses
everything, becomes an outcast, suffers illness, and resigns
himself to his inability to comprehend the god's ways. After
an attempted exorcism and superhuman visitations, the noble
recovers [summarized in Crenshaw, OTW, 230].

For the somber Ecclesiastes, death casts its specter over all
and denies wisdom's fundamental value. Nonetheless, Ecclesiastes
finally avoids nihilism. It offers a final, heroic ethic, a **carpe diem.**
Despite the torments and solitudes of existence, Ecclesiastes believes
enough in humans to assert that they can courageously seize
momentary happiness in the face of death.

Figure 16: **Sirach and the Wisdom of Solomon**

The Wisdom of Jesus ben Sira has two notable sections, an anthology of proverbs (1-42) and an eulogistic catalogue of famous men (44:1-50:24). Unlike Proverbs, Sirach **identifies wisdom specifically with Torah** (cf. 24:8-12, 23) as part of its nationalizing of earlier wisdom's universalism. Thus, the "praise of famous men" identifies "our ancestors" and makes wisdom active in Israel's history as well as creation. In short, Sirach merges the wisdom traditions with the basic biblical story.

By contrast the Wisdom of Solomon extends wisdom toward Greek thought in its fervent belief in the **immortality of the righteous** (e.g., 1:12-15; 2:21-24; note also the Greek virtues in 8:7). Wisdom has three major sections. The first section (1-5) presents the drama of the other-worldly triumph of the suffering righteous over the persecuting wicked. In the second section (6-9), Solomon extols the merits of **personified wisdom** (cf. Prov 8; Sir 24) and exhorts rulers to seek this immortality-conferring wisdom. The third section (11-19) highlights wisdom's involvement in Israel's history (particularly in the exodus).

Job's optimism about humans is more complex. Job's search for God has led most interpreters to discuss Job in terms of **theodicy**. Job does present in one form or another almost every conceivable theodicy. The sin-theodicy is given, by far, the most air-time in the friends' unending, relentless pursuit of the guilty Job. Of course, the prose introduction emasculates that theodicy.

In fact, the adversary's haunting question and the overwhelming whirlwind **reject the human search for theodicy**. Instead, they pose the fundamental question of religious life, the **nature of piety**. In short, does Job serve God "for naught?"

Summarized so, Job **challenges all myths and moralisms** [Tsevat, 365-72]. If Job serves God "for naught," there is no necessary connection between good and goods. If humans lose (Job 1-2) or receive goods (42) according to divine whim (or grace), there is no necessary connection either. In fact, Job reduces the connection to human fantasy. Job is part of a world far beyond his imagining and control. The Lord giveth, taketh away, and giveth again.

Job's only recourse, as a religious person, is repentance (faith). If this be theodicy, it is incredibly practical. It is, of course, no more practical than Ecclesiastes' **carpe diem** ethic. It is, however, more fundamentally religious.

Despite Job's lack of control and his final submission to forces larger than himself, Job, like the other wisdom materials, retains a fundamental faith in humankind. For Job, humans can serve God "for naught." In fact, even **God trusts Job**.

ANET: Fundamentally Different Anthropologies

The wisdom world-view's optimism, materialism, hedonism, and prudence correspond closely to what sociologists have described as the modern "sensate" perspective of empiricism, secularity, humanism, pragmatism, utilitarianism, and hedonism [Berger, Rumor, 1]. Ecclesiastes' cynicism in the face of the absurd also strikes responsive chords in modernity.

Nevertheless, wisdom's world-view is not modern. Its hedonistic materialism is actually a **sacramentalism**, the result of living in harmony with a divinely established order. Further, its optimistic anthropology is hardly the philosophical liberalism undergirding individualism, democracy, and dialogue. Wisdom belongs to a **closed, hierarchical traditional society** (cf. the treatment of women). Wisdom humans remain biblical humans, **humans before God**.

In short, wisdom is **the world of Job's repentance**. That religious submission surprises and frustrates most modern readers [see figures 5 and 6]. The submission is, of course, totally appropriate if one assumes a divine sovereignty ideology. In fact, Job wrestles with theodicy as much as that ideology will allow. It is, of course, that myth which separates wisdom from modernity. Even Ecclesiastes' cynicism does not challenge the divine sovereignty.

Review Questions

1. Apply the reading method of chaps. 3-4 to the wisdom literature. List its genre, plot shape, conflict, depiction of God, mythic function, and ANE problems.
2. Describe the wisdom world-view. In what sense is it optimistic? In what sense is it religious?
3. How are proverbs comparisons?
4. What is disinterested righteousness? How does the adversary's question differ from the question of theodicy?
5. Given the dramatic form of Job, how does the reader know what the narrative standards are?
6. Compare the implied stories of Proverbs and Ecclesiastes. Is Ecclesiastes' practical advice truly different from that of Proverbs? From that of Job?
7. What questions dominate Job? Are these questions answered?
8. How does Job challenge all myths and moralisms?
9. Is Ecclesiastes religious?

Questions for Alternate Reading and Reflection

1. How does the wisdom world-view compare to that of other sections of the HB? To that of modernity?
2. At what points do Job and Ecclesiastes challenge the wisdom world-view? Do they deconstruct it?
3. How does the prose framework interpret the poetic dialogue of Job? What would Job mean without the prose? Could the prose

stand alone? What would the prose mean without the poetry?

4. Is Job disinterestedly righteous? Is the repentance in Job's best interests or not? If so, is he moral?

5. Why would the imagery of Job be less conventional than that of Psalms and Proverbs? Do the functions of the various pieces differ? Do they expect different relationships with their implied readers?

6. Is the God of Ecclesiastes or of Job good?

7. Compare wisdom and Deuteronomy on the act-consequence.

8. How do specific cultural (socio-economic) provenances effect wisdom? How do specific mythic locations effect wisdom? Religion generally?

9. Categorize wisdom's ethic philosophically.

10. Compare Ecclesiastes and existentialism.

11. Is the wisdom God deistic?

12. In what directions do Job and Ecclesiastes threaten to take the wisdom traditions? In what directions do Sirach and the Wisdom of Solomon take wisdom?

For Further Reading

For a criticism of the scholarly category, "wisdom literature," see Alexandra Brown, 409-12.

For definitions of wisdom, see Crenshaw, "Wisdom," 369; **idem**, OTW, 62-63; Scott, Way, 52; and Rad, Wisdom, 289.

For ANE wisdom texts, see Pritchard. For discussion and comparison to the HB, see Crenshaw, OTW, 212-35; Lambert; Williams, "Wisdom"; and Oriential Wisdom. For a cross-cultural analysis of wisdom, see Rudolph, "Wisdom."

For a discussion of wisdom's optimistic, anthropomorphic ideology, see Brueggemann, In Man. On reason and revelation in wisdom, see Rylaarsdam; and Rad, Wisdom, 60-69. On wisdom as a search, see Crenshaw, OTW, 62-64. On wisdom and transcendence, see Brueggemann, In Man, 20-21, 52, 63, 113; and Rad, Wisdom,

106.

On the proverb as a teaching tool, see Alter, Poetry, 163-67. The teacher may well have given the first line of a proverb and expected the student to "cap" the proverb with a second line. For discussion of wisdom's "school" setting, see Clements, Hundred, 101-04; and Crenshaw, "Wisdom," 369-73. On Israelite education, see Kaster; Rad, Wisdom, 17-20.

For understandings of the sages as persons other than teachers, see Whybray, 59-70 (educated, gentleman farmers); and McKane, Prophets, 35, 46-48, 126-29 (realistic statesmen).

On wisdom's secularity, see McKane, Proverbs, 11-20; and **idem**, Prophets. For a defense of its religiosity, see Rad, Wisdom, 54-62, 98-109.

On wisdom for order and for chaos, see Crenshaw, OTW, 56-57, 93-99; Rad, Wisdom, 237-39; Williams, Ponder, 35-63; and Beardslee, Literary, 36-39.

On wisdom's vices and virtues, see Crenshaw, OTW, 19-20, 82-91. On the ontological good in wisdom, see Murphy, "Kerygma"; and Rad, Wisdom, 77-79. On the act-consequence relationship, see Koch, "Doctrine," 57-62.

On the proverb genre and style, see Scott, Hear, 7-13; Crenshaw, OTW, 67-69; Scott, Way, 53-56; and McKane, Proverbs, 22-23. On proverbial patterns, see Scott, Way, 59-63; and Alter, Poetry, 169-79. On the structure of the book of Proverbs, see Crenshaw, OTW, 72-76; and Scott, PE, xix.

On Job's poetry, see Alter, Poetry. On literary progression, see Greenberg, 287-97. On Job as an answered lament, see Crenshaw, OTW, 120-23.

For interpretations of Job's theophany, see Williams, "You"; Robertson, "Book"; Otto, 79-80; Terrien, Job, 236-39; Rad, Wisdom, 223-26; Tsevat, "Meaning," 365-72; Greenberg, 298-99; and Alter,

Poetry, 104-06. On Job's irony, see Williams, "You," 231-55; and Robertson, "Book," 467-68. On disinterested righteousness, see Tsevat, "Meaning," 365-72; and Crenshaw, OTW, 116-19.

On Ecclesiastes' genre, see Crenshaw, OTW, 144-45; Scott, Way, 174; and Eissfeldt, 494. On its structure, see Wright, "Riddle"; and Ginsberg, Studies, 1-5. For its use of proverbs, see Gordis, 95-108.

On the God of Ecclesiastes, see Crenshaw, "Eternal," 44-49. On meaning in a meaningless world, see Gordis, 84, 123-31; and Scott, PE, 193, 203-06. Cf. Becker, Denial. For a comparison to existentialism, see Gordis, 112-31.

On theodicy, see Scott, Way, 142-47; Crenshaw, "Theodicy," 895-96; and **idem**, Theodicy.

INTRODUCTION TO THE GOSPEL

The NT is the Christian addition to and **interpretation of the HB** [see chap. 1, different]. While the NT begins in Judaism, it rewrites Jewish symbols in an exilic situation and, thus, rejects this world in favor of a **world beyond** (e.g., kingdom of God, *apocalypticism*, *gnosticism*).

Figure 1: **Post-Exilic Judaism**

Except for the brief Hasmonean Kingdom, post-exilic Jews lived under the control of foreign empires (Persia, Greece, and Rome). Some carved out a **modified natural religion**, a temple state in cooperation with the imperial powers [cf. chap. 13]. Others **resisted** the foreign powers passively or violently. Others **withdrew into privatized faith or sects** [cf. chap. 15]. In the NT era, the Sadducees were an upper-class, priestly group in coalition with the Romans. By contrast, the Essenes withdrew from the corrupt world to found a pure sect in the desert at Qumran. Various brigands, outlaws, revolutionaries, and Zealots resisted or revolted against the Romans (particularly in 66 CE). The Pharisees sponsored an intriguing movement taking the Torah to the people and imposing the priestly purity regulations upon all. While the Jewish-Roman war of 66-73 CE destroyed most other options, later rabbis refined the Pharisees' program and created Classic or Rabbinic Judaism (of which the classic statement is the Talmud).

Where the HB often espouses natural religion and materialistic, this-worldly notions of the ontological good, the NT postpones the good. As the NT is "disenchanted with the world," it *ironizes* where the HB symbolizes. The NT's most fundamental symbols, then, invert, twist, and turn. Blessed are the poor. The master serves. The first are last. The righteous suffer. Death comes through life. The cross is good news.

Figure 2: **Irony**

While symbol points to a reality beyond the immediately observable, irony renames observable reality. Irony asserts a discrepancy between words/events and meaning from some perspective transcending the immediate context. Thus, verbal irony calls the large man, "Tiny"; the bald man, "Curly"; the stupid man, "Einstein." In Mark, when those who crucify Jesus acclaim him as the "King of the Jews," they speak ironically because they do not believe him to be king (Mk 15:13-32). By contrast, for the ironic NT, Jesus is Lord despite his death at the hands of the powers-that-be. The NT Jesus is akin to the **eiron**, the underdog hero of Greek comedy, whom the narrative shows to be more than he appears as he triumphs over braggart opponents [cf. Popeye and Bluto].

The NT consists of twenty-seven books in two sections, the Gospel and the Apostle. The Gospel consists of four stories of Jesus (Matthew, Mark, Luke, John). The Apostle consists of one history (Acts), twenty-one letters and essays, and one apocalypse (Revelation).

Mythically, the most important is the Gospel. *Gospel* translates a Greek word which first meant "the reward given to one bringing good news" and, then, "the **good news**" itself. Roman inscriptions use the word to announce the emperor's "coming of age, accession, or impending visit." Similarly, Mark uses the word to announce the arrival of God's kingdom:

> Now after John was arrested, Jesus came to Galilee,
> proclaiming the good news of God, and saying, "The
> time is fulfilled, and the kingdom of God has come
> near; repent, and believe in the good news." (1:14-15)

For Paul, the gospel is "the **message about Jesus**":

> Now I would remind you . . . of the good news that I
> proclaimed to you . . . that Christ died for our sins in
> accordance with the scriptures, and that he was
> buried, and that he was raised on the third day in
> accordance with the scriptures . . . (1 Cor 15:1-5)

In the second century, Christians used the word to designate the "literary genre of Jesus-stories" including Matthew, Mark, Luke, and John. Those works depict Jesus' public career after the fashion of **ancient biographies**.

Figure 3: **Ancient Biography**

An ancient biography depicts a public official or philosopher's **public career** in a chronological order into which it inserts **anecdotes and sayings** revealing the hero's character. The biography typically portrays its hero as a **type of social values** which it legitimates or condemns [see chap. 11, figure 2].

The Gospel present Jesus' **public ministry and his Jerusalem passion** as a new **deus ex machina** establishing a new mythic order. As the last public (historical) event of the Gospel is

Jesus' death at the hands of the authorities, the Gospel must speak ironically [see figure 2]. Not content with irony, however, the Gospel goes on to assert that God raised Jesus from the dead establishing an esoteric order available for private faith, in sectarian worship, or in imminent apocalypse [cf. figure 1].

Figure 4: **The Gospel Tradition**

Scholars refer to Matthew, Mark, and Luke as the **Synoptic gospels** because they are so similar. Most critics explain these gospels' similarities and differences according to the **two-source hypothesis**. This proposal asserts that Matthew and Luke depend upon Mark (the earliest gospel) and a now lost gospel called Q, short for **Quelle** (German for "source"). The evidence for the dependence upon Mark relies upon Mark's commonness. When one of the three gospels diverges, **Mark is always in the majority** (cf., e.g., Mt 3:17; Mk 1:11; Lk 3:22). Further, when Matthew or Luke appears to change Mark, one can often account for the change as an attempt to **improve Mark**. The evidence for Q depends upon **verbal agreements** between Matthew and Luke when Mark is not involved (cf., e.g., Mt 5:3-12 with Lk 6:20-23; 14:34-35).

Form critics argue that the gospels are also the result of a rich oral tradition of Jesus' stories and sayings. Orality necessitated stereotyped forms still discoverable in the gospels: miracle stories, legends, pronouncement stories (short stories providing a context for a saying), proverbs, eschatological sayings, Torah-sayings, I-sayings, and parables.

Redaction critics examine the gospels' editing of earlier traditions to discern the gospels' particular theological emphases and their distinctive portraits of Jesus.

The Gospel, then, does not only re-symbolize the HB in light of the frustrations of exile. It also re-symbolizes in light of Jesus.

The Gospel **founds Christianity with a Jesus-story**. The Gospel or Jesus, then, is the mythic center of the NT. For the Gospel, Jesus is the vehicle to the sacred, mythic paradigm, and evaluative norm by which all others are judged.

Figure 5: **Four Gospels or One?**

Although the NT contains four different gospels presenting Jesus in distinct fashions, the church asserts that there is only one Gospel. Texts from the second century and thereafter, then, title each of the four canonical gospels as "the Gospel according to . . . ." Further, the apostolic church **harmonizes** any discrepancies between the four. Outside the apostolic church, one might **privilege one gospel** over the others (as Marcion did with Luke) or **rewrite one new, integrated gospel** from the four (as Tatian did with the Diatessaron, "According to the Four"). By contrast, modern scholars privilege the distinctive features of the individual gospels [see figure 4].

Review Questions

1. Compare the HB and the NT.
2. How does the focus on Jesus transform the NT?
3. What is irony?
4. What is a gospel?
5. Describe an ancient biography.

Suggestions for Alternative Reading and Reflection

1. Compare the HB and the Old Testament.

2. Compare the God of the HB and the Jesus of the NT.

3. Why are four gospels a problem for the church? What possible solutions are there to this problem?

4. Describe the gospel tradition. What are the respective contributions of source, form, and redaction criticism to the study of the gospels?

For Further Reading

On post-exilic Judaism and the Judaism of the NT era, see Duling and Perrin, 35-97; Ackroyd, Exile; Smith, Parties; Reicke; Koester, NT, 1:205-80; and Horsley and Hanson.

On irony, see Muecke; and Booth, Irony.

On "gospel," see Kuemmel, Introduction, 35-37; Hennecke and Schneemelcher, 1:71-80; and Koester, Ancient, 1-48.

On the genre of the gospels, see Suggs; Koester, Ancient, 24-31; Talbert, What; and Aune, NT, 17-76.

For the critical analysis of the gospel tradition, see Barr, NT, 197-213; Kuemmel, Introduction, 38-80; Beardslee; McKnight, What; and Perrin, What.

On the interpretation of the gospels in the ancient church, see Grant and Tracy, 38-82; and Barr, NT, 194-97.

On the noncanonical gospels, see Cameron; and Hennecke and Schneemelcher.

CHAPTER 17

WAITING FOR JESUS
Mark

Introduction: An Abrupt, Apocalyptic Gospel

The **passion dominates Mark**. Mark foreshadows the passion early (3:6) and has the main character predict it repeatedly (8:31-33; 9:30-32; 10:33-34). Dramatically, the passion ends Mark's story. Jesus does not speak after the cross. As a result, the present becomes a time of suffering, the new ages' **"birth pangs"** (13:7-23).

Plot Conflict and Shape: The Ironic King and Kingdom

Jesus arrives amid prophetic fanfare (1:2-11) announcing that the "kingdom of God has come near" (1:15). That kingdom brings miraculous benefits for the possessed, sick, and hungry in Galilee (1:14-8:26). Demonic opposition (1:12-13, 21-28) and establishment resistance (2:1-3:6) create the narrative **conflict about divine authority**, power, and representation (Mk. 3:20-35).

While the reader knows Jesus to be the divine king (Christ or Son of God) because of the introduction and the baptismal voice (1:1-11), Jesus overwhelms story-characters. As a result, story after story ends with silence, amazement, awe, or befuddled questions.

Only those with **supernatural knowledge**, the demons (and readers), know Jesus rightly, but Jesus silences them (1:25, 34; 3:12). Further, he pointedly refuses any public demonstration of his identity (8:11-12). He withdraws from crowds (1:39-45; 6:30-52). In public, he speaks only in parables:

> To you has been given the secret of the kingdom of God, but for those outside, everything comes in parables; in order that "they may indeed look, but not perceive, and may indeed listen, but not understand; so that they may not turn again and be forgiven." (4:10-12)

Even instructed insiders (4:33-34; 7:17-23), like the disciples, can become outsiders in ironic Mark:

> Do you still not perceive or understand? Are your hearts hardened? Do you have eyes, and fail to see? Do you have hears, and fail to hear? (8:17-18)

Figure 1: **Secret Mark**

For Wilhelm Wrede, Jesus' "**messianic secret**," his public silence and esoteric teaching, is actually a Markan theological device created to reconcile Jesus' un-messianic life with the community confession that Jesus was the Messiah. Instead, one might observe that the motif is in keeping with Mark's **esoteric apocalypticism** and with its rhetorical design of gradually unveiling the ironic, dying Christ. For Mark, one can know Jesus as the Christ only as he publicly suffers.

In addition to the canonical, public Mark, Clement of Alexandria knew a **secret Mark** for the enlightened, which included Jesus' resurrection, baptism, and nocturnal teaching of a young man dressed only in a linen cloth (cf. 14:51-52) [see Cameron, 70-71].

Mercifully, at that point, revelation occurs. **Peter confesses** Jesus as the Messiah (Christ, king; 8:27-9:1). For the very first time, a character identifies Jesus rightly as the divine representative. The transfiguration stamps an immediate divine approval upon this confession. In contrast to the baptismal voice's privacy, this heavenly voice is also for the disciples (9:7-8; contrast 1:11).

Two miracles of sight restored (8:22-26; 10:46-52) bookend Mark's central section. The first comes between disciples' blindness and disciples' confession. The latter includes the only pre-passion, public confession of Jesus as king (son of David). The sight-miracles dramatize the theme of Mk 4:10-12 that only the supernaturally enlightened can see.

Still, confusion remains. Peter falls away from the "things of God" and "thinking humanly" sides with Satan (8:33). He knows that Jesus is king, but he does not see him as the ironic king. Mark's central section, then, displays Jesus as **the king who serves** (9:33-37; 10:32-45) **and dies** (8:31; 9:31; 10:33-34). Followers, too, must be willing to suffer. In fact, **life comes only through death** (8:34-9:1). These ironies escape the disciples who follow confusedly (9:18-19) and fearfully (9:32; 10:32) to the passion in Jerusalem.

For ironic Mark, **the passion reveals Jesus as the king** and judge. The triumphal entry symbolizes the king's arrival (11:1-10). Then, the judge appears to cleanse/reject the temple (11:11-26), to refute the authorities (11:27-12:40), and to predict apocalyptic judgments (13).

Dramatically, Jesus finally publicly admits his messianic status before the high priest (14:53-65). He names himself the king who comes in judgment (uniting Ps 110:1 and Dan 7:13). The authorities, of course, reject his revelation and try, mock, and kill him as a king claimant (15:1-26). Ironically, then, Jesus' opponents proclaim his kingship without accepting it.

For Mark, Jesus is king in his death. Thus, in an important scene, a woman anoints Jesus (14:3-9). Anointing, of course, suggests kingship as the Hebrew word, "Messiah," means the "anointed one." Mark's Jesus, however, denies this association and says instead that "she has anointed my body beforehand for its burial" (14:8). Mark's Jesus is the Messiah/king who dies. Esoteric words to the disciples corroborate this ironic kingship (14:22-25; cf. 10:45). Mark does not clearly indicate why

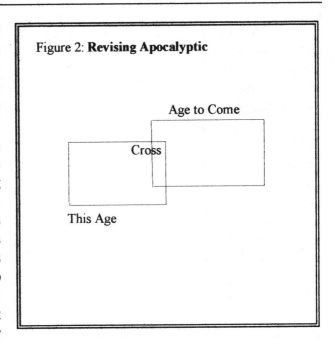

Figure 2: **Revising Apocalyptic**

Age to Come

Cross

This Age

this death is efficacious, but the apocalyptic discourse ties present suffering closely to future glorification (13). In fact, the **death is the linch-pin which will usher in the kingdom** (cf. 12:8-9). For Mark, Jesus' death is the decisive eschatological moment. With the cross, apocalyptic's new age begins.

Jesus' opponents have plotted his death for some time (3:6); and with Judas' connivance, they arrest, convict, and crucify Jesus. But for Mark, the cross is also **a divine act**. It is the divine plan. Thus, the Markan Jesus repeatedly predicts his death (8:31; 9:9, 31; 10:33-34, 45; 12:8; 14:8; 14:22-25) as part of the divine program (8:33). Further, Mark has Jesus describe the passion as fulfilling scripture (9:11-13; 12:10; 14:21, 27, 49). Larger patterns corroborate more subtly. Jesus is the type of the rejected prophet (6:1-6, 14-29; 9:11-13; 12:1-11) or the suffering righteous (8:34-9:1; 13; 15:34). At Gethsemane, Jesus reluctantly, privately affirms death as God's program (14:32-42). Finally, Mark portrays the death itself in the theophanic language of darkness, torn temple veil, and an opponent's acclamation (15:33-39). For Mark, **the cross is the theophany**.

Thus, the opponents' success ushers in the kingdom which destroys them. They assist the divine program by c r u c i f y i n g J e s u s . Ironically, then, the opponents act as disciples. They confess (15:39) and bury (15:40-47; cf. 6:29).

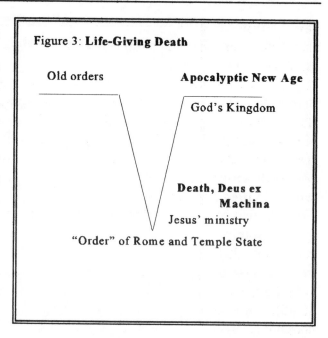

Figure 3: **Life-Giving Death**

Old orders

Apocalyptic New Age

God's Kingdom

Death, Deus ex Machina

Jesus' ministry

"Order" of Rome and Temple State

By contrast, the disciples are nowhere to be found. More problematically, at the climactic theophanic moment, Jesus asserts God's absence with his anguished "My God, my God, why have you forsaken me?" (15:34). Of course, in worlds of radical exile, the hidden God can be known only in death. The cross, then, e n t h r o n e s **Jesus**. In Mark's ironic

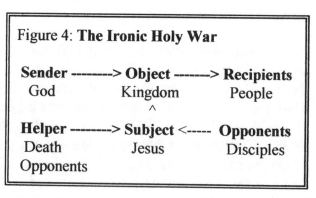

Figure 4: **The Ironic Holy War**

Sender --------> **Object** -------> **Recipients**
God   Kingdom   People
           ^

Helper --------> **Subject** <----- **Opponents**
Death   Jesus   Disciples
Opponents

passion, the opponents' mockery is the truth (15:16-19, 31-32). Jesus is truly known as king (son of God) only at his death.

Figure 5: **The Forsaken Jesus**

Jesus' last words in Mark are the anguished cry from the cross (15:34). As these words also open Ps 22, many see them as a lament (faith in the depths), rather than as a cry of desolation [cf. chap. 14; genre]. One should not, however, minimize the depths of the alienation. After all, God does not save Jesus (or his disciples) from death. For Mark, the chosen must plumb the depths before the ages turn.

Although Jesus has been fully revealed, the apocalypse remains future (13). Mark, then, proceeds to its **puzzling denouement.** An opponent buries. Women prepare to anoint. A mysterious young man reports the resurrection and reminds the women of Jesus' promised reunion. As Mk 16:9-20 is a later addition, Mark ends shockingly with **silent, frightened women**. While the work may be incomplete or the end mysteriously lost, this ending fits Mark's abrupt style and message. In particular, it focuses attention on the passion, dramatizes human dependence and the divine sovereignty, and intensifies the urgent apocalyptic atmosphere. The end (the appearance of Jesus) is nigh.

Characters: Thinking the Things of God

Mark depicts characters according to an ethical dualism centering in Jesus. As Jesus is the king who dies, Mark has, in effect, two touchstones: **Jesus and death**. Characters respond to Jesus and to death and, thereby, determine their fate. Those who identify Jesus rightly "think the things of God." Ethically, these "lose their life" for Jesus. Others think "the things of men" and live "lives of anxious self-concern" [see Tannehill, "Disciples"].

Mark, of course, rings **ironic changes** upon this simple

dualism. Expected insiders--the religious leaders--are outsiders. Outsiders--the dispossessed--are insiders. Thus, Jesus, who represents God, is the king who dies God-forsaken (15:34). Thus, the religious leaders demonically resist the kingdom, yet they assist the coming of the kingdom by their very opposition. They confess and bury while the disciples betray, deny, and flee.

Figure 6: **Mark's Ethical Dualism**

Think the things of God	**Think the things of men**
Jesus is Christ who dies	Jesus is of Beelzebul
Kings suffer and serve	Kings conquer and rule
Life comes through death	Anxious self-concern
Blind who see	Blind
Deaf who hear	Deaf
Faith	Hardened hearts
Suffering	Rich, powerful

Touchstones
Jesus
Death
fear?

Narrator			Demons
Jesus	<----	disciples --->	Establishment
Healed			

Mark's **disciples are**, perhaps, **the most surprising characters**. Their portrait is strikingly unfinished. They leave home, family, and occupation to follow Jesus and share his ministry (1:16-3:19). They are privy to the kingdom "secrets" (4). They, like little jesuses, travel Galilee preaching, healing, and exorcizing (6:7-13, 30). To this point, it appears that they stand with Jesus.

Two feeding scenes (6:30-44; 8:1-10) and three boat scenes (4:35-41; 6:47-52; 8:14-21), however, unmask their shallowness. By the third boat scene, the disciples are "**outsiders**" (cf. 8:17-21 with 4:11-12). After this debacle, Peter's confession surprises (8:29). Neither he nor the other disciples, however, are able to grasp the ironic king and kingdom (throughout 8:27-10:52). Peter rebukes Jesus. The inner circle wishes to remain on the mount of transfiguration. They fail to understand resurrection, "Elijah," and passion. They fail at an exorcism. They quarrel for positions of prestige. They **fear, but they still follow** (9:32; 10:32).

Figure 7: **The Disciples**

Some suggest that Mark characterizes the disciples as bumbling stooges to debunk them on behalf of a community which did not accept their authority. Others think Mark created such disciples as a literary device to allow the narrator to explain the myth at great length (cf. Socrates' dialogue partners). Still others think that Mark's disciples are ethical models. They warn readers that anyone can fail (13:20; 10:26-27). More optimistically, they may encourage faltering believers that even the disciples wavered. In every case, they inculcate Mark's lessons about the divine sovereignty and the need for faith (10:26-27; 13:20).

The passion distances them further. The contrast between Peter and Jesus is particularly telling. Despite Jesus' prediction that all will desert him, Peter boasts that he will stand (14:31). Juxtaposed to this boast, is Jesus' Gethsemane struggle where he fears (14:34, NRSV, "grieved"), resists, but ultimately accepts death while the disciples sleep (cf. 13:32-37). After the arrest, both Peter and Jesus appear on trial in a strikingly intercalated scene (14:53-72). While Jesus makes his only public confession of his identity, Peter denies his master.

Mark's disciples end with **betrayal** (14:43-46), **denial** (14:53-72), and **flight** (14:50), all predicted by Jesus (14:18-21, 27-31). The disciples never return. Only Jesus' promise of reunion and his remembrance of them binds them to him (14:28; 16:7). Of course, in a narrative in which everything depends upon the divine sovereignty, this is of little matter (cf. 10:27; 13:20). After all, Jesus' predictions, like those of the prophets of old, do invariably come true (see 11:1-6, 14, 20-24; 14:13-16, 18-21, 27-31, 43-50, 66-72).

The unfinished story does, however, leave the disciples' fate hanging. They are poised at the boundary, rather than clearly on either side of the Markan ethical dualism. They, like people who read stories, are "**on the way**" [cf. Malbon, "Fallible"].

Figure 8: **Fully God**

Mark does not contradict the church's creeds. It antedates the christological controversies which they reflect. Mark's Son of God, then, is not that of the Nicene Creed which affirms belief:

> . . . in one Lord Jesus Christ, the only-begotten Son of God, Begotten of the Father before all the ages, Light of Light, true God of true God, begotten not made, of one substance with the Father, through whom all things were made; who for us men and for our salvation came down from the heavens, and was made flesh of the Holy Spirit and the Virgin Mary, and became man, and was crucified . . .

Myth: Jesus, the Touchstone

Mark centers mythic identity in Jesus. Jesus is the

king/Messiah (Son of God) and apocalyptic judge (Son of Man).

The heavenly voice (1:11; 9:7), demons (3:11; 5:7), and the centurion at the cross call Jesus the Son of God. For Mark, this phrase designates Jesus as God's chosen king. The enthronement psalms (e.g., Ps 2; 89; cf. 2 Sam 7:14) so designate ancient Israelite kings [see chap. 10, figure 11]. In fact, the baptismal voice quotes Ps 2:7 (merging it with Isa 42:1). In short, for Mark, Son of God is equivalent to Messiah or Christ (cf. Mk 1:1 in some texts; as well as the expansion of 8:29 in Mt 16:16).

Son of man either designates Jesus enigmatically as a human being or identifies him as the apocalyptic judge of Dan 7:13-14. Mark uses the phrase to designate Jesus in his ministry (2:10, 28; 10:45?), in his passion (8:31; 9:12, 31; 10:33; 14:21, 41), and in his *parousia* (8:38; 13:26; 14:62).

Figure 9: **The Birth Pangs**

Mark 13 both provides the absent end of Mark and previews the disciples' (and the reader's) apocalyptic future:

1) the arrival of false-Messiahs (5, 21-22);
2) the birth-pangs: wars, earthquakes, famines (7-8);
3) the disciples' activity: suffering and preaching (9-13);
4) the desolating sacrilege (14);
5) flight and general suffering (14-20); and
6) the end: astral signs, the Son of Man, and the gathering of the elect (24-27).

Most importantly, for Mark, Jesus is the ironic king/Christ who dies. Followers' identities imitate that of Jesus, the mythic-archetype. For Mark, a Christian (to speak anachronistically) must live as Jesus did:

> If any want to become my followers, let them deny
> themselves and take up their cross and follow me.
> For those who want to save their life will lose it, and
> those who lose their life for my sake, and for the sake
> of the gospel, will save it. (8:34-35; cf. 10:42-45)

Figure 10: **Waiting for Godot**

Expectancy is not restricted to apocalyptic. In Samuel
Beckett's well-known play, Waiting for Godot, two hapless
men wait interminably at a crossroads for Mr. Godot. As they
wait, the bored men strive unsuccessfully to divert their
attention from the monotony of their life "unto death." The
result is clear-sighted confusion:

> Was I sleeping while the others suffered? Am I
> sleeping now? To-morrow, when I wake, or
> think I do, what shall I say of to-day? . . . .
> Astride of a grave and a difficult birth. Down
> in the hole, lingeringly, the grave-digger puts
> the forceps. We have time to grow old. The air
> is full of our cries. But habit is a great
> deadener. [58-59]

Not surprisingly, the play ends with a failed suicide attempt.
The pessimistic tone of this expectancy, of course, differs
dramatically from that of Mark's apocalyptic hope.

Christian suffering is part of the "**birth pangs**" ushering in
the kingdom. For Mark, Christians live in the ironic atmosphere of
apocalyptic. Apocalyptic, while it provides a powerful theodicy,
offers little in terms of a succession mechanism. Mark does not

imagine a lengthy period beyond Jesus. In fact, Mark merges the time of Jesus, of the reader, and of apocalypse (cf. 9:1; 13:14). The **time of Jesus and the time of the church are the same**.

Mark's abrupt end creates this effect wonderfully. The absence of resurrection appearances and the promise of Jesus' return leave the disciples and the reader in a similar situation, **waiting for Jesus**. Both live in the apocalyptic anteroom.

Those who suffer and serve **for the gospel** are the ones who follow Jesus (8:35). This is the mythic succession mechanism. Not surprisingly, Jesus and the gospel merge (1:1; 8:35; 10:29; 13:9-13; 14:9). Response to the gospel is response to Jesus. Jesus gospels (1:14-15). His followers gospel (3:13-19; 6:7-13; 13:10; 14:9; 16:15). Mark gospels (1:1). The gospel, ultimately Mark itself, maintains connections with the sacred, primeval time for Mark's apocalyptic community.

Style and Time: Episodic Suspense

Mark's style is episodic, hurtling from incident to incident with minimal connections (i.e., *parataxis*). The incidents themselves are action-oriented. Mark seldom pauses to offer lengthy teachings from Jesus (but see 4; 13). This frenetic pace and the tendency for incidents to end with silence, amazement, or questions create **suspense**. This style matches Mark's apocalyptic message. Mark is urgent because the end (the kingdom) has come near. Mark's apocalypticism also leads to an **esoteric** style. While Mark is not coded like Daniel or Revelation, Mark's message comes only through revelation.

Narrator and Implied Reader

Mark's narrator stands both with God (e.g., 1:11; 8:33; 9:7) and with Jesus. Thus, almost the entire narrative takes place "over the shoulder" of Jesus [so Petersen, "Point"]. That is, the narrative unfolds from Jesus' physical perspective. The narrative steps away from this perspective only to set stages (e.g., 1:1-8), to build the story's conflict (e.g., 3:6; 6:17-29; 14:1-2, 10-11), or to allude to the readers' later situation (6:12-13; 11:4-6; 13:5-27; 15:40-16:8).

Figure 11: **Intercalations**

Mark interprets stories by intercalating them, by placing one story within another. Mark so connects Jairus' daughter and the hemorrhaging woman (5:21-43), the cursed fig tree and temple (11:12-25), and Peter's denial and Jesus' confession (14:53-72). Placed together, the stories resonate with one another. Thus, the fate of the cursed tree augurs ill for the temple, and Peter's denial is made more heinous by its juxtaposition with Jesus' one public confession. While not technically an intercalation, the placement of the revelation of the ironic Christ to the disciples (8:27-10:45) within two miracles of sight restored (8:22-26; 10:46-52) seems equally interpretative.

The physical commitment to Jesus, the presentation of Jesus as God's representative, Jesus' awesome powers (miracles and prophecy), and his integrity in the face of death are persuasive rhetoric on behalf of the narrative's ideological perspective. One **learns to see "with Jesus"** and, thus, to "think the things of God."

Mark's narrator, God, and Jesus provide a **trinitarian** (three, yet one) ideological **perspective** (narrative standards). The narrator and Jesus are so closely united that the narrator can use Jesus'voice for his most important addresses to the narratee and implied reader (13:14; the inclusive, general language in 4:9; 8:34-38; 10:43-45; 13:37). This flexible narrative boundary--where a character speaks to the reader--like Mark's ironies, **imperialistically incorporates the**

reader. The reader becomes part of the story-world listening to and **waiting for Jesus**.

Figure 12: **Mark's Uncomfortable Reader**

Mark's ambiguity, silences, questions, and intercalations force the reader to construct meanings. They also drag the reader into the narrative world as she fills-the-gaps with supernatural knowledge (provided by God, the demons, and the narrator). Trained esoterically with the disciples, the reader may also find herself left ironically "outside." For example, in Mk 4, while Jesus interprets parables for the disciples, the reader receives no interpretation of 4:26-32. **Is the reader "in the know" or not?** A similar crux occurs at 8:15, 21 with the "leaven of the Pharisees." Clearly, the disciples do not understand and find themselves left outside, but where is the reader? While the esoteric training of 8:27-10:52 brings the reader inside again, she must face the trauma of the disciples' failure. The abrupt end leaves the story with the reader. What will she make of and do with the women's silence?

ANET: The Coming Divine Kingdom

In Mark, humans have little power. Revelation is a divinely capricious affair (4:10-12). The divine program escapes human understanding (8:33). Humans flounder (8:17-21; 9:32). Those who would follow cannot. Disciples (and women?) fail. The opponents' plot is taken up into the larger divine program. Even Jesus becomes grist for the divine mill.

The **divine sovereignty overwhelms**. After all, Mark is about the coming of the (ironic) kingdom. All humans can do is align themselves with that terrible power and wait (9:29; 10:27; 13:20). Outside that power--for example, with boasting disciples and arrogant establishment--there is only failure. Even within the divine rule, death remains (14:32-42; 15:34). For Mark, however, that **death is life** (8:35). Beyond (or through) failed disciples, forsaken and absent Jesus, and fearful women, there is gospel.

Figure 13: **The Gospel of Peter**

In contrast to Mark's public death, frightened women, and postponed apocalyptic vindication, the apocryphal Gospel of Peter offers a public, miraculous vindication of the risen Jesus. After the Jewish people crucify Jesus, miracles lead them to doubt their actions. Their qualms cause the leaders to place a guard around the tomb. As a result, **the resurrection occurs publicly** in full view of the people and leaders, leading the Romans to confess that Jesus is the Son of God (cf. Mk 15:39):

> . . . they saw again three men come out of the
> sepulchre, and two of them sustaining the
> other, and a cross following them, and the
> heads of the two reaching to heaven, but that of
> him who was led of them by the hand
> overpassing the heavens. And they heard a
> voice out of the heavens crying, "Thou hast
> preached to them that sleep," and from the
> cross there was heard the answer, "Yea."
> [10.39-42, in Cameron, 80-81]

This message offends modernity to its depths. Instead of the divine sovereignty, modernity offers a **gospel of human possibility**. In place of death and the possibility of defeat, (American) modernity promises success without tragedy. In the American myth, there is no room for defeat, tragedy, or death. To moderns, then, Mark's gospel emasculates human responsibility. Mark's death-gospel is **macabre** and a confession of failure.

Figure 14: **O'Connor's Epiphanies**

In Flannery O'Connor's "A Good Man is Hard to Find," the grandmother vainly tries to convince the Misfit that he is a good man so that he will not murder her:

> . . . the grandmother's head cleared for an
> instant. . . . "Why you're one of my own babies.
> You're one of my own children!" She reached
> out and touched him on the shoulder. The
> Misfit sprang back as if a snake had bitten him
> and shot her three times through the chest.
>
> "She would of been a good woman," the Misfit
> said, "if it had been somebody there to shoot
> her every minute of her life." [132-33]

In that horrific moment, both characters find self-knowledge. For O'Connor, **suffering and death may create epiphanies**. Not surprisingly, then, O'Connor's narrative worlds, like Mark's, are ironic and confrontational (cf. e.g., her caricatured, yet surprising characters including believing atheists, ethical murderers, and visionary hypocrites).

Finally, Mark's expectation of an imminent apocalyptic end has been disappointed (9:1; 13:30). Neither the death of Jesus nor the destruction of the temple ushered in the kingdom. To date, all **predictions of the end have been frustrated**. The church handled this failed hope by becoming an institution in the world, a part of the establishment. To that institution, Matthew, Luke, and John are far more important than Mark.

What, then, of Mark's intense expectation today? Does Mark elude middle-class modernity? Should readers reduce Mark to institutional domesticity or should they form an apocalyptic sect and await the end?

Review Questions

1. Apply the reading method of chaps. 3-4 to Mark. List its genre, plot shape, conflict, depiction of Jesus and God, mythic function, and ANE problems.

2. Describe Mark's apocalyptic world-view. How does this view differ from Jewish apocalyptic (like Daniel)?

3. Give examples of Mark's irony. What is the central irony for Mark? Who is Mark's Jesus? When does the kingdom come?

4. Who are Jesus' opponents?

5. What decides a character's fate in Mark?

6. Do Jesus' disciples fail? If so, are they redeemed?

7. What is the significance of Jesus' death for Mark?

8. What comes after Jesus' death in Mark? What does this say about the time of the reader?

Suggestions for Alternative Reading and Reflection

1. Is anyone safe from Mark's ironies?

2. What is the messianic secret?

3. How does secret Mark differ from canonical Mark?

4. Why are Jesus' last words, "My God, my God, why hast thou forsaken me?"

5. Why does Mark end as it does?

6. How does Mark's understanding of the Son of God differ from that of the creeds?

7. How does Mark's expectancy differ from that in Waiting for Godot?

8. Tell the story of a reader reading Mark. Where is she surprised? Where is she included in the tale? Where is she made

uncomfortable?

9. How does Mark's revelatory moment compare with that of the Gospel of Peter and with those of Flannery O'Connor?

For Further Reading

For a historical treatment of Mark's interpretation, see Kealy. For short applications of recent literary methodologies, see Anderson and Moore. For an interesting narrative critical introduction, see Rhoads and Michie. For modified structuralist approaches, see Via, Kerygma; and Malbon, Space. For a reader-response treatment, see Fowler, Let. For a deconstructive reading, see Moore, Mark. For socio-political readings, see Ched Myers; and Waetjen.

On the apocalyptic nature of Mark, see Duling and Perrin, 295-327; Kee, Community; and Marxsen, Mark.

On the messianic secret, see Wrede.

For a discussion of the feedings and sea crossings, see Fowler, Loaves.

For a discussion of the theological nature of Mark's settings, see Marxsen, Mark; and Malbon, Space.

On Mark's ethical dualism, see Petersen, "Point"; **idem**, Literary, 62-63; Rhoads and Michie, 44; Tannehill, "Disciples"; and **idem**, "Christology."

On Mark's use of Christological titles, see Kingsbury, Mark.

On literary models for Mark's passion, see Nickelsburg, "Genre."

On Mark's disciples, see Weeden; Robbins; Boomershine, "Apostolic"; Kelber, Story; **idem**, Oral; and Malbon, "Fallible." On the desire to avoid death, see Tannehill, "Christology."

On Mark's style, see Tolbert, <u>Sowing</u>.

On Mark's abrupt end, see Metzger, <u>Textual</u>, 122-26; Petersen, "When"; Boomershine, <u>Story-teller</u>; **idem**, "Apostolic"; and Magness.

CHAPTER 18

FOLLOWING JESUS' TORAH
Matthew

Introduction: Relationship to Mark and Overall Structure

Matthew tells the same story that Mark does (but notably omits Mk 4:26-29; 7:31-37; 8:22-26), but Matthew expands Mark with **infancy materials** (1-2), **five teaching sections**, and a **resurrection appearance** (28:8b-20).

> Figure 1: **Outlining Matthew**
>   [see Kingsbury, Structure, 1-25]
>
> 1. Presentation of the Messiah (1:1-4:16)
> 2. Messiah's Ministry to Israel and
>   Israel's Rejection (4:17-16:20)
>   a. Preaching and Healing (4:17-11:1)
>   b. Conflict over Identity (11:2-16:20)
> 3. Messiah's Journey to Jerusalem and
>   his Passion (16:21-28:20)
>   a. Teaching on the Way (16:21-20:34)
>   b. Passion (21:1-27:66)
>   c. The Risen Lord's Commission (28)

Plot Shape and Conflict: Response to the Kingdom

Matthew opens with an interpretation of the Messiah's genealogy:

> So all the generations from Abraham to David are fourteen generations; and from David to the

deportation to Babylon, fourteen generations; and from the deportation to the Messiah, fourteen generations. (1:17)

The precise enumeration implies **the unfolding of a providential plan** in four steps: Abraham, David, exile, and Messiah. The Messiah is the son of Abraham and David who finally ends the exile. Thus, he is named Jesus, the Greek form of the Hebrew Joshua, **"Yahweh is salvation"**--designating the one who "will save his people from their sins" (1:21). For those in exile, he is the very **presence of God** (1:23; cf. 12:28).

Figure 2: **Son of God and David**

Matthew's nativity story presents Jesus as divinely engendered and adopted as Son of David. By contrast, ancient Hebrew kings were literally the Son of David and were adopted as Son of God at their enthronement (e.g., Ps 2; 110). While Matthew uses Son of David more often than any other gospel, Son of God is the more important title. The narrator (2:15), God (3:17; 17:5), the disciples (14:33; 16:16), the centurion (27:54), and Jesus himself (11:27; 21:37; 26:63-64; 28:19) declare Jesus to be such. On this point, his opponents test him (4:3, 6; 26:63; 27:40, 43). As Son of God, Jesus makes God present (1:23). As this, Jesus addresses God as his father (e.g., 7:21) and calls others to sonship (e.g., 5:43-48; 6:9-15). Thus, Matthew's language is far closer to the Christian creeds than is Mark's (cf. 11:27; 28:17-19).

Surprisingly, Herod responds murderously (2). That rejection and the Baptist's call to repentance underscore the people's desperate, sinful condition (3:1-12; cf. 1:21). As in Mark, the kingdom arrives in Galilee as a holy war against the powers of evil represented by Satan, sin, disease, demons, and death (4-10).

Unlike Mark, Matthew includes **five long teaching discourses** in Jesus' public ministry. For Matthew, the kingdom comes to Galilee in teaching (4:23; 5-7) as well as in miracle (4:23; 8-9). The famous **Sermon on the Mount** (5-7) is a resume of Jesus'

Figure 3: **The Teaching Sections**	
Sermon on the Mount	5-7
Missionary Discourse	10
Parables of the Kingdom	13
Ecclesiological Discourse	18
Eschatological Discourse	24-25

preaching in Galilee. It describes the life of those in the kingdom as both divinely favored (5:1-11) and challenged (5:12-7:27). In particular, Jesus calls his followers to lives of "greater righteousness" (5:17-20) and obedience (7:21-27). The Galilean miracles, many of which are collected into one section (8-9), continue the theme of kingdom blessing.

The crowds become so great in Galilee (9:35-38) that Jesus makes his disciples his joint-participants in the gospel-healing ministry to Israel (10:6-7). Jesus warns his emissaries that they, too, will be divinely favored (10:26-42) and will be both received and rejected by their audience (10:14-23).

Matthew's central section dramatizes the recurring dual responses to the revelation (11:2-16:20). Beginning and ending with incidents discussing **Jesus' identity**, the section moves the reader to Matthean faith from John's question (11:2-19) to the disciples' confession (16:13-20). The opposition, of course, rejects this revelation, names Jesus a blasphemer (9:3; 10:25; 12:24), and plots his death (12:14). As in Mark, the Beelzebul story identifies the opposing camps in this **myth war plot** (12:22-37, 46-50).

Matthew uses the parables, the third teaching section (13), to mark the great divide. The revelation demarcates an ongoing conflict between **the kingdom of heaven and the kingdom of evil** (13:36-43). From this point on, Jesus' teaching becomes markedly esoteric (cf. 13:36-52 with 13:1-35). The subsequent discourses are for the disciples alone (18; 24-25).

Figure 4: **Parables of the Kingdom** (13; 24-25)

Matthew's parables (13) reveal the kingdom's demand for a decision (soils, hidden treasure, and pearl), the kingdom's fate (soils and tares), the kingdom's demand for absolute commitment (hidden treasure and pearl) and the kingdom's eschatological judgment (tares and net). The latter is Matthew's distinctive teaching. For Matthew, the community needs this warning, for **the judgment will purge evil from the kingdom itself** (13:41, 49). Matthew's expansion of Mark's apocalyptic discourse with parables about responsible living in the interim between gospel and judgment makes the same point. To be prepared for the unexpected end (24:36-25:13) demands serving the king (25:14-30) and loving the brother (25:31-40). This statement of love as devotion to God and concern for the brother, of course, reiterates the basic themes of the opening sermon (5-7) yet again.

The rest of Matthew plays out the conflict between these two kingdoms. The trip to Jerusalem (16:21-20:34) trains the Matthean community of "little faith" (8:26; 14:31; 15:8) as **scribes of the kingdom** (13:52). They learn that Jesus' death is part of the divine plan (16:21; 17:22-23; 20:17-19) and that his disciples are called to a **humble service** (18:1-14) **and forgiving love** (18:21-35) which greatly conditions their authority and that of the later church (among the gospels, only Matthew actually mentions the church; in 16:18-20; 18:15-20).

The dramatic conflict continues only after Jesus arrives in Jerusalem with a teaching and healing ministry (though see the conflicts in

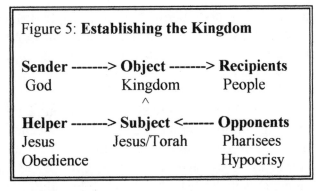

Figure 5: **Establishing the Kingdom**

Sender -------> **Object** -------> **Recipients**
God   Kingdom   People
                           ^

Helper -------> **Subject** <------ **Opponents**
Jesus   Jesus/Torah   Pharisees
Obedience   Hypocrisy

17:24-27; 19:3-10, 16-22). Matthew has the same five conflict incidents that Mark does (11:27-12:40) but also includes two additional parables (21:28-32; 22:1-14) and a lengthy final attack on the Pharisees (23). These additional materials provide a dramatic contrast to the Sermon on the Mount by pronouncing **judgment woes** (not beatitudes) upon hypocrisy (not obedience). Jesus' final teaching is quite fittingly a private warning for his disciples [see figure 4].

At this point, both sides know that Jesus must die. The opponents put Jesus to death as a blasphemer (26:63-68). By contrast, for Matthew, Jesus **dies for the sins of his people** (26:28; 1:21). Israel rejects her king (27:15-26) and

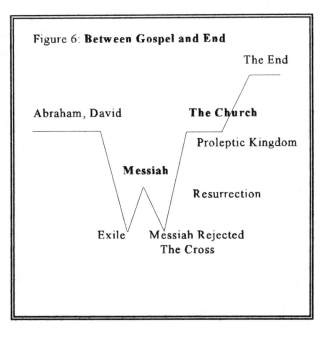

Figure 6: **Between Gospel and End**

The End

Abraham, David   **The Church**

Proleptic Kingdom

Messiah

Resurrection

Exile   Messiah Rejected
The Cross

takes his blood upon her (cf. 23:29-39). Ironically, this rejection-murder leads to the destruction of the order which the leaders have tried to save (cf. 3:9-10; 8:11-12; 21:33-44; 22:7; 23:29-39; 27:25).

For Matthew, however, the passion-resurrection establishes the kingdom for "another people" (21:43), echoing the words about new sons of Abraham (3:9; 8:11-12; cf. 28:18-20). The resurrection continues Jesus' **presence in the church** (18:20; 28:20b) for the community of "little faith." Nevertheless, they must still live through the birth pangs (24:8), remain obediently alert (24:15-46), and face their own judgment (13:37-43).

Characters: Jesus as Fulfillment and Standard

For Matthew, Jesus **fulfills OT prophecy** and is God's eschatological response to exile. He is the new divine act (**Emmanuel**). Not surprisingly, then, Jesus is an authoritative figure in word (7:28-29) and deed (9:8, 33). He forgives sin (9:1-8) and pronounces judgment

---

Figure 7: Fulfilling the Hebrew Bible

HB	Life of Jesus (Matthew)
Isa 7:14	Virgin birth (1:22-23)
Mic 5:1	Bethlehem birth (2:5-6)
2 Sam 5:2	Bethlehem birth
Hos 11:1	Flight to Egypt (2:15)
Jer 31:15	Innocents killed (2:17-18)
Unknown	Nazareth home (2:23)
Isa 40:3	The forerunner (3:3)
Isa 9:1-2	Galilee ministry (4:14-16)
Isa 53:4	Healings (8:17)
Isa 42:1-4	Healings (12:17-21)
Isa 6:9-10	Obduracy (13:14-15)
Ps 78:2	Parables (13:35)
Isa 62:11	Triumphal entry (21:4-5)
Zech 9:9	Triumphal entry
Zech 11:12-13	Judas' fate (27:9-10)

(11:2-24). He is greater than the temple (12:6) and lord of the sabbath (12:8). He is "more than a prophet" (11:9; 16:13-20). He founds (16:18-20; 18:15-20) and commissions his church (28:18-20; 9:36-10:42). Most importantly, he is **the Lord worshiped** by the church (28:17; cf. 14:33, and other miracle stories) and still present in the church (18:20; 28:20). In short, he has "all authority in heaven and on earth" (28:18).

Figure 8: **The Virgin Birth**

Matthew reads the OT freely. In the virgin birth passage (Mt 1:22), for example, Matthew reads the LXX Isa 7:14, where "virgin" occurs, rather than the HB which reads "young maiden." Throughout, Matthew reads the HB/LXX as a collection of oracles independent of their historical and literary context. For Matthew, **their important context is the eschatological act of God in Christ**. Thus, Matthew re-oracles the prophetic words in a new context. Where Isaiah offers an oracle of assurance to Israel promising divine aid before a newly born child comes of age, Matthew applies the words to Jesus' divine engendering.

Perhaps, most importantly, his word is **the authoritative interpretation of Torah**:

> Do not think that I have come to abolish the law or the prophets; I have come not to abolish but to fulfill. For truly I tell you, until heaven and earth pass away, not one letter, not one stroke of a letter, will pass from the law until all is accomplished. Therefore, whoever breaks one of the least of these commandments, and teaches others to do the same, will be called the least in the kingdom of heaven; but whoever does them and teaches them will be called great in the kingdom of heaven. For I tell you, unless

your righteousness exceeds that of the scribes and Pharisees, you will never enter the kingdom of heaven. (5:17-20)

Figure 9: **Qumran and Barnabas**

The rabbis read the HB in the context of an oral tradition interpreting Torah as relevant to everyday life as an **ethical and ritual guide** [cf. chap. 8, figure 9]. By contrast, Matthew and the sectarians at Qumran, responsible for the Dead Sea Scrolls, read the ancient texts in an **eschatological context** [see figure 8]. Thus, for example, the sectarians thought that the phrase "that he may run who reads" (in Hab 2:1-2) referred to their Teacher of Righteousness who clarified the prophets' mysteries [Longenecker, 41]. Others, like the Epistle of Barnabas read even more **extravagantly**. Thus, for Barnabas, the scapegoat and calves of Jewish ritual are Jesus [Barnabas, 7-8], and food laws are ethical injunctions to avoid sinners [10]. Barnabas' apologetic point is that the Jews misunderstand their own scripture (cf. 2 Cor 3-4; Heb 8-10). Ignoring its historical and literary context, such readings make the HB/LXX into the Christian OT.

Myth: The Narrow Path

Whereas for Mark the dying Christ is the touchstone of an ethical dualism, Matthew's touchstone is Jesus' Torah. One either **obeys the Torah and lives or one dies** (11:28-30). Matthew, of course, exhorts to life:

Enter through the narrow gate; for the gate is wide and the road is easy that leads to destruction, and there are many who take it. For the gate is narrow and the road is hard that leads to life, and there are few who find it. (7:13-14)

Figure 10: **The Sermon on the Mount**

The Sermon on the Mount encapsulates the Matthean Jesus' teaching and the Matthean myth. It describes the lifestyle appropriate to the kingdom as the life of "**greater righteousness**" (5:17-20) in deliberate contrast with past applications of Torah (note the antitheses of 5:21-48 and the critique of hypocritical piety in 6:1-18). Concisely, the sermon demands an **absolute devotion** to God and the brother with revolutionary results:

> Preoccupation with concerns dictated by apparent self-interest, with its attendant hubris, must be replaced by faith in God, love of neighbour (including the enemy), forgetfulness of self. The common thread binding together poverty of spirit and meekness, detachment from and generosity with wealth, turning the other cheek and loving the enemy, hiding what the right hand does from the left and praying in secret, is self-abnegation, the mortification of all egocentric thinking and doing . [Davies and Allison, "Reflections," 305]

The teaching sections provide detailed instructions in the way:

> To hear and internalize Jesus' speeches is to be conformed to the shape of his life. This, then, is the chief purpose of Jesus' great speeches: to bring the life of the disciple, or the implied reader, into conformity with the shape of Jesus' life. . . . By

internalizing the speeches of Jesus, the disciple, or the implied reader, who through Jesus has become a "son of God" (5:45), realizes this saying in his or her life: In single-hearted devotion to God the Father, he or she serves the neighbor and indeed all humankind. [Kingsbury, Story, 111]

In short, obedience to Jesus' Torah means loving God and the neighbor.

Mythic Characters: Hypocrisy

For Matthew, characters are **models of obedience or examples of hypocrisy**. Despite scathing criticisms by Jesus (e.g., 11:20-24), the crowds function like a **Greek chorus**. They emphasize key ideas and dramatic moves. Thus, they remark on Jesus' authority (e.g., 7:28-29) or are a foil for the disciples' enlightenment (13:1-52). Perhaps, most importantly, they dramatize Jesus' final repudiation as they opt to side with their leaders (26:47, 55; 27:15-26).

These religious leaders are Jesus' opponents. They consider Jesus a demonic blasphemer (9:3, 34; 10:25; 12:24; 26:63-66) and strive to kill him (12:14; 26:3-5; 26:63-66; 27:1-2; 21:33-46). Given Matthew's ethical dualism, this hostile opposition reveals them to be part of the kingdom of evil (e.g., 12:33-42; 13:37-43).

If the opening Sermon on the Mount depicts the greater righteousness, Jesus' **closing woes on the religious leaders** illustrate hypocrisy (23). Confessing divine goals, the leaders pursue human standards (23:1-12; contrast 6:1-18). Their hypocrisy deludes them (23:16-28) and leads to their **self-destructive** opposition to God's representative (23:15, 29-39).

The passion charts their **self-deceptive** bloodiness in great detail (26:14-15, 59-61; 28:11-15). Trying to save their life, they bring innocent blood upon themselves (27:25; cf. 23:29-39). The result of this bloody self-deception can only be destruction (cf. 21:43; 22:7; 24:1-2).

Figure 11: **Memorable Hypocrites**

Unfortunately, the gospels have made "Pharisee" a synonym for hypocrite. Sinclair Lewis's immoral evangelist, Elmer Gantry, is equally memorable. Despite protestations about service, Gantry is the ultimate "user." The contrast between his actions and his speech creates ludicrous scenes. The conclusion is typical:

> He turned to include the choir, and for the first time he saw that there was a new singer, a girl with charming ankles and lovely eyes, with whom he would certainly have to become well acquainted. But the thought was so swift that it did not interrupt the paean of his prayer: "Let me count this day, Lord, as the beginning of a new and more vigorous life, as the beginning of a crusade for complete morality and the domination of the Christian church through all the land. . . . We shall yet make these United States a moral nation!" [416]

Steve Martin's character in the recent movie Leap of Faith is more complex. Despite his false promises of rain and staged miracles, Martin's character finally encounters an inexplicable miracle when a crippled boy walks. Broken by this experience, the healer flees, hitch-hiking out of town as the rains begin. Unlike Elmer Gantry, Leap of Faith ends with a sign of transcendence.

Mythic Characters: Obedience

The disciples follow Jesus' model and path. They know him as the Son of God (14:33; 16:16) and understand his teaching (11:25-27; 13:51-52; 16:12). Through esoteric training, they become **scribes of the kingdom of heaven** (13:52) and teachers of his commandments (28:20). Despite their passion failures, they are reunited with and commissioned by the resurrected Lord. Beyond resurrection, they are those who judge, who "bind and loose," in Jesus' stead (16:18-20; 18:15-20).

These disciples are not, however, perfect. They fail to appropriate the teachings about suffering service and quibble about positions of authority (19:13-15, 27-30; 20:24-28; contrast 6:22-34). In the passion narrative, they betray, flee, and deny. Lacking faith (trust), they overestimate their own abilities (26:33-35). Appropriately, Matthew's disciples are **"men of little faith"** (6:30; 8:26; 14:31; 16:8; 17:20; cf. 21:20-22; 28:17).

The disciples, then, remain in process. They and the church **still face the eschatological judgment** which will weed out the evil from the kingdom (13:36-43, 47-50; 18:23-35; 24-25).

Mythic Succession and Implied Reader

The commissioning of the disciples closes Matthew (28:16-20) and separates later readers from Jesus. Of course, the **authoritative teaching of the disciples' church** connects later readers with Jesus (13:52; 16:18-20; 18:15-20; 28:16-20). In Jesus' absence, the disciples' church interprets Torah. They are the ones who bind and loose. Whereas Jesus is the only teacher during his ministry (note teaching's absence in 10:7-8), the disciples' church teaches after the commission (28:20). If one asks what these disciples teach, the answer is what Matthew's Jesus taught (28:20). That content is, of course, Matthew itself or, more specifically, the **teaching discourses** in which the Matthean Jesus continues to speak to new generations.

Figure 12: **The Sermon's Relevance**

The sermon's demands seem impossibly ideal to moderns. Who can keep these stringent words? Not surprisingly, various interpretations exist [see Connick, 260-64]. **Absolutists** say that the demands are literal and apply universally. **Hyperbolists** argue that the sermon contains exaggerated, dramatic demands which must be applied carefully and relatively. **Two-realmists** restrict the sermon's demands to the church and to spiritual life while denying its application to the secular, political realm. **Interimists** aver that these radical demands apply only to the extremely short time between the gospel and the apocalypse. Finally, **repenters** opine that the demands illustrate human ethical failures in order to drive humans to divine grace.

Style: Didactic, Typological

Matthew's numerous teaching sections create a **didactic** tone quite appropriate for a text which makes so much of obedience to the word (5:17-20; 7:21-27). Where Mark tries to convert, Matthew strives **to train scribes** and teachers:

> Therefore every scribe who has been trained for the kingdom of heaven is like the master of a household who brings out of his treasure what is new and what is old. (13:52)

Not surprisingly, then, Matthew often pedantically explains Mark's riddles. Thus, Matthew explains why John baptized Jesus (3:14-15), explains more carefully the relationship between unbelief and the absence of miracles (13:58 // Mk 6:5-6), and identifies the leaven of the Pharisees (16:6, 12 // Mk 8:15).

Figure 13: **The Didache**

The Didache is the early church's most famous catechetical manual. It contains a two-ways exhortation and an early church order (including baptism, the eucharist, and the role of prophets). The church order goes beyond Matthew (cf. Mt 18), but the Didache's two-ways ethic resembles Matthew closely. Its most concise ethical synopsis also recalls Matthew:

> Thou shalt love first the Lord thy Creator, and
> secondly thy neighbour as thyself; and thou
> shalt do nothing to any man that thou wouldst
> not wish to be done to thyself. [1]

The explanatory style is equally evident in the citation of fulfilled OT prophecies. The quotations connect Jesus *typologically* to Israel. In fact, they place Matthew's Jesus-story within the larger story of God and Israel:

> . . . the very existence of Matthew's book and its
> power to make sense depend on the prior existence of
> another book, which . . . needs completion.
> [Kermode, in Alter and Kermode, 398]

Genre: Didactic Biography

Some scholars have opined that Matthew was a catechetical document, a **training manual for young converts**. While Matthew does not fit that pattern exactly, this gospel does move beyond the typical biography pattern with its inclusion of such lengthy teaching sections. As a result, one might think of it as a didactic biography.

Figure 14: Borges

Context determines meaning. Thus, Borges' fictional "Pierre Menard, Author of Don Quixote" imagines two different authors writing the same words with different meanings:

> ... truth, whose mother is history, rival of time, depository of deeds, witness of the past, exemplar and adviser to the present, and the future's counselor. [43]

For the seventeenth-century Cervantes, the words are "rhetorical praise of history." For Menard, on the other hand, the same words are sheer pragmatism:

> History, the mother of truth: the idea is astounding. Menard, a contemporary of William James, does not define history as an inquiry into reality but as its origin. Historical truth, for him, is not what has happened; it is what we judge to have happened. [43]

ANET: Matthew's Torah

Matthew's criticism of the Jewish religious leaders (e.g., 23) and his remarks about Jesus' "innocent blood" (27:24-25) smack of anti-semitism. Read carefully, however, Matthew is not guilty of that charge. Like the Hebrew prophets, Matthew's **judgment is for everyone**. Jew and Gentile alike stand under the coming judgment (e.g., 25:31-46). Perhaps, more importantly, even the church faces the coming judgment (e.g., 13:37-43, 47-50; 18:23-35; 24:45-25:30). Of course, it cannot be denied that Matthew presents the Jewish obduracy more dramatically and, hence, far more memorably.

Still, of all the gospels, Matthew has the most positive view of the law (5:17-20; 23:2-3). For Matthew, the **Torah remains in force** (e.g., contrast Mk 7 with Mt 15). In fact, Matthew has a "regulatory" ethical style, not unlike the later rabbis [cf. Davies, Setting, 413-14].

Unlike the rabbis, however, Matthew reads Torah **eschatologically**. That is, Matthew reads Jesus as the fulfillment of Torah. As a result, Matthew often ignores the historical context of passages (e.g., 2:15 ignores the reference to Israel's exodus), their literary context and style (e.g., 21:4-5 ignores the Hebrew parallelism), and sometimes the best text (e.g., the "virgin" of 1:22 is the LXX, not the Hebrew). In fact, Matthew may even create texts (nothing like 2:23 is now known). In short, in light of Jesus, Matthew's Torah has an immediate, charismatic meaning. For moderns, particularly academics, the Torah is not such a contemporary text. Where Matthew reads prophetically and typologically, modern academics read historically and contextually.

Review Questions

1. Apply the reading method of chaps. 3-4 to Matthew. List its genre, plot shape, conflict, depiction of Jesus and God, mythic function, and ANE problems.
2. How does Matthew's structure differ from Mark's?
3. What is the point of Matthew's genealogy?
4. How do Matthew's teaching sections contribute to its plot?
5. Rewrite the Sermon on the Mount in one sentence.
6. Explain Matthew's two-ways myth and its mythic characters.
7. How does Matthew's Son of God differ from Mark's?
8. What does it mean to say that Matthew has a pedantic style?

Suggestions for Alternate Reading and Reflection

1. Compare the myths, Jesuses, and expectations of Christians in Matthew and Mark.

2. Can one follow the dictates of the Sermon on the Mount in the modern world?

3. Explain Matthew's "reading" of the OT. How does it differ from that of the rabbis and from modern historical or literary critics?

4. Can one reread ancient texts without rewriting them? How does typology differ from allegory? On what grounds would one condemn or praise allegory?

5. Is Matthew anti-semitic? Can one rewrite Matthew and make it less so? How might a modern Jewish reader object to Matthew?

For Further Reading

On the infancy narratives, see Brown, Birth; and Stendahl, "Quis."

On Matthew's use of Son of David, see Duling, "Therapeutic." On Matthew's use of Son of God, see Kingsbury, Structure, 136-37, 166.

On Matthew's structure, see Bacon; Kingsbury, Structure, 1-25; **idem**, Story, 43-93; Davies, Setting, 14-25; Barr, NT, 179-81; and Carter, 463-65.

For a brief introduction to the discourses, see Kingsbury, Story, 105-13.

For discussions of the sermon, see Davies, Setting; Guelich, Sermon; Betz, Essays; and Davies and Allison. Guelich has a helpful review of historical and contemporary views on the sermon in "Interpreting," 117-30.

On Matthew's parables, see Kingsbury, Parables.

On Matthew's two ways, see Rhoads, "Matthew," 453-61; and Via, Self-Deception.

On rabbinic, school, or scribal elements in Matthew, see Dobschuetz; Stendahl, <u>School</u>; and Cope.

On Matthew's use of the OT, see Brown, <u>Birth</u>, 97-98; and Gundry.

On Matthew's genre, see Shuler.

On Matthew's plot, see Powell, "Plot"; and Kingsbury, <u>Story</u>, 4-8, 71-75.

On Matthew's characters, see Kingsbury, <u>Story</u>, 9-18; and David Bauer. On the Matthean disciples, see Luz; Kingsbury, <u>Story</u>, 129-46; and Edwards.

For translations of the apostolic fathers, including the <u>Didache</u> and the <u>Epistle of Barnabas</u>, see Radice.

CHAPTER 19

IMITATING JESUS
Luke-Acts

Introduction: Relationship to Mark and Overall Structure

Compared to Mark, Luke adds an infancy narrative (1-2), a travel narrative (9:51-19:27), and resurrection appearances (24:13-53). Even where sharing "common" material, Luke departs from Mark more often than Matthew did. In particular, Luke omits Mk 6:45-8:26 and has a distinctive passion narrative.

Figure 1: **Outlining Luke**

1. Introduction of the Prophet (1:5-4:13)
   Infancy (1-2)
   Baptism and Temptation (3:1-4:13)
2. Galilean Ministry: Acquiring Witnesses
   (4:14-9:50) (Opening Sermon, 4:16-30)
3. On the Way to Jerusalem (9:51-19:27)
4. Jerusalem Ministry (19:28-24:53)
   Witnessing in the Temple (19:45-21:38)
   Last Supper and Passion (22-23)
   Resurrection/Ascension Narrative (24)

Plot Shape and Conflict: God's Salvation and Israel's Tragedy

Luke opens with the arrival of divine salvation:

Do not be afraid; for see--I am bringing you good
news of great joy for all the people: to you is born this
day in the city of David a Savior, who is the Messiah,

> the Lord . . . . And suddenly there was with the angel
> a multitude of the heavenly host, praising God and
> saying, "Glory to God in the highest heaven, and on
> earth peace among those whom he favors." (2:10-14)

From the beginning, this salvation reaches **beyond Israel** (2:10?, 32) to "all flesh" (3:6, only Luke continues the Isaiah quotation to this point).

Figure 2: **The Infancy**

Luke's infancy narrative is a story of **two births**, those of John and Jesus. Both are announced by Gabriel (1:6-25, 26-38) and call forth **hymns of praise**. Unlike Matthew, Luke includes no trace of opposition to the divine salvation begun by these miraculous births. Instead, the pious worshipfully receive God's salvation. Thus, the story often employs a temple setting (1:8-23, 59-79; 2:21-39, 41-51) and includes famous hymns (Magnificat, 1:46-55; Benedictus, 1:67-79; Gloria, 2:14; and Nunc Dimittis, 2:29-32).

The Galilean ministry begins with a similar announcement by Jesus in his hometown synagogue (4:16-30):

> The Spirit of the Lord is upon me,
>   because he has anointed me
>   to bring good news to the poor.
> He has sent me to proclaim release to the captives
>   and recovery of sight to the blind
>   to let the oppressed go free,
>   to proclaim the year of the Lord's favor. (4:18-19)

For Luke, Jesus' ministry begins with opposition. When Jesus recalls grateful Gentiles, the synagogue erupts into a murderous rage

(4:22-30). This early incident with its themes of **Jewish rejection and Gentile salvation** is the story of Luke-Acts in microcosm. In fact, throughout the Galilean ministry, synagogue opposition contrasts with peaceful teaching in houses.

After the disciples properly identify Jesus, Jesus predicts his passion (9:18-27, 44-45) and begins a lengthy journey (9:51-19:27) to Jerusalem. This lengthy travel narrative presents Jesus as always on his way to Jerusalem (13:22, 33; 17:11; 18:31) and creates a situation of crisis where salvation is available to those who act decisively.

Figure 3: **The Travel Narrative**

Luke's travel narrative is a useful framework for the inclusion of miscellaneous teachings. These teachings **interpret Jesus' impending death**. For Luke, Jesus goes to Jerusalem because that is where prophets die (13:33; 18:31-33). The journey to death also creates a crisis situation demanding decisive action (9:57-62; 13:22-30; 16:1-13). Not surprisingly, then, **supplicants seek salvation** (17:12-19; 18:18-30; 19:1-10), and even a "wicked" generation asks for signs (11:16, 29-32). Finally, the travel narrative instructs one in the **absolute commitment** required of disciples (9:23-27, 57-62; 10:25-42; 11:27-28; 12:13-34; 13:22-30; 14:7-35). Discipleship precedes all other concerns, even family and economics. The persistent demands for steadfastness strike a similar chord (11:5-13; 12:35-38; 14:25-33; 18:1-8; 19:11-27). Only the humble (14:7-14) and the repentant (13:1-9; 15:11-32; 18:9-14) can follow.

While many unexpected characters accept God's salvation, Israel does not. As a result, Jesus joins a long line of **rejected prophets** (6:22-23; 11:47-51; 13:34; 20:9-19; Acts 7:2-53). As a result, the kingdom is not yet (19:11; Acts 1:6-11). In fact, as Jesus arrives in Jerusalem, Luke makes painfully clear the connection between the innocent, rejected prophet's death and Israel's own destruction (19:41-44; 23:27-31).

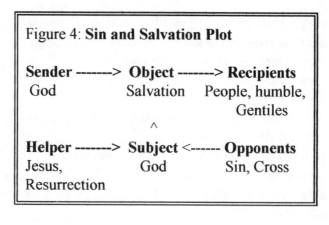

Figure 4: **Sin and Salvation Plot**

Sender ------> **Object** ------> **Recipients**
God   Salvation   People, humble,
                                        Gentiles

                                ∧

Helper ------> **Subject** <------ **Opponents**
Jesus,   God   Sin, Cross
Resurrection

As Israel does "not recognize the time of (her) visitation by God" (19:44), the glorious beginning of the infancy narratives does not come to fruition. As a result, Luke-Acts has a **sin plot** depicting **Israel's tragedy** (13:33-35), not at all unlike the Former Prophets.

Acts, however, **continues the story**. Witnesses, prepared by the resurrected Christ (Lk 24; Acts 1), offer continuing opportunities for repentance. A series of rejections lead, however, to the tragic, penultimate words of Acts in which Paul rejects Israel by quoting Isa 6:9-10 (cf. Mk 4:11-12) and turns to the Gentiles:

> Let it be known to you then that this salvation of God
> has been sent to the Gentiles; they will listen.
> (28:25-28; cf. 13:46; 18:6; Lk 20:16)

Thus, the Lukan **God finds those to save**. Luke-Acts is, then, also a salvation story for the humble (Jesus' teaching), the outcast (Jesus' miracles), the faithful (apostles), and the Gentiles. If God's salvation is put into question by Jesus' death and Israel's tragedy, it is gloriously realized in Acts by the church (2:43-47; 4:32-35; 5:11-16).

Acts is triumphal. The church lives in the midst of God's

salvation
(2 : 4 3 - 4 7 ;
4 : 3 2 - 3 5 ;
5:11-16). The
church has
witnessed God's
victory in the
resurrection
(2:23-24; 3:15;
13:28-33) and in
the apostles'
continuing
miracles (e.g.,
3:1-10; 14:8-18;
multiple
near-escapes).
Further, the
spirit makes the

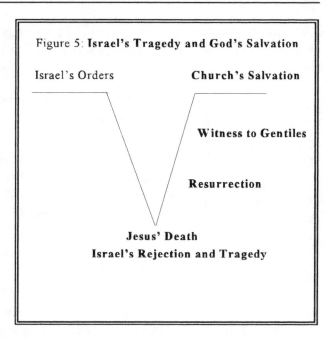

Figure 5: **Israel's Tragedy and God's Salvation**

Israel's Orders   **Church's Salvation**

Witness to Gentiles

Resurrection

Jesus' Death
Israel's Rejection and Tragedy

divine intensely present. It fills every important character (e.g., 4:8; 7:5, 55; 9:17; 13:9) and visibly guides the church at important junctures to new missions both geographically and ethnically (2:4; 8:17; 10:44-48; 11:15-18; 13:4; 15:8, 28; 16:6-11; 19:6; 20:22). Even persecution leads to expansion (e.g., 8:2).

The triumph is, however, incomplete. Acts ends with Paul languishing in prison and with growing Gentile opposition to the gospel (e.g., Acts 16:16-24; 19:23-40).

Volume Two: The Expansion of the Church

Unlike the other gospels, Luke is the first volume of a **two-volume work**. The **opening prefaces** indicate the close relationship of Luke-Acts (cf. Lk 1:1-4; Acts 1:1-5).

Further, Acts **fulfills Luke's promises**. Thus, the inclusion of the Gentiles (Lk 2:30-32; 4:16-30), the salvation to all flesh (Lk

3:6), and the promised spirit (3:16-17) arrive only in Acts. In an important way, then, Acts completes or "confirms" Luke [so Van Unnik].

Larger structural connections are also apparent. First, **Jerusalem is the center** of the two-volume work. If Luke hurtles toward Jerusalem, Acts moves ever

---

Figure 6: Outlining Acts

1. Witness in Jerusalem (1:12-8:1)
2. Witness in Surrounding Areas with returns to Jerusalem (8:2-12:25)
3. Witness to the Nations (13:1-19:20)
    Paul's mission and returns to Jerusalem
4. Journey to Rome via Jerusalem (19:21-28:31)

---

away from Jerusalem to the nations (1:8). Interestingly, the move does not begin until Acts 8:2 and, then, only as the result of persecution, not in obedience to the mandate of 1:8. Acts 8:2-12:25 is a **boundary crossing section** where the gospel goes to eunuchs, Samaritans, and Gentiles. These forays prepare for the Pauline **move to the Gentile world**. Even in the Pauline mission, however, as the story moves into the Gentile world, Jerusalem remains central. Thus, the Jerusalem church must approve of Paul's mission work (Acts 15), and Paul continues to return to Jerusalem throughout his missionary endeavors.

Throughout, **the church expands** geographically from Jerusalem to Rome, ethnically from Jew to Gentile, ritually from the Jerusalem temple to an independent Christian community, and institutionally from the church of the apostles to the church of the elders [so Tyson].

Second, the characters of Acts resemble those of Luke. John the Baptist, Jesus, Peter, Stephen, and Paul are all **rejected repentance-prophets** (Lk 11:47-51; 20:9-19; Acts 3:22-26; 7:2-53). Empowered by the spirit (Jesus in Lk 1:4-4:13; apostles in Acts 1:5-

2:47), they speak (call to repentance) and act (miracles, near-escapes) alike. The result is a succession of prophets similar to that in the Former Prophets.

Figure 7: **The Speeches and Near-Escapes of Acts**

   While the numerous speeches in Acts are by different characters, to different audiences, and of varying types (e.g., evangelism, defense), they are all **Lukan creations**. Thus, the speeches explain Luke-Acts' understanding of God's triumph in Jesus and the witnesses. In fact, the evangelistic sermons even have a similar structure. After introductory statements pertinent to the narrative context, the sermons stress the **Jewish crucifixion** of Jesus, **God's resurrection of Jesus**, and the apostolic witness to it (2:22-24; 3:13-15; 10:36-42; 13:23-25). They offer supporting **scriptural evidence** (2:25-31; 3:22-26; 10:43; 13:32-27) and **call for a decision** (2:38-39; 3:17-20; 10:42-43; 13:38-41).

   The triumph of God is also evident in a number of stories in which the disciples narrowly escape death (e.g., 12:1-24; 16:16-40; 19:23-40; 27) [cf. Pervo, 12-23]. Such stories are examples of the **deus ex machina** vindication of the suffering righteous. Acts knows two different kinds of vindication: deliverance from death and triumph beyond death (Jesus' resurrection).

Characters: Prophet, Benefactor Jesus and the Lowly

   More so than any other gospel, Luke portrays **Jesus as the prophet** (e.g., 4:24; 7:16, 39; 9:8, 19; 24:19; Acts 3:22-26; 7:37) thereby locating him within ongoing Jewish history:

> Moses said, "The Lord your God will raise up for you
> from your own people a prophet like me. You must

listen to whatever he tells you. And it will be that everyone who does not listen to that prophet will be utterly rooted out of the people." . . . You are the descendants of the prophets . . . . When God raised up his servant, he sent him first to you, to bless you by turning each of you from your wicked ways. (Acts 3:22-26, citing Deut 18:15-16)

Figure 8: **The Rejected Prophet**

Luke's distinctive passion does not attribute salvific significance to Jesus' death. Thus, Luke's parallel to Mk 10:45 and Mt 20:28 does not contain the final words, "to give his life a ransom for many" (22:24-27). More importantly, some ancient texts of Luke omit 22:19b-20 from the last supper [see Metzger, Textual, 173-77]. More obviously, the speeches of Acts uniformly attribute Jesus' death to human malice (e.g., 2:23; 3:13-14; 13:28; but see Acts 20:38). For Luke-Acts, it is God's resurrection which makes the forgiveness of sins possible (e.g., Lk 24:47; Acts 3:28; 4:11; 5:31). Jesus' death is simply **typical for a prophet** (e.g. 6:22-23; 11:47-51; 13:34; 20:9-19; Acts 7:52-53).

Correspondingly, Luke stresses **Jesus' innocence** (Lk 23:4, 14, 15, 22, 41, 47) and the Jewish leaders' culpability (22:66; 23:1-2, 10, 13, 18, 21, 23, 24). Even the Romans know Jesus to be innocent (23:4, 14-15, 22, 47).

Israel's rejection of the innocent prophet brings her **ruin** as two distinctive doom-oracles surrounding the passion make clear (19:41-44; 23:27-31). Even more ominously, two statements about the kingdom's non-occurrence form a wider frame for the passion (19:11; Acts 1:6-8).

As a prophet, Jesus **engenders a crisis which will save or engulf Israel**. His message, then, is the characteristic prophetic "repent!" (e.g., 5:32; 13:3, 5; 15:7, 10; 16:30; 17:3-4; 24:47; cf. Lk 3:8, 10-14;

Acts 2:37-38; 11:18; 17:30). Of course, as Luke continues "biblical history," prophet foreshadows the doom of both Jesus and Israel (Acts 7:37-53; Lk 11:47-51; 13:34-35; 20:9-19).

Prophet alone, however, does not capture Jesus' significance. Jesus is also "Lord" both in the gospel (see 7:13, 19; 10:1, 39, 41; 11:39; 12:42; 13:15; 17:5-6; 18:6; 19:8; 22:61) and in Acts. Jesus is a powerful (spirit-inspired, 4:1, 14, 18; 10:21) figure who actualizes **salvation** particularly **for the lowly** (e.g., Lk 1:51-53; 4:18-21; 6:20-26; 7:21-22; 16:19-31). Luke's Jesus is for sinners and tax-collectors (5; 7:36-50; 15; 18:9-14; 19:1-10; 22:31-32), for the poor (1:52-53; 4:18; 6:20-26; 16:19-31), for Samaritans (9:51-56; 10:30-37; 17:11-19), and for women (7:12-15; 8:2-3; 10:38-42; 23:27-31).

The outcast and lowly supply Luke with wonderful minor characters including Mary and Martha, Zacchaeus, the prodigal, the good Samaritan, and the repentant thief. Of course, these characters are primarily foils for Lord Jesus, the **benefactor** who bestows goods on his followers [cf. Danker].

Characters: God's Return

God figures more prominently in Luke than the other gospels because of Luke's **emphasis upon God's salvation** (1:47, 77; 2:30), the portrayal of the praying Jesus (3:21-22; 5:16; 6:12; 9:18; 11:1; 22:41-46), and the description of the Jesus-event as God's act in the sermons of Acts (2:22-24, 32-36; 10:38-40; 13:23, 30). Notably, God raises Jesus from the dead, but God's story continues even in Jesus' absence (Acts).

Luke portrays God as **liberator**, rather than orderer. When Israel rejects her prophet, Luke's **innovative, ironic God** finds surprising people to save. Not even the church can keep up with the surprising God who would include even Gentiles (Acts 8-11; 15).

The Gentiles' inclusion **depicts God universally**. God is the God of all peoples (Acts 15:14; 18:10; 20:28; cf. Lk 3:6). Luke-Acts hardly, however, forsakes the biblical traditions. The message goes first to Jews and only then to Gentiles. When the message does go to Gentiles, it is carried by repentant Jews. In short, Luke-Acts depicts a **missionary monotheism** similar to that of Second Isaiah.

Despite prophets and miracles, the dominant conception of providence is **cultic**. Temple and synagogue settings (as well as house churches) are common. More importantly, the resurrection scenes resemble (found?) Christian worship as they include the revelatory breaking of bread and scripture interpretation characteristic of that worship (Lk 24:13-53). Luke's God is known in worship (cf. Lk 4:16-30).

Given the emphasis upon God, Jesus, not surprisingly, becomes **the first Christian**. Like his followers, Jesus is filled with the spirit, worships, and prays. He expects them to ask for the spirit (11:13). He teaches them to pray (6:28; 10:2; 11:1-3; 18:1-18; 21:36). In fact, it is probably not too far-fetched to see the resurrected Jesus as the first Christian priest as he breaks bread and interprets scripture (Lk 24:13-53). In short, Jesus is **the model of Lukan piety** (9:27).

The Disciples: Transformed into Apostles

Luke's disciples do not understand the cross (9:45; 10:34; 24:25) or service (e.g., 9:46-50; 18:15-17; 22:24-27). Unlike Mark's disciples, however, they **do not flee the passion**. Although they betray and deny, they stand with the women and watch (23:49).

The resurrection and the spirit, of course, **transform them**. The resurrected Christ's revelation disperses their pre-passion ignorance (24:30-32, 45-49; cf. Acts 9:3-6). The empowering spirit vanquishes their fear (24:49; Acts 1:8; 2:1-42; cf. Paul's experience in 9:1-22). In short, they become powerful **witnesses** of all that they have seen (hence, their necessary presence at the cross). They also become powerful **benefactors** like Jesus (3:1-10; 5:12-16; 9:36-43; 14:8-13; 19:11-12; 20:9-12).

Peter undergoes a particularly dramatic change. Although he once fearfully denied Jesus (Lk 23), the spirit recreates him as a powerful witness for Jesus before people and authorities (Acts 1-5). His witness, with that of John and Stephen, **completes Jesus' prophetic ministry to Jerusalem**. In them, Jerusalem gets a second chance to repent which she again rejects by stoning Stephen (Acts 7) and imprisoning Peter (3-4; 12).

Figure 9: **Imitating Jesus**

The apostles are **types of Jesus**. They, too, are rejected repentance-prophets. Not surprisingly, then, the apostles also resemble one another [Talbert, Patterns, 23-24]:

	Peter	**Paul**
Empowered by the spirit	2:1-4	13:1-3
Opening sermon	2:14-40	13:16-40
Healing of a lame man	3:1-26	14:8-17
Confront a magician	8:9-24	13:6-12
Raise the dead	9:36-43	20:9-12
Restrain Gentile worshipers	10:25-26	14:13-15
Mission to the Gentiles	10-11	13-21
Confer the spirit	8:14-24	19:1-6
Imprisonment	12	21-28
Miraculously delivered	12:6-11	16:24-26

Paul, too, is a dramatic transformation. After his involvement in the stoning of Stephen and the persecution of the church, a reordering vision on the road to Damascus (9) makes Paul yet another witness of the risen Christ. This particular story is so important to Luke that it is twice repeated (22:4-16; 26:9-18).

Figure 10: **Paul**

Paul is the most prominent character in the last half of Acts and, according to tradition, the author of thirteen NT letters [see chap. 21]. The portraits of Paul in those two places, however, differ at various points. For example, Acts never mentions Paul's letters or his collection for the Jerusalem poor. Further, if Acts 15 and Gal 2 describe the same assembly, they disagree about its timing (how many times had Paul been to Jerusalem?), its nature (public or private?), and its results (Paul mentions no apostolic decree).

The decisive difference, however, is the **Jerusalem orientation** of Acts. In Acts only, Paul's missionary journeys begin from and return to Jerusalem. That focus, of course, supports the Lukan notion of the **Una Sancta Apostolica** centered in Jerusalem. In fact, Acts so homogenizes Paul that he is indistinguishable from Peter [see figure 9]. As a result, the Paul of Acts is **more Jewish** than the Paul of the letters (e.g., 15:19-29; 21:15-26). While he does suffer, he is a figure of miracles and near-escapes, not one who glories in his suffering (cf. 1 Cor 1-4; 2 Cor 10-13). Finally, his sermons in Acts center on the **resurrection, not the cross**. In short, the Paul of Acts is a Lukan character.

Paul is also **the incarnation of the move to the Gentiles**. The boundary crossings of Acts 8-15 and Peter's work with Cornelius (10-11) are only precedents. Paul has the real work and accomplishes the mandate of 1:8 (cf. 13:47; 19:10).

The Jews: Called to Repent

For Luke, the Jews are those to whom the repentance-prophets appeal. Although the religious leaders are nefarious opponents, some **Pharisees become believers** (Acts 15:5) or assist the believers in other ways (5:34-39; 23:9). Most importantly, of course, Paul is a transformed Pharisee and serves as a model for other conversions.

While the crowds facilitate Jesus' death (23:13-25), they quickly lament that death (Lk 23:27, 48). In Acts, then, conversions are massive (2:41, 47; 4:4; 5:14; 6:1, 7; 12:24).

These conversions incite the leaders to new violence (4:5-18; 5:17-42; 6:11-8:4; 9:1-2) which, in turn, leads to a successful Gentile mission. Even there, Jewish opposition continues (13:45, 50; 14:2, 4, 19; 17:5, 13; 18:6, 12-17; 19:9; 20:19; 21:11). Ultimately, both Stephen (7) and Paul face Jewish trials and "passions" (21-26). Finally, on three occasions, Paul **rejects the Jews** and declares his intention to turn to the Gentiles (13:46-47; 18:6; 28:28).

The last rejection, the penultimate words of Acts, is particularly ominous and seems to signal the end of Jewish opportunities for repentance. Against this "final solution," however, stand the constant notes about Jewish believers (e.g., 21:20; 28:24) as well as the **apostles' own Jewishness**.

In Acts, Peter and Paul worship in the temple and observe Jewish purity regulations. They go to the Gentiles only when it is clearly divinely mandated. Luke, in fact, imposes sojourner regulations (regulations for foreigners in the land) upon all Gentiles (15). Taken with this zealousness for the law, the biblical atmosphere of Luke-Acts hardly suggests a clean break with tradition. Rather, in typical prophetic style, **judgment continues God's history** with his people (cf. Rom 9-11; Deut 29-30). Acts 28:28, then, is not final rejection, but typical **prophetic critique**.

Genre: Late, Biblical History

Luke's gospel biography is **prophetic**, rather than apocalyptic or didactic. Further, Luke-Acts expands the biography to include a prophetic succession of John the Baptist, Stephen, Peter, and Paul. In short, Luke-Acts moves beyond biography to history. While the literary prefaces, the speeches of Acts, and the synchronisms with Roman history (2:1; 3:1; Acts 11:28; 18:2; 26:26) resemble ancient history generally, Luke-Acts' **closest generic companion is the Former Prophets**. Thus, for example, Lk 1-2 closely resembles 1 Sam 1-2. Far more obviously, Luke's characters (rejected repentance-prophets) and plot (Israel's tragedy) resemble those of the Former Prophets.

The addition of Acts also **historicizes** and institutionalizes Luke's Jesus-story. Acts makes Jesus part of the remote past. The story of the church's expansion separates him from the readers of Luke-Acts [see narrator]. In fact, for Luke, Jesus becomes "the middle of time" following Israel (Lk 16:16) and preceding the church [Conzelmann, 16-17]. Not incidentally, for Luke, Satan is absent from this mythic golden age of salvation (Satan departs in Lk 4:13 and returns only at 22:3). Of course, by this standard, the age of the apostles and subsequent ages are lesser days (cf. Acts 20:18-38) [cf. Talbert, Patterns]. This **fall from a golden age pattern** ultimately became the classic Christian myth of history [cf. Wilken, Myth].

Luke-Acts' three-stage **history of salvation** also differs notably from apocalyptic's two-age scenario. It distances the reader from the end. The time of the Gentiles (21:24), or the time of the church, separates Jesus from the end. The kingdom, then, is not yet (cf. Lk 19:11; Acts 1:6-8; 20:18-35).

Myth: Imitating Jesus and Prophetic Realism

Acts also **institutionalizes** the Jesus' story, for Jesus becomes the witnesses' property. They testify to and remember Jesus. Their control is not absolute, however. The story of successive repentance-prophets establishes a textual control over (later) witnesses. Later messages and lives must model the mythic founders' prophetic calls to repentance. While this is not yet apostolic succession, it is a significant move toward an institution. Of course, Luke's repeated emphasis upon the spirit enthuses this institution and prevents it from becoming a deadly bureaucracy [cf. Dunn, Unity, 356-57].

Figure 11: **Early Catholicism**

Compared to apocalyptic sects, Luke-Acts is more willing to accommodate to the world and is more concerned with apostolic harmony (an **Una Sancta Apostolica**) and apostolic succession/tradition. As a result, some scholars describe Luke-Acts as typical of early catholicism. That label should not obscure, however, the enthusiastic church in Acts. Put simply, **the spirit dominates the church**. It fills every important character (e.g., Acts 4:8; 7:5, 55; 9:17; 13:9) and visibly guides the church at important junctures to new missions both geographically and ethnically (2:4; 8:17; 10:44-48; 11:15-18; 13:4; 15:8, 28; 16:6-11; 19:6; 20:22). In short, Acts is not only the story of the growth of the apostolic institution, it is also the story of **Pentecost**(s) (cf. 2; 10; 19).

Unlike apocalyptic sectarians, this institutional church is at home in the world and, therefore, concerned with its relationship to Rome. As a result, Luke-Acts depicts the **innocence of its major characters before Rome** (Lk 23:4, 14, 20, 22; 23:47; Acts 16:38-39; 18:15-16; 19:35-41; 23:28-30; 25:24-27; 26:30-32). Paul's statement before Festus summarizes this apologetic motif: "I have in no way committed an offense against the law of the Jews, or against the temple, or against the emperor" (25:8). In short, Luke-Acts argues that Christians are of no concern to Rome.

Institutionalization does not mean non-critical acceptance of the world. For Luke, a higher sovereign bends imperial decrees to his purposes (Lk 2:1-7). God, rather than Jewish wickedness and Roman complicity, determines Jesus' death. God, rather than Rome, determines the fate of wicked Jerusalem (e.g., Lk 19:41-44; 20:16; Acts 3:23). In short, Luke reads political, imperial events in light of God's purposes.

Figure 12: **Innocent Victims Before Rome**

According to Luke-Acts, Romans repeatedly recognize the innocence of the Christian heroes. The resulting characterization of these Roman officials is, however, hardly positive. At best, they are uninterested in the apostles (cf. Acts 18:12-17). More often, even when Roman officials recognize the prophets' innocence, they are too **self-serving** to act on their behalf (cf. Lk 23:24-25; Acts 24:27; 25:9). In fact, these officials incarnate Luke's negative values, pride, complacency, and opposition to the gospel (e.g., 16:16-24; 19:23-40). The "innocent victim" motif, then, is **hardly an effective apology** for Christianity before Rome.

What identity, then, does Luke-Acts prescribe for Christians? In short, the time of the Gentiles calls for steadfast endurance and faithful witness (e.g., Lk 21:12-19, 34-36; Acts 4:23-31; 5:41-42; 14:22). That is, Christians are called to **the rejected lives of repentance-prophets**. In short, they are to live the life of Jesus and his first witnesses. Not surprisingly, then, they are called "Christians" (Acts 11:26).

More specifically, followers are to be **humble** (14:7-14) and repentant (13:1-9; 15:11-32; 18:9-14). **Outcasts**, sinners, women, tax-collectors, Samaritans, the poor, and the Gentiles accept Luke's salvation. The proud, complacent, and wealthy do not (e.g., Lk 12:13-34; 15; 16:14-31; 18:18-30).

Figure 13: **Anti-Semitism and Complacent Gentiles**

Luke-Acts' constant attribution of the death of Jesus to the Jews and Paul's rejection of the Jewish mission in favor of the Gentiles smack of anti-semitism. At the very least, Luke-Acts seems to function as a **foundational myth for early Gentile Christianity**.

Such Gentile complacency, however, would itself come under attack from Luke-Act's constant **critique of pride** and wealth. In short, as Gentile Christianity becomes the dominant religious form, it becomes, in turn, subject to all of the Lukan Jesus' strictures against the religious establishment of his day.

The founding and the prophetic critique allow Luke-Acts to be both for the institutional powers-that-be and for the humble outcasts. Or, more appropriately, it can be read in either way. Put differently, Luke-Acts can stand alongside medieval figures who cry "Christ-killers" or with the prophets who critique all complacent powers.

Narrator/Narratee: Distance and Succession

The Lukan narrator is **more self-conscious** and intrusive than the other gospel narrators. He interjects himself into the story through the prefaces (Lk 1:1-4; Acts 1:1-5) and in the "we-passages" in Acts (16:10-17; 20:5-15; 21:1-18; 27:1-28:16; but cf. Jn 1:14-16; 21:24).

Despite this involvement, the narrator remains at some **remove from Jesus**. He was not a witness of the events, but interviewed the witnesses (Lk 1:1-4). Further, as the "we-passages" begin only in the story of Paul's journeys to the Gentile world, the narrator is closer to his Gentile narratee (Theophilus) and to his readers in space and time than he is to Jesus.

Luke-Acts itself does, however, **provide a connection to the founding times** for its readers. The narrator shares an ideological perspective with Jesus and the apostles. Like those characters, he calls readers to repentance and to humble dependence upon the ironic God who relentlessly pursues and finds surprising people to save.

Figure 14: **Magical Realism**

Biblical realism strikes modern readers as fantastic because it incorporates miracle and presumes the divine sovereignty. As a result, biblical realism **subverts modern readers' realities**. Modern magical realism, a trend in recent Latin American fiction, similarly combines miraculous events with matter-of-fact narration. Gabriel Garcia Marquez's One Hundred Years of Solitude is, perhaps, the most famous example. That novel traces the tragic history of a family and its village from Eden to apocalypse. Along the way, the "realistic" narrative includes quite fantastic elements. People fly on magic carpets. Murdered ghosts live happily with their murderers. An insomnia plague strikes the village. A gypsy returns from the dead because he cannot bear the solitude. A room remains untouched by time. A virgin ascends to heaven. It rains butterflies and dead birds. Perhaps, most magically, the book ends as family and village end apocalyptically and the last family member translates the story the reader has just read from ancient Sanskrit.

ANET: The Tyranny of the Past and Prophetic Realism

Like traditional myths generally, Luke-Acts views the time of Jesus and the apostles as a past golden age (cf. Acts 20:29-30). To modern eyes, however, such views allow the past to impose tyrannically upon the present. By contrast, since at least the nineteenth century, modernity has found meaning in an innovative look to the future. It is **the new**, not the past, **which dominates** modernity [cf. Wilken, Myth].

Figure 15: **Parables**

Luke has the most distinctive, memorable parables in the gospel tradition: the Good Samaritan (10:29-37), the rich fool (12:13-21), the prodigal son (15), the unjust steward (16:1-13), the rich man and Lazarus (16:9-31), the unjust judge (18:1-18), and the Pharisee and the publican (18:9-14). These stories are often quite subversive. Thus, the good Samaritan makes mockery of a Jewish lawyer's notion of neighbor. The prodigal son critiques the Pharisees' notion of God's mode of dealing with sinners.

These semi-independent, realistic stories advance Luke's world-view. Given the presence of divine salvation, the Lukan heroes are those who act decisively in crisis (the prodigal, the unjust steward). The rich fool is, of course, an anti-hero. As in Luke as a whole, the humble are heroes (the prodigal, Lazarus, the tax-collector) while the complacent and the proud (the rich fool, the rich man, the Pharisee) come to bad ends.

More importantly, Luke-Acts is not palatable to modernity because it prophetically critiques the world in which it lives. For Luke-Acts, the empire is not final. Thus, Luke-Acts' mythic models are rejected repentance-prophets living uneasily in the time of the Gentiles. For Luke-Acts, as for all biblical history, the empires are "under God." For modernity, this prophetic realism is nothing short of fantasy.

Style and Atmosphere: Type Scenes

Luke-Acts is a far more integrated narrative than the other gospels. The parallels in both teaching and career between the various prophets supply a connective framework as do the themes (e.g., Gentile salvation) presaged by volume one and confirmed in volume two.

Various type-scenes also provide connective tissue [cf. Tannehill, Narrative, 1:170-71, 2:201-03]. Jesus and the other witnesses do the same things (preach, miracles) in the same settings. Jesus worships and teaches in the temple or synagogue, withdraws to pray, and teaches at meals. The same kinds of settings continue in Acts. Two are particularly worthy of note.

First, confrontations in Jewish worship settings persist (e.g., 3-4; 13-14; 21-22). Paul's rejection in the synagogue and his subsequent turn to the Gentiles, in particular, resemble the setting and themes of Jesus' opening synagogue sermon (Lk 4:16-30).

Second, trial scenes like those in Lk 22-23 play an even more prominent role in Acts (e.g., 4:1-22; 5:12-42; 6:8-8:1; 21:27-26:32). The result is an aura of controversy not unlike that created by the gospel's controversy stories and exorcisms. Unlike the gospel, however, Acts extends the conflict into a Gentile world. There, the apostle and his message must also contend with Roman administration (e.g., 16; 18; 24-25; 28), Greek philosophy (17), and Greek religion (16; 19).

Review Questions

1. Apply the reading method of chaps. 3-4 to Luke-Acts. List its genre, plot shape, conflict, depiction of Jesus and God, mythic function, and ANE problems.
2. How does Luke's structure differ from Mark's?
3. How is Luke's passion narrative distinctive?

4. Compare the story in Luke to that in Acts.

5. Describe the expansion of the church in Acts.

6. Compare Luke's view of history to that of apocalyptic.

7. How does Luke distance Jesus from the reader? How does Luke connect the reader with the time of Jesus?

8. In what ways is the Jesus of Luke-Acts the first Christian?

9. Describe the structure of the sermons in Acts.

10. Compare Luke-Acts to the Former Prophets in genre, plot, character, and theodicy.

Figure 16: **The Sayings of Jesus (Q)**

No copies of Q exist [see gospel, figure 4], but most scholars believe that Luke best preserves the hypothetical document. According to Kloppenborg, the following Lukan passages are Q material: 3:7-9, 16-17; 4:1-13; 6:20b-49; 7:1-10, 18-28, 31-35; 9:57-62; 10:2-24; 11:2-4, 9-52; 12:2-14, 16-31, 33-34, 39-59; 13:18-21, 24-30, 34-35; 14:16-24, 26-27, 33-34; 15:3-7; 16:13, 17-18; 17:1-6, 23-37; 19:12-27; 22:28-30 [92].

Traditionally, scholars have seen these sayings as apocalyptic and concluded, therefore, that Jesus was an apocalyptic prophet. More recently, scholars, like Kloppenborg, have argued that the apocalyptic sayings are actually later church additions to an original layer of wisdom sayings. Therefore, some scholars now conclude that Jesus was a sage (possibly of a counter-culture variety given the subversive nature of passages like 6:20b-49), rather than an apocalyptic seer.

Suggestions for Alternative Reading and Reflection

1. What incidents or passages in Luke foreshadow the contents of

the second volume?

2. Is God more important to Luke-Acts than to Matthew or Mark?

3. Is Luke-Acts anti-semitic? Compare the ethnocentrism of Luke-Acts to that of Torah.

4. Is Luke-Acts "at home" in the world?

5. Is Luke-Acts an institutionalist? Charismatic? Traditionalist?

6. Compare Luke-Acts' politics to those of Josephus, Chronicles, and Eusebius.

7. Is Luke-Acts for the poor and against the rich? Can one read Luke-Acts as a text of liberation (i.e., an ideological reading)?

8. How successful is Luke-Acts as an apology to Rome?

9. Compare magical and biblical realism.

10. What world-view do the sayings of Jesus reflect?

For Further Reading

For an excellent literary introduction to Luke-Acts, see Tannehill, Narrative. On Luke, cf. also Talbert, Reading. For Acts, see Haenchen.

On Luke's infancy narratives, see Brown, Birth; and Minear, "Luke."

On connections between Luke and Acts, see Talbert, Patterns; Tannehill, Narrative, 1:298-301; Van Unnik; and Parsons.

On the tragedy of Israel in Luke-Acts, see Tannehill, Narrative, 1:156, 160, 192-94, 283-89; 2:89-92, 348-49. For a discussion of the connection between Jesus' death and the destruction of Jerusalem, see Tiede, 65-96.

On Luke's emphasis upon God's salvation, see Marshall; and Tannehill, Narrative; 1:2-3.

On the expansion of the church in Acts, see Tyson.

On Jesus as a prophet, see Tannehill, Narrative, 1:96-99, 285-89; and Tiede, 97-125.

On Jesus as savior, see Danker.

On the Jews in Acts, see Haenchen, 101-02, 122, 728-29; Sanders, Jews, 81-83; Jervell, 41-74, 153-83; and Brawley, 68-83, 155-59.

On the genre of Luke-Acts, see Talbert, What; **idem**, "Luke-Acts"; Aune, NT, 77-157; and Pervo.

For comparisons of Luke-Acts and biblical history, see Aune, NT, 96-111; Beardslee, Literary, 42-46; Tannehill, Narrative, 2:86-97; and Gasque.

On Luke's view of history, see Conzelmann; Marshall; and Talbert, "Luke-Acts."

On Luke as a successionist, see Talbert, Gnostics; and **idem**, Patterns, 89-110.

On Luke and early catholicism, see Bultmann, Theology, 2:95-326; Kaesemann, "Paul," 236-51; Kuemmel, "Current," 131-45; and Dunn, Unity, 351-59.

On the relationship between Luke-Acts and later churches' myth of history, see Talbert, Patterns, 99-103; Wilken, Myth; and Walsh, "Reconstructing."

On the sermons in Acts, see Dibelius, Studies; Dodd, Apostolic; and Aune, NT.

On Luke's literary style, see Cadbury, Style; and **idem**, Making.

For an argument that the perspectives of Jesus and the Lukan narrator are dissimilar, see Dawsey.

On Q, see Koester, Ancient, 128-71; and Kloppenborg.

CHAPTER 20

ABIDING IN CHRIST
John

Introduction: Comparison to the Synoptics

John shares generic similarities with the Synoptics. In addition to a common protagonist, John shares an **overall structure** of events with those narratives [cf. Kysar, Maverick, 11]. Nevertheless, John differs strikingly from the other gospels. It omits common elements and adds its own own special materials [Barr,

Figure 1: **Common Gospel Order**

The Baptist	Mk 1:4-8; Jn 1:19-36
Feeding	Mk 6:30-44; Jn 6:1-13
Water walking	Mk 6:45-52; Jn 6:16-21
Confession	Mk 8:29; Jn 6:68-69
Entry/anointing	Mk 11:10; 14:3-9; Jn 12:1-15
Passion	Mk 14:43-16:8; Jn 18:1-20:29

Figure 2: **John's Omissions and Additions**

Omissions	**Additions**
Baptism	Wedding at Cana
Temptation	Nicodemus
Transfiguration	Samaritan woman
Lord's Supper	Healings in Jn 5; 9
Gethsemane	Long Dialogues
Parables	Raising of Lazarus
Exorcisms	Farewell Discourse

NT, 255-56].

John also differs in overall presentation. Thus, instead of a last supper, John gives the feeding of the multitude an eucharistic overtone (6:22-71). Instead of a single transfiguration, all of Jesus' ministry reveals the divine glory (cf. 12:28; 17). More importantly, John handles differently both the **location** of Jesus' ministry (Jerusalem, not Galilee) and the **content** of Jesus' teaching (his identity, not the divine kingdom).

Narrative Time (Order): A Jerusalem Festival Orientation

The Synoptic Jesus has a public Galilean ministry followed by a Jerusalem passion. By contrast, the Johannine Jesus is early and often in Jerusalem. In fact, the narrative flows back and forth to Jerusalem.

Figure 3: **Back and Forth to Jerusalem**			
Outside Judea		**Jerusalem**	
1:19-2:12	>	2:13-3:36	>
4:1-54	>	5:1-47	>
6:1-7:9	>	7:10-10:39	>
10:40-12:11	>	12:12-20:29	>
21:1-23			

Jewish rituals also provide important settings. The resulting Jerusalem festival orientation depicts Jesus against a backdrop of important Jewish symbols. Thus, Jesus' first miracle turns water into a wine superior to the old, depleted wine. Ominously, the next event is the temple-cleansing. While Jewish leaders are bemused, Samaritans and Gentiles accept Jesus' salvation (3-4). Despite Jewish resistance, Jesus claims to provide in truth that which various Jewish festivals symbolize. Thus, Jesus is bread (Passover in 6), water and light (Tabernacles in 7-9), and the dedicated one (Dedication in 10). This process is nothing less than **deliberate**

symbol inversion. Jesus, not Torah or temple, is the source of life and meaning (light) (cf. 1:17-18; 14:6).

Figure 4: **Ritual Orientation**

Festival (Text)	**Event (Discourse)**
Wedding (2:1-12)	Turns water into wine
Passover (2:13-25)	Cleanses the temple
Sabbath (5)	Healing of lame (Work)
Passover (6)	Feeds multitude (Bread)
Tabernacles (7-9)	Heals a blind man (Light)
Dedication (10)	(Good Shepherd)
Funeral (11)	Raises Lazarus (Life)
Passover (12)	Passion (Farewell Discourse)
Sunday (20)	Resurrection [a Christian holy day]

Narrative Time (Pace): Signs and Discourses

The Synoptic gospels present Jesus' ministry and teachings episodically. By contrast, John ruminates with long discourses over a few notable events, called signs. Where Mark has thirty plus miracles, John has only **seven signs**. These signs are symbols pointing to **Jesus' identity** (e.g., 2:11; 3:2; 5:36-38; 7:31), rather than

---

Figure 5: **The Signs**

Water into wine (2:1-11)
Healing an official's son (4:46-54)
Healing a lame man (5:1-15)
Feeding the multitude (6:1-15)
Walking on the water (6:16-21)
Healing a blind man (9)
Raising Lazarus (11)

miracles manifesting the kingdom (as in the Synoptics).

Like Mark's parables, these signs are revelatory **touchstones** (cf. Jn 12:36-43 with Mk 4:10-12). They reveal the witnesses' characters discriminating between those who are selfishly blind (12:36-43; 6:26; 11:47; 3:19-20), those who see and are led to faith (2:11, 25; 20:30-31), and those who believe without the need of signs (4:48; 20:29).

The discourses, often intimately connected with the signs, explain the **meaning of the key Johannine symbols**. The discourses indicate that the signs and symbols point to

Figure 6: **The Discourses**	
3:1-36	Born Again/From Above
4:1-42	Living Water and True Worship
5:1-47	Jesus' Union with the Father
6:1-71	The Bread of Life/From Heaven
8:12-9:41	The Light of the World
10:1-21	The Good Shepherd
11:1-53	The Resurrection and the Life
13-17	Jesus' Union with the Disciples

the life from above and to Jesus as the agent who makes that life available.

Not everyone grasps the **sacramental nature** of Jesus' signs and symbols. Thus, the Johannine discourses usually turn from dialogue **to explanatory monologue when some character misunderstands** Jesus' symbols. Typically, the misunderstandings arise because Jesus' dialogue-partner attempts to literalize a Johannine symbol or to understand the world above (the sacred) in this-worldly terms. Thus, Nicodemus misunderstands "born from above (again)" as re-entering the mother's womb. The Samaritan woman thinks that Jesus' living water will quench her physical thirst and make it unnecessary to draw water from a well. The satisfied crowd thinks that Jesus' bread from heaven will continually satisfy their physical hunger.

By contrast, those who penetrate the misunderstandings, who understand rightly--the disciples and the readers--break through to the Johannine other world.

Figure 7: **The Word**

In language recalling Gen 1, John's prologue praises the word (**logos**), the divine agent of creation, revelation, and redemption. Except for the "incarnation" of 1:14, the prologue's ideas were fairly common in the Hellenistic era. **Stoicism**, in particular, advocated a life of reason in harmony with the divine **logos** ("word, reason") which pervaded the universe. The **HB** also knows a creative assistant for God which it terms "wisdom" (e.g., Prov 8). Later Jewish texts even speak of wisdom's descent to earth, rejection, and return to heaven (cf. 1 En 42:2). The first century Jewish philosopher **Philo** has a **logos** which unites a dualistically Platonic world:

> To his Logos, his chief messenger [angelos], highest in age and honour, the Father of all has given the special prerogative, to stand on the border and separate the creature from the Creator. This same Logos both pleads with the immortal as suppliant for afflicted mortality and acts as ambassador of the ruler to the subject. . . . [He is] neither uncreated as God, nor created as you, but midway between the two extremes, a surety to both sides. [Philo, Who is the Heir of Divine Things, 205-06, cited in Barr, NT, 351]

Plot Shape and Conflict: The Rejected Revealer's Community

John begins with an impressive prologue identifying its protagonist as the divine, creative word (1:1-18). John's Jesus is nothing less than that word which **descends from God to reveal** the life from above in signs (1-12) and **ascends again**

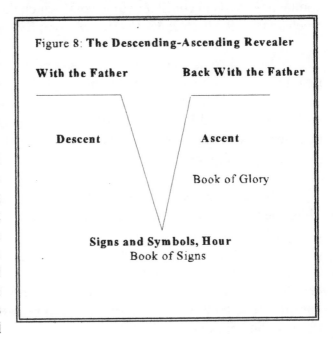

Figure 8: **The Descending-Ascending Revealer**

With the Father   **Back With the Father**

Descent   **Ascent**

Book of Glory

Signs and Symbols, Hour
Book of Signs

to the Father in glory (13-21) [see Brown, John, 1:cxxxviii-cxliv]. Characters recognize this revealer immediately. In Jn 1 alone, various characters can already identify Jesus as the Lamb of God, Son of God, Rabbi, Christ, the one of whom Moses and the prophets wrote, the king of Israel, and the Son of man.

While most reject this revealer (1:10-13), John reflects the small community of believers which accepts the revelation and tells the

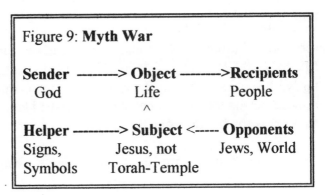

Figure 9: **Myth War**

Sender ------> **Object** ------->**Recipients**
  God   Life   People
                        ∧

Helper --------> **Subject** <----- **Opponents**
Signs,   Jesus, not   Jews, World
Symbols   Torah-Temple

revealer's tale (1:14; 20:30-31; 21:24-25). Unfortunately, this community exists in conflict with a world which does not accept its revelation (cf. 9:22; 16:2; 13-17) [see Martyn; Brown, Community].

John, then, is a **myth war** dramatizing conflicting claims to represent God. John's replacement of temple and Torah with Jesus as the source of life and light (meaning) indicates a storied conflict with a Jewish establishment. That is, John's dominant narrative question is **whether Jesus or the temple-Torah establishment presents the life from above**.

John, of course, presents this issue from a biased stance. Thus, the alternative to John's understanding that Jesus is life does not appear in the narrative until Jn 5. John, then, encloses the opposition's position that Jesus is a blasphemer within its own loftier, more inclusive position. Interestingly, John also encloses the passion, the opposition's best case, within the esoterically interpretative frames of the farewell discourses (13-17) and the resurrection appearances (20-21).

In John's **central conflict section** (5-12), two dramatic episodes (5; 8-9) portray **Jesus providing witnesses** for himself against his accusers, the Jews, in trial-like scenes. In those cases, Jesus (and thus John) call various witnesses for the Johannine case including John the Baptist, Jesus' works (signs), the Father, Moses (scriptures, Torah), Jesus himself (symbolic discourse), and the blind man.

Ironically, John's Jewish opponents do not know their own scriptures. Further, **a blind man sees while the sighted do not** (cf. Mk 8:22-10:52). John, of course, is not presenting the opponents fairly. It speaks for them. Thus, even Caiaphas ironically becomes a spokesperson for the Johannine perspective (11:47-53). John offers **three reasons for the revealer's rejection**.

First, humans are blind concerning the world above. The

pervasive literalistic misunderstandings of the revelation demonstrate that the spiritual world is simply **beyond the ken** of the physical-material world (e.g., 3:1-21). If this were not the case, there would be no necessity for a revealer. Ultimately, the revelation itself is only in signs and symbols.

Second, those who do not respond appropriately are evil. Their failure locates them mythically. They are **from below** (8:23). They do not belong to God (5:42; 8:47). Not surprisingly, they did not and do not believe Moses either (5:45-47; 7:19). They love darkness rather than light (3:19). They are of their Father the Devil (8:44). They seek human, rather than divine, glory (5:44; 7:18; 11:43). Such language, of course, betrays John's basic **ethical dualism** which opposes the world above (God and Jesus) to the world below (human and demonic opposition).

Finally, of course, mythic location depends upon **the divine sovereignty**. Some are called, and some are not (6:44, 65). Some are sheep belonging to the Shepherd, and others are not (10:26-27). While the Father gives to the Son those who belong to him (6:39; 17:2, 6, 9), he blinds others (see 12:36-43 which includes a citation of Isa 6:9-10). Ultimately, for John, only supernatural action can explain the revealer's rejection.

Characters: The Descending-Ascending Revealer

The Johannine Jesus is the **Son from above**, the descending-ascending revealer. John conceives this revealer in terms of an extremely high christology as the prologue [see figure 7] and the famous "I am-sayings" indicate.

John's "**I am-sayings**" appear in three forms: without predicate (8:24, 28, 58; 13:19), with an implied predicate, "he" (6:20; 18:15), and with a predicate nominative. The predicate nominatives include the bread of life (6:35, 51), the light of the world (8:12; 9:5), the door (10:7, 9), the good shepherd (10:11, 14), the resurrection and life (11:25), the way, truth, and life (14:6), and the true vine (15:1, 5).

The predicate nominative sayings suggest that Jesus is a vehicle to or a symbol of the sacred. Thus, Jesus is the way to the Father (14:1-6; the sacred's vehicle). To see him is to see the Father (1:14-18; 14:7-10). Clearly, Jesus is **God's agent**.

Figure 10: **The Creed and Incarnation**

While their language is similar, the creeds [see chap. 17, figure 8] reflect later struggles and more intense philosophical speculation than does John. In particular, John is not struggling in light of Stoic and Platonic philosophy **to harmonize an immutable God and a historical revelation** (Jesus Christ) which has become the basis of Christian worship.

Further, at the time of the creed's formation, John was not uniformly read. Those favoring an **incarnational christology** (from the Latin for "in the flesh") stressed the "became flesh" of Jn 1:14 and the Son's divine functions. The **docetists**, who thought that Jesus was a divine, spiritual being who appeared (from the Greek **dokein**) on earth without taking genuine human form, stressed the "beheld his glory" of 1:14 [see Kysar, Fourth, 185-99]. The **subordinationists** stressed those elements which subordinated Jesus to God and argued that the Son was the first creation. Incarnational christology (the creed) won the day after theologians pointed out that Christian worship was idolatry and that Christian salvation (understood as deification at this point) was questionable unless Jesus Christ was divine.

When the predicate becomes life itself (11:25; 14:6; cf. 5:21, 26), the distinction between Jesus and God is blurred. Jesus takes over **divine functions** (1:4; 3:13-15; 5:19-24). The sayings with implied predicates, which resemble Hebrew Bible theophanic language, and the absolute usage, which resembles **Yahweh**'s "I am" (e.g., Isa 47:8, 10), confuse the issue further. At times, John simply refuses to distinguish between the Father and the Son. They are one (10:30, 38; 1:2).

Ultimately, however, John does distinguish the two (14:28). John's favorite title, **the Son**, best depicts the revealer's connection with and distinction from the Father. Thus, for John, the Son is sent by and goes to the Father, is given authority and followers by the Father, is obedient to the Father, and is loved by and loves the Father.

Human Characters: Ethical Dualism

John's myth war plot divides human characters into two camps on the basis of their response to the mythic touchstone, the revealer Jesus. Those who see Jesus as the Son from above are aligned with the world above. Those who identify Jesus otherwise--the son of Joseph (6:42), the one from Galilee (7:41-41, 52), a blasphemer (5; 9)--are from the world below.

For John, characters are **symbols of faith or rejection**. **The Jews incarnate rejection**, the world's response to the revealer. Of course, John's myth war plot demands a foil like the Jews. The Jews are **the necessary foil** which allows John to explore the reasons for unbelief [see plot] and to explain the correct understanding of Jesus' identity.

By contrast, **the disciples typify faith**. They know from the very beginning who Jesus is (1:19-51). While his signs and symbols are often beyond them, they stand with him because he has the "words of life" (6:60-71). Their misunderstandings are only temporary (e.g., 2:21-22; 4:32-33; 9:2; 11:11-15; 12:16; 13:7, 36; 14:5, 8, 22). Beyond Jesus' glorification--the farewell discourse, the cross, the resurrection, and the spirit--they understand. They reach this point by maintaining their commitment. In short, **they abide** (15) [see myth]. Grounded in the spirit (20:22), their community continues to testify for Jesus (14:16-17, 26; 15:26; 16:14). Only Judas betrays and defects because,

Figure 11: **Ethical Dualism**

World Above	World Below
Life	Death
Spirit	Flesh
Light	Darkness
Truth	Lie
God	Satan
Jesus from above	From Galilee
Divine agent	Blasphemer
Faith	Unbelief
Blind see	Sighted don't

Touchstones
Jesus
Signs, Discourses

Narrator	Jews
Jesus, Disciples	
Implied Reader	

of course, he belongs to the world, rather than Jesus (6:70-71; 13:2, 27, 30; cf. 8:44).

While Peter denies (18:15-18, 25-27), a special resurrection appearance restores him (21:15-19). For John, however, Peter is not the ideal disciple. That role falls to **the beloved disciple**. He has the most intimate relationship with Jesus (13:23-26; 19:25-27). He mediates between Peter and Jesus (13:23-26). He sees more quickly than Peter (20:2-10; 21:7). Unlike the other named disciples, the beloved disciple never misunderstands or wavers in commitment. He alone stands at the cross (19:25-27). Not surprisingly, then, that disciple's testimony is the link between text, community, and Jesus (21:24).

Figure 12: **The Jews**

    Certain features mitigate John's hostile portrayal of the Jews. Importantly, not all Jews reject Jesus (8:31; 11:45; secret believers; crowds). There is, in fact, a great deal of **division about Jesus** (e.g., 7:12-43; 10:19-21). Further, Jesus and the disciples are themselves Jews. Finally, if "Jew" designates hostile rejection, "Israelite" designates those who receive Jesus rightly (1:31, 47; cf. 5:46).

    Judas demonstrates that John can imagine **movement between the poles** of its ethical dualism. So, too, do those who **almost believe** [see Culpepper, Anatomy, 146-48]. Thus, some come close to the Johannine perspective but ultimately fail either to commit (secret believers like Nicodemus and Joseph of Arimathea) or to understand (2:23-25; 6:66; the lame man). Misunderstandings alone, however, do not prevent discipleship. Thus, Nathaniel follows although he initially misunderstands Jesus' origins (1:45-51), and Peter continues despite his difficulties with Jesus' "hard sayings" (6:60-69).

Myth: Abiding in Jesus

    Johannine Christians are those who align themselves with the revealer from above or those who abide in Jesus (15:1-11). Beyond the narrative, the abiding is possible in the Johannine community and in the **Paraclete**, the Johannine word for the spirit (14:15-17, 26; 15:26-27; 16:7-11, 12-14). The **Paraclete** continues Jesus' presence (see 14:16). Like Jesus, the **Paraclete** comes from the Father (15:26; 16:7, 8, 13), will remain with and teach the disciples (14:17, 26; 16:13-14), and bears witness against the hostile world (14:17; 15:26; 16:8-11).

The emphasis upon the **Paraclete** and abiding indicate that Johannine Christians are **mystics** (loosely defined). They emphasize the spirit or the world above, rather than the world below. Not surprisingly, then, John does not emphasize the institutional church or the sacraments. The mystic does not need these vehicles to the sacred. For the mystic, the entire world becomes a sacrament (cf. 6:51-59). The spirit provides the continuing connection to both the world above and to the past revelation (Jesus). The primary physical vehicle providing connections to the sacred is, of course, the gospel itself (or the beloved disciple).

Figure 13: **Hellenistic Religion and Philosophy**

The demise of traditional religion in the face of the new world empires [cf. gospel, figure 1], as well as growing cosmopolitanism and individualism, created a general sense of religious frustration or alienation. In search of meaning, many turned to personifications of fate, to astrology, or to magic. Prophets, healers, and magicians were not rare.

Traveling philosophers offered meaning to the more intellectually venturesome. **Cynics** counseled people to forego mindless convention and to live naturally. Their outrageous flouting of custom led their opponents to call them dogs (Greek **kuon**, hence, "cynic"). **Stoics** called people to accept apathetically their place in the world. For Stoics, the world was permeated by the divine reason (**logos**). One could live reasonably by living in harmony with that natural force.

Interactions between the East and the West made available to the financially able a number of new salvific religions known collectively as **mystery religions**. Each offered power and immortality to those who underwent a secret initiation ritual uniting them with the cult hero (e.g., Demeter, Dionysus, Isis, or Mithra).

Myth: The World Above

The Johannine disdain for a hostile world (e.g., 15:18-16:33) reflects a sectarian viewpoint. The commitment to the world above indicates a **two-story cosmology**, rather than the two-age cosmology of historical apocalypses. This two-world notion is, of course, not uncommon in the ancient world (e.g., Plato) nor unknown in ancient Judaism (e.g., the Wisdom of Solomon, the Dead Sea Scrolls, and Philo). In fact, such dualism was quite common in the Hellenistic world and reflects that world's general sense of alienation or **"disenchantment with the world."**

Figure 14: **Gnosticism**

Gnosticism was the most radical form of Hellenistic dualism. It asserts that **matter is evil and spirit good**. For Gnostics, a host of spiritual beings emanate from a good spirit. These eons become less spiritual and more material as they are farther from the god of spirit. One of these lesser beings malevolently created the material world trapping many spirits in bodies. Fortunately, however, a **descending revealer** has presented the **spiritual elite** with a revealed knowledge (a **gnosis**) which gives them liberated lives now (either ascetic or antinomian) and promises them ascent through the spirit world upon their death.

While John has formal similarities with Gnosticism, John also includes non-Gnostic elements like creation (e.g., 1:3-4), incarnation (1:14), and apocalyptic remnants (e.g., 5:28-29). Put most concisely, John **does not separate the creative and redemptive acts** as Gnosticism does (see the prologue). John was, however, a favorite of the later Gnostics. The first (extant) commentary on John was by a Gnostic. Further, later conflicts probably indicate Gnostic tendencies in the Johannine communities themselves (see 1 Jn 4:2-3; 2 Jn 7).

Style: Irony

John's two-story world provides it with a transcendent perspective from which to comment ironically on the **discrepancies between appearance** (the world below) **and reality** (the world above). Not surprisingly, then, John portrays characters ironically who **fail to understand Jesus' symbols**. Invariably, they fail because they literalistically apply the symbols to this world, rather than to the world above (3:1-21; 4:1-26; 6:22-71). Thus, they wonder how anyone can enter the mother's womb again, how anyone can give water without a bucket, or how anyone can give human flesh as food.

Figure 15: **Realized Eschatology**

John minimizes apocalyptic motifs (though see 5:28-29; 6:39-40, 44, 54; 12:48). For John, judgment and life are already **present realities** (e.g., 3:18-21; 5:21-27; 12:31). Thus, while Martha merely hopes for the resurrection at the end (11:24; cf. 5:28-29), Jesus makes life present now (11:25-44). For John, then, eschatology is realized, not future: "the hour has come and now is."

Not surprisingly, John's most biting ironies are reserved for those who mistakenly think the one from above is from Joseph (6:42), from Galilee (7:41-42, 52), or of the devil (8:12-59). Thinking they know his lowly origins, they **miss his identity as the one from above**. For John, they are the truly blind (9:35-41).

Johannine irony is obvious as well in Caiaphas' sardonic comment that one man should die instead of the nation. For Caiaphas, this is merely hard-headed, clear-sighted realism: "Better him, than us." For John, however, Caiaphas' words are an unwitting prophecy of the cross' meaning. One dies for the many (11:49-53).

In this interpretation of Jesus' death, John celebrates the central NT irony that life comes through death (e.g., 3:14-15; 6:51-59; 10:11-18; 11:49-53; 12:24-33).

Figure 16: **The Date of the Passion**

The canonical gospels agree that Jesus died on Friday. For the Synoptics, this Friday is Passover. As Jewish reckoning begins the day at sundown, Thursday evening and Friday day make up the Synoptic Passover. In the Synoptics, then, **Jesus' last supper is the Passover meal**. By contrast, in John, Jesus dies on the day of preparation, the eve of Passover when the Passover lambs are being slain in the temple in preparation for the evening (the Jewish next day) Passover meal (19:14, 31, 42). When the Passover is celebrated, the Johannine Jesus lies in the tomb. Obviously, for the Synoptics, the point is that Jesus initiates a new meal celebration (the eucharist; e.g., Mk 14:1, 12-25). By contrast, for John, it is important to stress that **Jesus is the Passover lamb** (19:31, 42; cf. 1:29, 36).

Like Mark, John runs ironic changes upon the real king (18:33-38) mocked and crucified as a false claimant (18:33-19:22). John's peculiar irony, however, treats Jesus' death, not as a tragedy, but as **his lifting-up, his ascent, or his return** to the Father (e.g., 3:14-15; 8:28; 12:32-36; 13:31-14:7; but see 20:17). It is the passion which glorifies Jesus:

> The hour has come for the Son of Man to be glorified. Very truly, I tell you, unless a grain of wheat falls into the earth and dies, it remains just a single grain; but if it dies, it bears much fruit. Those who love their life lose it, and those who hate their life in this world will keep it for eternal life. . . . It is for this reason

that I have come to this hour. Father, glorify your
name. (12:23-25, 27b-28a; cf. 17:1)

Dramatically, for the only time in John, the divine voice, then,
corroborates: "I have glorified it, and I will glorify it again."

Biblically, glory often refers to **God's manifestation** (cf.
1:14; 11:40; 12:41; 17:24). The cross, then, is the ultimate
manifestation of God's love for humans (e.g., 3:14-16; 15:13). The
Johannine cross, then, differs dramatically from that of Mark. Put
simply, it is glory, rather than God-forsakenness. Here, God does not
abandon Jesus (16:32). Instead, then, of the Markan "My God,"
Jesus' last words in John are "It is finished" (19:30).

For John, the cross is **Jesus' action, not his passion**. Thus,
despite the manipulations of the opposition, Jesus alone decides the
time of his ascent. Thus, "the hour" is not yet (e.g., 2:4; 7:30; 8:20),
and, then, "the hour" has come (12:23, 27; 13:1; 17:1). For John,
then, Jesus lays down his life voluntarily. He is no victim (e.g.,
10:17-18; 12:27; 18:36).

Figure 17: **The Gospel of Thomas**

Thomas is a non-canonical collection of Jesus' sayings
with gnostic tendencies (contrast Q's apocalyptic orientation).
For Thomas, the kingdom is not future:

Rather, the kingdom is inside of you, and it is
outside of you. When you come to know
yourselves, then you will become known . . .
[3, in Robinson, NHL].

Salvation lies in knowing one's own true identity and in
rejecting the world [e.g., 56, 111]. Thus, Thomas exhorts its
narratees: "Become passers-by" [42].

Implied Reader: Johannine Faith/Sight

John uses irony to **bring the reader to Johannine sight/faith** (cf. 20:30-31). To this end, the farewell discourse (13-17) and the resurrection narrative (20-21) enfold the passion and teach the reader to read it Johanninely. The reader learns before and after the passion, then, that the passion is Jesus' glorification and his ascent to the Father.

Similarly, John's clarification of misunderstandings through extensive dialogues trains the reader to avoid literalism and materialism. The reader is brought to see the world above. Repeatedly, then, John tells the same story--someone meets the revealer and either believes or rejects the revelation--in order to **initiate the reader** and to provide a **sacramental reading guide** [so Culpepper, 88-89].

ANET: Forsaking the World

The Johannine revelation surpasses human understanding. Further, God opens some eyes and closes others. The final Johannine answer to unbelief is that God does not choose some. While this position is coherent with John's world-view and plot, it leaves little room for human effort, merit, or responsibility. To moderns, John smacks of **fatalism**.

John's treatment of the Jews as a symbol of unbelief also troubles. Like determinism, this treatment fits John's literary-mythic logic. Some foe is necessary for John's myth war and given the Judean setting of the story the Jews are realistic literary opponents. Despite this logic and John's softening of the portrayal, the symbol skates too closely to **anti-semitism**. Although John attempts a sketch of unbelief, not racism/nationalism, the gospel is too easily read in support of anti-semitism.

Figure 18: **Images of Jesus**

The traditional Jesus is the **Son of God** of the creeds who died to ransom humans from their sins and to provide them with eternal life. Modern critics have uncovered various images of Jesus prior to that traditional portrait. Clearly, the **various gospels** conceive Jesus differently. This recognition, as well as the development of modern historiography, has led many scholars to look for the **historical Jesus** behind the images. Three historical reconstructions are notable. First, nineteenth-century rationalists and liberals envisioned Jesus as the prophet of a rational religion (deism) or as a **teacher of an universal ethic** of love. Second, more recent scholars have imagined Jesus to be an **apocalyptic prophet** announcing the divine kingdom's presence or imminence. Finally, some recent American scholars have depicted Jesus as a **counter-cultural sage** acting out an egalitarian reform in the midst of ancient hierarchical society. Concerning these multiple images, Schweitzer's words still apply:

> . . . each successive epoch . . . found its own
> thoughts in Jesus; that was, indeed, the only
> way in which it could make him live.
>   But it was not only each epoch that found its
> reflection in Jesus; each individual created Him
> in accordance with his own character. There is
> no other historical task which so reveals a
> man's true self as the writing of a Life of Jesus.
> [4]

At best, then, the images of Jesus reflect human aspirations toward the ideal. The images of Jesus symbolize visions of the true, the good, and the beautiful [so Pelikan, 108].

Whether John is anti-semitic or only potentially so, its ethical dualism is rooted in a more **fundamental intolerance**. For John, there is only one path to the sacred for Jew, Samaritan, and Greek (14:6). While this stance may be missionary rather than exclusionary, it is not fashionable in the modern, pluralistic world.

Finally, and most importantly, John's basic dualism is foreign to modernity. For John, it is the world above/the spirit which is the real. For modernity, reality is the sensate, empirical world. In John's schema, modernity is committed to the world below. For modernity, John's spirit-gospel is mere fancy, mystical folderol lacking substance or hard evidence.

Review Questions

1. Apply the reading method of chaps. 3-4 to John. List its genre, plot shape, conflict, depiction of Jesus and God, mythic function, and ANE problems.
2. How does John differ from the Synoptics?
3. Compare Jesus' teaching in the Synoptics and John.
4. How are John's signs like Mark's parables?
5. Why do some characters reject Jesus?
6. Who are the beloved disciple and the **Paraclete**?
7. Compare John's world-view to that of apocalyptic.
8. List two examples of irony in John.
9. Compare the passions in Mark and John.
10. What does it mean to say that John is a "sacramental" reading guide?

Suggestions for Alternative Reading and Reflection

1. Compare the images of Jesus in the gospels. Are any of these images more historical than the others?
2. What are the important images of Jesus in the later West?
3. What is the intellectual world most similar to John's **logos**?
4. Compare John's christology to that of the creeds. What is an

incarnational christology?   What is a docetic christology?

5. Compare John and Matthew in terms of their relationship to Judaism.

6. Argue that John is or is not anti-semitic.

7. Compare John's community to those of Luke-Acts and Mark.

8. Compare John to Gnosticism.

9. Compare apocalyptic and Gnosticism.

10. Compare Q and Thomas.

11. What might a structuralist find to be the fundamental binary opposition in John? How is that tension resolved?

12. How might a contemporary Jew read John?

For Further Reading

For an introductory comparison of John and the Synoptics, see Kysar <u>Maverick</u>, 1-14; and **idem**, <u>Fourth</u>, 54-66. The classic comprehensive comparison is Barrett, <u>John</u>.

In addition to Barrett, Brown, <u>John</u>; Schnackenburg; and Bultmann, <u>John</u>, are important commentaries on John.

For a literary-critical analysis, see Culpepper, <u>Anatomy</u>.

On additions to John (e.g., 7:53-8:11; 21), see Metzger, <u>Textual</u>; and Brown, <u>John</u>, 1:332-38; 2:1077-82.

On possible displacements of the Johannine text (e.g., at 6:1 and 15:1), see Bultmann, <u>John</u>. For a concise summary, see Brown, <u>John</u>, 1:xxiv-xxvi.

For reconstructions of John's traditions and composition history, see Brown, <u>John</u>, 1:xxxiv-xl; Kysar, <u>Fourth</u>, 13-66; and Smith, "Johannine," 273-75.

Bultmann's famous commentary divided John into five strata: signs, passion, revelation discourses, scattered traditions, and the evangelist's work. On the signs source, see Fortna.

On the descending revealer, see Dodd, <u>Interpretation</u>, 241-49; · Talbert, "Myth," 418-40; and Meeks, "Man," 44-72.

On the **logos**, see Brown, <u>John</u>, 1:519-24; and Dodd, <u>Interpretation</u>, 263-85.

On the "I ams," see Brown, <u>John</u>, 1:533-38; and Kysar, <u>Fourth</u>, 119-22.

On Johannine christology, see also Kysar, <u>Fourth</u>, 178-206; and **idem**, <u>Maverick</u>, 22-46.

On Johannine signs, see Brown, <u>John</u>, 1:525-32; and Kysar, <u>Maverick</u>, 65-83. On symbols, see Dodd, <u>Interpretation</u>, 133-43, 170-78; and Culpepper, <u>Anatomy</u>, 190-98.

On Johannine faith, see Brown, <u>John</u>, 1:501-03, 512-15; Kysar, <u>Maverick</u>, 65-83; and Dodd, <u>Interpretation</u>, 151-69.

On Johannine misunderstandings, see Culpepper, <u>Anatomy</u>, 152-65.

On "realized eschatology," see Dodd, <u>Interpretation</u> (throughout); Brown, <u>John</u>, 1:cxv-cxxi; and Kysar, <u>Fourth</u>, 207-14.

For Hellenistic religion and philosophy, see Koester, <u>NT</u>, 1:141-204. For Gnosticism, see Jonas; and Rudolph, <u>Gnosis</u>. For texts, see Robinson, <u>NHL</u>.

For discussion of John's intellectual milieu, see Dodd, <u>Interpretation</u>, 3-130; Kysar, <u>Fourth</u>, 102-46; Brown, <u>John</u>, 1:lii-lxvi; and Smith, "Johannine," 276-79.

On Johannine irony, see Barr, <u>NT</u>, 243-44; Culpepper, <u>Anatomy</u>, 152-80; and Duke. On John's rhetoric, see Culpepper, <u>Anatomy</u>, 88-89, 97-98, 104, 145-48; Dodd, <u>Interpretation</u>, 165, 420-23; and Staley.

On the Johannine community, see Martyn; and Brown, <u>Community</u>.

On Thomas, see Robinson, <u>NHL</u>, 124-38; and Koester, <u>Ancient</u>, 75-128.

On the historical Jesus, see Schweitzer; Duling, Jesus; D. Harrington; and Luke Johnson. On images of Jesus, see Pelikan.

INTRODUCTION TO THE APOSTLE

The NT Apostle contains twenty-three books of **various genres** including one history, twenty-one letters, and one apocalypse. The unity of the section depends upon its type-character, the apostle. Except for Acts, every book is **attributed to an apostle** or first-generation (relative of J e s u s ?) C h r i s t i a n leader. Acts, of course, is the story of the apostles, the Lord's first missionaries.

Figure 1: **Genres and Books**
History: Acts
Pauline Letters: Romans; 1-2 Corinthians; Galatians; Ephesians; Philippians; Colossians; 1-2 Thessalonians; 1-2 Timothy; Titus; Philemon
General Letters: Hebrews; James; 1-2 Peter; 1-3 John; Jude
Apocalypse: Revelation

As a secondary mythic piece, the Apostle stands to the Gospel as the Prophets stand to Torah. That is, the Apostle **transmits and applies the founding myth** and its mythic identity to later days. While the Apostle which covers only a generation or so after the founding time does not provide great chronological breadth, the Apostle does extend the founding myth geographically (outside Palestine) and ethnically (beyond Judaism). The Apostle, then, takes the Jesus-story **to the Mediterranean nations**.

Like the Prophets, then, the primary mythic function of the Apostle is **succession**. Of course, the direct presence of Jesus diminishes as one moves away from the Gospel. Jesus remains as a story (tradition) character, as an experience in the church's worship, and as expected apocalyptic Lord. In the story itself, however, the apostles take center stage **as characters** (Acts) **or as narrators** (Letters, Revelation). Like the HB prophets, these characters are primarily mythic types and functionaries. Only Paul, who occupies more space than any NT character other than Jesus, truly escapes this type-casting. As both character (Acts) and implied author/narrator (Letters), he is truly a many-faceted character [see chap. 19, figure 10].

Figure 2: **The Apostle and Paul**

"Apostle" means **one who is sent**. Luke-Acts uses the term more narrowly to refer to the twelve disciples of Jesus who were **witnesses** both of his ministry/passion and of his resurrection. In this Lukan sense, Paul is hardly an apostle (cf. 1 Cor. 15:8-11). Ephesians uses the term to refer to the early group who **with Jesus founded the church** (2:20-22). The later Pauline church saw Paul in this fashion (cf. 1 Pet. 3:16-16). In the canon, Paul is virtually the Apostle because of his prominence in Acts and in the Letters. In later church tradition, only Peter rivals Paul.

The Apostle **addresses the early churches**. Their situation indirectly controls what appears in the Apostle, for the Apostle applies the founding myth to their contexts, problems, and questions. Without ever speaking, they shape the way the myth is transmitted. Their situations imply one of **two different church stories**. Revelation and Paul tell the story of the **pre-*parousia* church** awaiting the imminent apocalyptic end. By contrast, Acts, the Pastorals, and the Johannine letters tell the story of an **institutional church or mystic sect** more at-home in a continuing world largely unmoved by the appearance of Jesus.

Acts opens the Apostle and is arguably its most important book [see chap. 19]. Its canonical separation from its companion volume Luke indicates its apostolic importance. It provides the **textual bridge between the founding time and later generations**. It tells the tale of the early church. Its major characters--Paul, Peter, John, and James (?)--are the implied authors/narrators of the remainder of the Apostle. Further, Acts locates mythically the narratees/implied readers of the rest of the Apostle. Whoever and wherever they are, the divinely led expansion of Acts legitimizes them mythically. In the Letters, the Apostle speaks to specific church situations. Revelation, the final book of the Apostle, anticipates the mythic end, the divine kingdom and judgment to which the world and the churches go.

Review Questions

1. What makes the Apostle a literary, mythic unity?
2. What are the mythic functions of the Apostle?
3. What does the term "apostle" mean?
4. What are the implied church stories in the Apostle?

Reflection Questions

1. Do the stories of subsequent churches belong to the Apostle? Why or why not?
2. Compare the Apostle to the Prophets (Former and Latter) both literarily and mythically.

CHAPTER 21

THE APOCALYPTIC CROSS
Paul's Letters

Introduction: Genuine and Disputed Letters

Of the twenty-one NT letters, thirteen bear Paul's name in their salutations. Despite these salutations, most scholars doubt that Paul wrote all of these letters. Almost everyone rejects the Pauline authorship of the Pastoral letters (1-2 Timothy, Titus), many reject Ephesians, some reject Colossians, and a few deny 2 Thessalonians. The seven remaining are the undisputed, genuine letters: **Romans, 1-2 Corinthians, Galatians, Philippians, 1 Thessalonians, and Philemon**.

The Letter: Genre and Structure

Letters strive to **continue conversation despite absence** and distance with portable, written presences. The conversational model of letters is quite obvious in the formal, phatic language with which they begin and close.

In structure, Paul's letters resemble **other personal letters** of his day (cf. 1 Thess; Philem). Paul does, however, have a tendency to "Christianize" the phatic elements. Thus, Paul describes himself (apostle or slave of Christ Jesus) and his audience (saints) with terms reinforcing basic mythic identities. More pointedly, Paul changes the typical Greek salutation (**chairein**) to the Pauline grace (**charis**) and the Jewish peace (**shalom**).

Similarly, in Paul, the typical health wish becomes a thanksgiving praising God's creative and sustaining grace, reinforcing Christian virtues, and anticipating the letter's themes (for example, righteousness in Rom; spiritual gifts in 1 Cor; and joy in Phil). Notably, the thanksgiving does not appear at all in the harsh, angry Galatians.

Figure 1: Ancient Letters (and Paul)

Opening formulae
 Sender (with Christian epithets)
 Addressee (with Christian epithets)
 Greetings (Grace and peace)
 Health wish (Thanksgiving)
Body
 (Introductory formulas)
 (Travel Plans, Advice)
Closing formulae
 Greeting
 Health wish (Request for prayer)
 Farewell (Holy kiss)
 Date (Benediction)

The move from the formulaic opening to the body is not always easy to distinguish, but the body often begins with **an appeal** ("I urge you") **or a disclosure** ("I would have you know"). Typically, the body concludes with references to future, missionary **travel** (not present in 2 Thess; 1 Tim) and, on occasion, with major sections of ethical **advice** (Rom; Gal; Eph; Col; 1 Thess).

The letters end with final greetings (though not in Gal; Eph; 2 Thess; 1 Tim) and formal good-byes. Once again, Paul "Christianizes" the phatic language. Good-bye becomes a peace wish (not in 1 Cor; Philem) and a grace benediction. Other Christian elements--holy kiss, request for prayer, doxology--occur occasionally.

Media: Worship; Liturgical and Ethical Forms

The "Christianizing" is appropriate for the letters' worship medium:

And when this letter has been read among you, have it read also in the church of the Laodiceans; and see that you read also the letter from Laodicea. (Col 4:16; cf. 1 Thess 5:26-27)

Paul also incorporates other items--scripture [see rhetoric], liturgical elements (prayers, hymns, confessions), and ethical traditions (lists, household codes)--appropriate to that context.

The hymns and confessions are notable because of their poetic parallelism. In content, the **hymns** extol God (Rom 11:33-36; Eph 1:3-14; Col 1:12-14) or Christ (e.g., Col 1:15-20; 1 Tim 3:16). Philippians 2:6-11 is a famous example:

> who, though he was in the form of God,
>> did not regard equality with God
>> as something to be exploited,
> but emptied himself,
>> taking the form of a slave,
>> being born in human likeness.
> And being found in human form,
>> he humbled himself
>> and became obedient to the point of death--
>> even death on a cross.
> Therefore God also highly exalted him,
>> and gave him the name
>> that is above every name,
> so that at the name of Jesus
>> every knee should bend,
>> in heaven and on earth and under the earth,
> and every tongue should confess
>> that Jesus Christ is Lord,
>> to the glory of God the Father.

Jesus' death and resurrection is a frequent subject of the **confessions** (cf. 2 Cor 5:15; Rom 4:24-25; 8:34; 10:8-9; 14:9; 2 Tim 2:8):

> that Christ died for our sins
> in accordance with the scriptures,
> and that he was buried,
> and that he was raised on the third day
> in accordance with the scriptures . . . (1 Cor 15:3-4)

> who was descended from David
> according to the flesh
> and was declared to be the Son of God with power
> according to the spirit of holiness by the resurrection,
> Jesus Christ our Lord . . . (Rom 1:3-4)

Monotheism is another frequent subject (Rom 3:30; 1 Cor 8:4, 6; Gal 3:20; Eph 4:6; 1 Tim 2:5; cf. 1 Cor 8:6; Eph 4:5). By far the most common confession, however, is the simple "Jesus is Lord!" (e.g., Rom 10:9; 1 Cor 12:3; 2 Cor 4:5; Phil 2:11; Col 2:6).

On occasion, even longer liturgical patterns, like the Lord's supper (1 Cor 11:23-26) or baptism (e.g., Gal 3:27-28; 1 Cor 12:13; Col 3:11) are evident. Some ethical lists (e.g., the "put-on, put-off" of Col 3:1-17; vice-virtue contrasts like Gal 5:17-24; Eph 5:3-14) may also reflect baptismal liturgy.

The most common ethical traditions are simple lists of vice and/or virtue (e.g., vice: Rom 1:29-31; 1 Cor 5:10-11; Eph 4:31-32; 1 Tim 6:4-5; and virtue: Phil 4:8; Eph 6:14-17). A second kind of ethical tradition is **the household code**, which specifies the duties of various members of the household. In brief, these lists demand submission to hierarchical authority (Col 3:18-4:1; Eph 5:21-6:9; cf. Rom 13:1-7). With a little adaptation, this form becomes a community code or church order specifying the duties of the various members of the church (1 Tim 2:1-15; 5:1-21; 6:1-2; Titus 2:1-10).

Implied Author/Narrator: Apostolic Authority

The Pauline narrator resembles the prophetic in personality

and in authority. Like the prophets, Paul creatively reinterprets tradition in the light of his personal, **charismatic sense of divine authorization**: "So we are ambassadors for Christ, since God is making his appeal through us; we entreat you on behalf of Christ, be reconciled to God" (2 Cor 5:20; cf. 1 Thess 2:13).

Most often, Paul describes his vocation as **his apostleship** (e.g., Rom 1:1). For Paul, the apostle is the gospel's vehicle (Rom 1:16-17) and the gospel dictates the apostle's suffering, ministerial style (e.g., 1 Cor 1-4; 2 Cor 10-13). That is, the apostle **incarnates his message** of a dying-rising savior for his mission field. As a result, he can audaciously call others to imitate him (1 Thess 1:6; Phil 3:17; 1 Cor 4:16; 2 Cor 10:33-11:1; cf. 1 Thess 2:14).

Although Paul recognizes other apostles (cf. Gal 2:9; 1 Cor 15:8-11) and has many co-workers, Paul is the authority in his missionary field, the Gentiles (Gal 1:15-16). Here, he brooks no rival. After all, he is the founder/father of most of the churches to whom he writes (Galatia, Thessalonica, Philippi, and Corinth).

Paul's letters, then, are **apostolic administration of his mission field**. They thank churches for faithfulness and support (1 Thess; Philem). They try to garner support for future missionary endeavors (Rom). They support Pauline personnel and attack non-Pauline personnel and teachings (2 Cor; Gal; Col; 2 Thess; Pastorals). They attack apostates (Gal; 2 Cor). They deal with pastoral problems (1 Cor; Philem).

Put concisely, they call the churches to realize more fully or to return to the gospel. That is, Paul exhorts, advises, and counsels his churches **to act according to** his apostolic understanding of their **shared mythic identity** (hence, the frequent familial language).

Rhetoric: Purpose and Persuasion

As attempts to exercise apostolic authority and mythic

interpretation, the letters are **open-ended stories**. The communities may not heed Paul. They may not return slaves, support further mission work, continue in Paul's gospel, reject false apostles, forego meat offered to idols, and so forth.

Figure 2: **Ancient Rhetoric**

Ancient rhetoric had different contexts and purposes [see Barr, <u>NT</u>, 10-14]. **Forensic** (judicial) rhetoric argues truth, justice, and guilt in the courtroom as various speakers prosecute or defend an individual's past actions (cf. 2 Cor 10-13; Gal). **Deliberative** rhetoric argues issues of interest and expediency in the assembly as various speakers exhort to or dissuade from an action. The majority of Paul's letters fit this category. Paul asks his readers to return to their gospel/myth (Gal), to practice holiness (1 Thess; 1 Cor), to practice decorum in worship (1 Cor), to receive fellow-workers properly (Philem; letters of recommendation), to support missionary work (Rom), or to give to the collection (1 Cor 8-9; etc.). **Demonstrative** rhetoric exhorts the populace to hold or reaffirm a group-value (myth) at public celebrations. In the context of Christian worship, the Pauline letters could certainly be used to explore and celebrate mythic identities.

Paul's letters, then, must persuade his audience. In most cases, Paul does not seek to win an argument or to convert his audiences (though see Gal; 2 Cor). Instead, he reminds his audience of what they know and applies that to new situations. Paul, then, **rehearses mythic givens before advising future action**.

Not surprisingly, Paul justifies beliefs and actions by appealing to **the gospel**, the tradition of Jesus' death and resurrection (e.g., 1 Cor 15:1-7). This appeal warrants beliefs about the general resurrection (e.g., 1 Thess 4:14; 1 Cor 15), about humble, serving lifestyles (e.g., Phil 2:5-11; 1 Cor 1:18-31; 2 Cor 3-5), and about the newness of life in Christ (e.g., Rom 6; Gal 2:19-21). More rarely, Paul motivates belief (1 Thess 4:15), ritual (1 Cor 11:23-26), and ethic (1 Cor 7:10-11) with appeals to the words of the Lord.

Figure 3: "Letter From Birmingham City Jail"

Martin Luther King, Jr.'s famous letter exhorts white Southern clergy to act according to their Christian mythic identity. For King, the program of nonviolent civil disobedience and the goal of racial equality were logical corollaries of the gospel:

> But though I was initially disappointed at being categorized as an extremist, as I continued to think about the matter I gradually gained a measure of satisfaction from the label. Was not Jesus an extremist for love .... [297]
> There was a time when the church was very powerful .... In those days the church was not merely a thermometer that recorded the ideas and principles of popular opinion; it was a thermostat that transformed the mores of society. [300]
> Things are different now. So often the ... church ... is an archdefender of the status quo. ... If today's church does not recapture the sacrificial spirit of the early church, it will lose its authenticity ... [300]

Paul also appeals to his **followers' experiences**. Thus, as the Galatians received the spirit, freedom, and sonship through Paul's gospel of grace, they should not abandon that gospel for the law (Gal 3-5). Similarly, as one's place in Christ depends upon grace, there is no room for human pride or boasting (1 Cor 1-4; 12-14). Likewise, the baptismal experience can also justify certain ethical standards (e.g., Rom 6; Gal 3:27-27; Col 3:1-17).

Paul's own special, visionary experiences also warrant actions (Gal 1-2; Rom 1:1-6; 2 Cor 12:1-10?). His **apostolic status** is a warrant, then, in and of itself. As apostle, Paul speaks weighty words (cf. 1 Cor 7; 9:1-2). The fact that Paul's missionary style and the gospel cohere [see narrator] also buttresses his appeals and commands.

Style: Eschatological Perspective and Irony

Paul also substantiates his arguments with **appeals to scripture**. Paul, of course, understands scripture from a new, **eschatological perspective** available only in Christ:

> Indeed, to this very day, when they hear the reading of the old covenant, that same veil is still there, since only in Christ is it set aside. Indeed, to this very day whenever Moses is read, a veil lies over their minds; but when one turns to the Lord, the veil is removed. (2 Cor 3:14-16)

As for the ancient prophets, a new, definitive act of God makes old things new. Thus, the apostle knows that God speaks in scripture in seemingly insignificant passages "for us" (cf. 1 Cor 9:10; 10:11; Rom 15:4) [see chap. 18, figures 7-9]. This daring interpretation disparages the experience of Moses (2 Cor 3), claims Abraham as a precursor of gospel-faith (Gal 3; Rom 4), and shockingly reads the Jews as Hagar's children (Gal 4:21-31).

With eschatological hindsight, Paul sees God's activity as a whole so that God's story continues in Christ:

> God is the protagonist in the story, the one who has

> formed and sustained Israel from Abraham onward, the one whose promise of faithfulness stands eternally firm. Scripture is, then, a story about . . . God's righteousness, and God's righteousness is the ground of the narrative unity between Law and gospel. . . . God's act in Jesus Christ illuminates, Paul contends, a previously uncomprehended narrative unity in Scripture. . . . this unforeseen act of grace is the supremely fitting climactic action of the same God whose character and purposes are disclosed in the narrative of his past dealings with Israel. [Hays, Echoes, 157]

As a result, some older characters/incidents become **types of Christ**. The most important type is Adam (Rom 5:14). After the Christ, humans live either **in Adam or in Christ** (so Rom 5:12-21) [see myth]. For Paul, then, Jesus is a new Adam, a new beginning (2 Cor 5:17).

As the eschatological community continues to live in the midst of an unchanged world, Paul **ironizes**. Thus, "cursed" Jesus is the means of Christian blessing (Gal 3:10-14). His death is the fount of life (Rom 5:17-19). One must die in order to live (Gal 2:19-20; Rom 6:1-4).

Such ironic inversions are common in the NT. Others, like **the inversion of righteousness in Romans**, are more distinctively Pauline. There, after asserting quite traditionally that God is righteous when he condemns sinners (1:18-3:20), Paul lays out the gospel's striking reversal. Now, in Christ, God is righteous when he judges (or makes) the sinful righteous (3:21-26). That is, God is a righteous (just) judge both in condemnation and salvation.

Romans also contains another Pauline inversion. In Rom 9-11, Paul **ironizes Jewish history**. There, he asserts that the gospel's inclusion of the Gentiles is God's attempt to recoup Israel by inciting her to jealousy (10:19). For Paul, Israel's exclusion (judgment, death) is the way to her life (11:25-32) [cf. Hays, Echoes, 163-64].

These inversions, of course, rest in Paul's ironic gospel which offers divine strength in the **weakness of the cross**:

> For Jews demand signs and Greeks desire wisdom, but we proclaim Christ crucified, a stumbling block to Jews and foolishness to Gentiles, but to those who are called, both Jews and Greeks, Christ the power of God and the wisdom of God. For God's foolishness is wiser than human wisdom, and God's weakness is stronger than human strength. (1 Cor 1:22-25)

Correspondingly, Paul is a weak apostle (1 Cor 1:17-2:5; 2 Cor 4:7-12). His **boast is in his suffering** through which God's power flows (cf. 4:8-13; 2 Cor 11:16-30; Phil 1:27-2:18).

Style: Tangents

Paul's arguments have a tendency to meander. Paul's most obvious tangents occur in Phil 3:2-4:1 and in 2 Cor 6:14-7:1; 2:14-7:4. These sections differ markedly from their surroundings. The Philippians' section, for example, disturbs Paul's joyful letter with a warning more typical of Galatians or 2 Corinthians. Further, without these sections, the letters flow nicely: Phil 4:2 after 3:1; 2 Cor 7:2 after 6:13; and 2 Cor 7:5 after 2:13.

For this reason, many scholars find these letters **composite**. Scholars believe 2 Corinthians, in particular, to be a collection of several Pauline letters badly patched together. While this is likely the case in extreme situations, other tangents may simply reflect Paul's oral medium. Paul **dictated the letters** in the midst of a harried career (e.g., Rom 16:22; Gal 6:11). One may not always expect, then, a literate cohesiveness.

Figure 4: **Images of Paul**

The disputed epistles and Acts offer a "Paul" which differs from the one recoverable from the authentic letters. Those texts intensify Paul's traditional and world-accepting tendencies. In Wiles' apt phrase, they "**domesticate Paul**" in the service of the later institutional church [see Meeks, Writings, 207-13].

Other early Christians **radicalize Paul**. For Marcion, Paul was the only apostle to understand that Jesus revealed a new unknown God, a God of grace radically different from the God of the OT who was creator, lawgiver, and judge. That is, Marcion pushes Paul's tension between the law and the gospel to the breaking point [see Meeks, Writings, 184-93]. Other radicals push Paul's world-denying, ascetic tendencies in the direction of Hellenistic religious frustration and Gnosticism [see chap. 20, figures 13-14; Meeks, Writings, 193-207]. Of course, Jewish **reactionaries** chastise Paul as the great infidel, the Satanic enemy of the faith, because he does not treat God's past acts (Torah) with sufficient respect [see Meeks, Writings, 176-84].

Specific Narratees and Canonical Letters

Paul's letters are **to specific local churches** or officials which were a part of his missionary work in Asia Minor and Greece in the middle of the first Christian century. Generally, the letters deal with the specific identity crises faced by these young Christian communities.

Canonization made these occasional, particular documents into the property of a religious community with universal notions. In short, it invited all Christians to read the mail of a few particular churches. Interestingly, Paul's recommendation to churches to read each other's letters is already a step in this direction (see Col 4:16). Further, the salutation of 1 Cor 1:2 addresses all Christians. The blank in the oldest manuscripts of Eph 1:1, where "in Ephesus" stands, may also be an attempt at **generalizing a particular message**. Of course, the later church did not leave the matter implicit. Later church leaders simply opined that "when the apostle wrote to some he wrote to all" [Tertullian, cited in Aune, <u>NT</u>, 218; cf. 2 Pet 3:15-16].

Plot Shape and Conflict: Paul's Apocalyptic Cross

Paul's letters have little concern for Jesus' ministry, miracles, or teaching. For Paul, the story is Jesus Christ's **death and resurrection**. Thus, in Phil 2:5-11, the pre-existent Christ empties himself, obediently humiliating

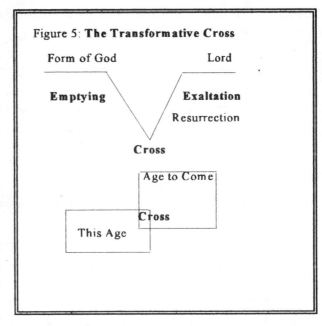

Figure 5: **The Transformative Cross**

himself even unto death, and is then exalted (cf. 2 Cor 8:9). The resulting shape is that of a typical hero myth, with the **cross as the crucial transition**.

The cross is also the key transitional moment for all those "in Christ": "So if anyone is in Christ, there is a new creation: everything old has passed away; see, everything has become new!" (2 Cor 5:17; cf. Gal 2:19-20; 5; Rom 5-8). Put differently, the cross is **the apocalyptic moment**. At the cross, the ages pivot.

Figure 6: **The Atonement**

While Paul relies on symbols to describe God's salvific act in Christ, later theologians describe the atonement more philosophically. The early church fathers often depict the innocent Christ's death as a **ransom** paid to Satan on behalf of guilty humanity. Others envisioned the innocent Christ as "bait" which Satan foolishly swallowed only to be forced to disgorge him along with the redeemed in Christ. Anselm's **satisfaction** theory describes the innocent Christ's death as the necessary satisfaction demanded by the feudal Lord's affronted honor. Christ's divinity makes possible the infinite payment necessary to God's honor, and Christ's humanity fulfills the necessary requirement that a human redress the offense. Abelard's **moral influence** notion argues that Christ's death demonstrates the infinite love of God and, thereby, draws sinners back to God.

Paul depicts this divine transformation as the disclosure of **God's righteousness** for those who believe:

> For there is no distinction, since all have sinned and fall short of the glory of God; they are now justified by his grace as a gift, through the redemption that is in Christ Jesus, whom God put forward as a sacrifice of atonement by his blood, effective through faith. He did this to show his righteousness, because in his divine forbearance he had passed over the sins previously committed; it was to prove at the present time that he himself is righteous and that he justifies

the one who has faith in Jesus. (Rom 3:22-26)

Paul's key symbols here are **justification, redemption, and atonement**. Justification reflects legal terminology for those declared innocent. Redemption recalls economic language describing the manumission of slaves. Atonement suggests ritual language for sacrifices obtaining forgiveness. All the symbols strive to indicate how the cross reconciles humans to God: "For our sake he made him to be sin who knew no sin, so that in him we might become the righteousness of God" (2 Cor 5:21).

Apart from Christ, humans are **estranged from God**. They live in sin, in the flesh, and under the powers of this age (the law and death). God's act in Christ, then, is a holy war delivering humans from these powers unto himself. **Reconciled to God** in Christ, humans have a new life of faith. They live in the spirit, in freedom, and at peace with God.

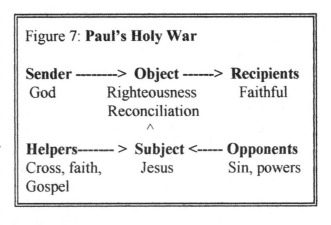

Figure 7: **Paul's Holy War**

Sender --------> Object ------> Recipients
God   Righteousness   Faithful
                Reconciliation
                     ^
Helpers------- > Subject <----- Opponents
Cross, faith,   Jesus   Sin, powers
Gospel

Myth: The Life in Christ

In short, Paul views human existence in terms of a basic ethical dualism. Humans are either apart from God or with God [see Bultmann, Theology, 1:185-352]. Paul symbolizes this as **life in Adam or in Christ**:

If, because of the one man's (Adam's) trespass, death

exercised dominion through that one, much more surely will those who receive the abundance of grace and the free gift of righteousness exercise dominion in life through the one man, Jesus Christ. Therefore just as one man's trespass led to condemnation for all, so one man's act of righteousness leads to justification and life for all. For just as by the one man's disobedience the many were made sinners, so by the one man's obedience the many will be made righteous. (Rom 5:17-19)

Figure 8: **Sola Fide (Faith Alone)**

Paul speaks to a world of chaos, not a mythically ordered world. Paul appeals to the **deus ex machina**, then, not to human responsibility [see chap. 16, figure 1]. Not surprisingly, then, reformers are the theologians who turn most often to Paul. In Harnack's famous summary, Paul is a "ferment" in the history of theology, not a "basis" [cited in Meeks, Writings, 436]. Thus, **Augustine** appeals to Paul against Pelagius' moralism. Again, **Karl Barth** employs Paul against the natural theology of Protestant liberalism [Meeks, Writings, 250-57]. And, of course, **Martin Luther** uses Paul against what he understood as the "Babylonian captivity" of the medieval Catholic church. For Luther, salvation was not in the church or any human work; it was by grace and faith alone:

> This faith cannot exist in connection with works . . . . Therefore the moment you begin to have faith you learn that all things in you are blameworthy, sinful . . . . When you have learned this you will know that you need Christ . . . ["Freedom" 280-81]

Although God's act is basic to human transformation, humans must respond to this grace. For Paul, the necessary response is **faith, alignment with or commitment to Christ** (e.g., Rom 3:21-4:25). Faith literally places one **"in Christ,"** Paul's favorite term for the Christian's basic mythic identity. Baptism objectifies that faith, ritualizes the entry into "in Christ," and symbolizes dying and rising in Christ (e.g., Rom 6:1-4).

Life "in Christ" is now, however, only partial. Christ's resurrection is only the first-fruits anticipating the general resurrection (e.g., 1 Thess 4:12-18; 1 Cor 15). Until then, the Christian

Figure 9: **Between the Ages**		
In Adam	**Interface**	**In Christ**
	Cross	
Flesh	Baptism	Spirit
Sin		Faith
Death		Life
Law		Freedom
Wrath		Peace
Apart from God		With God

lives on **the interface of the ages**, between Adam and Christ. Only when death is overcome will the Christian be fully victorious over the powers of this age (1 Cor 15; Rom 8:18-39).

Less symbolically, "in Christ" presently describes only the **social and symbolic world of a small sect**. That group lives in the midst of an unchanged world operating by vastly different myths. Only the end will ameliorate the tension between the myth of those "in Christ" and their larger social world (the Roman empire).

As Christians are "in Christ" but not fully transformed and as they live in **the midst of competing myths**, Paul's letters are replete with exhortations to live after the spirit and not the flesh (see Gal 5:16-26). In short, Paul's letters struggle to bring "in Christ," Christian mythic identity, to the fullest possible reality in the believer's experience.

Figure 10: **Paul's Theology**

   While Paul was a situational, rather than systematic
thinker, theologians have tried to organize his thought around
a cohesive center. Historically, "**justification by faith**" is the
most popular choice although Protestants (God declares the
guilty innocent) and Catholics (God makes the guilty
innocent) understand the term differently. Of course, one
might question whether justification is, in fact, the center of
Paul's thought. After all, it dominates only two letters (Gal;
Rom), both of which are clearly argumentative. Further, in
Romans [see plot], justification is only one of several symbols
describing God's act in Christ. Recently, then, scholars have
suggested other "centers" (e.g., **salvation history or
apocalyptic righteousness**). The larger question of Paul's
intellectual and religious **background** is also crucial to the
discussion (whether it be Judaism or Hellenism or some
particular form of either). More recently still, some scholars
forego the question of Paul's theology in favor of the
discussion of **the theology of particular letters** [see Furnish,
331-36; Bassler].

   In terms of **theodicy**, Paul has an interesting problem, the
justification of grace. To do so, Paul **rewrites his Jewish tradition**
as a story emphasizing the priority and precedence of the
promise/gospel over the law (cf. Gal 3-4; Rom 4). For Paul, the
gospel creates a new, but similar, salvation history. For both
versions, God's decisive act precedes the law. Neither Jew nor Paul
believes that the law alone will create a people of God. The
difference in the stories lies in their **different elective moments**. For
Paul, the cross shows that where there was no people God has now
created a new people. With this, of course, Jews cannot agree.

```
Figure 11: Competing Election Stories

        Jewish Story              Paul's Story

1. No people of God         1. Law will not work pre-elect
2. Election (Abraham)       2. Election in Christ
3. Law                      3. Apostle's teaching
4. Obedience maintains      4. Obedience maintains status
```

Actually, even Paul is not willing to go so far. In Rom 9-11, he simply refuses to close the books on Israel. There, he merges more closely the promises to Israel and the promises of the gospel. To reconcile the two, he adopts a prophetic, **Deuteronomic view of Israel's history**. For that tradition, Israel's history is characterized by disobedience, judgment, and salvation. Paul, then, reads the rejection of the gospel as the latest disobedience, portrays the turn to the Gentiles as a new exile/ judgment, and prophesies the ultimate salvation of Israel [cf. Hays, Echoes, 163-73].

Paul's theodicy, then, **declares temporary both law and Jewish exclusion**. For Paul, all God's promises--in Israel and in Christ--will be realized.

Paul, the Apostle

Paul **incarnates the gospel** for his communities [see narrator]. His life displays the gospel's grace and suffering. Thus, although once a persecutor of the church, God's "revelation" transformed Paul into the apostle to the Gentiles (Gal 1:13-17, 23). This recreation renders what was once considered "gain"--the highlights of his Jewish resume--a "loss" compared to life in Christ (Phil 3:4-11). Paul has begun anew, like his followers, dying to self in baptism in order to live anew in Christ (Gal 2:19-20; Rom 6:1-4).

466

This transformation gives the apostle's life a pattern not unlike that of his Jesus-story (Phil 2:5-11).

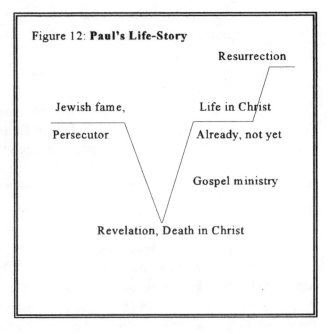

Figure 12: **Paul's Life-Story**

Resurrection

Jewish fame,   Life in Christ

Persecutor   Already, not yet

Gospel ministry

Revelation, Death in Christ

Paul's transformation is, however, hardly complete. His life still demonstrates the **already-not yet** quality of life in Christ. As an apostle and as a Christian, he now **shares Christ's suffering**. As an apostle, he shares sufferings in order to bring the gospel to his communities (1 Cor 4:8-13; 2 Cor 11:23-33). As a Christian, he shares the sufferings in hope of the resurrection of the death (Phil 3:10-11; Rom 6:5; 8:17-39; 2 Cor 4:7-5:10). That is, like all Christians, he awaits the full conformity of myth and social reality.

As Paul's life conforms to and incarnates his gospel, he can dare to **call his followers to imitate him**. For his communities, Paul is the spiritual father. Put differently, the apostle is the sacred vehicle and the mythic *tradent*. His communities can trust him to transmit faithfully that which he received (cf. 1 Cor 15:1-7).

The Community: Living in Christ

Paul has a dualistic understanding of mythic identity. One is either in Adam or in Christ [see myth]. The death of Christ and death in Christ releases the believer from this age's powers and actualizes divine power (spirit) within the believer.

Paul's communities live this story. They attempt with Paul's apostolic leadership to live "in Christ" and "in the spirit." Individual letters spell out the ramifications of that mythic identity in light of a hostile world (this age) and **competing myths** (either political, social, or religious).

Paul stresses **life consistent with "in Christ."** His exhortations and advice resemble the apodictic and conditional laws of Torah. Like those laws, his teachings attempt to preserve the community's sacred biosphere (in Christ) [see chap. 8, style]. Faith, love, and humility preserve the biosphere. Sin, selfishness, and pride destroy it.

In the face of error, Paul prescribes actions which restore the biosphere's integrity. Thus, the Galatians must return to the gospel. The Corinthians must cease boasting. They must excommunicate notorious cases of immorality. They must give up meat if it troubles the brother. They must not speak in tongues lest there is an interpreter.

In short, communities must live according to their transformed lives. They must **live the Pauline myth** regardless of the cost, whether that be imprisonment (Paul himself), persecution (1 Thess), foregoing personal liberties (1 Cor), or even economic loss (Philem). In short, Paul's churches must strive to become more "in Christ" and less "in Adam." They must enlarge either **the flesh or the spirit**. One way leads to death while the other leads to life.

Retelling Paul's Myth

If the disputed Pauline epistles are, in fact, non-Pauline, they apply Paul's myth to new, post-Pauline situations. In general, Ephesians and the Pastorals make Paul's myth more "**at home**" in the world by emphasizing **culturally acceptable ethics and faith's secure transmission**. In short, the disputed epistles enhance the aura of tradition in contrast to Paul's creative newness.   Paul's **eschatological**, charismatic community is becoming an institution more "at home" in the world.

Thus, the "household codes," which instruct each family member in his responsibilities, are virtually synonymous with the ethic of the surrounding culture (Eph 5:21-6:9; modified in Titus 2:1-14; 1 Tim 4:11-6:2).   The codes advocate **hierarchical relationships**, for example, for husbands and wives and for masters and slaves. Such an ethic is some distance from Paul's sometimes revolutionary egalitarianism:

> There is no longer Jew or Greek, there is no longer
> slave or free, there is no longer male and female; for
> all of you are one in Christ Jesus. (Gal 3:28)

While Paul is hardly consistent on this point (cf. 1 Cor 11:2-16; 14:33-36), his ethic does challenge the traditional hierarchies which these later texts support.

Titus and 1 Timothy adapt the household code to life in a hierarchical community with clearly defined offices and an overwhelming concern for order. They are, in fact, **church manuals**. They exhort to hierarchical submission, to order, to quiet lives, and to good citizenship (1 Tim 2:1-7).

Finally, these documents struggle with the secure transmission of tradition, **the deposit of faith** (e.g., 2 Tim 1:13-14; 2:2). This faith is closer to creed/tradition than to Paul's alignment with Christ (cf. 1 Tim 1:15; 3:1; 4:9; 2 Tim 2:11; Titus 3:8). Correspondingly, Paul is now one of the holy apostles who with the prophets and Jesus Christ founded the church (Eph 2:20; 3:5). Paul is **a guarantor of the tradition**, a mythic model.

Of course, readers can find traces of these elements in the

genuine epistles as well (cf., e.g., "imitate me"). The disputed epistles do, however, seem to offer a "Paul" of a different shade. They intensify certain trends in Paul (hierarchy, tradition) and diminish others (egalitarianism, prophetic creativity).

Figure 13: **Paul, the Feminist**

Paul's gospel of grace and faith (Gal 3:28) sounds a radically egalitarian revision of Jewish hierarchies. By the later epistles, however, the household codes reassert the subordination of wives and slaves (Col 3:18-4:1; Eph 5:22-6:9). Perhaps, not surprisingly, then, male-female equality is missing from this later baptismal formula:

In that renewal there is no longer Greek and
Jew, circumcised and uncircumcised,
barbarian, Scythian, slave and free; but Christ
is all and in all! (Col 3:11)

While the most radically egalitarian passages are in the genuine epistles and the most patriarchal are in the disputed (e.g., 1 Tim 2:8-15), it is unlikely that one should imagine a straight-line movement **from sectarian equality to institutional patriarchy** (though see Schuessler-Fiorenza, Her). After all, the genuine epistles also include conservative, traditional passages (e.g., 1 Cor 7). Paul both gives and takes away equality. While recognizing women prophets (deacons and apostles, e.g., Rom 16:1, 7), he also places them under patriarchal authority (1 Cor 11:2-16; though consider 11:11-12) and, finally, demands womanly silence (14:33-36). In short, Paul seems to have only flashing moments of egalitarian insight.

ANET: "In Christ" as Mythic and Social Reality

Paul's apocalyptic cross shares apocalyptic's "timing" problem. If declarations of the imminent end pale over time, so, too, do assertions that God's decisive, eschatological act has occurred. As history marches relentlessly on, Paul's "already-not yet" tension becomes more difficult to maintain. In short, how can a death two thousand years ago be the ages' crucial pivot? What is that death's significance when the powers of this age (sin, death, the imperial myth) continue unabated? How long can a myth live in tension with social reality?

Further, in what sense does that death reconcile the believer to God ? Assuming corporate personality, Paul blithely asserts that Adam's sin and Christ's obedience are mythic founding acts. Modern individualism flounders here. Put bluntly, **what does the death of a first century Jew have to do with modern life?**

Paul's churches created sub-communities, social realities, which gave empirical reality to Paul's myth. In them, one was truly "in Christ." The waning of the church in modernity has **removed much of this support structure**. Faith is left virtually alone to carry the burden of the symbolic union with Christ. Without objective support (the social reality of "in Christ" and its attendant rituals), modern literalism's problem with symbolism renders the significance of Christ's death difficult to appropriate. Apart from ritual, myth has difficulty surviving.

Review Questions

1. Apply the reading method of chaps. 3-4 to Paul's letters. List their genre, plot shape, conflict, depiction of Jesus and God, mythic function, and ANE problems.

2. Name the genuine and disputed Pauline letters.

3. How does Paul "christianize" the phatic language of ancient letters?

4. What are the most important traditional elements in Paul?

5. What is the most important "new" element for Paul?

6. Compare the prophetic and apostolic voices.

7. How is Paul ironic?

8. Compare Paul's myth with that of apocalyptic. How is Paul an "already, not yet" thinker? How does Paul's gospel/myth compare with that of Mark?

9. Is "in Christ" a description or a prescription?

10. How do the disputed epistles adapt Paul?

Suggestions for Alternate Reading and Reflection

1. Is Paul a *tradent* or a creative innovator?

2. What does it mean to say that Paul's myth is imperialistic?

3. How does Paul justify grace?

4. What is Paul's attitude to Judaism and the Torah? Compare this view with that of Matthew.

5. Describe Paul's theology.

6. How did early interpreters understand Paul? How has Paul been important in Western intellectual history?

7. How might a structuralist read Paul? What are the important binary oppositions in Paul? How does Paul resolve these tensions?

8. Can a modern individualist believe in the saving, apocalyptic cross? How is God's act in Christ and in the cross salvific?

9. Compare "Letter From Birmingham Jail" with Philemon.

10. Is Paul a feminist? Do the disputed epistles differ from the genuine on this point? Do Paul's letters justify subordination of certain groups?

For Further Reading

For the distinction between epistle (formal, public letter) and letter (private communication), see Deissmann, <u>Bible</u>, 1-59.

For discussions of the letter structure and genre, see Funk, <u>Language</u>, 250-74; Dahl, "Letter," 539-42; Duling and Perrin,

206-11; Doty, Letters; and Aune, NT, 158-225.

On Pauline thanksgivings, see Schubert; and O'Brien. Boers, "Letters," argues that the thanksgiving is part of the letter's body.

On the beginning of the body, see Doty, Letters, 34-36; and White, "Introductory."

On early Christian worship, see C. C. Richardson; and Martin, Worship.

On Paul's use of traditional items, see Duling and Perrin, 210-13; Doty, Letters, 49-63; Aune, NT, 192-97; Martin, "Liturgical," 556-57; Sanders, Hymns; Lohse, 154-63; and Balch, 25-50.

On Paul's apostolic authority, see Schuetz; and Holmberg. Schuetz deals primarily with the connection between apostle and gospel. Holmberg deals primarily with Paul's relationship to other human or institutional authorities.

On the canonical problem of the particularity of the Pauline letters, see Dahl, "Particularity"; and Gamble, Canon, 35-46.

On ancient and NT rhetoric, see Barr, NT, 10-14; Kennedy; and Betz, Galatians. For a comparison of Paul's exhortations and ancient philosophy, see Stowers, Letter, 42-43, 91-94, 107-09, 125-28; Malherbe, Thessalonians; and **idem**, Popular.

On Paul's attempt to extend the range of the gospel's influence in his churches' lives, see Petersen, Rediscovering, 141-49, 258-69.

On Paul's use of scripture, see Ellis; Longenecker, 104-32; and Hays, Echoes.

For brief introductions to Paul's theology, see Duling and Perrin, 248-55; Keck, Paul; and Beker, Gospel. For a detailed discussion of Paul's apocalyptic gospel, see Beker, Triumph. For a reading of Paul against the backdrop of Torah, see E. P. Sanders, Palestinian; and **idem**, Law. For a sociological interpretation see Meeks, Urban. For a sociology of knowledge (or mythic) treatment, see Petersen, Rediscovering. For a structuralist approach, see Patte, Paul's. For a feminist and ideological reading, see Castelli, Paul.

The modern classic on Paul's theology is Bultmann, Theology, 1:185-352. For recent appraisals and revisions, see Furnish, 331-38.

A recent innovation is the study of the theology of various Pauline letters, rather than an attempt to reduce Paul's theology to a systematic whole. See Bassler; Hay; and Johnson and Hay.

For discussion of Paul's life, see Duling and Perrin, 177-95; Bornkamm, Paul; and Furnish, 328-31.

Reconstructions depend primarily upon the letters or upon Acts. For treatments of Paul's life privileging the letters, see Knox, Chapters; Hurd; and Buck and Taylor. For critical treatments of the evidence in Acts, see Luedemann; and Jewett, Chronology.

Aune, NT, 190, lists the following autobiographical passages in Paul: 1 Thess 1:2-3:13; Gal 1:10-2:21; Rom 1:14-16a; 2 Cor 1:12-2:17; 7:5-16; 10:7-12:13; Phil 1:12-26; 3:2-14; 1 Thess 2:1-12.

For images of Paul (early interpretations), see Barr, NT, 157-87; Meeks, Writings, 149-213; and Beker, Heirs. On Deutero-Paulinism, see Duling and Perrin, 261-93.

On pseudonymity in antiquity, see Barr, NT, 69-71; and chap. 15, figure 6.

CHAPTER 22

CONTINUING THE APOSTOLIC TRADITION
Hebrews, James, Peter, John, and Jude

Introduction: The General and Pauline Letters

Scholars often call the non-Pauline NT letters the "general epistles" to indicate that most of these letters have broad audiences. Not surprisingly, then, the narrative voice and ethical demand are general. Collectively, these letters constitute **an appeal for a generalized apostolic tradition**.

Genre: The Sermon

The general epistles are remarkably free from the phatic language which structures letters. Thus, while Hebrews has a letter closing, it has no opening. Conversely, James lacks a closing. 1 John has neither opening nor closing. The remaining documents--1-2 Peter, 2-3 John, and Jude--are more clearly letters.

Of those, 2 Peter and Jude have quite **general addressees**:

To those who have received a faith as precious as ours through the righteousness of our God and Savior Jesus Christ . . . (2 Pet 1:1b)

To those who are called, who are beloved in God the Father and kept safe for Jesus Christ . . . (Jude 1b)

While James, 1 Peter, and 1 John are more specific, their addressees mark them as **encyclicals**. With the exception of 2-3 John, then, these epistles are not letters to specific addressees.

Not surprisingly, the body of these letters is not a specific response to a specific occasion. Rather, the letters are **sermons**, **which reflect upon the foundational traditions** of the authors/communities.

Figure 1: **Foundational Traditions**

Letter	Tradition
Hebrews	Jesus and scripture
James	Jewish wisdom
1 Peter	Christ, righteous sufferer
2 Peter	Petrine traditions
1-3 John	Johannine symbolism
Jude	Apostolic faith

The traditions are applied generally. In essence, the audiences should **hold onto their traditions**, resist apostasy, and live in accord with their tradition.

Figure 2: **General Appeal**

Letter	Appeal (Warning)
Hebrews	maintain original confession (avoid apostasy to Judaism(?))
James	live wisely and humbly (avoid foolishness and pride)
1 Peter	suffer righteously like Christ (avoid sin and unholiness)
2 Peter	maintain Petrine traditions (avoid heresy and immorality)
1-2 John	maintain Johannine Christology and ethic (avoid docetism and sin)
3 John	support Johannine missionaries (do not support non-Johannine)
Jude	maintain apostolic tradition (avoid heresy and immorality)

Narrator: Anonymous, Traditional Voices

The commitment to tradition creates a particular narrative voice. Whether apostle (1-2 Pet), servant (Jas; Jude; 2 Pet), or elder (2-3 Jn), that voice is **the authoritative guardian of tradition**.

These **priestly custodians** exhort within and for an already established conventional wisdom (Jas) or apostolic tradition (2 Pet; 1-3 Jn; Jude). They do not substantively extend or recreate myth. They strive to maintain it in the face of apostasy.

Naming these voices priestly does not denigrate them. The priest is as important to a religious tradition as the prophet. After all, without a continuing tradition, there are no new insights. Further, the priest's authority is more secure than the prophet's. His story is traditional and, therefore, less open-ended than that of the prophet. As a result, the general epistles tend to be less open-ended than the Pauline letters. They do not establish authority; they exercise it. The exception to this rule, of course, is 2 and 3 John which are tools in the elder's charismatic mission.

Given this traditional character, the narrative voice here is not as personal as the Pauline voice. The priestly apostle's experience is not as important as that of the prophetic apostle. Thus, Hebrews and 1 John are anonymous. Their texts need not name their narrator/voice. Similarly, little or nothing personal is known about James and Jude or necessary for their advocation of wisdom or apostolic tradition. Only 2 Peter relies upon an incident in the life of Peter. That incident serves merely to mark Peter as the approved, guaranteed mythic channel (cf. 1 Jn 1:1-5).

In this process, the apostle loses his individuality and becomes **one of the mythic founding heroes** (Jude; 2 Pet 3:2) [cf. chap. 19, disciples]. The anonymous result is a stress upon a **common apostolic tradition**. Thus, the narrator of 1 John speaks for the "we" who has witnessed the hierophany. Pauline figures appear in the closing remarks in Hebrews and 1 Peter. More importantly, 2

Peter reveres Paul's letters themselves as community-scripture (3:15-16). Finally, for Jude, the faith is simply apostolic. It needs no individual qualification:

> Beloved, while eagerly preparing to write to you about the salvation we share, I find it necessary to write and appeal to you to contend for the faith that was once for all entrusted to the saints. (Jude 3)

> But you, beloved, must remember the predictions of the apostles of our Lord Jesus Christ; for they said to you, "In the last time there will be scoffers" . . . . But you, beloved, build yourselves up on your most holy faith . . ." (Jude 17-20)

Narratee: The Church at Large

The addressee of these letters is even more anonymous than their voices (except for 2-3 Jn). Their generality makes these letters easily **adaptable to a canonical situation**. That is, these general epistles speak more easily to the continuing Church than do the specific, occasional Pauline letters [cf. chap. 21, specific]. Their rehearsal of traditional values and virtues, if not timeless, transfers easily to new situations.

Rhetoric: Rehearsing and Reaffirming Tradition

The general epistles' exhortation to traditional, well-known values resembles the style of demonstrative rhetoric. Such rhetoric **reaffirms a community's values and virtues on ceremonious, public occasions**. Hebrews' "cloud of witnesses" evokes this public setting (11-12) for its culminating appeal as do the references to the baptismal liturgy in 1 Peter. That letter repeatedly alludes to baptism, a decidedly public ceremony, in order to remind its hearers of their tradition of righteous suffering (life through death).

The chief warrant is, of course, the tradition itself [see figure 1]. The tradition's mythic founders and exemplars are Jesus (Heb 2:9-18; 12:1-4; 1 Pet 2:21-25; 3:18-33) and the apostles (1 Pet 1; 1 Jn 1:1-5; 2 Pet; Jude).

James and 1 John slightly modify this "backward" look. While James has examples from the past—Jewish heroes, but never Jesus—its appeal is really to the **eternal way of wisdom**. The ancient examples are merely models, not founders. 1 John modifies the turn to the past by appeals to its **audience's personal experiences**. It exhorts community members to act according to their indwelling spirit (2:20-27; 4:4, 13-16; 5:10). Similarly, Hebrews appeals to its audience's experiences of salvation (e.g., 2:1-4; 5:11-6:20).

For the general epistles, **scripture** is also part of the tradition. With the exception of James, the epistles **read** Jewish scriptures **eschatologically**. That is, only the Jesus-event makes scripture's true meaning clear (1 Pet 1:10-12; 2 Pet 1:19-21; Heb 7-10). Hebrews is an extended eschatological reading of several Jewish scriptures (particularly Ps 2; 110; and Jer 31:31-34) and a Jesus-story simultaneously. The use of Isa 53 in 1 Pet 2:21-25 is less extended and eschatological. It remains, however, a basic warrant for Peter's appeal to the decorum of righteous suffering.

Finally, apostolic tradition and Jewish scripture become one warrant. Thus, for 2 Peter, scripture (i.e., prophets) and apostles (i.e., Paul) agree when rightly and institutionally read:

> So we have the prophetic message more fully confirmed. . . . First of all you must understand this, that no prophecy of scripture is a matter of one's own interpretation . . . (1:19-20)

> So also our beloved Paul wrote to you according to the wisdom given him, speaking of this as he does in all his letters. There are some things in them hard to understand, which the ignorant and unstable twist to

their own destruction, as they do the other scriptures.
(3:15-16)

Atmosphere: Nostalgia

The appeal to and reaffirmation of tradition create a sense of living in a late world. The narrators and narratees stand at some **remove from the mythic founding times**. In fact, in some cases, the audiences are already in possession of written apostolic traditions (2 Pet; 1 Jn). At any rate, even the apostles are part of the past mythic founding time (2 Pet; Jude).

The epistles look back at this past with nostalgia. The past is a mythic **golden-age** from which later ages deviate only to their peril. Given this stable tradition (world), these epistles are seldom ironic. Even 1 Peter's call to righteous suffering is more a call to decorum than an ironic call to find life in death.

Only Hebrews handles its lateness with an ironic reading of earlier tradition. In particular, Hebrews re-symbolizes sacred Jewish scriptures in light of the Jesus-event and the world above:

> But Jesus has now obtained a more excellent ministry and to that degree he is the mediator of a better covenant, which has been enacted through better promises. For if that first covenant had been faultless, there would have been no need to look for a second one. (8:6-7)

> Since the law has only a shadow of the good things to come and not the true form of these realities, it can never, by the same sacrifices that are continually offered year after year, make perfect those who approach. (10:1)

For Hebrews, Jesus is a new priest offering a better sacrifice in the heavenly tabernacle (4:14-10:18; cf. Exod 25:10-40). As a result, he replaces earlier, inadequate models (8-9). In particular, Jesus makes God accessible. This access completes the pilgrimage to the promised rest begun, but left incomplete, by Moses-Joshua (3-4).

Style: Tapestry

The general epistles resist outline. Unlike the Pauline epistles which occasionally build an application section (an imperative) on an explanatory base (indicative), these epistles weave together their reflection and their application.

Hebrews, for example, routinely interrupts its description of the ritual access to the heavens made possible by Jesus with ethical exhortations based on points made in process (e.g., 2:1-4; 3:7-4:13; 6:1-20; 10:19-39). Such interruptions and the anticipatory suggestion of major points subsequently expanded create a tapestry (e.g., the priesthood and faithfulness of Jesus mentioned in 2:9-18 but expanded only in 4:14-10:18 and in 11-12 respectively).

James and 1 John return again and again to reflect upon a few interconnected, fundamental motifs. John builds a mosaic from obedience/righteousness (1:6-2:6; 2:29-3:10); love (2:7-11; 3:11-24; 4:7-21); and Johannine faith (1:1-5; 2:15-28; 4:1-6). Similarly, James is a densely interwoven reflection upon religious wisdom, faith and works, riches and poverty, and control of the tongue (see, e.g., Jas 1).

Character and Plot: The Apostolic Golden Age

For the tradition-epistles--1 John, 2 Peter, and Jude--Jesus is at such a distance that **the apostles, too, are part of the founding time**. They transmit the hierophany (2 Pet 1:16-18; 1 Jn 1:1-4). Jude has the most concise statement of this Jesus-apostle story:

Beloved, while eagerly preparing to write to you

about the salvation we share, I find it necessary to write and appeal to you to contend for the faith that was once for all entrusted to the saints. For certain intruders have stolen in among you, people who long ago were designated for this condemnation as ungodly . . . . But you, beloved, must remember the predictions of the apostles of our Lord Jesus Christ; for they said to you, "In the last time there will be scoffers, indulging their own ungodly lusts." But you, beloved, build yourselves up on your most holy faith . . . (3-4, 17-18, 20)

If the apostles are the mythic heroes which found, exemplify, and guarantee the myth (cf. Eph 2:20; 3:5), later teachers/believers **deviate at their peril**. In fact, deviate positions indicate the presence of the "last days" (e.g., 1 Tim 4:1-10; 2 Tim 3:1-9; 2 Pet 3; 1 Jn 2:18-25). That is, the community lives in **a time of institutional decay** at a remove from and less than the golden age of myth, but still in possession of the mythic tradition through the apostles.

Figure 3: **Mythic Decay**

Golden Age of the   **Maintain Tradition**

Apostles

Heresy

Apostasy

Last Days

Judgment

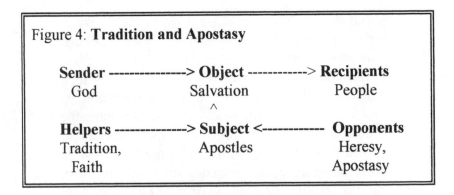

Figure 4: **Tradition and Apostasy**

Sender ----------------> **Object** ------------> **Recipients**
God   Salvation   People
                             ∧

Helpers --------------> **Subject** <------------ **Opponents**
Tradition,   Apostles   Heresy,
Faith   Apostasy

Character and Plot: Jesus as Founder

Unlike the tradition epistles, 1 Peter's emphasis is, like Paul's, on **Jesus' death-resurrection**. He, alone, founds the new order with his sufferings and is its chief mythic exemplar (2:21-25; 3:18-22). For 1 Peter, Jesus is the epitome of **the suffering righteous**.

For Hebrews, too, the death and resurrection of Jesus is the founding story. Like Paul, Hebrews has a three-stage Jesus-story characterized by a middle stage of suffering (e.g., 2:9-18). Unlike Paul, however, Hebrews

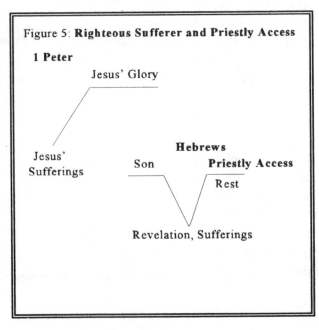

Figure 5: **Righteous Sufferer and Priestly Access**

1 Peter

Jesus' Glory

Jesus' Sufferings

Hebrews

Son   **Priestly Access**

Rest

Revelation, Sufferings

depicts the suffering and exaltation of Jesus in terms of **priestly**

sacrifice and approach to the heavenly tabernacle (4:14-10:18). Further, Jesus as the mythic-hero makes it possible for others to imitate his approach to God (10:19-39; cf. the "rest" of 3:1-4:13). To accomplish this goal, they, like Jesus, must also endure (cf. 10:19-13:7).

Myth: Mythic Order and Apostasy

The general epistles present a number of distinctive mythic identities. All of the general epistles, however, understand mythic identity in terms of **faithfulness to the community's traditions**. For these epistles, mythic order is an established fact in which believers can live. As a result, the epistles

Figure 6: **Mythic Identities**	
Letter	**Identity**
Hebrews	Enduring Priestly Pilgrims
James	Humble Wise
1 Peter	Righteous Sufferers
2 Peter/Jude	Faithful to Apostolic Tradition
1 John	Mystics Faithful to Johannine Tradition

imagine the continuing community story in "**two-ways**" terms. Believers will live out the myth and salvation that they have experienced, or they will apostasize from it.

ANET: Traditional, Hierarchical Institution

The general epistles are more "at home" in the world than are the Pauline apocalyptic communities. The general epistles represent "institutions," rather than sects. As a result, these epistles trouble modernity less than Paul's.

Nonetheless, the **hierarchical, traditional institution** of the general epistles remains unpalatable to modernity. First, modernity is not comfortable with the general epistles' strong commitment to tradition or their **myth of a golden past**. Instead, modernity prizes the new. Second, modern egalitarianism is profoundly disturbed by apostolic, **patriarchal hierarchies**.

The ethic of the general epistles may be even more profoundly troubling. Alongside the call to tradition is a positive and **acquiescent understanding of suffering** (endurance; cf. Jas 1:2-4; 1 Pet; Heb). Nothing could be more remote from modern reformism and triumphalism. Modernity does not accept suffering and defeat or see value in them. Modernity eliminates ardor and difficulty wherever possible. Modernity makes easy paths and cheap successes available for all.

Review Questions

1. Apply the reading method of chaps. 3-4 to the general epistles. List their genre, plot shape, conflict, depiction of Jesus and God, mythic function, and ANE problems.
2. Why are these letters known as "general epistles"?
3. What is the basic appeal of the general epistles?
4. How do these narrators differ from that of the Pauline letters?
5. How do these narratees differ from that of the Pauline letters?
6. Compare the atmosphere of these letters with that of apocalyptic.
7. Is the "last ages" of the tradition epistles the same as that of apocalyptic?
8. What other biblical texts have a general world-view and ethic similar to the general epistles?

Suggestions for Alternate Reading and Reflection

1. Which is more important to religion--a priest or a prophet?
2. What biblical evidence suggests that there was an early common

apostolic tradition? What evidence suggests there was not?

3. Compare 1 Peter's understanding of the suffering righteous with that of Paul.

4. Is James a Christian book?

5. Is Hebrews overly negative in its appraisal of other religions?

6. Did the later church fall from an early golden age? Did any reform movements successfully recover the golden age? Are there alternative ways to conceive Christian history?

7. Is Christianity closer to its original traditions when it exists as a sect or when it is an institution?

For Further Reading

On the idea of **Una Sancta Apostolica**, see chap. 2, tradition; and the bibliography at the end of the chapter.

On the continuance of the myth of the golden age in the West, see Wilken, Myth.

CHAPTER 23

GOD CONQUERS ALL
Revelation

Introduction: Revelation and Apocalyptic

Apocalyptic pervades the NT. Its motifs appear in the earliest
(1 Thess) and latest (2 Pet) NT documents. Further, apocalyptic is
the background for both Mark and the Pauline letters. The most
complete NT example of apocalyptic is Revelation, the very title of
which is **an English translation for the Greek "apocalypse."**

Genre: Apocalyptic Letters

While Revelation is a typical historical apocalypse (4:1-22:5),
it is set within **the framework of a letter**. It has, then, fairly typical
phatic opening (1:4-8) and
closing (22:6-21)
language. Within the
general letter frame, stand
seven letters to specific
churches (2-3).

> Figure 1: **The Letters to the**
> **Seven Churches**
>
> name of addressee
> symbolic description of Christ
> commendation/condemnation
> exhortation (endure, avoid
>   idolatry and immorality)
> promise

The letter frame is
thoroughly apocalyptic. A
vision of the risen,
judging Christ (1:9-20)
authorizes the specific
letters to the churches
(2-3). As a result, they are nothing less than **the words of the risen
Christ**. Further, as typical apocalyptic exhortation, these letters
counsel **endurance**. In fact, specific warnings about the assembly of

Satan and Jezebel anticipate the dragon and harlot of the central apocalyptic vision (17-19).

Structure: A Chinese Box

The **letter frame** is only the first of several shells in Revelation's "Chinese box"structure.

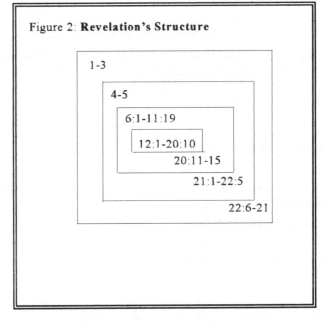

Figure 2: **Revelation's Structure**

1-3

4-5

6:1-11:19

12:1-20:10

20:11-15

21:1-22:5

22:6-21

A **worship frame** is the second layer (4-5; 21:1-22:5). Thus, the apocalypse proper begins with John's tour of heaven (4:1) where he witnesses worship at the heavenly throne of God (4) and the lamb (5). In a circular movement, the apocalypse ends with worship of this same God and the lamb in the new heaven and earth (21:1-22:5). The apocalypse is the story of the worshiped divine sovereignty "come to earth."

A **judgment frame** (6:1-11:19; 20:11-15) follows the worship box. The worshiped lamb (5) breaks the seven seals on the scroll of divine judgment (6:1-8:15 or 11:19). A similar judgment scene ends this frame at the great white throne where the books of works and life are opened (20:11-15).

Inside the letter, worship, and judgment boxes stands the **apocalyptic centerpiece** (12:1-20:10). That section (possibly the content of the "little scroll" of 10:1-11) details the ultimate conflict between divine and demonic forces. The story provides a series of opposed or **mirror visions**. For example, the dragon-beasts (12-13) oppose the heavenly woman and the Lamb (12:1-6; 14:1-5). The great whore (17-18) opposes the heavenly bride (21). The **final conflict** itself occurs between these last two opposites (19:11-20:10).

This conflict, like other biblical holy wars, is no real conflict. The conflict is **actually a divine judgment**. Thus, the conflict is set within a judgment frame (6:1-11:19; 20:11-15) and itself contains an impressive judgment section (14:6-16:21).

Media: Worshiped Reality

The worship frame connects the apocalyptic vision with the readers' reality. The sovereign that the believers already know in worship is now the heavenly reality (4-5) and will ultimately become earthly reality (21:1-22:5). Revelation **envisions worshiped and ideal sovereignty become reality**.

Worship scenes are even more dominant in the apocalypse than judgment. They, too, are part of the drama (e.g., 6:9-11; 7:9-17; 11:15-19; 14:1-5; 15:2-8; 16:5-7; 19:1-8). After the fashion of the **choruses of Greek drama**, these worship-scenes predict ensuing action and provide explanatory comments. Further, these scenes, particularly those involving martyred voices, motivate the apocalypse. That is, the judgment-conflict storied by the apocalypse arises logically from the opening throne vision (4-5) and from the martyrs' cries/blood (e.g., 6:9-11; 8:3-5; 11:12-13; 12:10-12; 16:6; 18:24; 19:2).

The worship scenes and frames have important connections with the letter frame. That outside box indicates that Revelation had a place in early Christian worship. Revelation was **written to be read in church worship**. The letter frame, then, leads the reader from actual worship to a vision report about heavenly worship becoming earthly reality. One moves, then, from worship into vision and back into worship. That experience transfigures worship in light of heavenly visions, and such worship itself transforms the earthly reality of the reader where dragons dwell. Earthly reality stands under heavenly (or worshiped) realities. Revelation, then, **provides in vision and in ritual the experience of the divine sovereignty**.

The worshiper desires to experience even more fully that sovereignty:

> The Spirit and the bride say, "Come,"
> And let everyone who hears say, "Come,"
> And let everyone who is thirsty come.
> Let anyone who wishes take the water of life as a gift.
>
> Amen. Come, Lord Jesus! (22:17, 20b)

Not incidentally, that last benediction may have introduced the eucharist in which, at least for the church, the slain, judging lamb truly came.

Style: Poetry and Apocalyptic Tradition

Three sets of seven judgments figure prominently in the apocalypse: seals (6:1-8:5), trumpets (8:6-11:19), and bowls (15:1-16:21). These three sets of seven are not a sequential progression. Rather, they replicate and expand one another. In other words, Revelation's dominant syntax is not logical, temporal progression. Instead, the apocalypse repeatedly reflects and expands a few motifs: divine sovereignty, worship, judgment, and conflict.

The clear progression is the realization on earth of the divine sovereignty known presently in worship and in vision (4-5). The mysterious judgments lead up to and give way to a theophany (21:1-22:5). Interestingly, the seventh item in each judgment-series also resounds with theophanic language (cf. 8:5; 10:6-7; 11:15-19;

16:17-21). Each judgment-sequence **symbolizes the divine interruption which rights the world**.

Figure 3: **Interpreting Revelation**

Readers of Revelation typically want to know if Revelation's visions are about to become reality. In short, is the bloody end nigh? There are three classic answers to this question. **Futurists** believe the end is near and interpret Revelation's symbols in light of current or imminent events [cf. figure 5]. By contrast, **historicists** argue that readers should interpret Revelation in light of the first-century Roman empire. From that perspective, the number of the beast (666 in Rev 13:18), for example, refers to **Neron Caesar**. If one transposes the letters of that name to Hebrew and allows the Hebrew letters their numerical value, the name adds up to 666 (dropping the final **n** would total 616, which is the number in some manuscripts of Revelation). **Symbolists** think that Revelation's symbols have no exact referent. On their reading, the story of Revelation occurs again and again whenever anyone arrogates divine prerogatives to himself.

The Chinese box structure and the repetitive, non-sequential judgment series make the apocalypse a circular tapestry. Everything opens out onto and explains its surroundings. Thus, the opening vision of the risen Christ (1:12-20) provides symbols both for the apocalyptic letters (2-3) and the victorious finale. The exhortation of the letters suggests the final conflict with Satan and the whore. The seventh seal opens onto the trumpets. The seventh trumpet is nothing other than the end itself. The seventh bowl depicts Babylon's fall which demands prophetic explanation (17) and taunt song (18). One can go on and on. This circular, repetitive syntax resembles the parallelism of biblical poetry. At least, the woven style of the apocalypse demands a similar kind of stereoscopic reading. That is, it does not call out so much for logical, progressive analysis (an outline) as much as its does for multiple perspectives.

Figure 4: **Symbols De-Coded**

Symbol	Referent
seven stars, lamps (1:13)	seven angels, churches
Sodom (1:17)	site of crucifixion
dragon (12:9)	Satan
666 (13:8)	number of a man
7 heads, 10 horns (17:9-15)	7 mountains, 10 kings
slain, risen Lamb (5)	Jesus Christ
white horse rider (19:11)	Jesus Christ
lamb's bride (21)	Christ's people
4 (number)	created world
7 (number)	perfection
10 (number)	wholeness
12 (number)	Israel
multiples of numbers	intensify
white	victory
red	war, blood
black	famine
pale	death

Revelation's semantics also resemble poetry. In fact, Revelation is so bizarrely symbolic that it frequently overwhelms readers. Fortunately, Revelation **interprets some of its own symbols** or relies on common Christian assumptions.

Other symbols rely on earlier **biblical tradition**. Thus, the throne vision (4) resembles and echoes the throne visions of Ezek 1-11 and Isa 6. The seven judgment sets have strong affinities with the Exodus plagues. The judgment of Babylon and the taunt song against her clearly reflect similar biblical prophetic genres. Finally, the depiction of the end (21:1-22:5) resembles the biblical beginning

(Gen 3).

Figure 5: **The Futurist Interpretation**

The most popular interpretation of Revelation is the futurist. It reads Revelation as a complete prediction of history from the time of Revelation itself to the end of time. In this schema, the seven churches of Rev 2-3 are stages representing the whole of **church history**, not actual first-century churches. The **rapture**, the translation of saints from earth to heaven (cf. 1 Thess 4:17), begins the apocalypse. As the rapture does not appear in the text of Revelation, futurists interject it at 4:1. After the rapture of the elect, the earth undergoes seven years of **tribulation** (4:1-19:10). **Armageddon**, the final great battle, ends the reign of evil (19:11-21; cf. 16:13-16) and ushers in the **millenium**, Christ's thousand-year reign upon the earth (20:1-6). After the release and defeat of Satan (20:7-10), the **great judgment** assigns everyone to their final destiny (20:11-15). The elect, of course, live blessedly in the **new heaven and earth** (21-22).

Most importantly, Revelation is a part of the apocalyptic tradition. That is, Revelation's symbols have apocalyptic symbols and myth as their larger frame of reference. Basic to that myth is the **ancient combat-enthronement myth**. Not surprisingly, then, Revelation tends to opposed visions of the dragon and the beasts against the lamb (or the whore against the bride).

Despite some fairly clear referents, Revelation's poetic symbols ultimately resist literalizing and allegorizing. Thus, as a whole, the symbolic visions are **ambiguous and evocative**, not precise cognitive communications [see figure 3].

> Figure 6: **Horror Movies and the Persistence of Evil**
>
> Curiously, the divine forces **defeat evil twice** (19:11-20:3; 20:7-10). The double defeat allows both Christ and God to figure in the climax. Further, as the two defeats bookend the millenium (20:4-6) and precede the final judgment (20:11-15), they also create space for both an earthly (20:4-6) and a heavenly (21:1-22:5) kingdom.
>
> The double defeat may also witness to **evil's persistence**. Thus, in popular suspense and horror movies today, evil dies hard. In movie after movie, the finale has the hero vanquish the villain/monster. When the hero turns away, however, the villain/ monster rises again often to dispatch an unnecessary sidekick or love interest. In a slightly different form, the motif allows sequels. The monster/robot, with regenerative powers, is not completely destroyed, and the movie ends with a shot of "the remains." In both popular horror movies and in apocalypse, Freddy, Jason, and Satan return.

Plot Shape: The Final Solution

Revelation envisions a **heavenly order supplanting earthly chaos**. A series of bloody divine judgments deposes the oppressive rule of the beasts and the whore. Ultimately, the divine sovereignty known at first only in worship and in heaven (4-5) comes to earth to replace this demonic rule (21:1-22:5). **God's sovereignty is all in all**. Nothing beside remains. Revelation's end in feasting and marriage celebrates the final, divine comedy.

As the end of the Christian Bible, Revelation provides **a mythic end which recalls the mythic beginnings** (Gen 1-3). Once again, God is directly present. Once again, there is a river and a tree of life (22:1-5). Now, however, there is a heavenly city as well (21; contrast Gen 11:1-9). Revelation is **the final solution** to exilic chaos. The Christian drama ends with Paradise Restored.

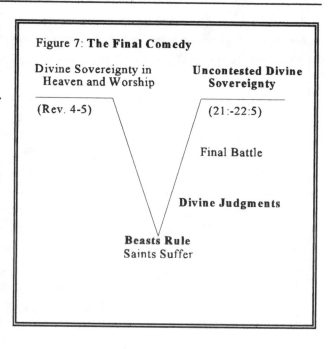

Figure 7: **The Final Comedy**

Divine Sovereignty in Heaven and Worship

Uncontested Divine Sovereignty

(Rev. 4-5)

(21:-22:5)

Final Battle

Divine Judgments

Beasts Rule
Saints Suffer

Plot Conflict: An Ironic Holy War

Revelation is a typical, biblical holy war. As such, the central narrative question concerns **the identity of the true sovereign** (cf. exodus). Do the dragon, beasts, and harlot rule? Is it the God of the martyrs and the churches' worship who rules? The comic finale resolves all doubt. God rules!

Ironically, however, **no real conflict** ever ensues. The penultimate conflict scene is a mere announcement of the conqueror's arrival (19:11-16) and the fate of his foolish enemies (19:17-20:3). The "final" conflict is a rain of fire from heaven (20:9). In short, the heavenly sovereign is never seriously challenged. The judgment frames (6:1-11:19; 20:11-15) which surround the conflict section make the lack of real conflict even more obvious [see figure 2]. Revelation stories **a divine punishment**, not a real conflict.

More ironically, **the conqueror is a slain Lamb** (5; cf. 21:9-22:5). Revelation dares to imagine a world in which lambs conquer dragons, in

```
Figure 8: Ironic Holy War

Sender --------> Object ------->Recipients
God          Divine sovereignty    World
                    ^
Helper --------> Subject <----- Opponents
judgments,      Lamb/Christ        Dragon,
martyrs, visions                Beasts, Babylon
```

which only the slain Lamb is worthy to judge, and in which the blood of the martyrs sparks Babylon's divine demise (e.g., 6:9-11; 12:11; 17:1-19:10). Evil's apparent victory becomes its defeat (e.g., 12:31; 16:6; 17:2, 6). Such ironies, of course, reprise the fundamental NT irony that life comes through death or that suffering precedes glory.

Revelation's conquering Lamb significantly rewrites the ancient combat myth. Nevertheless, the eventual and climactic advent of the rider on the white horse (19:11-21) undoes this irony. A warrior, not a Lamb, ultimately wins. The **return of the warrior** means that Revelation does not subvert the apocalyptic combat myth to the extent that Paul and Mark do. Both of them invert apocalypticism by recognizing the cross itself as the ultimate divine act ushering in the new age. By contrast, for Revelation, it is the warrior who turns the ages.

Divine Sovereignties

God figures more prominently in Revelation than in any other NT book (with the possible exception of Luke-Acts). God is not hidden behind Jesus as he is in the gospels. Thus, the apocalypse proper begins with a vision of God's sovereignty (4) and ends with the direct presence of God with the faithful (21:1-8).

Jesus is God's agent in the realization of the divine

sovereignty. Thus, the divine-throne vision (4) segues to the vision of **the slain, resurrected Lamb** who alone is worthy to judge (5-6). This depiction resonates strongly with the Christian tradition of the cross (1:5-6). Thus, the agent of the apocalypse is no less than the object of the church's worship (see 1; 22). This portrayal also connects Jesus with the martyrs, his suffering followers in the apocalypse itself.

Figure 9: **Star Wars**

The recently re-released and still popular Star Wars depicts a rebellion against an all-powerful empire by a few unlikely heroes (a boy, an old man, two robots, a girl, and an outlaw). The heroes have a nostalgic commitment to the force (an unseen, spiritual force) and bygone traditions (the republic, knight-errantry). Their opponent is the unseen emperor represented cruelly by the mechanistic Darth-Vader and the Death Star, the ultimate force in the universe. Going twice "into the belly of the whale," the heroes defeat the Death Star. The story ends with the rebel-heroes receiving various rewards.

The plot similarities to Revelation (12; 19-22) are unmistakable. The enemies are, of course, more mechanical than monstrous as befits modern fears. Despite the **deus ex machina** use of the force, the climactic conquest in Star Wars is also far more human than that in Revelation. Most importantly, however, Star Wars continues the externalization of evil and the resulting notions of innocent violence. Interestingly, the third movie in the trilogy, The Return of the Jedi, debunks this view of evil.

Jesus' depiction as **the divine warrior** (19:11-21) is, of course, more in keeping with general apocalyptic portrayals and, compared to other NT texts, is Revelation's most distinctive characterization of Jesus. This depiction bathes Jesus in supernatural hues. He is an incredibly powerful figure as the opening vision evidences (cf. 1:10-20 with Dan 7:9-14). Jesus, then, is not only like the martyrs, he is also the divine power which provides their remedy. Not surprisingly, then, the Lamb shares God's final sovereignty (21:1-22:5).

Thus, Jesus is the primary mediator between the heavenly sovereign and the demonic world of the martyrs. John and his vision report with its various characters (e.g., angels) are also important mediators, but **the apocalypse is Jesus' revelation** (1:1). Jesus is not only character in the apocalypse, but also **its narrative voice**.

Narrator and Rhetoric

Typically, apocalypses have ancient worthies as "fictional" narrators. For example, the second-century BCE Daniel has a sixth-century hero (Daniel) as its narrator. Such a device allows successful predictions because the text can offer history as prophecy.

Revelation's narrator is not such an ancient worthy. Instead, its narrator is John (1:9), a church-leader obviously well-known to its audience. Revelation has chosen another literary device as its primary authorization. John does not speak on his own. He introduces a vision-report of the speaking, risen Christ. Of course, in a Christian context, there is no more worthy ancient:

> The revelation of Jesus Christ, which God gave him to show his servants what must soon take place; he made it known by sending his angel to his servant John, who testified to the word of God and to the testimony of Jesus Christ, even to all that he saw. (1:1-2)

After advising the churches (2-3) and showing John (4:1-22:5) "what must soon take place," Jesus' last words are "Surely I am coming soon" (22:20b).

Other voices--for example, the angels (1:1; 17:1-20:11)--also speak, but are set within Jesus' authoritative voice. John, the appointed listener/seer and now secondary spokesperson, frames Jesus' voice as minimally as possible. John **"shows" Jesus speaking to the churches** and presents himself as a mere transmitter of the visionary experience within the work.

The visionary experience, however, marks the narrator-John as a **prophet** (e.g., 1:3; 10:11; 22:6, 9-10, 18). Like the prophets, then, John must convince his audience on the basis of his own religious experience. The **poetry/vision must entrap the reader**.

Mythic Atmosphere: The Presence of God

Revelation begins and ends in the world of church worship [see media]. The various Chinese boxes ultimately lead the reader deep within the prophet's visionary experience. In fact, Revelation is a textual attempt to **create that visionary world for its audience**.

That world is not "real," but a symbolic re-envisioning of the readers' worlds. The demonic forces and the world in which the faithful suffer and die symbolize the extra-worship reality of the alienated apocalyptic community. The heavenly world symbolizes the community's worship. The comic, apocalyptic resolution resolves these tensions with a new heaven and new earth in which the divine sovereignty is unopposed:

> See, the home of God is among mortals.
> He will dwell with them as their God . . . .
> he will wipe every tear from their eyes.
> Death will be no more . . . (21:3-4)

> . . . they will see his (God's) face, and his name will
> be on their foreheads. And there will be no more

night; they need no light of lamp or sun, for the Lord
God will be their light, and they will reign forever and
ever. (22:4-5)

In that mythic world, of course, no reader has ever lived.

Figure 10: **Evil as Seductive and Banal**

Revelation externalizes evil (except for Rev 2-3). The
resulting demonization of evil perilously misses evil's
seductiveness and banality. While Revelation's monstrous
beasts are terribly powerful, they are not alluring. By contrast,
Eden's forbidden fruit does tempt. Eve eats because she saw
"that the tree was good for food, and that it was a delight to
the eyes, and that the tree was to be desired to make one wise .
. ." (Gen 3:6). Revelation's powerful beasts also fail to treat
evil's banality. By contrast, for Hannah Arendt, Eichmann,
notorious Nazi war criminal, is horrible simply because he is
such an average person, not because he is a monster:

> The trouble with Eichmann was precisely that
> so many were like him, and the many were
> neither perverted nor sadistic, that they were,
> and still are, terribly and terrifyingly normal.
> From the viewpoint of our legal institutions and
> of our moral standards of judgment, this
> normality was much more terrifying than all the
> atrocities . . . [276]

> Eichmann was not Iago and not Macbeth, and
> nothing would have been farther from his mind
> than to determine with Richard III "to prove a
> villain" . . . He merely . . . never realized what
> he was doing. [emphasis in original, 287]

Myth: A Liberating Vision

Revelation offers the alienated community a liberating vision. Potentially at risk in the empire, the community has powerful connections. They belong to the ultimate, heavenly sovereign whom they know in worship and in vision. Further, if they suffer, they share a mythic identity with their mythic founder--the Lamb who was slain to receive glory and honor.

These **righteous sufferers** will ultimately share the Lamb's triumph. That hope is a classic **future-recompense theodicy**. The future apocalyptic reversal will right any present injustices. The present evil powers and the martyrs will both receive their just rewards.

In the interim, the faithful live in hope. Now, community worship and the apocalyptic text provide the only vehicles to the sacred. Only therein does the community find the experience of the divine sovereignty. Hope, however, resolves the continuing dissonance between mythic vision and imperial reality. Revelation's story completes the comic plot, but, of course, it is **only story**. Outside vision and worship, the beasts live on.

Figure 11: **Deconstructing Revelation**

Revelation resolves the tension between external imperial reality and the divine sovereignty known in worship with a vision of the ultimate divine victory. The depiction of the empire with demonic symbols rhetorically asserts the heavenly sovereign's superiority. The military imagery and the hellish fate of the opposition, however, threaten to deconstruct Revelation's rhetoric. If the slain Lamb could do without the rider on the white horse, Revelation would have an alternative imagination. The rider, however, suggests that Revelation **merely changes the names of those in power**, rather than replacing the imperial conceptions of reality.

Characters: The Demonic Opposition

Revelation's intensely supernatural conception of good--God, Christ, Spirit, and angels--has as its opponent an equally supernatural conception of evil--the beasts and Satan. This cosmic view of evil symbolizes the empire "from below," from the perspective of a **disenfranchised sect**. The lofty symbols reflect powers completely beyond this sect's manipulation.

Thus, the evil empire (Rome, of course) is Babylon, the archetypal destroyer of God's people. Opposed to the bride of Christ, she is no less than the great whore. Drunk on the blood of the martyrs, she is monstrous and, thus, demonically represented by great beasts and the dragon-Satan. The dragon-Satan represents the biblical remnant of the ancient combat myth (12-13; 20:1-10).

Figure 12: **Vengeance and Love**

Apocalyptic elevates the **human desire for vengeance** to a cosmic vision. Such fantasies are, of course, not rare. Tertullian, an early church father, once opined that watching the torments of the damned would be one of the delights of heaven. Similarly, Dante's famous Inferno consigns sinners and Dante's enemies to various levels of hell [see chap. 15, figure 3].

The line in the apostles' creed that Jesus "descended into hell" (cf. 1 Pet 3:19) contrasts with such vengeance. Here, Christ descends to **harrow hell**, not to consign to hell. Later folk tales depict the intercession of Mary and the saints for the damned. In short, some conceive God's love in terms of overpowering love, rather than as vengeance. Thus, Origen, the early Alexandrian theologian, thought that God would ultimately redeem all, even Satan.

ANET: The Empire Strikes Back

Like apocalyptic generally, Revelation has a notion of **innocent, redemptive violence**. As evil is largely external to the sectarian community (though see 2-3), Revelation imagines a "surgical strike" removing evil's pestilent influence and righting the world (cf. 19:11; 20:9).

While Revelation is an alienated community's cry for release and vengeance, the **fantasy remains imperial**. While Revelation imagines the names of the rulers changing, it leaves the imperial structure in place. Ironically, then, the empire strikes back.

Figure 13: **Tours of Hell**

Tours of hell are a prominent feature of Western literature (e.g., in the Odyssey, the Aeneid, The Divine Comedy, and Ulysses). Such a journey also provides the structure for Conrad's Heart of Darkness and for the movie, Apocalypse Now (loosely based upon the novel). In both cases, hero-narrators travel up a river into the jungle to find and retrieve or kill a mysterious, dangerous figure. Both stories can be read either psychologically or socially. That is, the journey into darkness may symbolize **an investigation of the evil within**. Alternatively, the story can serve as an **indictment of the imperialism** (European or American) which created the context for the ruthless figure of the quest. In either case, these quests have less external views of evil than Revelation.

Review Questions

1. Apply the reading method of chaps. 3-4 to Revelation. List its genre, plot shape, conflict, depiction of Jesus and God, mythic

function, and ANE problems.

  2. What is the effect of Revelation's frames?

  3. What is Revelation's connection to worship?

  4. How does Revelation answer Gen 2-3?

  5. Explain the tension between vision and reality in Revelation.

  6. How does Revelation characterize Jesus Christ?

  7. Explain the tension between the slain Lamb and the rider on the white horse.

  8. What is an externalization of evil?

Suggestions for Alternative Reading and Reflection

  1. Do Revelation's symbols refer to an external reality? If so, is that reality past or future?

  2. Compare Revelation to apocalyptic generally.

  3. Compare Revelation to Paul's letters and Mark.

  4. What would a historical-critic or a literary-critic say about the futurist interpretation of Revelation?

  5. How is the notion that God is love in tension with Revelation?

  6. What is the basic bipolar tension resolved by Revelation?

  7. Offer a deconstructive reading of Revelation.

  8. Critique Revelation's depiction of evil.

  9. Name popular stories or movies which resemble Revelation.

For Further Reading

For apocalyptic bibliography, see chap. 15. In addition, see A. Y. Collins, Early; and Minear, Apocalyptic.

For an introductory overview of interpretation, see Pilch; Efird, Daniel; and Clouse. For more advanced commentaries, see Summers; and Caird, Revelation.

On Revelation's symbols, see Barr, "Symbolic."

On Revelation's cultural setting, see Collins, <u>Crisis</u>; and Schuessler Fiorenza, <u>Revelation</u>.

On Rome and the Christians, see Frend; and Wilken, <u>Christians</u>.

CHAPTER 24

THE CONTINUING BIBLE
The Relevance and Truth of the Bible

The Relevance of the Bible

As an ancient myth, **the Bible is in "decay"** in the modern West.

First, it **no longer provides the world-view** by which individuals understand and interpret life. For pre-modern Westerners, the Bible actually provided the "story" in which individuals lived [see Frei]. Individuals literally lived after the Gospel and before the Apocalypse. Further, the Bible was an unchallenged authority in whatever area it spoke (science, history, and so forth).

Modernity destroyed this "story" both intellectually and socially. The "will-to-believe," to accept the traditional authority, was gradually replaced by the "**will-to-truth**," as truth was humanly perceived (science) and deduced (philosophy) [see Harvey, 38-42; Krentz, 10-16]. Not surprisingly, then, other stories (myths) now provide the overarching narratives within which individuals locate themselves and with which they interpret the world [see figure 1].

Second, the Bible **no longer provides the "social glue"** for society. Biblical mythic identities and rituals no longer locate individuals in the larger community, nor do they ameliorate social tensions. The demise of the Bible as the West's social charter has left the West somewhat adrift, for the modern replacement myths lack transcendence and universal appeal. Compared to the biblical myth, they are shallow, failing to transport humans beyond themselves, and narrow, failing to connect humans with one another.

Figure 1: **Modern Myths**

According to Lyotard, there are two modern myths, the liberation of humanity and the speculative unity of all knowledge. One might state these stories more concisely as **individualism and rationalism** or as one of their many corollaries:

Individualism	**Rationalism**
Freedom	Science
Rise of Middle Class	History
Liberalism	Unity of Knowledge
Subjectivism	Urbanization
Pluralism	Industrialization
Egalitarianism	Bureaucracy

Modern humans consider individualism and rationalism **self-evident goods**. Such evaluation indicates, of course, their mythic status. Not surprisingly, post-modernism challenges these mythic values.

As a result, humans are left with **private religious experiences** and beliefs. Anyone can believe anything she likes as long as it does not effect society. Such a religion, of course, is a denuded, emasculated affair of little mythic and social consequence. Further, society becomes largely an affair of **mutual alienation** [see Bellah, Habits]. At its worst, society is a collage of competing tribal groups, virulent natural religions brought violently together in and by the modern, pluralistic world.

Third, and perhaps most importantly, the Bible no longer provides the **vehicle to the sacred**. Modern individuals do not find the Bible the pathway to power and meaning. For these ends, they pursue reason, science, technology, individual freedom, political power, materialism, and so forth.

Figure 2: **The American Myth**

The American myth is a virulent form of the modern myth. It **intensifies individualism** with emphases on the new and on equality. The emphasis on **the new** tends to value youth, innocence, revolution, independence, change, and progress. It is also one of the foundations of modern consumerism. All these values are supported and transmitted by major American institutions (e.g., the mass media, corporations, politics, education, and psychotherapy).

Anyone could decipher the American myth by asking questions about **American assumptions** regarding value (meaning), purpose, and power: Where do Americans find power and meaning? What do they consider the good life? How do they obtain it? What institutions support or hinder these values and goals?

In sum, the Bible is an alien myth in the modern West. Once the triumphant, subliminal master-story of the West, it has given way to new world-views, social charters, and vehicles to the sacred. Nevertheless, the Bible remains in modernity as the founding myth of sub-communities, as aesthetic and ethic debris in Western culture, and as an alternative imagination.

Sub-communities, communities existing within the larger modern Western community, continue to claim the Bible as their founding myth. Their existence within the modern West and their actual use of the Bible, however, demonstrate a rationalization of the biblical myth in light of modernity. That is, they adapt and interpret the Bible in light of their larger cultural location.

Thus, fundamentalists, despite their allegiance to the inerrant

Thus, fundamentalists, despite their allegiance to the inerrant Word of God, read that word in light of and in defense of nineteenth-century Protestant America. Likewise, academics who read and study the Bible as myth and as ANET invariably read the Bible from the standpoint of the modern academic myth. To claim the Bible's relevance, they invariably *demythologize* the Bible and re-mythologize it in light of their own myth (e.g., liberalism or existentialism).

This new cultural determination typically results in a selective, piecemeal use of the Bible. The Bible is no longer the founding myth or the subliminal myth, even for religious sub-communities. Rather, it is used selectively as a warrant for an argument. That is, the Bible becomes a **rhetorical device**.

Figure 3: **The History of Myths**

According to Richard Moore, myths have three-stage lives [19-21]. In the first or **compelling** stage, a new myth captivates an audience with a liberating message. The dispossessed and disenchanted flock to it (e.g., Christianity in its first centuries). If it emerges as the triumphant myth of a society, it enters the second or **subliminal** stage. It becomes the acknowledged, unspoken way of looking at the world. It becomes the establishment (e.g., Medieval Christianity). If a new compelling myth arises, the old subliminal myth decays. If it survives at all, it does so by entering the third or **rationalized** stage. It adapts to the new subliminal myth (e.g., post-Enlightenment Christianity). It is at the mercy of more powerful myths which set the rules for the game. The Bible, of course, is in such a situation today with modernity's individualism (egalitarianism) and rationalism (science).

This use testifies to the Bible's continuing appeal in culture.

There, the Bible continues as **mythic debris**. Its citation in political campaigns and in social debates about abortion and other matters demonstrates the Bible's continuing power as **ethical lodestar**. People, for example, still revere the Ten Commandments even if they cannot cite them or keep them.

Further, biblical symbols (Adam, Christ) and patterns (quest, deliverance, Christ-figures, etc.) remain as **aesthetic** (and religious) **fodder** for new artistic creations in both literature and film. Artist after artist struggles with modern identity and theodicy using biblical symbols (e.g., Moby Dick) and patterns (e.g., One Flew Over the Cuckoo's Nest).

In short, the Bible remains relevant in the West because the West dimly remembers the Bible as one of its historical roots.

Finally, quite ironically, the alien Bible has an **educational relevance**. At the very least, acquaintance with the Bible can inform moderns of the nature and limitations of their own cultural myths. As struggling with a foreign language casts a native grammar into relief, wrestling with the alien Bible **illumines the modern world-view**.

Beyond such illuminations lie revelatory possibilities. The Bible is to modernity a **revelation from afar**. It speaks, if not directly from God, at least from another culture.

In short, the Bible demythologizes modern culture by providing it with a critical interlocutor. Such dialogue may promise liberation from cultural captivity and from blinding ethnocentrism. By offering modern culture an **alternative imagination**, the Bible subversively "keeps the present provisional and refuses to absolutize it" [Brueggemann, Prophetic, 45]. Even in such limited transcendence lies the possibility for moderns to confront their own age critically while retaining their capacity for laughter and play [Berger, Rumor, 96].

> Figure 4: **Conceptions of Truth**
>
> Philosophical discussions usually include three different conceptions of truth. The **correspondence** view holds that a statement is true if it agrees with observed reality. This notion dominates the scientific method. The **coherence** view finds a statement true if it agrees with other statements already known to be true. This conception is important in mathematics. If neither of the former views of truth is decisive, the **pragmatic** view holds a statement to be true if the statement proves to be useful or productive.

The Truth of the Bible

The combination of the Bible's status as ancient myth and its continuance raises the question of its truth. Truth refers to statements' conformity to reality/actuality or their adherence to a standard. That is, truth is a human judgment. That judgment is invariably dependent upon a particular perspective. Put bluntly, **truth is myth dependent**. The question of the Bible's truth depends upon the myth in place in a given community.

In the communities which created the Bible, the question of the Bible's truth did not arise. The Bible (or some part of it) was the truth which created the communities. It was the standard of truth, not subject to truth-evaluation.

Sects, of course, have more difficulty maintaining this position than do *natural religions*. Sects, by definition, cherish a truth which exists in an antagonistic relationship with the larger community. Sectarian truth is always under attack and defense. The Bible is in just this rationalized, defensive situation in its sub-communities today whether those sub-communities be committed to inerrancy or to demythologizing.

In modernity at large, the question of the Bible's truth is even more extreme. Secular, pluralistic, and individualistic modernity can hardly consider the sacred, exclusive, authoritarian Bible truth without denying itself. In fact, given this mythic conflict, the continued use of the Bible by modern religious sub-communities borders on the miraculous. Of course, its continuance is partly the result of powerful institutions still accepted in modernity (e.g., the church and the academy).

Ironically, however, **modern pluralism leaves a place for the Bible**. Despite its secularity, modernity tolerates, while it does not value, religious experience. The proto-typical modern response, then, to the question of the truth of the Bible is that it is a **personal matter**. Individuals decide for themselves whether or not the Bible is true. While this is an extremely popular position, its potential for solipsism is palpable.

Myth-ritual communities avoid such solipsism by creating **communities of like-minded people**. In those cases, the communities' declarations of the Bible's truth become descriptions of the communities, rather than of the Bible.

The academy avoids solipsism by critically treating the Bible in light of other cultures, religions, and myths (including its own). The academy presumes a limited relevance for the Bible as part of the West's cultural foundation and as aesthetic, ethical debris. Likewise, the academy awards the Bible a limited truth status by continuing to engage it as a field for **cultural enhancement** and as an enduring, **transcultural wisdom** in the perennial human questions.

If the academy wishes to pursue the question of the Bible's truth more rigorously, it must do so in discussions of the truth of religious language or of foundational assumptions. Reasoned discourse on the latter results in judgments about the truth of myth/Bible in a fashion similar to philosophy's discussion of the truth of rival metaphysics or science's discussion of the truth of rival theories. Thus, a scholar chooses a myth/metaphysic/theory among rivals by choosing the one which is coherent, comprehensive, explanatory, fruitful, and so forth. In short, a scholar chooses a myth which is true to and creative of her individual and social experience.

Figure 5: **Truth and Religious Language**

Some twentieth-century philosophers have rejected the discussion of the truth of religious language as a dead end. They hold that religious language is **not subject to falsification** (and, therefore, not true). For these thinkers, religious language is **only emotive or expressive**. It may be meaningful as ethical prescription and so forth. Others, however, argue that religious language does make truth claims which will **someday be empirically verifiable**. At the "end," religious claims will be either true or false [so Hick]. For others, while religious language is not always subject to empirical validation, it is **capable of rational evaluation** [so Barbour]. Such evaluation extends beyond correspondence and coherence to pragmatic notions of truth. In fact, it questions the complacency and the lack of mythic sophistication of the correspondence and coherence theories.

The academy avoids solipsism here through **reasoned debate**. That is, in terms of biblical truth, the academy can offer only reasoned discussion. Honesty should require the academy to admit, however, that this is merely to take refuge in the academy's myth of reason and tolerance.

If reason, like truth, advances from a mythic starting-point, the crucial question becomes mythic (and self-) evaluation. Whether or not this is an attainable goal is an intriguing question. Some have argued nihilistically that it is simply the vanity of the academic myth (the quest for self-knowledge) to think so.

Certainly, as humans are mythic (cultural) creatures, their foundational assumptions are partly determined by their culture. Even prophets and madmen are more like their culture-fellows than the alien. The myth in which a human lives is a social, not merely an individual, affair. As a result, even individualistic moderns have myths which they can **only minutely adapt**. For example, they may vary the modern myth in light of religious faith or commitment to the liberal arts. Even such tinkering, however, has to do with allegiances to significant sub-communities (the church, academy).

Such mythic tinkering depends upon new social alignments or upon severe experiences of dislocation and evil. After all, mythic theodicies tend to be quite effective and elastic. Only when theodicies fail is there conversion to another myth. In sum, only **those moderns disenchanted with modernity** to some degree will look for or find truth in the Bible.

Reflection Questions

1. How is the Bible irrelevant to the modern West? How is it relevant to sects and to culture as a whole?

2. Give examples of the continuance of the Bible in recent art, literature, and cinema.

3. Give examples of the Bible's rhetorical use in contemporary ethical, political, and religious debate.

4. Does the Bible offer anything constructive or destructive to the modern West?

5. How can one avoid solipsism on the question of the Bible's truth?

6. Describe the modern, American, and academic myth. Critique the myth of the academy.

7. Why do humans change their myths?

For Further Reading

On the relevance of the Bible, see Bultmann, "Mythology";

Carroll; Kelsey; Frei; and Nineham.

On the Bible as a demythologizing presence in modernity, see Schniedau; Crossan, <u>Dark</u>; and Girard, <u>Scapegoat</u>.

On modern myths, see Lyotard; R. May; J. Robertson; Bellah, <u>Habits</u>.

On truth and religious language, see Hick, 68-96; and Frazier, 273-340. On truth and myth, see Barbour.

APPENDIX 1

A READING GUIDE TO THE PROPHETS

A History of Israel's Prophetic Tradition
[cf. Blenkinsopp, History]

1) Although the beginnings of Israelite prophecy are no longer recoverable, Israel's traditions depict **Moses as the founding prophet** (e.g., Deut 18:15-18).

2) Early Israelite prophets were **war prophets** who blessed their own nation and cursed the enemy (cf. Balaam, Num 22-24; the war prophets of Joshua and Judges).

3) Later, the prophets were important **cultic officials** leading communities to confession, penitence, thanksgiving, and assurance and providing responses to questions concerning cultic purity and so forth (e.g., Isa 1:10-17; Am 5:21-27; Zech 7:1-7; Mal).

4) When the monarchy began, prophecy was **closely connected with the king** (cf. 1 Sam 9:9; Samuel; etc.).

5) Tradition remembers the prophets, however, primarily as **charismatic critics of cult, court, school, and prophecy** itself. Thus, the prophets are often associated with Rechabites (Jer 35) and nazirites (Am 2:11), both of whom had lifestyles rejecting Canaanite customs (Num 6:1-21; 2 Kings 10:15-28). The Elijah and Elisha stories in 1-2 Kings indicate the conservative nature of Israelite prophecy (rejecting Canaanite religion and politics).

6) The **classical prophets** (essentially the Latter Prophets) date from the Assyrian and Babylonian crises (8th - 6th cent.). Amos, Hosea, Micah, and Isaiah responded to the Assyrian crisis (8th cent.). Zephaniah, Nahum, Habakkuk, and Jeremiah spoke during Babylon's hegemony (late 7th and 6th cent.). Ezekiel, Obadiah, and Second Isaiah were exilic prophets.

7) During the exile, **the Deuteronomists** provided a rationale for earlier prophets by seeing them as unheeded prophets whose lack of

hearing led to the exile. They may also have published a prophetic corpus, possibly including Amos, Hosea, Isaiah, Micah, Zephaniah, and Jeremiah. They may even be responsible for the salvation through judgment pattern.

8) In the restoration period, prophecy was reabsorbed into the cult (Haggai, Malachi, Joel), became the property of sectarian groups (Third Isaiah), and was itself criticized (Jonah; Zech 13:2-6).

9) Finally, **textualization** made prophecy a thing of the past. For these scribal groups, interpretation of texts (not new oracles) was the pathway to divine knowledge.

Reading Guide to Isaiah

First Isaiah (1-39) accuses Judah of social injustice (cf. Amos) and predicts her military destruction. Despite external aggression, Isaiah calls Judean kings--Ahaz and Hezekiah--to **faith**, to dependence upon God, rather than political-military alliances. This audacious advice depends upon Isaiah's vision of God's overpowering holiness ("**the Holy One** of Israel"). Lacking faith, Judah will go into Assyrian exile. In that event, God will bring a purified **remnant** back to the land.

Key passages: 6-7; 9:2-7; 11:1-8; 28-31

Outline
1. Judgment oracles against Judah (1-12)
2. Foreign nation oracles (13-23)
3. Isaiah apocalypse (24-27)
4. Judgment (28-31) and salvation oracles (32-35)
5. Story of Jerusalem's deliverance from Assyria and prediction of her coming destruction by Babylon (36-39)

Reading Notes
1. Note the salvation through judgment pattern (1-12; 13-23; 24-27).
2. Isaiah 6-11 presents in a condensed form Isaiah's key symbols (cf. 28-31).

3. Isaiah 35-39 anticipates the symbols of Second Isaiah and facilitates the transition from Isaiah's unfulfilled prediction of Assyrian exile/return to the rude fact of Babylonian exile/return.

Second Isaiah comforts the exiles with predictions of a **new exodus**. The incomparable **Creator** has appointed Cyrus as Babylon's destroyer. Israel, **the servant**, will reveal God to the nations as the Lord, the God of the whole earth.
Key passages: 40; 42; 48-49; 53; 55

Outline
1. The return from exile (40-48)
2. The Servant and the nations (49-55)

Reading Notes
1. Isaiah 40-48 opens with preparation for God's coming (40:1-11) and closes with God's call for the people to leave Babylon (48:17-21). The section states God's incomparable power (40-44), appoints Cyrus as the people's deliverer (44:24-45:13), highlights Babylon's vanity and useless idols (46-47), and predicts God's new exodus (48).
2. Isaiah 49-55 depicts God's relation to the nations through the servant. Readers see the servant variously as Cyrus, Israel, a remnant, or the prophet himself (see the so-called "servant songs," 42:1-4; 49:1-6; 50:4-11; 52:12-53:12; outside these songs, the servant is more clearly Israel). Both the servant and Israel suffer and are vindicated before the nations. Importantly, the servant's fate accomplishes good for others (e.g., 42:5-9; 49:6-12; 53:4-12). Not surprisingly, early Christians saw the servant as a prophecy of Jesus.
3. Note that Second Isaiah concludes with cultic assurance (54-55).

Third Isaiah (56-66) attributes the failure of the glorious hopes of Isa 40-55 to the people's sins and calls the community to proper living--**sabbath observance**, fasting, social justice--and to **repentance** that God might act.
Key passages: 56:1-8; 59; 61; 65

Outline
1. Call to repentance and Zion's exaltation (56-62)
2. Hymns and concluding comments (63-66)

Reading Notes
1. The work has an obvious cultic flavor. Various cultic instructions (56-58) and a call to repentance (59) culminate in **Zion's exaltation** (60-62). Then, a cry for God's help (63-64) similarly leads to a section on the exaltation of Zion (65-66).
2. In 65-66, God's servants are repentant (57:14-21; 59), humble, mourners (57:18), tremblers, and those hated by their own people (66:2, 5).

Reading Guide to Jeremiah

Jeremiah predicts Babylon's destruction of Judah because she is apostate and has **failed to heed the prophets**. Not surprisingly, his audience does not accept his message gratefully, and **Jeremiah suffers for his words**.
Key passages: 1; 7; 21-22; 25-29; 30-31; 44

Outline
1. Judgment oracles on Jerusalem and Judah (1-25)
2. Biographical narratives (26-45, 52)
3. Foreign nation oracles (46-51)

Reading Notes
1. Jeremiah 1 (and 25) anticipate Jeremiah's major themes. Thus, according to Jer 1, Jeremiah is called as a prophet to the nations (cf. 25:12-38; 46-51), is reluctant (cf. the laments), is both a destroyer (cf. judgment oracles) and a planter (cf. 30-33; 50-51), predicts destruction from the north (cf. 25:8-11; 4-6; 20-22; 25-29; 37-38), condemns Judah's apostasy (cf. 25:5-7; 2-3; 5-7; 11), and suffers (cf. 25:3-8; the "passion narrative").
2. Salvation oracles are infrequent (though see 23:1-8; 30-33; 50-51). The Book of Consolation (30-31) does, however, predict the

reversal of previous judgments so that the exiled return. God, then, sets up a **new, everlasting covenant** with his people.

3. Much of Jeremiah is a third-person narrative about Jeremiah. Poetic oracles dominate only in 1-10; 30-31; 46-51. This approach makes **Jeremiah himself the message**. He is the **emblematic rejected prophet** (particularly 7:25-28; 25:1-7; cf. 2 Kings 17) whose sufferings authenticate his message. The famous **laments** (11:18-12:6; 15:10-21; 17:14-18; 18:18-23; 20:7-18) express his alienation from his fellows and his God who is to him a "deceitful brook" and a "terror."

4. His people plot his death (11:18-12:6), imprison him (20:1-6; 32-33), reject his message (25-36), treat him as a traitor (37-38), and carry him unwillingly to Egypt (42-44). Jeremiah's audience treats him so because Jeremiah rejects Judah's **natural religion** and its institutions, the temple (7; 26), the covenant (11), the kings (21-23), and cult prophets (27-28).

5. Jeremiah's story ends with an inversion of the Hexateuch story. The people return to Egypt and reject God (44).

Reading Guide to Ezekiel

Ezekiel describes God's coming destruction of Judah and her temple for religious abominations. Later, God's glory reanimates the people and **the temple**.

Key passages: 1-3; 8-10; 18; 20; 37; 43; 47

Outline
1. Judgment oracles against Jerusalem (1-24)
2. Foreign nation oracles (25-32)
3. Restored kingdom and temple oracles (33-48)

Reading Notes
1. Vision reports structure the book as a story of the departure and return of God's glory. God's concern for his glory (honor) also leads to judgment and to salvation (20:41; 36:21-23; 38:16, 23; 39:7-8).

a. In an introductory vision of God's **throne/chariot glory** in

Babylon (1-3), God commissions Ezekiel to prophesy to a rebellious people.

    b. Ezekiel has a vision of the temple's abominations and destruction (8-11). Ominously, the **glory departs** the temple.

    c. Ezekiel has a vision of God's reanimation of Israel from a "valley of dry bones" (37) and a vision of the restored temple to which God's **glory returns** (40-48).

  2. Ezekiel is a "maker of allegories" (20:49) castigating the people for their rebellious history (16; 20; 23) and is prone to dramatic symbolic acts which give concreteness to his message (e.g., 4; 5; 12; 24:15-27).

Reading Guide to Hosea

    Hosea understood his **marriage to an adulterous woman** as a symbol of God's relationship with Israel who committed apostasy by worshiping Baal. As a result, God will forswear his disloyal people and leave her to the Assyrians. God's long-suffering love, however, will eventually restore the people through a **new exodus** from their new Egypt (i.e., Assyria).

    Key passages: 2; 6:6; 11

Outline
  1. Symbolic story of Hosea's marriage (1-3)
  2. Oscillating judgment and salvation oracles (3-14)

Reading Notes
  1. Hosea's marriage (1-3) is the basis for the judgment-salvation oracles which follow it (4-14).

  2. Hosea oscillates between judgment (1:2-8; 2:1-13; 3:1-11:7; 12-13) and salvation (1:10-11; 2:14-23; 11:8-11; 14), rather than presenting a salvation through judgment structure.

Reading Guide to Joel

Joel interprets a **locust plague** as God's judgment. A **national fast** will bring a deliverance which is depicted in terms of God's **apocalyptic exaltation of Zion**. The book is cultic. Calls to repent or to fast (1:8-20; 2:12-17) follow the descriptions of the plague (1:2-7; 2:1-11) and elicit God's deliverance (2:18-27 (or 3:21?)).

Key passages: 2:12-29

Outline
1. Locust plague as an occasion for repentance (1:2-2:27)
2. **Day of Yahweh** as exaltation of Zion (2:28-3:21)

Reading Guide to Amos

Amos describes **God's coming holy war against Israel for her sins of social injustice**. Amos laments an Israel already dead.

Key passages: 2:6-3:2; 5 (particularly 5:18-24)

Outline
1. Foreign nation oracles (1-2)
2. Judgment oracles on Israel (3-6)
3. Five judgment visions (7-9)

Reading Notes
1. Amos uses a **rhetoric of reversal**. Thus, its foreign nation oracles play the typical cursing the enemy game until Israel herself becomes God's enemy (2:6-16; cf. 4:12; 5:17; 7:8; 8:2; 9:1-4). This reversal sets the tone for others (cf. 3:1-2; 5:18-20; 9:7).
2. Amos' visions justify the **doom-message** (cf. 7:7-9 with 7:1-6).

Reading Guide to Obadiah

As Edom had assisted the Babylonian destruction of

Jerusalem, the **holy war prophecy** of Obadiah gleefully anticipates **Edom's destruction**. Interestingly, Obadiah takes pains to justify Edom's judgment as the result of her atrocities (3-4, 10-15).

Outline
1. God calls nations to destroy Edom (1-16)
2. Zion is exalted over Edom (17-21)

Reading Guide to Jonah

Jonah is a story about a **reluctant prophet** who does not wish to offer hated Assyria an opportunity to repent. Unable to avoid his commission, he **sulks when Nineveh repents**. He is angry with **God's mercy**.

Key passage: 3:6-4:11

Outline
1. Rejection of the divine commission (1:1-3)
2. Divine judgment (1:4-17)
3. Repentance and deliverance (2)
4. Second commission and reluctant obedience (3:1-4)
5. Nineveh's repentance and deliverance (3:5-10)
6. God's justification of mercy (4)

Reading Notes
1. Jonah has two repentance-deliverance stories, that of Jonah (2) and that of Nineveh (3:5-10). Ironically, the prophet, not Nineveh, requires persuasion.

2. The story climaxes with God's attempts to justify his repentance (3:9-10). After all, grace requires as much justification as evil does. The story mocks those who would accept mercy but not allow it to others. Such a story is easily read as a critique of Israelite nationalism or as a critique of prophetic pretensions to control God. Neither Israel nor prophet controls the divine sovereign.

Reading Guide to Micah

Micah criticizes Samaria and Jerusalem for **oppressing the poor** and predicts their military destruction.

Key passages: 3:1-3, 9-12; 6:6-8

Outline
1. Judgment oracles on Samaria and Jerusalem (1-3)
2. Glorious **exaltation of Zion and David** (4-5)
3. God's controversy with Israel/Judah (6:1-7:7)
4. Cultic prayer for forgiveness/vindication (7:8-20)

Reading Notes
1. Micah oscillates between judgment (1:2-2:11; 3:1-12; 6:1-7:7) and salvation (2:12-13; 4-5; 7:8-20).

2. The oscillation makes judgment the birth-pangs of salvation (4:9-5:15). The enemy's triumph will reverse on him (7:8-9). The reversal turns on a **deus ex machina**, an unlikely hero who comes from Bethlehem, not Jerusalem (5:2-6).

3. Micah 6:6-8 is a classic summary of the ethical concerns of the prophets and of the major themes of the eighth century prophets (justice, Amos; love kindness, Hosea; and walk humbly, Isaiah).

Reading Guide to Nahum

Nahum **celebrates the coming destruction of Nineveh**, the capital of Assyria (612 BCE), as God's just judgment of a wicked, bloody nation. This foreign nation oracle "comforts" (cf. the meaning of Nahum) God's people.

Key passages: 1; 2:8; 3:18-19

Outline
1. The coming of the Divine Warrior (1:1-14)
2. God's arrival and Nineveh's destruction (1:15-2:13)
3. Taunt song over Nineveh (3)

Reading Note
1.   Nahum's structure reflects a ritual setting with an opening processional (1:2-8) and address to the relevant parties (1:9-14), with a ritual curse liturgically enacting the war (1:15-2:13), and with a concluding celebration taunting Nineveh (3).

Reading Guide to Habakkuk

Habakkuk struggles with **God's justice** in the face of the rise of the evil Babylonian (the Chaldeans) empire (605 BCE). He learns that God's ways are **beyond human ken** and that God expects his people to **await his deliverance faithfully**.
Key passages: 1:2-4, 13; 2:2-4

Outline
1.   Dialogue on divine justice (1:2-2:5)
2.   Five woes on a wicked nation (2:6-20)
3. Thanksgiving hymn celebrating God's deliverance (3)

Reading Notes
1.   Habakkuk's dialogue about the divine justice provides divine responses to prophetic questions.
   a.   Prophetic question (1:2-4) and divine response (1:5-11).
   b.   Prophetic question (1:12-17) and divine response (2:2b-5).
2. Habakkuk 2-3 also responds to the question of divine justice with the traditional judgment of the nations (2) and salvation of Judah (3).
   3.   Like a lament, Habakkuk's complaints give way to praise (3).

Reading Guide to Zephaniah

Zephaniah condemns Judah's **religious syncretism** and adoption of foreign customs (the practices of Manasseh and Amon). He asserts that the **Day of Yahweh** will destroy Judah with the nations. Only the **humble** and the repentant will escape.
Key passages: 1:2-2:3; 3:11-13

Outline
1. **Day of Yahweh** as universal judgment (1)
2. **Day of Yahweh** as day of judgment for foreign nations and of salvation for humble (2)
3. Judgment of Jerusalem and salvation of humble (3)

Reading Notes
1. Zephaniah oscillates judgment (1:2-18; 3:1-7) with salvation for the humble (2:1-15; 3:8-20).
2. Zephaniah climaxes with a celebration of God's enthronement. Zephaniah functions as **a cultic call to humility**, including a confession of sin, a waiting on God, and a praise of God.

Reading Guide to Haggai

Haggai, **campaigning for a rebuilt temple**, links that event with God's exaltation of Zion and of **Zerubbabel as Davidic king**. **Key passages**: 1:3-10; 2:20-23

Outline
1. Rebuilding the temple (1)
2. The temple and God's age of prosperity (2)

Reading Guide to Zechariah

Zechariah adds detailed **visions of God's cosmic, universal upheaval** establishing a new priestly age to the campaign for **rebuilding the temple**. **Key passages**: 1:1-6; 7-8

Outline
1. Previous judgments, the temple, and future salvation (1:1-7; 6:9-8:23)
2. Eight night visions (1:8-6:8)
3. Two independent, later salvation oracles (9-11; 12-14)

Reading Notes
1. Zechariah has two independent sections (1-8; 9-14).

2. The **night visions** are the crux of part one. They follow a common **apocalyptic** pattern of vision, question, and angelic explanation. They also depict the typical pattern of the judgment of the nations and the exaltation of Zion.

3. Part two describes the nations' judgment and Zion's exaltation even more apocalyptically (9-10; 12; 14). This section also includes material reflecting intra-community conflict between wicked and suffering **shepherds** (11; 12:10-14; 13). "Shepherd" bears several significations (cf. 10:2-3; 11:4-17; 13:7-9). If there is a progression, it is from wicked shepherds, through rejected/suffering shepherds, to God as shepherd (king in 14:9).

Reading Guide to Malachi

Malachi condemns the **corrupt worship** in the second temple. People and priest cheat God of proper sacrifices and tithes. Proper ritual would lead to blessing, so Malachi calls the people to prepare for God's coming.

Key passages: 1:6-14; 3-4

Outline
1. God's love for Israel (1:1-5)
2. Judgment on tainted worship (1:6-2:16)
3. Coming of the Judge (2:17-4:3)
4. Closing notes (4:4-6)

Reading Notes
1. Malachi responds to the queries of hypothetical opponents.
   a. Query (1:2) and response (1:2-5)
   b. Query (1:6) and response (1:7)
   c. Query (1:7) and response (1:7-14)
   d. Query (2:14) and response (2:14-16)
   e. Query (2:17) and response (2:17)
   f. Query (3:7) and response (3:8-12)

g. Query (3:13) and response (3:14)

2. To that basic structure, Malachi adds a condemnation of the priests (2:1-9), a plea to repent before the divine coming (3:1-7), and a section describing the coming of God who brings life and death (3:16-4:3).

3. Malachi 2:17-4:3 fittingly concludes the prophets. The prophets are God's messengers preparing his coming (3:1-2). Two appendices emphasize the prophets' Mosaic heritage (4:4) and continuing tradition (4:5-6).

APPENDIX 2

A READING GUIDE TO THE LETTERS

Reading Guide to Romans

Many consider Romans the classic statement of **Paul's gospel**. As Romans is a request to a non-Pauline church for support for a new Western mission (15:14-33), it offers an introduction to Paul and his gospel (1:1-17). Written in the style of a diatribe, Paul engages an **imaginary Jewish opponent in mock dialogue**. Paul strives to demonstrate that the new apocalypse of **God's righteousness** in Christ is compatible with God's previous acts with Israel. Not surprisingly, this argument involves Paul repeatedly in the fundamental NT irony of life-through-death (3:21-26; 5; 6:1-4) and in the ironic depiction of God as **the justifier of the ungodly** (3:26; 4:5).

Key passages: 1:16-17; 3:21-26; 5:12-21; 8; 11:11-36

Outline: The Revelation of God's Righteousness
1. In Wrath (1:18-3:20)
2. In Christ (3:21-8:39)
3. With Israel (9-11)

Reading Notes
1. In terms of formal letter structure, Romans has an unusually long salutation (1:1-7) and closing greetings (16:1-23). Both are appropriate for Romans as a letter of introduction. Further, Romans is an excellent example of a letter with an exhortation at the body's close (12:1-15:13).
2. Romans' unifying motif is God's righteousness (1:16-17). The motif's pervasiveness is somewhat obscured by the fact that English lacks a verb form to match the adjective "righteous." As a result, English translations use various words ("just, righteous, justify,

justice, and righteousness") to translate Greek words from the **dikaiein** root.

3. Romans has **three major movements**. Movement one (1:18-3:20) sets out the conflict between God's righteousness and human sinfulness. Movement two (3:21-8:39) depicts God's apocalyptic resolution of that problem begun at the cross. Movement three reconciles God's apocalyptic (in Christ) and historical (with Israel) righteousness.

4. Paul's myth as set out in Romans is replete with irony (e.g., God the justifier of the unjust; life-through-death). Put differently, Paul's myth is characterized by **dramatic reversals** (e.g., cross, then resurrection; death, then life; baptism, then glorification; sufferings, then glory; Israel's judgment, then salvation).

5. These reversals issue from the divine freedom. Paul's emphasis on the divine sovereignty is evident in his themes of revelation, election (3:1-8; 9:6-29), grace, and faith. The abrupt transition escapes language. Romans symbolizes it with justification, redemption, atonement, and reconciliation.

6. Movement two is Paul's composite attempt at sketching the transition from beginning (cross, baptism) to end (adoption, glorification). This movement is Paul's apocalyptic age to come which is "already, but not yet." Put differently, movement two depicts the life "in Christ" which Paul describes as freedom from sin, wrath, the law, and death (the perils of movement one).

7. Movement three, Paul's ironic view of Israel's future history (9-11), is similar to the Deuteronomic previews of judgment, exile, and salvation (e.g., Deut 29-30; 1 Kings 8).

Reading Guide to 1 Corinthians

Here, Paul the pastor offers spiritual advice on a host of problems including factions, immorality, sex and marriage, food regulations, worship order, spiritual gifts, the resurrection of the body, and so forth. Some scholars think that these problems are merely symptoms of the underlying problem of **spiritual enthusiasm or pride**. In short, the Corinthians have inflated opinions of themselves. Paul counters this pride with his **ironic gospel** of the God of grace who brought all good gifts through the weakness and folly of the cross. The ethical corollary of this theology is love or concern for the brother and the community's edification.   For Paul, **grace/faith/love** is the opposite of pride (boasting, self-glorification).

Key passages: 1:18-2:16; 4:7-13; 10:23-11:1; 12-13; 15

Outline
1. Paul's Ironic Gospel vs. Spiritual Pride (1-4)
2. Applying the Gospel to Particular Problems (5-15)
   A. Social Responsibility (Decorum and Love) (5-10)
   B. Worship Decorum (Community Edification) (11-14)
   C. The Consummation (15)

Reading Notes
1.   First Corinthians 1-4 (with review in 8-14) combats the Corinthians' spiritual pride by reviewing the ironic gospel (1:18-25) of grace (4:7) and Paul's lowly apostolic style (2:1-4). Their spiritual pride simply does not match their father's life (4:8-21). More pointedly, Paul wonders how they can be so proud given their lowly beginnings (1:26-31) and their spiritual ignorance, made obvious in their prideful factions (3:1-4).

2.   First Corinthians 5-15 (and 16:1-4) applies the gospel of grace/faith to a multitude of specific problems. Beginning with 7:1, the problems seem to be matters on which the Corinthians have requested advice (see the repeated "now concerning").   In the process, Paul demonstrates his **gospel's ethical corollary--love**. The "graced" should not jockey for hierarchical superiority.

3. Paul's handling of the specific problems also illustrates a rather **conservative concern for decorum**. It matters how the church appears to outsiders (e.g., 5-7). Given Paul's apocalyptic gospel, current social status is not terribly important (7). The concern for decorum is also evident in the section on worship (11-14) and motivates, at least, partly Paul's dicta on women, the Lord's supper, and spiritual gifts. Paul would have order!

4.   **Apocalyptic** balances Paul's social decorum (7).   The apocalyptic presuppositions with which Paul addresses Corinthian

problems is most evident in the famous chapter on the resurrection (15; cf. 6:14).

Reading Guide to 2 Corinthians

Second Corinthians is hard to read as a literary whole. **Notable breaks** occur at 2:14, 6:14, 7:2, 7:5, and 10:1. Further, three concerns dominate separate sections of the letter: reconciliation (1-7), the collection (8-9), and rebellion (10-13). As a result, many scholars read 2 Corinthians as a **composite** of several Pauline letters [see outline]. One historical reconstruction says that Paul dealt first with internal opposition at Corinth (2:14-6:13; 7:2-4). When this letter and a "painful visit" was unprofitable, "super-apostles" led the church further from Paul. Paul, then, sent a "harsh letter" (10-13) and Titus. En route to Macedonia, Paul met Titus with news of the church's reconciliation whereupon he wrote the letter of reconciliation (1:1-2:13; 7:5-16). Read as a canonical whole, 2 Corinthians now tells the story of the apostle's **successful recovery of an erring church**. The letter of reconciliation now provides the "title" under which the sordid tale is read.

Key Passages: 3:4-5:20; 11:16-12:10

Outline
1. A Letter of Reconciliation (1:1-2:13; 7:5-16)
2. A Defense of Paul's Apostleship (2:14-6:13; 7:2-4)
3. A Warning against Relationships with the Immoral (6:14-7:1)
4. Two notes on the Collection (8-9)
5. Harsh Letter to a Rebellious Church (10-13)

Reading Notes
1. In the letter of reconciliation (1:1-2:13; 7:5-16), there is an interplay between affliction and consolation as well as a historical review of the Corinthian "troubling" of Paul.
2. Paul defends his apostleship (2:14-6:13; 7:2-4) by arguing that God's glory is now revealed in the ministry of the new covenant in

such a way that it surpasses the glory of Moses (3:4-18). In a typical Pauline irony, that **glory is manifest in the gospel and in the apostle's sufferings** (4:1-5:20). The apostle's suffering ministry of reconciliation will ultimately usher in the new creation.

3. The collection notes (8-9) challenge the Corinthians to publicly commit to Paul and the gospel. Paul uses shame (8:1-7; 9:1-5), Jesus' example (8:8), a sense of justice (8:10-15), and proverbial wisdom (9:6-15) to encourage them.

4. The letter to the church in rebellion (10-13) combats the seductive appeal of the "super apostles" with the threat of an impending apostolic visit (10:1-11; 12:14-13:10), a reminder that the church belongs to Paul, a catalogue of his sacrifices for them (10:12-11:15; 12:11-21), and Paul's foolish boasting (11:16-12:10 or 12:13). Of course, Paul ironically boasts only in human weakness (12:10), so his boasting is a **catalogue of suffering** (11:23-28) and attaches human weakness even to the greatest revelations (12:1-10).

Reading Guide to Galatians

The Galatians' apostasy to another gospel (1:6-9) is the occasion for the letter. This other gospel entails circumcision. If 2:4, 2:12, and 1:7 all refer to the missionaries of this gospel, they are traveling Jewish Christians from Jerusalem, traditionally known as **the Judaizers**. In response, Paul defends his own divinely-originated gospel and apostleship and the **free sonship** which it has brought the Galatians. As a result, Galatians may be the classic statement of the biblical idea that divine sovereignty (grace) founds human freedom.

Key Passages: 1:6-17; 2:15-21; 3:23-4:7; 5:1, 13-26

Outline
1. Gospel History (1-2)
   A. Galatian Apostasy (1:6-10)
   B. Divine Origin of Paul's Gospel (1:11-17)
   C. Paul/Gospel Accepted, Then Rejected (1:18-2:14)
   D. Gospel Reiterated (2:15-21)

2. Experience and OT for the Gospel (3:1-5:1)
   A. Spirit-experience Proves Gospel (3:1-5)
   B. Abraham's Example Proves Gospel (3:6-18)
   C. The Law as Pedagogue (3:19-24)
   D. The Freedom of God's Sons (3:25-5:1)
3. The Freedom Ethic of Grace/Faith/Spirit (5:2-6:10)

Reading Notes

1. The recounting of the Galatian history proceeds in reverse order from apostasy (1:6-10) to gospel (2:15-21). In between, Paul offers his own experience which provides the true gospel order from grace/revelation to obedience (1:11-2:14). This story includes a typical biblical reversal (persecutor to evangelist) and a typical lonely prophet story (only Paul stands with the gospel unadulterated).

2. The statement of the gospel in 2:15-21 provides in a brief, difficult passage most of the Pauline terms (explained with greater care in Romans).

3. The argument for the gospel in 3:1-5:1 depends upon the Galatians' experience of the spirit, which makes them God's sons, and a rather tedious interpretation of OT passages. Paul's reading of Torah makes much of Abraham's faith preceding the law and the singular "seed" in Gen 12:7 (cf. Rom 4). Clearly, as 3:10-14 indicates, this interpretation is possible only after the apocalypse of Jesus Christ turns everything topsy-turvy. The extent of the disarray is evident in 4:21-31 where Jews become children of Hagar and Christians become children of Sarah.

4. The highpoint of the argument is clearly 3:23-4:7 where Paul asserts the **spirit-sonship available in Jesus Christ** (cf. Rom 8). The result, of course, is secondary status for the law (3:19-4:31; cf. Rom 7).

5. The fruits of the flesh/spirit suggest the two spheres of Rom. 5-8. The imperatives in this section indicate that the life of the spirit is only partially realized (already/not yet) and reject any antinomian interpretations of Paul's gospel (cf. 6:2)

Reading Guide to Ephesians

Despite numerous parallels to other Pauline letters (particularly to Colossians; cf. 4:1-2 with Col 3:12-13; 5:19-20 with Col 3:16-17; and 6:21-22 with Col 4:7-8), Ephesians seems to post-date Paul. The church is now a Gentile-Jewish unity (2), and the apostles and prophets are parallel mythic figures (3:5). In fact, Ephesians has little contact with a specific situation. This church, unlike other Pauline churches, is **the one universal church** (1:22; 3:10, 21; 5:24, 25, 27).

Key passage: 1:15-3:21

Outline
1. The Mystery of the Church's Unity (1:15-3:21)
   A. Prayer for Knowledge (1:15-23)
   B. Formation of Church Through Transformation and Reconciliation of Gentiles (2)
   C. Prayer for Knowledge (3)
2. Exhortation (4:1-6:20)
   A. Exhortation to Unity (4:1-16)
   B. Put-on, Put-off Exhortations (4:17-5:20; 6:10-20)
   C. Household Code (5:21-6:9)

Reading Notes
1. Prayers for enlightenment bookend the first major section (1:15-23; 3:14-21) and give to the whole a stately, liturgical character. The heart of the first section is the **mystery of the reconciliation of Gentiles and Jews** into God's one household/temple (2:19-22). The mystery, although only lately revealed to Paul (3:1-6), has always been God's eternal plan (1:3-14; 3:7-13).

2. Chapter 2 sets out the Gentiles' reconciliation in a stately "before-after" pattern comparable to Pauline reversal-stories. This reversal pattern and the initiation-into-mystery aura suggests a **baptismal liturgy** as do the "put on, put off" exhortations.

3. The vice-virtue lists (5:1-20) and the household code (5:21-6:9) indicate **a church at-home in the Hellenistic world**. The ethic is

little more than civilized decorum. The outstanding or **characteristic appeal is for unity** (4:1-16) which, along with baptism-mystery, provides the unifying motif of the letter.

Reading Guide to Philippians

Philippians is a lengthy Pauline **thank-you** to a Pauline community for its continued financial and personal (Epaphroditus) support of Paul and his mission (cf. Romans as a request for support). Paul's celebration with this enduring, successful church makes **joy the letter's dominant motif**. By contrast, the warning in 3:2-4:1 represents a notable change in tone. If it is not a tangent, it represents a letter fragment included here.

Key Passages: 1:12-26; 2:5-11

Outline
1. Shared Joy in the Gospel (1:3-26)
2. Exhortation to a Gospel Lifestyle (1:27-4:1)

Reading Notes
1. Paul measures his life by the gospel. As a result, he can have joy even while in prison (1:12-26; cf. 4:10-14) and counts other values as loss by comparison (3:4-16).

2. Paul also calls others to this gospel lifestyle or to the "**mind of Christ**." Thus, appeals to live worthy of the gospel (2:27-2:5; 2:12-18; 3:17-4:1) surround the positive examples of Jesus Christ (the famous hymn of 2:5-11) and Paul himself (3:4-16). In the midst of all of this is the negative example of the circumcizers (3:1-4). Both Christ and Paul are worthy of imitation (2:5; 3:17) because they incarnate the gospel-pattern of emptying/suffering, reversal, glorification.

4. Paul's amazing reversal of values in Christ (3:4-16) provides much of what is known about Paul's life (cf. also Gal 1:11-2:14; 2 Cor 11:16-12:13).

Reading Guide to Colossians

While Colossians is a **miniature version of Ephesians**, it differs notably. First, while Ephesians appeals for unity (4:1-16), Colossians demands allegiance to the tradition/faith in a time of heresy (2:6-20). Second, Colossians, unlike Ephesians, is clearly a genuine letter. It contains a typical Pauline thanksgiving (1:3-8) and closing greetings (4:7-17). It is, however, unusual in the Pauline corpus in that it is to a non-Pauline church (though cf. Romans). Many question the Pauline authorship of Colossians because of its Christology (cf. 1:15-20 with Phil 2:5-11) and its sacramental, baptismal ethic.

Key Passage: 1:15-3:4

Outline
1. Sufficiency of Christ (1:15-2:5)
2. Exhortation (2:6-4:1)
   A. Live According to Tradition, Not Heresy (2:6-20)
   B. Baptismal Exhortations (2:20-3:17)
   C. Household Code (3:18-4:1)

Reading Notes
1. Ephesians' mystery is the reconciliation of the Gentiles. By contrast, Colossians' mystery is "Christ in you" (1:25-2:3).
2. Colossians' major appeal is to maintain the faith versus a heresy which questions the **sufficiency (fullness) of Christ** and the fullness found by believers in him (2:8-10, 17-20; 3:4).

Reading Guide to 1 Thessalonians

First Thessalonians is a ritual-like **thanksgiving** (1-3) celebrating the faithfulness of a young church in the face of opposition and despite Paul's abrupt absence (1:6; 2:14; 3:3-4). The remainder of the letter exhorts the church to holy love (4:1-12) and to hope (4:13-5:11). Thus, the trinity in 1:3 (cf. 5:8) provides a rough outline of the letter.

Key Passage: 4:13-18

Outline
1. Thanksgiving for the Thessalonians' Faith (1-3)
2. Appeal for Holy Love (4:1-12)
3. Clarification of Hope (4:13-5:11)

Reading Notes
1.   Thanksgiving prayers (1:2-10; 3:9-13) surround a lengthy reminiscence of Paul's ministry with the Thessalonians describing his evangelism (2:1-12),   their conversion (2:13-16), Paul's forced absence (2:17-20), and Timothy's interim ministry and report of their faithfulness (3:1-6).

2. Paul recalls their conversion according to a typical reversal pattern and an already/not yet tension (1:9-10). This passage may also supply a synopsis of Paul's evangelistic preaching.

3. The clarification of Christian hope (4:13-5:11) avers that God's power extends beyond the grave to include **dead Christians** and that the time of the end cannot be calculated.

Reading Guide to 2 Thessalonians

Like 1 Thessalonians with which it has strong verbal similarities, 2 Thessalonians is a thanksgiving with insertions and a concluding exhortation.   Where 1 Thessalonians encourages, 2 Thessalonians warns. Further, while 1Thessalonians comforts those troubled by Christian deaths, 2 Thessalonians   emphasizes **apocalyptic signs** and the grand reversal for those troubled by announcements that the end has already come. If Paul wrote both letters, the church must have changed suddenly and dramatically.

Key Passage: 2:1-12

Outline
1. Thanksgiving for Faith (1-2)
    With Apocalyptic Scenario (1:5-2:12)
2. Exhortation (3)

Reading Notes

1. The apocalyptic scenario depicts present woes, a grand reversal, and signs (particularly apostasy) portending the end.

2. The **exhortation for steadfastness** is appropriate to the letter's apocalyptic tenor. In fact, persecution/suffering is welcomed as a mark of the apocalyptic faithful. By contrast, suffering in 1 Thessalonians is seen more often as a chance to imitate Jesus/Paul.

Reading Guide to the Pastorals

Scholars refer to **1 Timothy, 2 Timothy, and Titus** as the Pastoral Epistles because they are **letters to church leaders** (pastors) exhorting the leader to **maintain the Pauline tradition** and to act to insure proper **church order**. Here, apocalyptic sects have given way to institutions at home in the world. Thus, faith becomes tradition maintenance (e.g., 2 Tim 2:1-7) and the virtues are sobriety, godliness, and "quiet, peaceable lives" (e.g., 1 Tim 2:1-12). Paul has become a mythic hero in whose absence heresy becomes increasingly problematic (cf. Acts 20:18-35) in these "last days" (e.g., 1 Tim 4:1-10; 2 Tim 3:1-9). All of this, of course, leads to the unanimous scholarly conclusion that the Pastorals were written by a later follower of Paul.

Reading Guide to 1 Timothy

First Timothy has a rudimentary letter format with a minimal opening and closing (1:1-2; 6:21b). The letter is actually a **church manual** with interlocking, rotating appeals for adherence to the Pauline tradition (1:3-20; 4:1-12; 6:3-21) and for the maintenance of decorous church order (2-3; 5:1-6:2). The former casts Paul's good, sound example versus the bad example of the false teachers of the last days. The latter appeal calls for "quiet, peaceable" living in the world and affirms a **hierarchical ethic** not unlike that of the Hellenistic world at large (cf. 2:8-15; Ephesians).

Key Passages: 1:3-2:15; 6:3-21

Outline
1. The Pauline Tradition (1)
2. Appeal for Decorum (2)
3. True and False Leaders/Teachers (3-4)
4. Community Code (5:1-6:2)
5. Final Appeal for Timothy to Teach and Model (6:3-21)

Reading Notes
1. The letter implies a typically **"late" Christian view of history** in which a mythic golden age (the time of Paul) is followed by a later decadent time (the time of the church befuddled by heretics in the "last days").
2. The letter progresses from Paul as teacher and model (1-2) to **Timothy as teacher and model** (clearly in 6:3-21, but probably from 4:11 through 6:21, as the teaching concerns "duties"). Between the two, stand the Pauline descriptions of true and false leaders/teachers (3-4) which amounts to a two-ways teaching.

Reading Guide to 2 Timothy

Second Timothy is a genuine letter with numerous personal references and a lengthy closing greeting section (4:9-22). The letter depicts **Paul as Timothy's mythic exemplar** and exhorts Timothy to remember and remind others of the glorious past (Paul and Jesus) and to resist false teaching. The dominance of military metaphors is particularly striking (1:13-14; 2:1-7; 4:7-8).
Key Passages: 1:3-14; 4:1-5

Outline
1. Mythic Remembrance (1:1-2:13)
2. Mythic Duty in the "Last Days" (2:14-4:8)

Reading Notes
1. The letter moves **from mythic remembrance** of Paul and Jesus, as well as Timothy's own sacred initiation and training (1:3-2:13), to Timothy's **mythic responsibility** as a Pauline tradent (2:14-4:8).

Thus, Timothy is first to remember, rekindle, continue, and only then to teach (first in 2:14).

2. Two appeals to courage and sound teaching (2:1-16; 3:14-4:5) surround a lengthy section on the "last days" (2:17-3:9).

Reading Guide to Titus

Like 1 Timothy, Titus is a **church manual** appealing for sound doctrine and order. Here, decorum is **self-control and good works** (2:11-3:11).

Key Passage: 2:11-3:11

Outline
1. True and False Leaders and Teaching (1)
2. Community Code (2:1-10)
3. Appeal for Self-Control and Good Works (2:11-3:11)

Reading Guide to Philemon

Paul writes to a specific slave owner, Philemon, on behalf of a specific runaway slave, Onesimus. Paul's rhetoric transforms the "slave" into "my child," "useful," "my heart," and "your brother." While Paul does not explicitly demand the slave's freedom, his intentions are clear (see 13-14, 20-21). The letter asks Philemon to demonstrate publicly (before the church of v. 2) his Christian faith and love. Philemon is to operate according to the Christian myth of brotherhood, rather than the imperial myth of slavery.

Reading Notes
1. "Useful" (11) and "benefit" (20) are puns based on the meaning of the name Onesimus.
2. While Paul seeks Onesimus' freedom, he does not challenge the institution of slavery.

Reading Guide to Hebrews

Against a background of **Jewish history** (the revelation and rest of 1-4) **and ritual** (the priests, sacrifices, and sanctuary of 5-10), Hebrews aggressively **asserts the superiority of the Christian confession** of Jesus Christ, the faithful Son-Priest who acted once for all to open the heavenly (real) sanctuary and to establish a better covenant. The sermon exhorts those in danger of apostasy to **steadfastness to the Christian confession**.
    Key Passages: 1:1-4; 2:14-18; 4:14-5:10; 8-10

Outline
1. The Son as the Superior, Faithful Mediator (1:1-4:13)
2. Jesus as the Superior Priest (4:14-10:39)
3. Jesus as the Supremely Faithful One (11-12)

Reading Notes
1. Hebrews alternates explanation and exhortation. Many English translations note the move to explanation with "therefore" (cf. 2:1-4; 3:7-4:13; 6:1-20; 10:19-39; 12:1-29).
2. Hebrews is a sermon explaining earlier scriptures (particularly, Ps 2; 110; Jer 31:31-34; and Ex 25:10-40).
3. Hebrews has a three-stage Jesus' story including lofty state, humiliation, and exaltation (see, e.g., 1:1-4; 2:9-18; 4:14-5:10). For Hebrews, Jesus is essentially **the mythic sacrifice-maker** (4:14-10:19). Hebrews argues that Jesus is a priest after the order of **Melchizedek**, not Levi, in an incredibly convoluted reading of the HB (Heb 7 reflects upon Ps 110 and Gen 14:17-20).
4. For Hebrews, Jesus is a **superior priest** because he is the mediator of a new covenant (7:1-22; throughout 8-10), because he is a permanent (7:23-25), perfect (7:26-28), and heavenly minister (8-10), and because he offered a single, effective sacrifice of his own blood (9-10). Jesus' priestly transit makes possible Christian **access** to the heavens (e.g., 4:11, 16; 6:20; 7:19; 10:19-22; 12:18-24; 13:13-16).

Reading Guide to James

James continues **the HB wisdom tradition**. It has the typical wisdom sense of life as a trial to be endured properly (i.e., "wisely") through humility and faith. The notion of God as the giver of good gifts and the warnings about/to the rich are merely reverse sides of **humble faith**. **Self-control** (epitomized in speech) is, perhaps, the best symbol for James' moral vision. While the anti-rich elements are not typical of Hebrew wisdom, they do reflect the Jesus' sayings-tradition of which there are numerous echoes in James (cf. 1:5, 17 with Mt 7:7-12; 1:22 with Mt 7:2-27; 4:12 with Mt 7:1; and 5:12 with Mt 5:36-37).

Key Passages: 1; 2:14-26; 3:13-4:12

Outline
1. Call to Wisdom Virtues (1)
2. Clarifications (2:1-3:12)
   A. The Rich (2:1-13)
   B. Faith and Good Works (2:14-26)
   C. Self-Control and the Tongue (3:1-12)
3. Two-Ways: Divine Wisdom vs. Pride (3:13-5:6)
4. Call to Wisdom Virtues (5:7-20)

Reading Notes
1. James is essentially a series of fifty-plus imperatives.
2. James is unique for its freedom from the Christian tradition. Only echoes of the Jesus-sayings, two references to Jesus Christ (1:1; 2:1), and a running **argument with the Pauline tradition** (2:14-26) are notably Christian. The **lack of reference to the death-resurrection** is particularly peculiar. HB saints, not Jesus, act as mythic exemplars.

Reading Guide to 1 Peter

First Peter calls its audience to be **righteous sufferers** like

Jesus Christ, the mythic exemplar for the community (2:21-25; 3:18-22). Although 1 Peter expresses a sense of **alienation** (cf. 1:17; 2:11; 4:12-19; 5:6-11), it also insists on a **decorum** which will give the community a good reputation (e.g., 2:11-17; 3:13-22). The result is a rudimentary household/community code (2:18-3:7; 5:1-5). In short, 1 Peter sounds (5:1-5) like a Petrine pastoral letter.

Key Passages: 1:13-21; 2:9-12; 3:16-22; 4:12-19

Outline
1. Call to New Life of Holiness (1:13-2:10)
2. Call to Righteous Suffering (2:11-5:11)

Reading Notes
1. Part one (1:13-2:10) begins and ends with **calls to holiness** for a newly created people (cf. also the blessing in 1:3-12). Frequent references to birth, children, progress to maturity, baptism, and before-after patterns may reflect a **baptismal liturgy**. All of this also resembles Ephesians.

2. Part two (2:11-5:11) contains the paradoxical conjunction of aliens/exiles called to this-worldly decorum. The section begins and ends with a recognition of alienation based on the newness of the community's life which recalls part one (2:11; 4:1-6) and a concluding apocalyptic hope (4:7-19; 5:6-11). The instruction to elders in 5:1-5 interrupts this conclusion, but recalls the centerpiece on decorum (2:12-3:22).

3. The suffering of 4:12-19 is present while previous references are to potential suffering. As a result, some suggest that a baptismal homily was updated for a crisis situation.

Reading Guide to 2 Peter

Like the Paul of 2 Timothy, this Peter asserts his **tradition** (1:3-21) on the eve of his death **against the apostasy of "the last days"** (2:1-3:10).

Key passages: 1:3-21; 3:1-13

Outline
1. Grow unto Godliness (1:3-11)
2. Recall the Petrine Tradition (1:12-21)
3. Apostasy of the Last Days (2:1-3:10)
4. Grow unto Godliness (3:11-18)

Reading Notes

1. The letter begins and ends with an exhortation to godliness and the Petrine tradition (1:3-11; 3:11-18). The central section (1:12-3:10) depicts Peter as the mythic exemplar and mythic vehicle of the tradition (1:12-21) and contrasts him with the apostates of the last days (2:1-3:10).

2. Peter is a guarantor of the tradition because he is an eyewitness of mythic events (1:16-18) and because he **agrees with other mythic vehicles** including the prophets (1:19-21; 3:2), apostles (3:2), and Paul (3:15-16).

3. Those who wrangle with Peter are known as false teachers because of their immorality (2) as well as their distance from the Petrine tradition. Chapter 2 edits Jude.

Reading Guide to 1 John

First John is a sermon on life in the Johannine tradition (life, light, and love). It calls its audience to obedience and love.

Key Passages: 1:1-5; 3:11-4:21

Outline
1. Life in the Johannine Tradition (1:1-2:14)
   A. The Tradition (1:1-5)
   B. Abide in the Light (1:6-2:14)
2. The Children of God (2:15-5:13)
   A. Life Against the World and Apostates (2:15-28)
   B. Life in Righteousness (2:29-3:10)
   C. Loving One Another (3:11-24)
   D. Recognizing the Spirit of Truth (4:1-6)
   E. Life in Love (4:7-21)

F. Life in Belief in the Son of God (5:1-13)

Reading Notes

1. First John exhorts believers to a belief and a lifestyle appropriate to the tradition through a **twice-repeated pattern**: a) avoid sin (1:6-2:6), love the brother (2:7-11), and believe properly (2:15-28), and b) avoid sin (2:29-3:10), love the brother (3:11-24), and believe properly (4:1-6). After a final love section (4:7-21), the concluding chapter deals again with belief and sin (5).

2. After an initial statement (1:1-5), the Johannine tradition takes place in counterpoint to the false teaching of the last days (2:18-29; 4:1-6). The false teachers, who have left the community, **deny that Jesus** is from God and/or that he **has come in the flesh**. Notably, the primary attack against this false teaching is that it does not agree with the believer's internal testimony! The spirit of truth lives in them.

Reading Guide to 2 John

Second John is a genuine letter applying the themes of 1 John to a specific situation. The elder warns a community **not to give hospitality to false teachers**.

Reading Guide to 3 John

Third John is an administrative letter commending Gaius and Demetrius who support the elder's mission and criticizing Diotrophes who challenges it.

Reading Guide to Jude

Jude reminds its readers of the **common apostolic tradition** (faith, salvation) faithfully handed down and warns them about the apostates who have arisen in the "last days." In fact, Jude contains in its most concise NT form the **fall from an earlier golden age** pattern (3-4, 17-20). The critique of the false teachers in vv. 5-19 appears to be an earlier form of that appearing in 2 Pet 2:4-3:3. While both passages use HB examples, Jude also uses examples from apocalyptic traditions which 2 Peter purges. The critique of the false teachers is little more than name-calling, focusing on their immorality and their similarity to ancient "criminals."

APPENDIX 3

LIST OF FIGURES

GLOSSARY AND KEY TERMS INDEX

Allegory is a *hermeneutic* which ignores *literal* and historical meanings in order to find some other hidden meaning more palatable to the interpreter. The traditional reading strategy uses this method in order to find proper, spiritual meanings in recalcitrant texts. 26-27, 82, 295, 314; cf. *symbol*; *typology*.

Androcentrism refers to language or *world-view* which privileges male perspectives over female. It differs from *patriarchy* as ideology differs from social structure. 127, 200.

Anomie is the experience of chaos or purposelessness.

Anthropology refers to a conception of the nature of humanity and the human condition. 105, 351-52.

Anthropomorphic means "in human form." Some biblical *theophanies* are anthropomorphic. 57, 103.

Apocalypticism is a *world-view* characterized by a belief in the imminent, supernatural end of the present world order. The present is an evil time in which the good are persecuted, but the coming end will rectify those injustices and punish the current world rulers. Apocalyptic groups often produce apocalypses, written vision reports symbolically depicting the imminent world change (e.g., Dan 7-12; Rev). 7, 31, 284, 310-28, 365-66, 371-73, 379, 459-61, 486-504; cf. *eschatology*; *millenarian*; *sect*.

Apocrypha is the designation for the "hidden books" of the Christian Church. These extra books were included in the LXX, but not in the HB. Jerome gave them the name "apocrypha" during the process of translating them for the *Vulgate*. 2.

Apostasy means "to rebel" or "to fall away." It is *faith*'s opposite. In the HB, it often refers to a violation of *henotheism*. 94, 166-67, 183-84, 222-23, 226-27, 230-32, 480-82; cf. *faith*; *henotheism*.

Apotheosize means "to deify" a person. In a lesser sense, it can mean "to glorify" or "to idealize." 226.

Atmosphere is a story's setting or world. It defines the realm of the possible within the story. Biblical story-worlds range from mythic to realistic. 62-64.

Biosphere is a sphere of life. The Sinai *covenant* and *cult* create a biosphere in which Israel can live safely and well. 154-55, 207-08.

Bureaucracy is a rationalized, administrative system for the delivery of goods or services. *Torah*'s *cultic* materials define a *sacred* bureaucracy making the *holy* available through stated offices and procedures. 172.

Canon is a list of books with sacred authority or a scripture. The word itself comes from a Greek word meaning "reed" or "measuring-stick." The evolution to "standard" is obvious. The canon of scripture is an authority or standard for the religious community. 6, 9-10, 19; cf. *scripture*; *word of God*.

Character refers to a *story*'s actors. The chief biblical character is God, the Lord of life and meaning. Human characters are arranged around God according to a simple *ethical dualism*. Human characters model *mythic* identities for the worshiping community. 53-62, 67, 102-05, 120-27, 132, 140-44, 167-72, 188-95, 210-18, 232-35, 263-65, 277-83, 302-04, 320-23, 346-48, 367-73, 386-88, 390-93, 398, 405-11, 429-33, 465-67, 480-83, 495-97, 501.

Charisma refers to the appeal and power of remarkable individuals who have an authority unto themselves without institutional standing. Religious authorities tend to be either charismatic (e.g., prophets, seers, or miracle-workers) or institutional (e.g., office-holders or priests). Charisma comes from a Greek word meaning "gift." Biblical charismatics are empowered not by their innate abilities but by God or the spirit (e.g., judges and prophets). 33, 88, 143, 189-90, 191-93, 202, 215, 249-51, 269, 452; cf. ***prophet***.

Christian Bible is the sacred scripture of the Christians. It consists of two parts, the ***Old Testament*** and the ***New Testament***. 2.

Cleanness is one of the ethical expectations of biblical humans. This corollary of God's ***holiness*** initially indicated the ***ritual purity*** necessary to approach God. Ultimately, however, cleanness came to have ethical overtones as well (e.g., Lev 19). Cleanness is an ethical, ***ritual*** necessity in closed, traditional societies which are obsessively concerned with maintaining order (keeping things in their proper place). 60-61, 173-74, 175-76, 179; cf. ***purity***.

Cosmogony means "the generation of order (cosmos)." ***Torah*** provides Israel both with a general cosmogony (Gen 1-11) and with the cosmogony of Israel itself (the ***epic***). 93, 105-06, 107-11.

Covenant is a formal agreement similar to a modern contract although with far more religious overtones. The most important biblical covenant is the Sinai covenant which imposes obligations upon Israel in light of God's Exodus-deliverance. This covenant is the heart of ***Torah*** and Judaism. Jeremiah's oracle about a new covenant beyond exile (31:31-34; cf. Heb 8:8-12; 10:16-17) is apparently the biblical basis for the name given to the early Christian writings (the ***New Testament***) in the third century. 93, 119-20, 131, 150-57, 178.

Cult is a worship system. It is the *bureaucracy* or channel of the *holy*. 150-51, 170, 172-74, 179, 258-59, 278-79, 283-86, 291-92; cf. *ritual*.

Demythologize, a term popularized by Rudolf Bultmann, means "to read a myth or mythic element in light of another *world-view*." Thus, Bultmann attempted to re-state the NT Gospel in terms of modern *existentialism*. 141, 508.

Deus ex machina literally means "god in the machine." The term was originally used to refer to a dramatic device by which an author resolves *plot* complications by inserting a deity in the story at the last moment. On stage, a machine lowered the actor-deity to the stage to resolve the issue. Here, the term describes the tendency of biblical *story* to make God the *plot* motivation (particularly in liberation stories). 51-52, 136-37, 275-76, 321, 345; cf. *hierophany*; *miracle*.

Deuteronomic History is a scholarly designation for the *Former Prophets* (and sometimes Deuteronomy). It describes the work's *genre* and two-ways *world-view* in which obedience (*henotheism*) leads to life and *apostasy* leads to death. 180, 183, 184-85, 201, 465; cf. *Former Prophets*.

Discourse is the "how" of *story*. It is *story*'s packaging or expression as compared to its content. The primary biblical discourses are *ritual* and *verbal* although various aesthetic discourses have been important in the Western world (art, opera, ballet, and cinema). As a broad term, discourse includes a work's *medium*, *genre*, *narrator*, *time*, *style*, and *narratee*. 45, 68-92.

Divine sovereignty is the rule of God. This notion is the central assumption and assertion in the biblical myth and the fundamental difference between the biblical *world-view* and that of modernity. The Bible understands this notion relationally--i.e., God's rule is that of a Father or King--not philosophically--i.e., as divine determinism. 10-12, 53, 56-57, 67, 102, 104-05, 144-47, 193-95, 323-24, 339-41, 375-77, 429, 489, 493-97.

Election is the theological term for God's choice of a particular people for himself (see Gen 12:1-3; Ex 19:3-6). The notion symbolizes dramatically the freedom of God. 59-60, 93-94, 119-20, 123-25, 128-30, 131, 206-07, 218-19.

Epic designates long, narrative poems (the Greek root means "song") depicting the lives of heroes who are particularly important to a people/nation's early history (e.g., the Iliad, the Aeneid, and Paradise Lost). Although not poetic, *Torah* resembles epic. 114-15, 131.

Eponymous indicates one who gives his name to a city, state, etc. Jacob/Israel is the eponymous ancestor of the Israelites. 114.

Eschatology refers to the "last things." It can be used adjectivally to suggest the goal of a project or sequence of events or to suggest a matter of ultimate concern (i.e., an *existential* matter). 83, 310-11, 395-96, 435, 455-57, 478, 492; cf. *apocalypticism*; *existential*.

Ethical dualism is a simplistic, "black-white" value structure dividing events and characters into clearly defined good or evil categories. Biblical ethical dualism divides humans into "with God" or "apart from God" groups. 51, 58-59, 148-49, 196, 303-04, 309, 322-23, 367-70, 379, 429, 431-33, 461-65, 466-67; cf. *ethnocentrism*; *natural religion*; *sect*; *xenophobia*.

Ethnocentrism is the assumption that one's culture is superior to others. It parochially restricts one's perspective and values to the nation or group of which one is a part. It engenders an "Us vs. Them" mentality. It is typical of *natural religion* groups. 16, 94, 171, 196, 307, 323, 324-26, 415, 439-41; cf.

ethical dualism; *natural religion*; *sect*; *xenophobia*.

Etiology designates stories which explain the causes or origins of something. *Cosmogonic myths* provide etiologies for many of the important elements and customs in a society. 98, 144.

Existential pertains to existence, to the very fact of life. Existential questions are those which humans must answer by virtue of their human existence (e.g., quests for identity, meaning, order, and *theodicy*). Existentialism is also a twentieth-century philosophical movement stressing human existence over human essence. For Sartre and others, one's existence (choices) determines one's life, not one's essence (some kind of universal human nature). 16, 342.

Faith is one of the ethical expectations of biblical humans. This corollary of the *divine sovereignty* indicates the unalloyed allegiance which the sovereign expects of his subjects. Biblically, faith refers to commitment, loyalty, or *henotheism* (cf. Ex 20:3). Only after institutionalization and Western rationalization did faith come to mean adherence to a creed or believing seven impossible things before breakfast. 60, 67, 101, 106, 122-24, 132, 143-44, 217-18, 462, 468; cf. *henotheism*.

Former Prophets is a canonical designation for Joshua, Judges, 1-2 Samuel, and 1-2 Kings. These books are considered *prophets* because they provide a prophetic succession connecting the Mosaic *Torah* and the synagogue. 180-81; cf. *Deuteronomic History*.

Genre refers to a type or kind of literature. Genre describes a work's form, content, function, and reading conventions. As a whole, the Bible belongs to the genre of *myth*. More precisely, the Bible includes various kinds of stories, essays, lists, sayings, and poetry. 70, 74-77, 91, 97-98, 114-15, 184-85, 203, 224-27, 244-49, 292-96, 311-13, 327, 332-41, 354-

55, 358-59, 361, 394-95, 398, 411-12, 421, 445, 448-49, 471-72, 474-75, 486-87.

Gnosticism refers to a radically dualistic world-view popular during the Hellenistic era. It takes its name from the Greek word **gnosis** which means "knowledge." The esoteric knowledge of Gnosticism concerns the division of the world into spirit (good) and matter (evil) and reveals the way to the spirit's liberation from matter. 435, 438, 443.

Gospel is the generic designation for early Christianity's cult biographies of Jesus. The term also means "good news," and depicts the life, death, and resurrection of Jesus as such. In the canon, gospel designates Matthew, Mark, Luke, and John. 356-61.

Halakah, from a Hebrew word meaning "to walk," indicates God's prescriptions for Jewish life. 161, 388; cf. *Mishnah*.

Hebrew Bible is the sacred scripture of the Jews, named the HB because of its dominant language. It consists of three parts: *Torah*, *Prophets*, and *Writings*. 1-2, 5-7.

Henotheism: 54-55, 96, 147, 151; cf. *apostasy*; *faith*; *monolatry*.

Hermeneutic refers to a system of interpretation or a way of reading. It can be the rationalized set of rules which govern a reading strategy or the interpretative perspective which a *myth* establishes for reading the world. 30, 309.

Hexateuch is a scholarly designation for the first six books of the HB. The promise of the land, given to Abram and fulfilled in Joshua's wars, connects the books thematically. 183.

Hierophany is a manifestation of the *sacred*. 13-14, 54, 135, 255; cf. *symbol*; *theophany*.

History, as distinct from fiction, purports to describe "what actually happened" at a particular time and place. Ancient history differs radically from modern in its *world-view* or view of the "possible." In particular, biblical history assumes the *divine sovereignty*. 27-31, 74-75, 91, 180, 184-85, 203, 220, 224-27, 242, 318, 411-12, 421.

Holy is the awesome, attractive power which is the heart and aim of religious systems. It is the source of both life and meaning for a particular community. In biblical texts, God is the holy. Humans are holy by extension and association. 53-54, 60-61, 103, 175-76; cf. *sacred*; *transcendence*.

Holy war is an ideology that defines war as a ritual act requiring priestly devotion and purity from its soldiers and that asserts that God fights with and for the troops. 51, 137-39, 185-87, 260-61, 276-77, 320, 344-46, 459-61, 493-95.

Implied author refers to the persona which an author assumes or the ethical and aesthetic choices which an author makes in order to create a *story*. The implied author, then, is a text's perspective, its norms and standards. Readers infer the implied author as they read. 77, 91, 451-52.

Implied reader refers to the audience an author/text expects to find. It is the persona which the reader assumes or the ethical and aesthetic choices which a reader makes in order to read a *story*. 77, 86-89, 91, 341, 373-75, 392-93, 439.

Inerrancy is the guiding assumption in fundamentalist *hermeneutic*. It asserts that no part of scripture is or should be read in such a way that it appears to be in error in any way. 33-34.

Irony asserts that reality is different than it appears. Thus, a *theodicy* ironically asserts order in the face of chaos. Biblical stories without the luxury of the *ontological good* often create ironic *atmospheres*. Such ironic texts often have to invert the meaning of old biblical *symbols*. Thus, some texts say that the righteous suffer and that death comes through life. Undoubtedly, the fundamental biblical irony is the relentless assertion of the *divine sovereignty*. Irony invariably creates the impression that the *narrator* knows more than the *narratee*. Further, irony invites (or seduces) the reader to accept the text's perspective. 64, 88-89, 357, 361, 362-68, 407, 436-38, 443, 455-57, 494-95.

Kerygmatic comes from the Greek word for "preaching." It suggests the Bible's evangelistic, imperialistic *style* which intends to foist its *world-view* upon the reader.

Lament is a complaint or a psalm *genre* with the typical form of address, lament (complaint, confession, and petition), and vow to praise. 137, 293-96, 337.

Legend refers to stories about ancient heroes (customs, or events). Its content is thus distinct from that of *myth*, which can be defined as a story of the gods. The stories of the patriarchs, the judges, the prophets, and the apostles can be read as legends.

Literal is the opposite of figurative, *symbolic*, or *allegorical*. It often refers to the obvious or plain sense of a text. Obviously, the literal meaning of a text depends upon the reader's own perspective or *world-view*. 26-27, 33, 85; cf. *allegory*; *symbol*; *realistic*.

Masoretic Text is one of the texts of the HB, named for the Masoretes who preserved both the consonantal Hebrew text and a tradition for pronouncing it for centuries. Masorete comes from the Hebrew word for tradition. 6-7.

Medium is the means through which and by which *story* is transmitted. The basic biblical medium is orality. 69-74, 90-91, 255-58, 291-92, 308, 334, 449-51, 488-89.

Melodrama refers to romantic, sensational stories with strong emotional appeals which end in ways that satisfy popular appetites for justice. In melodrama, the wicked are punished and the righteous are rewarded. 100-02, 212, 215, 323.

Metaphor refers to a strong comparison without benefit of like or as (a simile). It asserts a hidden similarity between two diverse objects or experiences. Its effect is often dramatic and revelatory. Metaphor is a new vision as opposed to *myth*'s *traditional* perspective. 89, 297, 309; cf. *symbol*.

Millenarian comes from the Latin meaning "a thousand." Millenarian is often used as a synonym for *apocalyptic*. More technically, it refers to groups who believe that God will ultimately rule on earth for a thousand years (see Rev 20:1-6). Cf. *apocalypticism*; *sect*.

Miracle popularly means a violation of natural law. Biblically, miracles are manifestations of the *divine sovereignty*. They reveal the divine purposes and actualize the divine program. The Bible contains four types of miracles: nature miracles, healings, resuscitations, and exorcisms. 145-46, 234; cf. *deus ex machina*; *hierophany*.

Mishnah is the second century CE codification of Jewish oral tradition explaining and applying the *halakah* demands of *Torah*. 7, 25, 159, 161, 179, 388.

Monolatry or henotheism refers to the worship of one God to the exclusion of all others (see Ex. 20:3). For the HB, this demand is synonymous with *faith*. The demand is particularly frequent and central to Deuteronomic thought. 54-55; cf. *faith*; *henotheism*.

Monotheism is the belief that only one God exists. Religions based upon the biblical stories are monotheistic although many biblical stories are not. In fact, most biblical stories are *henotheistic*. 55-57, 263-65.

Multiple perspectives describes the Bible's tendency to describe an event from multiple, apparently competing perspectives, rather than describing a matter through a strict logical progression. 84-85; cf. *parataxis*.

Mysticism refers to a type of religion which seeks either communion with or absorption into the sacred. 7, 265-66, 433-34; cf. *charisma*; *Gnosticism*; *prophet*.

Myth is a community's master story which serves as its narrative repository of power and meaning and which incarnates its *world-view*. 13-17, 20, 22, 39-40, 47-49, 58-59, 62-65, 74, 87, 89, 97-98, 105-06, 112, 127-28, 144, 164-65, 170-72, 172-74, 190-91, 207-10, 225-27, 235-38, 261-63, 283-86, 288, 301-02, 303-05, 323, 329-32, 348-51, 370-73, 388-93, 412-15, 433-35, 461-65, 467-69, 483, 498-500, 505-14.

Narratee refers to the ear listening to a tale. Biblical narratees are both anonymous and specific. The mythic community easily sees itself as the anonymous narratee. Some interpretative work is necessary for the community to see itself as the recipient of works with specific narratees. 86-89, 91, 251-55, 458-59, 477.

Narrator refers to the voice through which a tale is told. In reliable narration, the narrator expresses the *implied author*'s perspective. Typically, biblical narrators speak from a divine perspective giving biblical story a *word of God* effect. 77-80, 91, 161-64, 249-51, 300-01, 317-18, 341-42, 373-75, 415-16, 421, 451-52, 476-77, 497-98.

Natural religion describes a religion of "blood and soil," a situation in which culture and religion are synonymous. Such religions do not require distinguishing names. They are the religion for a particular culture. In such settings, *ontological views of the good* dominate. 4, 54, 95, 128, 145, 148-49, 197-98, 277, 284, 286-88, 307, 309, 319-20, 346, 510; cf. *ethical dualism*; *ethnocentrism*; *xenophobia*.

New Testament is the sacred scripture of Christianity. Its addition to the HB (or the LXX) forms the *Christian Bible*. Some scholars feel that Second Testament is a less offensive, parochial term. 2, 8-10.

Old Testament is the Christian name for the HB (Protestant) or LXX (Catholics). Christians read that earlier testament in light of the *New Testament*. 2.

Ontological good refers to the view that "good" is a noun or verb, not a mere adjective. Such a good is a life-giving sphere into which one can move by following cultural conceptions of ethics and religion. Put simply, the notion asserts that if one does the good, one will have it good (prosper). It is a fundamental component in both Deuteronomic and Wisdom thought. Many argue that it is the common sense wisdom of many, if not most, cultures. 4, 175-76, 319-20, 331-32, 344-46; cf. *biosphere*; *natural religion*.

Paradigm is Thomas Kuhn's term for the imaginative perspective by which a community interprets data. Chapter two uses the term to symbolize the differing governing images which communities use as a basis to interpret the Bible (e.g., myth, word of God, and literature). 22.

Parallelism is a form of repetition sometimes called "thought rhyme." It indicates an ideological relationship between two lines of a couplet. The second line may restate (synonymous), oppose (antithetical), or build upon (stair-step) the first. 76, 298-99, 333-34.

Parataxis literally means "placed alongside." It describes a syntax characterized by juxtaposition or coordination, rather than subordination. The latter is known as periodic syntax. Parataxis is characteristic of speech and oral narratives. In texts, it creates a "run-on" effect. 84-85; cf. *multiple perspectives*; *parallelism*.

Parousia means "arrival" or "presence." Early Christian texts use the term to refer to Jesus' second coming as the warrior-judge who will end this evil age and inaugurate God's reign. 371, 446.

Patriarchy refers to social structures which privilege males over females. Typically, in such structures, females are understood to be "embedded" in males. That is, they are dependent upon males and take their identity from their association with significant males (as wife, mother, or daughter). 106, 127, 200, 469; cf. *androcentrism*.

Peripetia is the "turning point" in tragedy when fortunes reverse and/or when the protagonist recognizes his fate. 212.

Plot is the causal arrangement of a *story*, the "why" of a story. Biblical plots are either revelations of *mythic* orders and characters or resolutions of conflicts between God and outsiders (holy war plots) or insiders gone astray (sin plots). 47-52, 66-67, 100-02, 119-20, 137-39, 166-67, 185-87, 206-07, 230-32, 260-61, 275-77, 301-02, 320, 342-46, 362-67, 381-86, 398, 399-405, 427-29, 459-61, 480-83, 493-95.

Poetry is a rhythmic, often-rhyming, playful yet constrained, and affective use of language. Biblical poetry does not use recognizable Western poetic conventions (particularly rhyme). In translation, the most noticeable feature of biblical poetry is *parallelism*. Like all poetry, biblical poetry is *symbolic*. 76, 91, 253-55, 269, 297-99, 309, 333-35, 354, 489-93; cf. *parallelism*; *symbol*.

Priest is the prototypical institutional figure in biblical texts. The priests and Levites operate the *cult* and make the *sacred ritually* accessible. In the HB, the priesthood begins with Aaron, the founding priest, and continues as long as the tabernacle and, then, temple last. 163-64, 280-82, 476-77.

Prophet is the prototypical biblical *charismatic*. The prophet has an intimate relationship with God and mediates between God and people. The prophet delivers divine messages, provides access to the *sacred*, and *symbolizes faith/henotheism*. In the HB, prophecy extends from Moses, the founding prophet, through the character-prophets in the Former Prophets to the classical prophets (the prophets associated with the books of oracles known as the Latter Prophets). 141-43, 162-63, 180-82, 191-93, 214-15, 233-35, 243-72, 281-82, 405-07, 409, 414, 421, 515-27; cf. *charisma*.

Providence refers to the divine control and direction of the world. Biblical stories assume divine providence. *Stories* portray it both directly, in stories in which God is a character, and indirectly, in stories in which God is the hidden effector of events. 57, 121-22, 141, 169, 189-90, 210-14, 233, 277-78, 303, 320-22, 346-48, 408, 498-99.

Purity refers to *ritual cleanness*, the requisite for safely approaching God in the *cult*. 60-61; cf. *cleanness*.

Realistic refers to a story-world which resembles the reality of the reader. Verisimilitude is a better term. 62-64, 203, 212-14, 416; cf. *atmosphere*.

Rhetoric is the art of persuasion. Biblical rhetoric combines that suitable to public celebrations which encourages the reaffirmation of *mythic* identities (demonstrative) and that suitable to public assemblies which encourages expedient action (deliberative). Its warrants are both *charisma* and *tradition*. 88, 92, 251-55, 452-55, 472, 477-79, 497-98.

Ritual refers to the *sacred, symbolic drama* which enacts the founding *myth* of a community, makes the sacred and its benefits available to worshipers, and provides condensed, symbolic identities for worshipers (i.e., "we are the ones who do such and such"). 68-69, 89, 90, 137, 144, 172-74, 179, 185-86, 304-05, 308, 309, 423-24, 449-51, 472, 488-89; cf. *cult*.

Sacred: 13-14, 19-20, 53-54, 172-74, 179, 207-08; cf. *holy*; *transcendent*.

Scripture is a community's *sacred* text. It mediates the sacred and constitutes a sacred authority. 1-2, 7, 19, 94; cf. *canon*; *word of God*.

Sect refers to a disenfranchised, protesting religious group. Unlike *natural religions*, sects are separate from the economic, social, and political powers, and, thus, they resist rather than support the dominant culture. 7, 322, 327, 501, 507-08, 510.

Septuagint (LXX) is the earliest Greek translation of the HB. The translation of *Torah* dates to the third century BCE. Early Christian churches used this translation, and the Christian OT follows its ordering and naming of the HB books. 2.

Sin is the opposite of *faith*. Sin rejects God's sovereignty rather than loyally accepting it. It is the egoistic attempt to make the self, rather than God, the center and ruler of the world. Sin provides the Bible's basic *theodicy*. 50-51, 100-02, 106, 112-13, 166-67, 180-81, 185-87, 190-91, 230-32, 235-40, 246, 260-61, 262-63, 288, 402; cf. *apostasy*; *faith*; *henotheism*.

Soliloquy is a dramatic speech delivered by a character alone on stage. It provides "inside views." 161-62.

Story is a type of literature, a narrative as opposed to an essay. It is the content of a piece of literature or a summary of its contents. It is the "what" of literature as opposed to its "how," its *discourse*. In this sense, story includes a narrative's *plot*, *characters*, and *atmosphere*. 45-67.

Style refers to the distinctive aesthetic, artistic expressions of a work or to its flavor. Overall, the Bible has a *mythic* style. Its semantics is *symbolic* and its syntax is *paratactic*. 84-86, 98-99, 115-16, 134-36, 154-61, 211, 224-29, 276, 297-99, 314-17, 332-41, 373, 380, 393-94, 418, 421, 457, 480; cf. *parataxis*; *symbol*.

Symbol refers to something, either verbal or physical, which represents something else. Religious symbols represent the *sacred*, its benefits, or the *mythic* identity of the worshiping community. As the *sacred transcends* human experience, it can be spoken of only symbolically. 14, 20, 66, 84-86, 91, 251, 297, 314-17, 327, 423-27, 443, 489-93, 503; cf. *allegory*; *hierophany*.

Talmud is the fifth and sixth century CE codification of rabbinic oral tradition explaining the *halakah* requirements of *Torah*. 7, 25, 159; cf. *Mishnah*.

Tanak is a synonym for the *Hebrew Bible*. It is an acronym derived from the first letters of the Hebrew names of the three parts of the HB (*Torah*, Prophets, and Writings). 1.

Theodicy refers to the question of God's justice in the face of evil and *anomie*. It is a reassertion of order and meaning in the face of the harsh limitations on human life. The dominant biblical theodicy is *sin*, but mystic (e.g., Job) and future recompense versions (e.g., apocalyptic) also occur. 16, 50-51, 87-88, 106, 180-81, 190-91, 235-40, 288, 296, 304, 323, 340-41, 350-51, 355, 464-65, 500; cf. *sin*.

Theophany refers to a manifestation of God. In biblical texts, theophanies are either meteorological or *anthropological*.

57-58, 67, 121-22, 131, 247, 262-63, 338, 340-41, 354-55, 365; cf. *hierophany*; *symbol*.

Time concerns the relationship of *discourse* time to *story* time. Biblical stories are episodic. The discourse skips over years of story to concentrate on important moments. The discourse also provides story material out of order in flashforwards (prophecy) and flashbacks (*typology*). 80-83, 91, 164-65, 373, 423-26.

Torah is from the Hebrew for "revelation" or "instruction." It can refer to the first five books of the HB, to the whole of the HB, or to the totality of Jewish revelation. 1, 93-95, 153-54, 387-88, 388-90.

Tradent is one who hands on a tradition. 255, 466.

Tradition is that which is handed on. A *myth-ritual* community creates a tradition by handing on a *mythic* identity and *hermeneutic* from one generation to the next. The Bible's tendency to reuse *symbols* and patterns also creates a tradition and facilitates *typological* interpretations. 24-27, 28, 46, 88, 89, 248, 269, 475, 480-82, 483-84.

Tragedy is a drama which recounts the catastrophe of a person of significance. For Aristotle, this change could not be motivated by "sin." Later critics and tragedies were not so strict. Tragedy can also be used to describe any story with a "tragic vision." Such works typically create characters who meet the inevitable defeat and suffering associated with humanity with dignity and courage. 99-101, 112, 212, 215, 221, 230-32, 343-44, 402, 420; cf. *melodrama*; *sin*.

Transcendence suggests the otherness and superiority of the sacred through a vertical, spatial metaphor. 14, 20, 89, 103-04; cf. *holy*; *sacred*.

574

Typology asserts an interpretative connection between one event or ***character*** and another. The first item signifies the second and the second repeats or fulfills the former. 82-83, 91, 386-87, 393-94, 455-56; cf. ***allegory***; ***symbol***.

Voluntary religion refers to religions of creed and code, rather than religions of "blood and soil." They center in charismatic leaders, beliefs, or ethics, rather than in race, state, or place. Their freedom from place gives them missionary and expansionist opportunities. Further, as the name suggests, voluntary religions are more individual and subjective (interior) than ***natural religions***. The historic (major world) religions are usually voluntary.

Vulgate is the most important Latin translation of the Bible. Much of it stems from the work of Jerome and is usually dated to the early fifth century CE. The Vulgate was the Bible of the Western world until nationalism, the printing press, and the Reformation made "vulgar" translations available. 2.

Word of God is a Western synonym for ***scripture***. It reflects the Western world's personal conception of the ***sacred***. 13-14, 22, 24, 77-78; cf. ***word of God***.

World-view refers to a culture's "taken for granted" perspective on the world, the lens through which it interprets and evaluates life. It is both the ideology and the ***hermeneutic*** supplied by a ***myth***. 10-13, 15-16, 20, 72, 73, 106-11, 128-30, 144-47, 168, 175-76, 195-99, 218-19, 238-40, 265-68, 286-88, 305-07, 323-26, 339, 351-52, 375-78, 395-96, 416-17, 439-41, 470, 483-84, 502, 505-14.

Xenophobia is the fear of the alien or strangers. 184, 187, 197-98; cf. ***ethical dualism***; ***ethnocentrism***; ***natural religion***.

Yahweh is the modern, scholarly rendering of the name of Israel's God (see Ex 3:14). Because of the HB's textual transmission, only the consonants are certain. As a result, scholars sometimes speak of the Tetragrammaton (YHWH). 4, 54-55, 140, 144.

BIBLIOGRAPHY

Abba, R. "Priests and Levites." In Buttrick, 3:876-89.

Abrams, Meyer Howard. A Glossary of Literary Terms. 4th ed. NY: Holt, Rinehart and Winston, 1981.

Achtemeier, Paul J., ed. Harper's Bible Dictionary. San Francisco: Harper & Row, 1985.

Ackroyd, Peter R. Exile and Restoration. Philadelphia: Westminster, 1968.

_____. "The Historical Literature." In Knight and Tucker, 297-323.

_____. "History and Theology in the Writings of the Chronicler." CTM 38 (1967):501-15.

Adams, Hazard, ed. Critical Theory Since Plato. 2nd ed. Fort Worth: Harcourt Brace Jovanovich, 1992.

Adams, Hazard and Searle, Leroy, eds. Critical Theory Since 1965. Tallahasse: Florida State, 1986.

Albright, William F. Yahweh and the Gods of Canaan. Garden City: Doubleday, 1968.

Alt, Albrecht. "The Origins of Israelite Law." In Alt. Essays on OT History and Religion. Garden City: Doubleday, 1967. Pp. 101-71.

Alter, Robert. The Art of Biblical Narrative. NY: Basic, 1981.

_____. The Art of Biblical Poetry. NY: Basic, 1985.

_____. "The Characteristics of Biblical Poetry." In Alter and Kermode, 611-24.

_____. The World of Biblical Literature. NY: Basic, 1992.

Alter, Robert and Kermode, Frank, eds. The Literary Guide to the Bible. Cambridge: Harvard, 1987.

Anderson, Bernhard W., ed. Creation in the OT. Philadelphia: Fortress, 1984.

_____. Creation versus Chaos. NY: Association, 1967.

_____. "God, Names of." In Buttrick, 2:407-17.

_____. "Jehovah." In Buttrick, 2:817.

_____. Out of the Depths. NY: Board of Missions, United

Methodist Church, 1970.

_____. Understanding the OT. 4th ed. Englewood Cliffs: Prentice-Hall, 1986.

_____. The Unfolding Drama of the Bible. 3rd ed. Philadelphia: Fortress, 1988.

Anderson, Janice Capel and Moore, Stephen D. Mark and Method. Minneapolis: Fortress, 1992.

Arendt, Hannah. Eichmann in Jerusalem: A Report on the Banality of Evil. Rev. ed. NY: Penguin, 1965.

Aristotle. The Poetics. Loeb Classical Library. Vol. 17. Translated by W. H. Fyfe. Cambridge: Harvard, 1965.

Auerbach, Erich. Mimesis. Princeton, 1953.

Augustine. Confessions. Translated by Henry Chadwick. NY: Oxford, 1992.

Aune, David E. The NT in Its Literary Environment. Philadelphia: Westminster, 1987.

Bacon, Benjamin W. Studies in Matthew. London: Constable, 1930.

Bainton, Roland H. Christian Attitudes Toward War and Peace. Nashville: Abingdon, 1960.

Bal, Mieke. Murder and Difference: Gender, Genre, and Scholarship of Sisera's Death. Bloomington: Indiana, 1988.

Balch, D. L. "Household Codes." In David E. Aune, ed. Greco-Roman Literature and the NT. Atlanta: Scholars, 1988. Pp. 25-50.

Barbour, Ian G. Myths, Models, and Paradigms. NY: Harper & Row, 1974.

Barr, David L. "The Apocalypse as Symbolic Transformation of the World: A Literary Analysis." Interp 38 (1938):39-50.

_____. New Testament Story. 2nd ed. Belmont: Wadsworth, 1995.

Barr, James. Fundamentalism. Philadelphia: Westminster, 1977.

Barrett, C. K. The Gospel According to St. John. London: SPCK, 1958.

_____. The NT Background: Selected Documents. Rev. and expanded ed. San Francisco: Harper, 1989.

Barthes, Roland. Mythologies. NY: Hill & Wang, 1972.

Barton, John. Reading the OT. Philadelphia: Westminster, 1984.

Bartsch, Hans Werner, ed. Kerygma and Myth. NY: Harper & Row,

1961.

Bassler, Jouette M. Pauline Theology, Volume 1: Thessalonians, Philippians, Galatians, Philemon. Minneapolis: Fortress, 1991.

Bauer, David R. "The Major Characters of Matthew's Story." Interp 46 (1992):357-67.

Bauer, Walter. Orthodoxy and Heresy in Earliest Christianity. Philadelphia: Fortress, 1971.

Beardslee, William A. Literary Criticism of the NT. Philadelphia: Fortress, 1970.

Becker, Ernst. The Denial of Death. NY: Free Press, 1973.

Beckett, Samuel. Waiting for Godot. NY: Grove, 1954.

Beker, J. Christiaan. Heirs of Paul: Paul's Legacy in the NT and in the Church Today. Minneapolis: Fortress, 1991.

_____. Paul's Apocalyptic Gospel. Philadelphia: Fortress, 1982.

_____. Paul, the Apostle: The Triumph of God in Life and Thought. Philadelphia: Fortress, 1980.

Bellah, Robert N. Beyond Belief. NY: Harper & Row, 1970.

_____. The Broken Covenant. NY: Seabury, 1975.

_____. "Civil Religion." In Bellah, Beyond, 168-89.

_____. "Religious Evolution." In Bellah, Beyond, 20-50.

Bellah, Robert N., et al. Habits of the Heart. Berkeley: University of California, 1985.

Bercovitch, Sacvan. "The Biblical Basis of the American Myth." In Gunn, 219-29.

Berger, Peter L. A Rumor of Angels. Garden City: Anchor, 1969.

_____. The Sacred Canopy. Garden City: Anchor, 1969.

Berlin, Adele. Poetics and Interpretation of Biblical Narrative. Sheffield: Almond, 1983.

Berman, Art. From the New Criticism to Deconstruction. Urbana: Illinois, 1988.

Betz, H. D. Essays on the Sermon on the Mount. Philadelphia: Fortress, 1985.

_____. Galatians. Philadelphia: Fortress, 1979.

Birch, Bruce C. The Rise of Israelite Monarchy. Missoula: Scholars, 1976.

Black, Matthew, and Rowley, H. H., eds. Peake's Commentary on the Bible. Rev. ed. London: Thomas Nelson and Sons, 1962.

Bleich, David. Subjective Criticism. Baltimore: John Hopkins, 1978.

Blenkinsopp, Joseph. A History of Prophecy in Israel. Philadelphia: Westminster, 1983.

_____. Prophecy and Canon. Notre Dame, 1977.

Boers, Hendrikus. "The Form Critical Study of Paul's Letters: 1 Thessalonians as a Case Study." NTS 22 (1976):140-58.

Boomershine, Thomas E. "Biblical Megatrends: Towards a Paradigm for the Interpretation of the Bible in Electronic Media." SBLSP 26 (1987):144-57.

_____. "Mark 16:8 and the Apostolic Commission." JBL 100 (June):225-39.

_____. Mark the Story-Teller: A Rhetorical-Critical Investigation of Mark's Passion and Resurrection Narrative. Ph.D. Dissertation. Union Theological Seminary, 1974.

_____. Story Journey: An Invitation to the Gospel as Storytelling. Nashville: Abingdon, 1988.

Boone, Kathleen C. The Bible Tells Them So. Albany: SUNY, 1989.

Booth, Wayne. The Rhetoric of Fiction. 2nd ed. Chicago, 1981.

_____. A Rhetoric of Irony. Chicago, 1975.

Borges, Jorge Luis. "Pierre Menard, Author of Don Quixote." In Borges. Ficciones. NY: Grove, 1962. Pp. 45-55.

Bornkamm. Guenther. Paul. NY: Harper & Row, 1969.

Boulding, Kenneth E. The Image. Michigan, 1956.

Brandon, S. F. G. Creation Legends of the Ancient Near East. London: Hodder & Stoughton, 1963.

Braun, R. L. "Solomonic Apologetic in Chronicles." JBL 92 (1973):503-16.

Brawley, Robert L. Luke-Acts and the Jews. Atlanta: Scholars, 1987.

Bright, John. A History of Israel. 3rd ed. Philadelphia: Westminster, 1981.

Brockway, Robert W. Myth from the Ice Age to Mickey Mouse. Albany: State University of New York, 1993.

Brown, Alexandra. "Wisdom Literature: Theoretical Perspectives." In Eliade. ER, 15:409-12.

Brown, Douglas C., ed. The Enduring Legacy: Biblical Dimensions in Modern Literature. NY: Charles Scribner's Sons, 1975.

Brown, Raymond E. The Birth of the Messiah. Garden City: Image, 1979.

_____. The Community of the Beloved Disciple. Ramsey: Paulist, 1979.

_____. The Gospel According to John. The Anchor Bible. Garden City: Doubleday, 1966.

Brown, Raymond E., Fitzmeyer, J. A., and Murphy, Roland E., eds. Jerome Biblical Commentary. Englewood Cliffs: Prentice-Hall, 1969.

Brown, Robert M. Unexpected News: Reading The Bible with Third World Eyes. Philadelphia: Westminster, 1984.

Bruce, F. F. The Books and the Parchments. Rev. ed. Revell, 1963.

_____. The English Bible: A History of Translations. Rev. ed. NY: Oxford, 1970.

Brueggemann, Walter. "From Hurt to Joy, From Death to Life." Interp 28 (1974):3-19.

_____. Genesis. Interpretation. Atlanta: John Knox, 1982.

_____. In Man We Trust. Atlanta: John Knox, 1972.

_____. Praying the Psalms. Winona: St. Mary's, 1982.

_____. "Presence of God, Cultic." In Crim, 680-83.

_____. The Prophetic Imagination. Philadelphia: Fortress, 1978.

_____. "Psalms and the Life of Faith." JSOT 17 (1980):5-10.

_____. "Yahwist." In Crim, 971-75.

Buck, Charles and Taylor, Greer. Saint Paul: A Study of the Development of His Thought. NY: Charles Scribner's Sons, 1969.

Bultmann, Rudolf. The Gospel of John. Philadelphia: Westminster, 1971.

_____. History of the Synoptic Tradition. Rev. ed. NY: Harper & Row, 1963.

_____. "NT and Mythology." In Bartsch, 1-44.

_____. Theology of the NT. 2 vols. NY: Charles Scribner's Sons, 1955.

Bury, J. B. The Ancient Greek Historians. NY: Dover, 1958.

Buttrick, George Arthur, et al. The Interpreter's Dictionary of the Bible. 4 vols. Nashville: Abingdon, 1962.

Cadbury, Henry J. The Making of Luke-Acts. London: SPCK, 1961.

_____. The Style and Literary Method of Luke. Cambridge: Harvard, 1920.

Caird, G. B. The Language and Imagery of the Bible. Philadelphia: Westminster, 1980.

_____. The Revelation of St. John the Divine. Harper's NT Commentaries. NY: Harper & Row, 1966.

Cameron, Ron. The Other Gospels. Philadelphia: Westminster, 1982.

Campbell, Anthony and O'Brien, Mark A. Sources of the Pentateuch: Texts, Introductions, Annotations. Minneapolis: Fortress, 1993.

Campbell, Joseph. The Hero with a Thousand Faces. Princeton: 1968 (1949).

_____. "The Masks of God." In Frazier, 161-69.

Campenhausen, Hans von. The Formation of the Christian Bible. Philadelphia: Fortress, 1972.

Camus, Albert. The Rebel. Rev. ed. NY: Vintage, 1956.

Capps, Walter H. Religious Studies: The Making of a Discipline. Minneapolis: Fortress, 1995.

Carroll, Robert P. The Bible as a Problem for Christianity. Philadelphia: Trinity, 1991.

Carter, Warren. "Kernels and Narrative Blocks: The Structure of Matthew's Gospel." CBQ 54 (1992):463-81.

Castelli, Elizabeth. Imitating Paul: A Discourse of Power. Philadelphia: Westminster, 1991.

Castelli, Elizabeth A. et al, eds. The Postmodern Bible: The Bible and Culture Collective. New Haven: Yale, 1995.

Charles, R. H. Apocrypha and Pseudepigrapha of the OT. 2 vols. Oxford: Clarendon, 1913.

Charlesworth, J. H. "From Messianology to Christology." In Charlesworth. Messiah, 3-35.

_____, ed. The Messiah: Developments in Earliest Judaism and Christianity. Minneapolis: Fortress, 1992.

_____, ed. The OT Pseudepigrapha. 2 vols. Garden City: Doubleday, 1983.

Chatman, Seymour. Story and Discourse: Narrative Structure in Fiction and Film. Ithaca: Cornell, 1978.

Cheetham, Erika. The Prophecies of Nostradamus. NY: G. P. Putnam's Sons, 1974.

Childs, Brevard S. The Book of Exodus. OT Library. Philadelphia: Westminster, 1974.

_____. Introduction to the OT as Scripture. Philadelphia: Fortress, 1979.

Clements, Ronald E. Abraham and David. Naperville: Alec R. Allenson, 1967.

_____. Exodus. Cambridge Commentary on the NEB. Cambridge, 1972.

_____. One Hundred Years of OT Interpretation. Philadelphia: Westminster, 1976.

_____. Prophecy and Tradition. Atlanta: John Knox, 1975.

Clouse, Robert G. The Meaning of the Millenium: Four Views. Downers Grove: InterVarsity, 1977.

Coggins, R. J., and Houlden, J. L., eds. A Dictionary of Biblical Interpretation. Philadelphia: Trinity, 1990.

Cole, G. D. H., ed. Rousseau's The Social Contract and Discourses. Everyman's Library. NY: E.P. Dutton, 1950.

Collins, Adelo Yarbo. Crisis and Catharsis: The Power of the Apocalypse. Philadelphia: Westminster, 1984.

_____, ed. Early Christian Apocalypticism: Genre and Social Setting. Semeia 36. Decatur: Scholars, 1986.

Collins, John J., ed. Apocalypse: The Morphology of a Genre. Semeia 14. Missoula: Scholars, 1979.

_____. The Apocalyptic Imagination. NY: Crossroads, 1987.

_____. "Apocalyptic Literature." In Kraft and Nickelsburg, 345-70.

Connick, C. Milo. Jesus: The Man, the Mission, and the Message. 2nd ed. Englewood Cliffs: Prentice-Hall, 1974.

Conzelmann, Hans. The Theology of St. Luke. Philadelphia: Fortress, 1961.

Cope, Oliver Lamar. Matthew: A Scribe Trained for the Kingdom of God. Washington, D.C.: CBA, 1976.

Corbett, J. Elliott. The Prophets on Main Street. Rev. ed. Atlanta: John Knox, 1978.

Cox, Harvey. On Not Leaving it to the Snake. NY: Macmillan, 1964.

Crapanzano, Vincent. "Spirit Possession." In Eliade. ER, 14:12-19.

Crenshaw, James L. "The Eternal Gospel (Eccl. 3:11)." In Crenshaw and Willis, 25-55.

_____. OT Wisdom: An Introduction. Atlanta: John Knox, 1981.

_____. "Prophecy, false." In Crim, 201-02.

_____. Prophetic Conflict. Berlin: Walter de Gruyter, 1971.

_____, ed. Studies in Ancient Israelite Wisdom. NY: KTAV, 1976.

_____. "Theodicy." In Crim, 895-96.

_____. Theodicy in the OT. Philadelphia: Fortress, 1983.

_____. "The Wisdom Literature." In Knight and Tucker, 369-407.

Crenshaw, James L. and Willis, John T. Essays in OT Ethics. NY: KTAV, 1974.

Crim, Keith, et al. The Interpreter's Dictionary of the Bible: Supplementary Volume. Nashville: Abingdon, 1976.

Croatto, J. Severino. Exodus: A Hermeneutics of Freedom. Maryknoll: Orbis, 1981.

Cronbach, Abraham. "Worship in NT Times, Jewish." In Buttrick, 4:894-403.

Cross, F. L. and Livingstone, E. A., eds. The Oxford Dictionary of the Christian Church. 2nd ed. London: Oxford, 1974.

Cross, Frank M. Canaanite Myth and Hebrew Epic. Cambridge: Harvard, 1973.

Crossan, John Dominic. The Dark Interval. Niles, IL: Argus, 1975.

_____. The Historical Jesus: The Life of a Mediterranean Peasant. San Francisco: HarperCollins, 1991.

Culler, Jonathan. On Deconstruction. Ithaca: Cornell, 1982.

_____. Structuralist Poetics. Ithaca: Cornell, 1974.

Culley, Robert C. Studies in the Structure of Hebrew Narrative. Philadelphia: Fortress, 1976.

Culpepper, R. Alan. Anatomy of the Fourth Gospel. Philadelphia: Fortress, 1983.

Dahl, N. A. "Letter." In Crim, 539-42.

_____. "The Particularity of the Pauline Epistles as a Problem in the

Ancient Church." In Neotestamentica et Patristica: Eine Freundsgabe, Herrn Professor Dr. Oscar Cullmann zu seinem 60 Geburtstag. Leiden: E. J. Brill, 1962. Pp. 261-71.

Damrosch, David. The Narrative Covenant. San Francisco: Harper & Row, 1987.

Danby, Herbert. The Mishnah. London: Oxford, 1933.

Danker, Frederick W. Benefactor: Epigraphic Study of a Graeco-Roman Semantic Field. St. Louis: Clayton, 1982.

Davies, G. Henton. "Theophany." In Buttrick, 4:619-20.

Davies, W. D. The Setting of the Sermon on the Mount. Cambridge, 1964.

Davies, W. D. and Allison, Dale C., Jr. "Reflections on the Sermon on the Mount." SJT 44 (1991):283-309.

Davis, Charles. "The Theological Career of Historical Criticism of the Bible." Cross Currents 32 (1982):267-84.

Dawsey, James M. The Lukan Voice. Macon: Mercer, 1986.

Deissmann, Adolf. Bible Studies. Edinburgh: T & T Clark, 1901.

Detweiler, Robert. "What is a Sacred Text?" Semeia 31 (1985):213-30.

DeVries, Simon J. "A Review of Recent Research in the Tradition History of the Pentateuch." In K. H. Richards. SBLSP 1987. Atlanta: Scholars, 1987. Pp. 459-502.

Dibelius, Martin. From Tradition to Gospel. 2nd ed. NY: Charles Scribner's Sons, 1934.

_____. Studies in the Acts of the Apostles. London: SCM, 1956.

Dobschuetz, Ernst von. "Matthew as Rabbi and Catechist." In Stanton, 19-29.

Dodd, C. H. The Apostolic Preaching and Its Development. Hodder & Stoughton, 1936.

_____. The Interpretation of the Fourth Gospel. Cambridge, 1953.

_____. The Parables of the Kingdom. Rev. ed. NY: Charles Scribner's Sons, 1961.

Dollimore, Jonathan and Sinfield, Alan, eds. Political Shakespeare: New Essays in Cultural Materialism. Ithaca: Cornell, 1985.

Dostoevski, Fydor. Crime and Punishment. Translated by Sidney Monas. NY: Signet Classic, 1968.

Doty, William. Letters in Primitive Christianity. Philadelphia:

Fortress, 1973.

_____. Mythography. Tuscaloosa: University of Alabama, 1986.

Douglas, Mary. Natural Symbols: Explorations in Cosmology. NY: Pantheon, 1982.

_____. Purity and Danger: An Analysis of the Concepts of Pollution and Taboo. London: Routledge & Kegan Paul, 1966.

Dubrow, Heather. Genre. London: Methuen, 1982.

Duke, Paul D. Irony in the Fourth Gospel. Atlanta: John Knox, 1985.

Duling, Dennis C. Jesus Christ Through History. NY: Harcourt Brace Jovanovich, 1979.

_____. "The Therapeutic Son of David." NTS 24 (1978):392-410.

Duling, Dennis C. and Perrin, Norman. The NT: An Introduction. 3rd ed. NY: Harcourt Brace Jovanovich, 1994.

Dundes, Alan, ed. Sacred Narrative. Berkeley, 1984.

Dunn, James D. G. Unity and Diversity in the NT. Philadelphia: Westminster, 1977.

Edwards, Richard A. "Uncertain Faith: Matthew's Portrait of the Disciples." In Segovia, 47-61.

Efird, James M. Daniel and Revelation: A Study of Two Extraordinary Visions. Valley Forge: Judson, 1978.

Eichrodt, Walther. Theology of the OT. 2 vols. OT Library. Philadelphia: Westminster, 1961, 1964.

Eissfeldt, Otto. The OT: An Introduction. NY: Harper & Row, 1965.

EJ. NY: Macmillan, 1971.

Eliade, Mircea, ed. ER. NY: Macmillan, 1987.

_____. Essential Sacred Writings from Around the World. San Francisco: Harper & Row, 1977.

_____. "Methodological Remarks on the Study of Symbolism." In Ellwood, 136-41.

_____. The Myth of the Eternal Return. NY: Pantheon, 1954.

_____. The Sacred and the Profane. NY: Harcourt, Brace, 1959.

Elliot, John H. "Social-Scientific Criticism of the NT and its Social World: More on Method and Models." Semeia 35 (1986):1-33.

Ellis, E. Earle. Paul's Use of the OT. Edinburgh: Oliver and Boyd, 1957.

Ellul, Jacques. "Modern Myths." Diogenes 23 (1958):23-40.

Ellwood, Robert S., Jr. Readings on Religion. Englewood Cliffs: Prentice-Hall, 1978.

Emerson, Ralph Waldo. "Self-Reliance." In Hollinger and Capper, 1:274-88.

Epp, Eldon Jay and MacRae, George W., eds. The NT and Its Modern Interpreters. Philadelphia: Fortress, 1989.

Eusebius. EH (or The History of the Church). Translated by G. A. Williamson. NY: Penguin, 1965.

Exum, J. Cheryl, ed. Tragedy and Comedy in the Bible. Semeia 32. Decatur: Scholars, 1984.

Fetterley, Judith. The Resisting Reader: A Feminist Approach to American Fiction. Bloomington: Indiana, 1978.

Feyerabend, Paul K. Against Method. London: New Left Books, 1975.

Fisch, Harold. Poetry With a Purpose. Bloomington: Indiana, 1988.

Fish, Stanley E. Is There a Text in This Class? Cambridge: Harvard, 1980.

_____. Self-Consuming Artifacts. Berkeley: California, 1972.

Fishbane, Michael. Biblical Interpretation in Ancient Israel. Oxford: Clarendon, 1985.

Fiske, John and Hartley, John. Reading Television. London: Meuthen, 1978.

Flanders, Henry Jackson, Jr., Crapps, Robert Wilson, and Smith, David Anthony. People of the Covenant. 3rd ed. NY: Oxford, 1988.

Fornara, C. W. The Nature of History in Ancient Greece and Rome. University of California, 1983.

Forster, E. M. Aspects of the Novel. NY: Harcourt, Brace, & World, 1927.

Fortna, Robert. The Gospel of Signs. Cambridge, 1970.

Foucault, Michel. The Archaeology of Knowledge. NY: Pantheon, 1972.

Fowler, Robert M. Let the Reader Understand: Reader-Response Criticism and the Gospel of Mark. Minneapolis: Fortress,

1991.

_____. Loaves and Fishes: The Function of the Feeding Stories in the Gospel of Mark. SBLDS 54. Chico: Scholars, 1981.

_____. "Who is 'the Reader' in Reader Response Criticism?" Semeia 31 (1985):5-23.

Frazier, Allie M., ed. Issues in Religion: A Book of Readings. 2nd ed. Belmont: Wadsworth, 1975.

Freedman, David Noel. "The Chronicler's Purpose." CBQ 23 (1961):436-42.

Frei, Hans W. The Eclipse of Biblical Narrative. New Haven: Yale, 1974.

Frend, W. H. C. Martyrdom and Persecution in the Early Church. Oxford, 1967.

Fretheim, Terence E. The Suffering of God. Philadelphia: Fortress, 1984.

Friedman, Richard Elliot. Who Wrote the Bible? NY: Harper & Row, 1987.

Froelich, Karlfried, ed. Biblical Interpretation in the Early Church. Philadelphia: Fortress, 1984.

Frye, Northrop. The Anatomy of Criticism. Princeton: 1957.

_____. The Great Code. NY: Harcourt Brace Jovanovich, 1982.

Frye, Roland, ed. Is God a Creationist? NY: Charles Scribner's Sons, 1983.

Funk, Robert W. Language, Hermeneutic, and Word of God. NY: Harper & Row, 1966.

_____. The Poetics of Biblical Narrative. Sonoma: Polebridge, 1988.

Furnish, Victor Paul. "Pauline Studies." In Epp and MacRae, 321-50.

Gamble, Harry Y. The NT Canon: Its Making and Meaning. Philadelphia: Fortress, 1985.

Gammie, John G. Holiness in Israel. Minneapolis: Fortress, 1989.

Gasque, W. Ward. "A Fruitful Field: Recent Study of the Acts of the Apostles." Interp 42 (1988):117-31.

Gaster, Theodor. Festivals of the Jewish Year. NY: William Sloane, 1953.

_____. Passover: Its History and Traditions. Boston: Beacon, 1962.

_____. Thespis: Ritual, Myth, and Drama in the ANE. NY: 1961.

Geertz, Clifford. The Interpretation of Cultures. NY: Basic, 1973.

Genette, Gerard. Narrative Discourse: An Essay in Method. Ithaca: Cornell, 1980.

Gerhart, Mary. "Generic Studies: Their Renewed Importance in Religious and Literary Interpretation." JAAR 45 (1977):309-25.

Gerhart, Mary and Williams, James G., eds. Genre, Narrativity, and Theology. Semeia 43 (1988).

Gerstenberger, Erhard S. "The Lyrical Literature." In Knight and Tucker, 409-44.

Ginsberg, H. Louis. Studies in Koheleth. NY: Jewish Theological Seminary of America, 1950.

Girard, Rene. The Scapegoat. Baltimore: John Hopkins, 1986.

_____. Violence and the Sacred. Baltimore: John Hopkins, 1977.

Glatzer, Nahum N. The Passover Haggadah. Rev. ed. NY: Schocken, 1969.

Goldberg, Jay and Goldberg, Nancy Marmer, eds. The Modern Critical Spectrum. Englewood Cliffs: Prentice-Hall, 1962.

Good, Edwin M. Irony in the OT. Philadelphia: Westminster, 1965.

Gordis, Robert. Koheleth--The Man and His World. 3rd augmented ed. NY: Schocken, 1968.

Gottwald, Norman K. The Hebrew Bible: A Socio-Literary Introduction. Philadelphia: Fortress, 1985.

_____. "Poetry, Hebrew." In Buttrick, 3:829-38.

_____. The Tribes of Yahweh. Maryknoll: Orbis, 1979.

Grant, Michael. The Ancient Historians. NY: Charles Scribner's Sons, 1971.

_____. The History of Ancient Israel. NY: Charles Scribner's Sons, 1984.

Grant, Robert M. and Tracy, David. A Short History of the Interpretation of the Bible. 2nd ed. Philadelphia: Fortress, 1984.

Greenberg, Moshe. "Job." In Alter and Kermode, 283-304.

Greenstein, Edward L. In Eliade. ER, 12:38-45.

Greimas, A. J. Structural Semantics: An Attempt at a Method. Lincoln: Nebraska, 1983.

Guelich, R. A. "Interpreting the Sermon on the Mount." Interp 41 (1987):117-30.

_____. The Sermon on the Mount. Waco: Word, 1982.

Guettgemanns, Erhardt. Candid Questions Concerning Gospel Form Criticism. Pittsburgh: Pickwick, 1979.

Gundry, Robert H. The Use of the OT in St. Matthew's Gospel. Leiden: E. J. Brill, 1967.

Gunkel, H. The Psalms: A Form-Critical Introduction. Philadelphia: Fortress, 1967.

Gunn, Giles, ed. The Bible and American Arts and Letters. The Bible in American Culture. Philadelphia: Fortress, 1983.

Habel, Norman. Literary Criticism of the OT. Philadelphia: Fortress, 1971.

Hadas, Moses. A History of Greek Literature. NY: Columbia, 1950.

Haenchen, Ernst. The Acts of the Apostles. Philadelphia: Westminster, 1971.

Hals, R. M. "Ruth, Book of." In Crim, 758-59.

Hanson, Paul D. "Apocalypse, Genre." In Crim, 27-28.

_____. "Apocalypticism." In Crim, 28-34.

_____. "Apocalyptic Literature." In Knight and Tucker, 465-88.

Harrelson, Walter. The Ten Commandments and Human Rights. Philadelphia: Fortress, 1980.

Harrington, Daniel J. "The Jewishness of Jesus." CBQ 49 (1987):1-13.

Harrington, Michael. The Politics at God's Funeral. NY: Holt, Rinehart, and Winston, 1983.

Harvey, Van A. The Historian and the Believer. Philadelphia: Westminster, 1966.

Hassan, Ihab. The Postmodern Turn. Columbus: Ohio State, 1987.

Hay, David M. Pauline Theology, Volume 2: 1 and 2 Corinthians. Minneapolis: Fortress, 1993.

Hayes, John, ed. OT Form Criticism. San Antonio: Trinity, 1974.

Hays, Richard B. Echoes of Scriptures in the Letters of Paul. New Haven: Yale, 1989.

Heidel, Alexander. The Babylonian Genesis. 2nd ed. Chicago, 1951.

_____. The Gilgamesh Epic and OT Parallels. 2nd ed. Chicago, 1949.

Hellholm, D., ed. Apocalypticism in the Mediterranean World and the Near East. Tuebingnen: J. C. B. Mohr, 1983.

Hennecke, Edgar and Schneemelcher, Wilhelm, eds. NT Apocrypha. 2 vols. Philadelphia: Westminster, 1963.

Henry, Patrick. New Dimensions in NT Study. Philadelphia: Westminster, 1979.

Herodotus. The History. Translated by David Greene. Chicago: 1987.

Hertzberg, H. W. The Books of Samuel. OT Library. Philadelphia: Westminster, 1964.

Herzog, Avigdor. "Psalms, Book of." In EJ 13:1303-33.

Heschel, Abraham J. The Prophets. 2 vols. NY: Harper & Row, 1969.

Hick, John. Philosophy of Religion. 2nd ed. Englewood Cliffs: Prentice-Hall, 1973.

Hirsch, E. D. Validity in Interpretation. New Haven: Yale, 1967.

Hoffman, Michael and Murphy, Patrick, eds. Essentials of the Theory of Fiction. Duke: 1988.

Holland, Norman. Five Readers Reading. New Haven: Yale, 1975.

Hollinger, David A. and Capper, Charles. The American Intellectual Tradition. 2 vols. NY: Oxford, 1989.

Holman, C. Hugh and Harmon, William. A Handbook to Literature. 6th ed. NY: Macmillan, 1992.

Holmberg, Bengt. Paul and Power. Philadelphia: Fortress, 1978.

Homer. The Iliad. Translated by Richmond Lattimore. Chicago, 1951.

Horsley, Richard A. and Hanson, John S. Bandits, Prophets, and Messiahs: Popular Movements at the Time of Jesus. Minneapolis: Winston, 1985.

Hrushovski, Benjamin. "Hebrew Prosody." In EJ, 13:1200-02.

Huffmon, H. B. "Prophecy in the ANE." In Crim, 697-700.

Huizinga, Johan. Homo Ludens: A Study of the Play Element in Culture. Boston: Beacon, 1950.

Humphreys, W. Lee. Crisis and Story. 2nd ed. Palo Alto: Mayfield, 1990.

_____. "Esther, Book of." In Crim, 279-81.

_____. "A Life-Style for Diaspora: A Study of the Tales of Esther and Daniel." JBL (1973):211-23.

_____. "The Tragedy of King Saul: A Study of the Structure of 1 Samuel 9-31." JSOT 6 (1978):23-66.

_____. The Tragic Vision and the Hebrew Tradition. Philadelphia: Fortress, 1985.

Hurd, John C., Jr. "Paul the Apostle." In Crim, 648-51.

Hyers, Conrad. The Comic Vision and the Christian Faith. NY: Pilgrim, 1981.

Ingarden, Roman. The Cognition of the Literary Work of Art. Evanston: Northwestern, 1973.

Iser, Wolfgang. The Act of Reading. Baltimore: John Hopkins, 1978.

Jacob, Edmond. Theology of the OT. NY: Harper & Row, 1958.

James, William. The Varieties of Religious Experience. Cleveland: Fountain Books, 1960. Original in 1902.

Japhet, Sara. "Chronicles, Book of." In EJ, 5:517-34.

Jenni, E. "Messiah, Jewish." In Buttrick, 3:360-65.

Jeremias, J. "Theophany in the OT." In Crim, 896-98.

Jervell, Jacob. Luke and the People of God. Minneapolis: Augsburg, 1972.

Jewett, Robert. The Captain America Complex. Philadelphia: Westminster, 1973.

_____. A Chronology of Paul's Life. Philadelphia: Fortress, 1979.

Jewett, Robert and Lawrence, John Shelton. The American Monomyth. Garden City: Doubleday, 1977.

Johnson, E. Elizabeth and Hay, David M. Pauline Theology, Volume 3: Romans. Minneapolis: Fortress, 1995.

Johnson, Luke Timothy. The Real Jesus: The Misguided Quest for the Historical Jesus and the Truth of the Traditional Gospels. San Francisco: Harper, 1996.

Johnson, Mark. Metaphors We Live By. Chicago, 1980.

Johnstone, Ronald L. Religion in Society. 3rd ed. Englewood Cliffs: Prentice-Hall, 1988.

Jonas, Hans. The Gnostic Religion. 2nd ed. Boston: Beacon, 1963.

Jones, Donald G. and Richey, Russell E., eds. American Civil Religion. NY: Harper Forum, 1974.

Josephus. The Jewish War. Translated by G. A. Williamson. Revised by E. Mary Smallwood. NY: Penguin, 1981.

Josipovici, Gabriel. The Book of God. New Haven: Yale, 1988.

Kaesemann, Ernst. "Paul and Early Catholicism." In Ernst Kaesemann. NT Questions of Today. Philadelphia: Fortress, 1969. Pp. 236-51.

Kaster, J. "Education, OT." In Buttrick, 2:27-34.

Kealy, Sean. Mark's Gospel: A History of Its Interpretation. NY: Paulist, 1982.

Keathley, Naymond, ed. With Steadfast Purpose. Waco: Baylor, 1990.

Keck, Leander. Paul and His Letters. Philadelphia: Fortress, 1979.

Keck, Leander J. and Martyn, J. Louis, eds. Studies in Luke-Acts. Nashville: Abingdon, 1966.

Kee, Howard Clark, ed. The Bible in the Twenty-First Century. NY: American Bible Society, 1993.

_____. Community of the New Age. Philadelphia: Westminster, 1977.

_____. Miracle in the Early Christian World. New Haven: Yale, 1983.

Keegan, Terence. Interpreting the Bible: A Popular Introduction to Biblical Hermeneutics. Mahwah, NJ: Paulist, 1985.

Kelber, Werner. Mark's Story of Jesus. Philadelphia: Fortress, 1979.

_____. The Oral and the Written Gospel. Philadelphia: Fortress, 1983.

Kelsey, David. The Use of Scripture in Recent Theology. Philadelphia: Fortress, 1975.

Kennedy, George A. NT Interpretation Through Rhetorical Criticism. Chapel Hill, 1984.

Kierkegaard, Soren. Fear and Trembling and the Sickness unto Death. Translated by Walter Lowrie. Princeton, 1968.

King, Martin Luther, Jr. "Letter From Birmingham City Jail." In James M. Washington, ed. A Testament of Hope: The Essential Writings and Speeches of Martin Luther King, Jr. San Francisco: Harper, 1991. Pp. 289-302.

Kingsbury, Jack Dean. The Christology of Mark's Gospel. Philadelphia: Fortress, 1983.

_____. Matthew as Story. 2nd ed. Philadelphia: Fortress, 1988.

_____. Matthew: Structure, Christology, Kingdom. Philadelphia:

Fortress, 1975.

_____. The Parables of Jesus in Matthew 13. Richmond: John Knox, 1969.

Kloppenborg, John S. The Formation of Q. Philadelphia: Fortress, 1987.

Knight, Douglas A. and Tucker, Gene M., eds. The Hebrew Bible and Its Modern Interpreters. Philadelphia: Fortress, 1986.

Knox, John. Chapters in a Life of Paul. Nashville: Abingdon, 1950.

Koch, Klaus. The Growth of the Biblical Tradition. NY: Charles Scribner's Sons, 1969.

_____. "Is There a Doctrine of Retribution in the OT?" In Crenshaw. Theodicy, 57-87.

_____. The Rediscovery of Apocalyptic. Naperville: Allenson, 1972.

Koester, Helmut. Ancient Christian Gospels: Their History and Development. Philadelphia: Trinity, 1990.

_____. Introduction to the NT. 2 vols. Philadelphia: Fortress, 1982.

Kort, Wesley. Story, Text, and Scripture. University Park: Pennsylvania State, 1988.

Kraft, Robert A. and Nickelsburg, George W. E., eds. Early Judaism and Its Modern Interpreters. Philadelphia: Fortress, 1986.

Kramer, Samuel Noah, ed. Mythologies of the Ancient World. Chicago: Quadrangle Books, 1961.

Krentz, Edgar. The Historical-Critical Method. Philadelphia: Fortress, 1975.

Kubo, Sakae and Sprecht, Walter. So Many Versions? Grand Rapids: Zondervan, 1975.

Kuemmel, Werner Georg. "Current Theological Accusations Against Luke." Andover Newton Quarterly 16 (1975):131-45.

_____. Introduction to the NT. Rev. ed. Abingdon: Nashville, 1975.

_____. The NT: The History of the Investigation of its Problems. Nashville: Abingdon, 1972.

Kugel, James. The Idea of Biblical Poetry. New Haven: Yale, 1981.

Kuhn, Thomas S. The Structure of Scientific Revolutions. 2nd ed. Chicago, 1970.

Kysar, Robert. The Fourth Evangelist and His Gospel. Minneapolis: Augsburg, 1975.

_____. The Maverick Gospel. Atlanta: John Knox, 1976.

Lakoff, George and Johnson, Mark. Metaphors We Live By. Chicago, 1980.

Lambert, William G. Babylonian Wisdom Literature. Oxford: Clarendon, 1961.

Lanser, Susan Sniader. The Narrative Act: Point of View in Prose Fiction. Princeton, 1981.

Laymon, Charles, ed. The Interpreter's One Volume Commentary on the Bible. NY: Abingdon, 1971.

Levi-Strauss, Claude. Structural Anthropology. NY: Basic, 1963.

Lewis, I. M. Ecstatic Religion. Hammondsworth, 1971.

Lewis, Sinclair. Elmer Gantry. NY: Harcourt Brace Jovanovich, 1927.

Lincoln, Abraham. "Second Inaugural Address." In Hollinger and Capper, 1:392-93.

Lind, Millard C. Yahweh as Warrior: The Theology of Warfare in Ancient Israel. Scottdale, PA: Herald, 1980.

Livingston, James C. Anatomy of the Sacred. 2nd ed. NY: Macmillan, 1993.

Lohse, Eduard. Colossians and Philemon. Hermenia. Philadelphia: Fortress, 1971.

Longenecker, Richard. Biblical Exegesis in the Apostolic Period. Grand Rapids: Eerdmans, 1975.

Luedemann, Gerd. Paul, Apostle to the Gentiles. Philadelphia: Fortress, 1984.

Luther, Martin. The Freedom of a Christian. In Martin Luther. Three Treatises. 2nd rev. ed. Philadelphia: Fortress, 1970. Pp. 261-316.

Luz, Ulrich. "The Disciples in the Gospel According to Matthew." In Stanton, 98-128.

Lyotard, Jean-Francois. The Postmodern Condition. Minneapolis, 1984.

Mack, Burton L. A Myth of Innocence. Philadelphia: Fortress, 1988.

Mack, Burton L. and Robbins, Vernon K. Patterns of Persuasion in the Gospels. Sonoma: Polebridge, 1989.

MacLeish, Archibald. JB. Boston: Houghton Mifflin, 1957.

Magness, J. Lee. Sense and Absence: Structure and Suspension in the Ending of Mark's Gospel. Atlanta: Scholars, 1986.

Malbon, Elizabeth Struthers. "Fallible Followers: Women and Men in the Gospel of Mark." Semeia 28 (1983):29-48.

_____. Narrative Space and Mythic Meaning in Mark. San Francisco: Harper & Row, 1986.

Malherbe, Abraham J. Paul and the Popular Philosophers. Minneapolis: Fortress, 1989.

_____. Paul and the Thessalonians. Philadelphia: Fortress, 1987.

Malina, Bruce. Christian Origins and Cultural Anthropology. Atlanta: John Knox, 1986.

Malinowski, Bronislaw. Myth in Primitive Psychology. NY: Norton, 1926.

_____. "Religion and Primitive Man." In Frazier, 149-58.

Mann, Thomas W. The Book of the Torah: The Narrative Integrity of the Pentateuch. Atlanta: John Knox, 1988.

Marsden, George M. Fundamentalism and American Culture: The Shaping of Twentieth-Century Evangelism: 1870-1925. NY: Oxford, 1980.

_____. Religion in American Culture. San Diego: Harcourt Brace Jovanovich, 1990.

Marshall, I. Howard. Luke: Historian and Theologian. Grand Rapids: Zondervan, 1970.

Martin, James P. "Toward a Post-Critical Paradigm." NTS 33(1987):370-85.

Martin, R. P. "Liturgical Materials." In Crim, 556-57.

_____. Worship in the Early Christian Church. 2nd ed. Grand Rapids: Eerdmans, 1974.

Martyn, J. Louis. History and Theology in the Fourth Gospel. Rev. ed. Nashville: Abingdon, 1979.

Marxsen, Willi. Mark the Evangelist: Studies on the Redaction History of the Gospel. Nashville: Abingdon, 1969.

May, Rollo. The Cry for Myth. NY: Norton, 1991.

Mays, James L. et al, eds. Harper's Bible Commentary. San Francisco: Harper & Row, 1988.

McCarter, P. K. I-II Samuel. The Anchor Bible. Garden City: Doubleday, 1980.

McCarthy, Dennis J. OT Covenant: A Survey of Current Opinions. Atlanta: John Knox, 1972.

McKane, William. Prophets and Wise Men. London: SCM, 1965.

_____. Proverbs. OT Library. Philadelphia: Westminster, 1970.

McKnight, Edgar. The Bible and the Reader. Philadelphia: Fortress, 1985.

_____. Post-modern Use of the Bible. Nashville: Abingdon, 1988.

_____. What is Form Criticism? Philadelphia: Fortress, 1969.

McLuhan, Marshall. The Medium is the Message. NY: Simon & Schuster, 1989.

Meade, David G. Pseudonymity and Canon: An Investigation into the Relationship of Authorship and Authority in Jewish and Early Christian Tradition. Grand Rapids: Eerdmans, 1986.

Meeks, Wayne. The First Urban Christians: The Social World of the Apostle Paul. New Haven: Yale, 1983.

_____. "The Man From Heaven in Johannine Sectarianism." JBL 91 (1972):44-72.

_____, ed. The Writings of St. Paul. NY: W. W. Norton, 1972.

Mendenhall, George E. "Covenant." In Buttrick, 1:714-23.

_____. Law and Covenant in Israel and the ANE. Pittsburgh: Biblical Colloquium, 1955.

_____. The Tenth Generation. Baltimore: John Hopkins, 1973.

Metzger, Bruce M. The Text of the NT. 3rd ed. NY: Oxford, 1992.

_____. A Textual Commentary on the Greek NT. United Bible Society, 1971.

Metzger, Bruce M. and Coogan, Michael D, eds. The Oxford Companion to the Bible. NY: Oxford, 1993.

Mihelic, J. L. and Wright, G. E. "Plagues in Exodus." In Buttrick, 3:822-24.

Miles, Jack. God: A Biography. NY: Alfred A. Knopf, 1995.

Miller, J. Maxwell. "Israelite History." In Knight and Tucker, 1-30.

_____. The OT and the Historian. Philadelphia: Fortress, 1976.

Miller, J. Maxwell and Hayes, John H. A History of Ancient Israel and Judah. Philadelphia: Westminster, 1986.

Miller, Patrick D., Jr. Interpreting the Psalms. Philadelphia:

Fortress, 1986.

Minear, Paul S. "Luke's Use of the Birth Stories." In Keck and Martyn, 111-30.

_____. NT Apocalyptic. Nashville: Abingdon, 1981.

Monk, Robert C., et al. Exploring Religious Meaning. 4th ed. Englewood Cliffs: Prentice-Hall, 1994.

Moore, Richard E. Myth America 2001. Philadelphia: Westminster, 1972.

Moore, Stephen D. Literary Criticism and the Gospels. New Haven: Yale, 1984.

_____. Mark and Luke in Poststructuralist Perspectives: Jesus Begins to Write. New Haven: Yale, 1992.

Morgan, Robert. Biblical Interpretation. Oxford, 1988.

Morrow, James. Towing Jehovah. San Diego: Harcourt Brace, 1994.

Mowinckel, Sigmund. He That Cometh. Nashville: Abingdon, 1954.

_____. The Psalms in Israel's Worship. 2 vols. NY: Abingdon, 1962.

Muecke, D. E. The Compass of Irony. London: Meuthen, 1969.

Murphy, Roland E. "The Kerygma of the Book of Proverbs." Interp 20 (1966):3-14.

Myers, Ched. Binding the Strong Man: A Political Reading of Mark's Story of Jesus. Maryknoll: Orbis, 1988.

Myers, Jacob M. 1 Chronicles. The Anchor Bible. Garden City: Doubleday, 1965,

Neil, W. "Jonah, Book of." In Buttrick, 2:964-67.

Neill, Stephen and Wright, Tom. The Interpretation of the NT: 1861-1986. 2nd ed. London: Oxford, 1988.

Nelson, John S., et al. The Rhetoric of the Human Sciences. Madison: Wisconsin, 1987.

Nelson, Richard D. First and Second Kings. Interpretation. Atlanta: John Knox, 1987.

Neusner, Jacob. The Idea of Purity in Ancient Judaism. Leiden: E. J. Brill, 1973.

_____. The Way of Torah: An Introduction to Judaism. The Religious Life of Man. Belmont: Dickenson, 1970.

Newsome, James D., Jr. The Hebrew Prophets. Atlanta: John Knox, 1984.

_____. "Toward a New Understanding of the Chronicler and His Purposes." JBL 94 (1975):201-17.

Neyrey, Jerome H. "Unclean, Common, Polluted, and Taboo." Forum 4 (December 1988):72-82.

Nickelsburg, George W. E. "The Genre and Function of the Markan Passion Narrative." Harvard Theological Review 73 (1980):153-84.

_____. Jewish Literature Between the Bible and the Mishnah. Philadelphia: Fortress, 1981.

Nickelsburg, George W. E. and Stone, Michael E. Faith and Piety in Early Judaism: Texts and Documents. Philadelphia: Fortress, 1983.

Niditch, Susan. Chaos to Cosmos. Chico, CA: Scholars, 1985.

_____. "Legends of Wise Heroes and Heroines." In Knight and Tucker, 445-63.

Niditch, Susan, and Doran, Robert. "The Success Story of the Wise Courtier: A Formal Approach." JBL 96 (1977):179-93.

Niebuhr, H. Richard. Christ and Culture. NY: Harper & Row, 1951.

Nineham, Denis. The Use and Abuse of the Bible. NY: Macmillan, 1976.

Nisbet, Robert. "Civil Religion." In Eliade. ER, 524-27.

_____. History of the Idea of Progress. NY: Basic, 1980.

Noth, Martin. The Deuteronomistic History. Sheffield: JSOT, 1981.

_____. The History of Israel. Rev. ed. Harper & Row, 1960.

O'Brien, Peter Thomas. Introductory Thanksgivings in the Letters of Paul. Leiden: E. J. Brill, 1977.

O'Connor, Flannery. The Complete Stories. NY: Farrar, Straus, & Giroux, 1971.

Ong, Walter J. Orality and Literacy. London: Meuthen, 1982.

Oriental Wisdom. JAOS 101.1 (1981).

Overholt, Thomas W. Channels of Prophecy. Minneapolis: Fortress, 1989.

Otto, Rudolf. The Idea of the Holy. NY: Oxford, 1958.

Parrinder, Geoffrey. "Charisma." In Eliade. ER, 3:218-22.

Parsons, Mikeal C. "The Unity of the Lukan Writings: Rethinking the Opinio Communis." In Keathley, 29-53.

Patrick, Dale. OT Law. Atlanta: John Knox, 1985.

_____. The Rendering of God in the OT. Philadelphia: Fortress, 1981.

Patte, Daniel. Paul's Faith and the Power of the Gospel: A Structural Introduction to the Pauline Letters. Philadelphia: Fortress, 1983.

_____. What is Structuralist Exegesis? Philadelphia: Fortress, 1976.

Pedersen, Johannes. Israel: Its Life and Culture. London: Oxford, 1926.

Pelikan, Jarislov. Jesus Through the Centuries: His Place in the History of Culture. New Haven: Yale, 1985.

Perrin, Norman. Jesus and the Language of the Kingdom. Philadelphia: Fortress, 1976.

_____. What is Redaction Criticism? Philadelphia: Fortress, 1969.

Perrine, Laurence. Story and Structure. 4th ed. NY: Harcourt, Brace, Jovanonvich, 1974.

Pervo, Richard I. Profit with Delight. Philadelphia: Fortress, 1987.

Petersen, Norman R. Literary Criticism for NT Critics. Philadelphia: Fortress, 1978.

_____. "Point of View in Mark's Narrative." Semeia 12 (1978):97-121.

_____. Rediscovering Paul. Philadelphia: Fortress, 1985.

_____. "When is the End not the End? Literary Reflections on the Ending of Mark's Narrative." Interp 34 (1980):151-66.

Pfeiffer, R. H. "Ezra and Nehemiah, Books of." In Buttrick, 2:215-20.

Pilch, John J. What Are They Saying About the Book of Revelation? NY: Paulist, 1978.

Plato. The Republic. Rev. ed. Translated by Desmond Lee. NY: Penguin, 1974.

Plutarch. The Lives of the Noble Grecians and Romans. Translated by John Dryden and revised by Arthur Hugh Clough. NY: Modern Library.

Poland, Lynn. Literary Criticism and Biblical Hermeneutics. Chico: Scholars, 1985.

Pope, M. H. "Devoted." In Buttrick, 1:838-39.

Powell, Mark Allan. "The Plots and Subplots of Matthew's Gospel." NTS 38 (1992):341-46.

_____. What is Narrative Criticism? Minneapolis: Fortress, 1990.

Prince, Gerald. "Introduction to the Study of the Narratee." In Tompkins, 7-25.

Pritchard, J. B., ed. ANET's Relating to the OT. 3rd ed. with supplement. Princeton, 1969.

Propp, Vladimir. Morphology of the Folktale. Austin: Texas, 1968.

Rad, Gerhard von. Deuteronomy. OT Library. Philadelphia: Westminster, 1966.

_____. Genesis. Rev. ed. OT Library. Philadelphia: Westminster, 1972.

_____. Der heilige Krieg im alten Israel. Zuerich: Zwingli, 1951.

_____. The Message of the Prophets. NY: Harper & Row, 1967.

_____. Moses. London: Lutterworth, 1960.

_____. OT Theology. 2 vols. NY: Harper & Row, 1962.

_____. Wisdom in Israel. Nashville: Abingdon, 1972.

Radice, Betty. Early Christian Writings: The Apostolic Fathers. Translated by Maxwell Staniforth. NY: Penguin, 1968.

Rauber, D. F. "Literary Values in the Bible: The Book of Ruth." JBL 89 (1970):29-37.

Reicke, Bo. The NT Era: The World of the Bible from 500 B.C. to A.D. 100. Philadelphia: Fortress, 1968.

Rhoads, David. "The Gospel of Matthew: The Two Ways: Hypocrisy or Righteousness." CTM 19 (1992):453-61.

Rhoads, David and Michie, Donald. Mark as Story: An Introduction to the Narrative of a Gospel. Philadelphia: Fortress, 1982.

Richardson, Alan. The Bible in the Age of Science. London: SCM, 1961.

_____. The Miracle Stories of the Gospels. London: SCM, 1941.

Richardson, C. C. "Worship in NT Times, Christian." In Buttrick 4:883-94.

Ricoeur, Paul. Freud and Philosophy: An Essay on Interpretation. New Haven: Yale, 1970.

_____. The Symbolism of Evil. Boston: Beacon, 1969.

Rimmon-Kenan, Shlomith. Narrative Fiction: Contemporary

Poetics. London: Metheun, 1983.

Ringgren, Helmer. The Faith of the Psalms. Philadelphia: Fortress, 1963.

_____. Israelite Religion. Philadelphia: Fortress, 1966.

_____. Religions of the Ancient Near East. Philadelphia: Westminster, 1973.

Rivkin, E. "Messiah, Jewish." In Crim, 588-91.

Robbins, Vernon. Jesus the Teacher. Philadelphia: Fortress, 1984.

Roberts, J. J. M. "The Ancient Near Eastern Environment." In Knight and Tucker, 75-121.

Robertson, David. "The Book of Job: A Literary Study." Soundings 56 (1973):446-69.

Robertson, James Oliver. American Myth, American Reality. NY: Hill & Wang, 1980.

Robinson, H. Wheeler. Corporate Personality in Ancient Israel. Philadelphia: Fortress, 1964.

Robinson, James, ed. The Nag Hammadi Library in English. 3rd rev. ed. San Francisco: Harper, 1990.

Rogerson, J. W. "Slippery Words: Myth." In Dundes, 62-71.

Rorty, Richard. Philosophy and the Mirror of Nature. Princeton: 1979.

_____. "Texts and Lumps." New Literary History 17 (1985):1-16.

Rosenberg, Donna. World Mythology. Chicago: National Textbook, 1992.

Rowley, H. H. The Relevance of Apocalyptic. Rev. ed. NY: Association, 1963.

Rudolph, Kurt. Gnosis: The Nature and History of Gnosticism. San Francisco: Harper & Row, 1983.

_____. "Wisdom." In Eliade. ER, 15:393-401.

Russell, D. A. Ancient Literary Criticism: The Principle Texts in New Translation. NY: Oxford, 1988.

Russell, D. S. Apocalyptic: Ancient and Modern. Philadelphia: Fortress, 1978.

Russell, Letty M., ed. Feminist Interpretations of the Bible. Philadelphia: Westminster, 1985.

Rylaarsdam, J. Coert. Revelation in Jewish Wisdom Literature. Chicago, 1946.

Sandeen, Ernest. The Roots of Fundamentalism. Chicago, 1970.

Sanders, E. P. Paul, the Law, and the Jewish People. Philadelphia: Fortress, 1983.

_____. Paul and Palestinian Judaism. Philadelphia: Fortress, 1977.

Sanders, Jack T. The Jews in Luke-Acts. Philadelphia: Fortress, 1987.

_____. The NT Christological Hymns. Cambridge, 1971.

Sanders, James A. Canon and Community. Philadelphia: Fortress, 1984.

Sarna, Nahum M. Understanding Genesis. NY: Schocken, 1970.

Sasson, Jack M. "Ruth." In Alter and Kermode, 320-28.

Saussere, Ferdinand de. Course in General Linguistics. London: Duckworth, 1983.

Schnackenburg, Rudolf. The Gospel According to St. John. 3 vols. NY: Crossroad, 1982.

Schneidau, Herbert N. Sacred Discontent: The Bible and Western Tradition. Baton Rouge: Louisiana State, 1976.

Scholes, Robert and Kellogg, Robert. The Nature of Narrative. London: Oxford, 1966.

Schubert, Paul. Form and Function of the Pauline Thanksgivings. Berlin: Toepelman, 1939.

Schuessler Fiorenza, Elizabeth. "The Ethics of Interpretation: De-Centering Biblical Scholarship." JBL 107 (1988):3-17.

_____. In Memory of Her. NY: Crossroad, 1983.

_____. Revelation: Vision of a Just World. Minneapolis: Fortress, 1991.

Schuetz, John Howard. Paul and the Anatomy of Apostolic Authority. Cambridge, 1975.

Schweitzer, Albert. The Quest of the Historical Jesus. NY: Macmillan, 1968.

Scott, Bernard Brandon. Hear Then the Parable. Minneapolis: Fortress, 1989.

_____. Hollywood Dreams and Biblical Stories. Minneapolis: Fortress, 1994.

Scott, R. B. Y. Proverbs, Ecclesiastes. Anchor Bible. Garden City: Doubleday, 1965.

_____. The Way of Wisdom. NY: Macmillian, 1971.

Segovia, Fernando F., ed. Discipleship in the NT. Philadelphia: Fortress, 1985.

Sheely, Steven. "The Narrator in the Gospels: Developing a Model." Perspectives in Religious Studies 16 (1989):213-23.

Shuler, Philip L. A Genre for the Gospels. Philadelphia: Fortress, 1982.

Silberman, Lou H., ed. Orality, Aurality and Biblical Narrative. Semeia 39 (1987).

Smalley, Beryl. The Study of the Bible in the Middle Ages. Oxford: Clarendon, 1941.

Smart, James D. The Strange Silence of the Bible in the Church. Philadelphia: Westminster, 1970.

Smith, D. Moody. "Johannine Studies." In Epp and MacRae, 271-96.

Smith, H. Shelton, Handy, Robert T., and Loetscher, Lefferts A. American Christianity: An Historical Interpretation with Representative Documents. 2 vols. NY: Charles Scribner's Sons, 1960.

Smith, Huston. Beyond the Post-Modern Mind. NY: Crossroads, 1982.

Smith, Mark S. The Early History of God: Yahweh and the Other Deities in Ancient Israel. San Francisco: Harper & Row, 1990.

Smith, Morton. Jesus the Magician. San Francisco: Harper & Row, 1978.

_____. Palestinian Parties and Politics That Shaped the OT. NY: Columbia, 1971.

Smith, Wilfred Cantwell. The Meaning and End of Religion. NY: Macmillan, 1963.

_____. What is Scripture? Minneapolis: Fortress, 1993.

Sontag, Susan. Against Interpretation and Other Essays. NY: Farrar, Straus & Giroux, 1966.

Staley, Jeffrey Lloyd. The Print's First Kiss. Atlanta: Scholars, 1988.

Stambaugh, John E. and Balch, David L. The NT in Its Social Environment. Philadelphia: Westminster, 1986.

Stamm, J. J. and M. E. Andrew. The Ten Commandments in Recent Research. Naperville, IL: Alec R. Allenson, 1967.

Stanton, Graham, ed. The Interpretation of Matthew. Philadelphia: Fortress, 1983.

Stendahl, Krister. "The Bible as Classic and the Bible as Scripture." JBL 103 (1984):3-10.

_____. The School of St. Matthew. Philadelphia: Fortress, 1968.

_____. "Quis et Unde? An Analysis of Matthew 1-2." In Stanton, 56-66.

Sternberg, Meir. The Poetics of Biblical Narrative. Bloomington: Indiana, 1987.

Stinespring, W. F. "Eschatology in Chronicles." JBL 80 (1961): 209-19.

Stowers, Stanley. Letter Writing in Greco-Roman Antiquity. Philadelphia: Westminster, 1989.

Strauss, D. F. The Life of Jesus Critically Examined. 3rd ed. Philadelphia: Fortress, 1975. Original in 1835.

Suggs, M. J. "Gospel, Genre." In Crim, 370-72.

Suleiman, Susan, and Crosman, Inge, eds. The Reader in the Text: Essays on Audience and Interpretation. Princeton, 1980.

Summers, Ray. Worthy is the Lamb. Nashville: Broadman, 1951.

Szikszai, S. "King, Kingship." In Buttrick, 3:11-17.

Talbert, Charles H. Literary Patterns, Theological Themes, and the Genre of Luke-Acts. Missoula: Scholars, 1974.

_____. "Luke-Acts." In Epp and MacRae, 297-320.

_____. Luke and the Gnostics. Nashville: Abingdon, 1966.

_____. "The Myth of a Descending-Ascending Redeemer in Mediterranean Antiquity." NTS (1976):418-40.

_____. Reading Luke. NY: Crossroads, 1982.

_____. What is a Gospel? Philadelphia: Fortress, 1977.

Talmon, S. "Ezra and Nehemiah." In Crim, 317-28.

Tannehill, Robert. The Disciples in Mark: The Function of a Narrative Role." JR 57 (1977):386-405.

_____. "The Gospel of Mark as Narrative Christology." Semeia 16 (1979):37-95.

_____. The Narrative Unity of Luke-Acts. 2 vols. Philadelphia: Fortress, 1986.

Tebbel, John William. From Rags to Riches: Hortio Alger, Jr. and the American Dream. NY: Macmillan, 1963.

Tennyson, Alfred Lord. "Idylls of the King." In Christopher Ricks, ed. The Poems of Tennyson. NY: W. W. Norton, 1969. Pp. 1460-1754.

Terrien, Samuel. The Elusive Presence. NY: Harper & Row, 1978.

_____. Job: Poet of Existence. Indianapolis: Bobbs-Merrill, 1957.

_____. Till The Heart Sings. Philadelphia: Fortress, 1985.

Tiede, David L. Prophecy and History in Luke-Acts. Philadelphia: Fortress, 1980.

Tillich, Paul. Dynamics of Faith. NY: Harper & Row, 1957.

Tillyard, E. M. The English Epic and Its Background. NY: Oxford, 1966.

Tolbert, Mary Ann. Sowing the Gospel. Minneapolis: Fortress, 1983.

Tompkins, Jane P., ed. Reader-Response Criticism: From Formalism to Post-Structuralism. Baltimore: John Hopkins, 1980.

Thompson, Leonard. Introducing Biblical Literature. Englewood Cliffs: Prentice-Hall, 1978.

Thucydides. The History of the Peloponnesian War. Edited and Translated by Richard Livingstone. Oxford, 1960.

Torgovnick, Marianna. Closure in the Novel. Princeton, 1981.

Tribble, Phyllis. God and the Rhetoric of Sexuality. Philadelphia: Fortress, 1978.

_____. Texts of Terror. Philadelpha: Fortress, 1984.

Tsevat, Matitiahu. "The Meaning of the Book of Job." In Crenshaw. Studies, 341-74.

Tucker, Gene M. Form Criticism of the OT. Philadelphia: Fortress, 1971.

_____. "Prophecy and Prophetic Literature." In Knight and Tucker, 325-68.

Turner, Victor. The Ritual Process. Chicago: Aldine, 1969.

Twain, Mark. "The War Prayer." In Justin Kaplan, ed. Great Short Works of Mark Twain. NY: Harper & Row, 1967. Pp. 218-21.

Tyson, Joseph B. "The Emerging Church and the Problem of Authority in Acts." Interp 42 (1988):132-45.

Uspensky, Boris. A Poetics of Composition. Berkeley: California,

1973.

Van Gennep, Arnold. The Rites of Passage. Chicago: 1960.

Van Seters, John. Abraham in History and Tradition. New Haven: Yale, 1975.

_____. In Search of History: Historiography in the Ancient World and the Origins of Biblical History. New Haven: Yale, 1983.

Van Unnik, W. C. "'The Book of Acts,' the Confirmation of the Gospel." NovT 4 (1960):26-59.

Velasquez, Manuel. Philosophy: A Text with Readings. 4th ed. Belmont: Wadsworth, 1991.

Veyne, Paul. Did the Greeks Believe in Their Myths? Chicago: 1988.

Via, Dan O., Jr. The Ethics of Mark's Gospel in the Middle of Time. Philadelphia: Fortress, 1985.

_____. Kerygma and Comedy in the NT: A Structuralist Approach to Hermeneutic. Philadelphia: Fortress, 1975.

_____. The Parables: Their Literary and Existential Dimension. Philadelphia: Fortress, 1967.

_____. Self-Deception and Wholeness in Paul and Matthew. Minneapolis: Fortress, 1990.

Waetjen, Herman C. A Reordering of Power: A Socio-Political Reading of Mark's Gospel. Minneapolis: Fortress, 1989.

Walsh, J. P. M. The Mighty From Their Thrones. Philadelphia: Fortress, 1987.

Walsh, Richard. "Reconstructing the NT Churches: The Place of Acts." In Keathley, 309-25.

Weber, Max. Theory of Social and Economic Organization. NY: 1946.

Weeden, Theodore J. Mark: Traditions in Conflict. Philadelphia: Fortress, 1971.

Weinfeld, Moshe. Deuteronomy and the Deuteronomic School. Oxford, 1972.

Weiser, Artur. The Psalms. OT Library. Philadelphia: Westminster, 1962.

Werner, E. "Music." In Buttrick, 3:459-61.

Westermann, Claus. Basic Forms of Prophetic Speech. Philadelphia: Westminster, 1967.

_____. Praise and Lament in the Psalms. Atlanta: John Knox, 1981.

_____. "Psalms, Book of." In Crim, 705-09.

Wheelwright, Philip. Metaphor and Reality. Bloomington: Indiana, 1962.

_____. "Poetry, Myth, and Reality." In Goldberg and Goldberg, 306-20.

White, James. The Legal Imagination. Boston: Little, Brown, 1973.

_____. "Rhetoric and Law: The Arts of Cultural and Communal Life." In John Nelson, 298-318.

White, John L. "Introductory Formulae in the Body of the Pauline Letter." JBL 90 (1971):91-97.

Whitman, Walt. Leaves of Grass: The 1892 Edition. NY: Bantam, 1983.

Whybray, R. N. The Intellectual Tradition in the OT. Berlin: Walter de Gruyter, 1974.

Wiesel, Elie. Night. NY: Avon, 1960.

Wilken, Robert L. The Christians as the Romans Saw Them. New Haven: Yale, 1984.

_____. The Myth of Christian Beginnings. Garden City: Doubleday, 1971.

Williams, James G. "The Social Location of Israelite Prophecy." JAAR 37 (1969):153-65.

_____. Those Who Ponder Proverbs. Sheffield: Almond, 1981.

_____. "'You Have Not Spoken Truth of Me,' Mystery and Irony in Job." ZAW 83 (1971):231-55.

Williams, R. J. "Wisdom in the ANE." In Crim, 949-52.

Wilson, Bryan. Magic and the Millenium. NY: Harper & Row, 1973.

_____. Religion in Sociological Perspective. Oxford, 1982.

_____. Religious Sects. NY: McGraw-Hill, 1971.

Wilson, Robert R. Genealogy and History in the Biblical World. New Haven: Yale, 1977.

_____. Prophecy and Society in Ancient Israel. Philadelphia: Fortress, 1980.

_____. Sociological Approaches to the OT. Philadelphia: Fortress, 1984.

Wimsatt, William K., Jr. and Beardsley, Monroe C. "The Intentional

Fallacy." In The Verbal Icon: Studies in the Meaning of Poetry. Lexington: Kentucky, 1954. Pp. 3-18.

Wink, Walter. The Bible in Human Transformation. Philadelphia: Fortress, 1973.

Wrede, William. The Messianic Secret. Cambridge: James Clarke & Co., 1971. Original published in 1901.

Wright, Addison G. "The Riddle of the Sphinx: The Structure of the Book of Qoheleth." CBQ 30 (1968):245-66.

Wright, G. Ernest. The Book of Deuteronomy. The Interpreter's Bible. Nashville: Abingdon, 1953.

Zimmerli, Walther. "The Place and Limit of the Wisdom in the Framework of the OT Theology." In Crenshaw. Studies, 314-26.

Zuesse, Evan M. "Divination." In Eliade. ER 4:375-82.